ALLIANCES AND TREATIES WITH INDIGENOUS PEOPLES OF QUÉBEC

The History of the Wolastoqiyik Wahsipekuk First Nation:
The Maliseet Nation of the St. Lawrence

ALLIANCES AND TREATIES WITH INDIGENOUS PEOPLES OF QUÉBEC

The History of the Wolastoqiyik Wahsipekuk First Nation:
The Maliseet Nation of the St. Lawrence

CAMIL GIRARD
CARL BRISSON

Translated by Kateri Aubin Dubois

Presses de
l'Université Laval

Financé par le gouvernement du Canada
Funded by the Government of Canada

Nous remercions le Conseil des arts du Canada de son soutien.
We acknowledge the support of the Canada Council for the Arts.

Conseil des arts Canada Council
du Canada   for the Arts

Each year, Presses de l'Université Laval receives financial support from the Société de développement des entreprises culturelles du Québec for their publishing programs.

SODEC
Québec

Bibliothèque et Archives nationales du Québec and Library
and Archives Canada Cataloguing in Publication

Title: Alliances and treaties with indigenous peoples of Québec: the history of the Wolastoqiyik Wahsipekuk First Nation: the Maliseet Nation of the St. Lawrence / Camil Girard, Carl Brisson ; translation, Kateri Aubin Dubois.

Other titles: Alliances et traités avec les peuples autochtones du Québec. English | History of the Wolastoqiyik Wahsipekuk First Nation

Names: Girard, Camil, 1950- author. | Brisson, Carl, 1958- author.

Description: Translation of: Alliances et traités avec les peuples autochtones du Québec: l'histoire de la Première Nation Wolastoqiyik Wahsipekuk: la nation Malécite du Saint-Laurent. | Includes bibliographical references.

Identifiers: Canadiana (print) 20240078020 | Canadiana (ebook) 20240078039 | ISBN 9782766302710 | ISBN 9782766302727 (PDF)

Subjects: CSH: Wolastoqiyik—Saint Lawrence River Valley—History. | CSH: Wolastoqiyik—Saint Lawrence River Valley—Treaties. | CSH: Wolastoqiyik—Saint Lawrence River Valley—Politics and government.

Classification: LCC E78.Q3 G5713 2024 | DDC 971.4004/9734—dc23

Groupe de recherche sur l'Histoire
Université du Québec à Chicoutimi

Linguistic Review: Anne Curry
Layout: Diane Trottier
Cover design: Laurie Patry

Translated by Kateri Aubin Dubois with the collaboration
of Bernadine McCreech and Camil Girard.

Cover illustration: *We Are of Lakes and Rivers (St John River)*.
Private collection, Camil Girard, 2020.

First published in French as *Alliances et traités avec les peuples autochtones du Québec. L'histoire de la Première Nation Wolastoqiyik Wahsipekuk: la nation malécite du Saint-Laurent* by Camil Girard and Carl Brisson. Presses de l'Université Laval, Québec, 2021.

© Presses de l'Université Laval 2024
All rights reserved
Printed in Canada

Legal deposit 2th quarter 2024
ISBN: 978-2-7663-0271-0
ISBN PDF: 9782766302727

Les Presses de l'Université Laval
www.pulaval.com

Any reproduction or distribution in whole or in part of this book by any means is forbidden without written permission of Presses de l'Université Laval.

... The history of contempt and negation of the *Other* is long and complex.
— Fernando Matamoros Ponce, Mexican sociologist
La pensée coloniale [...], 2007, 329.

Contents

List of maps XI

List of figures XIII

List of tables XIV

List of appendices XV

Preface XVII
Kévin Morais

Amsqahsewey XIX
Kévin Morais

Acknowledgements XXI

FOREWORD
The history of the Maliseet of Viger First Nation in Québec: Research orientation and methodology XXIII

Terms of reference XXIX

INTRODUCTION
The context of research with the Maliseet of Viger First Nation 1

The general context of the recognition of Indigenous Peoples and the claims of the Maliseet People of Québec 1

Methodology and new questions of the research 4

CHAPTER 1
From pre-contact to the first coastal meetings 11

The Etchemin/Maliseet: Hunters and fishers 12
The Maliseet: Hunters, fishers, and also farmers.. 13
First contacts with Indigenous Peoples (1500–1603)..................................... 15

CHAPTER 2
The Etchemin and the alliance of Indigenous Nations with France 25

The first treaty of alliance between France and Indigenous
Nations (1603)...26
Analysis of the commission of 8 November 1603 38
Recent readings of the 1603 alliance..50
The Innu presence on the ancestral lands of the Maliseet 64
Presence of the Maliseet on their traditional lands.......................................70
The French policy regarding alliances and treaties.....................................109
The Grande Paix de Montréal of 1701..117

CHAPTER 3
Maliseet Nations' treaties with the British, 1725–1760 121

The Treaty of 1725–1726: Neutrality and rights of Indigenous
Peoples confirmed and continued...122
The treaties of 1749 confirm the Treaty of 1725 and reiterate
the parties' commitment...127
The Treaty of 16 September 1752..127
The Treaty of 1760: Renewal and confirmation of the Treaty of 1725....127
Maliseet leaders recognize the Treaty of 1725 during celebrations
on 4 June 2016 129

CHAPTER 4
Managing land for agriculture and settlement 135

From 1534 to 1627...135
1627 to 1663 136
1663 to 1674 139

1723 to 1745 142
Management of land used for commercial purposes................................147

CHAPTER 5
The Conquest, the Royal Proclamation, and the recognition of Indigenous Nations........................... 151

The Royal Proclamation of 1763..151
The Crown commits to protecting traditional lands "possessed" by "Nations or Tribes" 152
Protest and ensuing recognition of the traditional lands of the Maliseet in the province of Québec (1765) 158
The King's Domain: Recognized as "Indian territory" in 1767 162

CHAPTER 6
The Maliseet: From recognition (1763) to oblivion and dispersal (1869) 169

Establishing the policies and legislation that excluded Indigenous Peoples from Confederation (1774–1876)..169
United Province of Canada and the implementation of a policy of municipalization..173

CHAPTER 7
From dispersal to the rebirth of the Wolastoqiyik Nation of the St. Lawrence 203

Wolastoqiyik Wahsipekuk First Nation (Maliseet Nation of Québec) 204
The 1969 White Paper and the creation of Indigenous advocacy organizations 205
The Constitution Act, 1982: Repatriation of the constitution, along with constitutional recognition and continuing exclusion of Indigenous Peoples...207
Amendment of the Indian Act (1985): The federal government's obsession with extinguishment (absolute surrender)................................210
Rebirth of the Maliseet of Viger First Nation, 27 and 28 June 1987 in Rivière-du-Loup..211
From the French regime to the present: Maliseet families that have made claims or and affirmed the culture of the Wolastoqiyik 215

General conclusion 231

The Maliseet People, from first contact to the nineteenth century:
A People of alliances and treaties 231
French regime: A policy of alliances and treaties 231
The British Regime: Recognition and the construction
of a discourse of continuing exclusion 234
United Province of Canada and the Canadian federation:
From oblivion to manipulated memory, or when Hunting
Grounds become "reserves" and Indigenous Nations become
"Indian bands" under trusteeship 235
The Maliseet/Wolastoqiyik Wahsipekuk Nation of Québec:
From forgotten memories (dispersal in 1869) to rebirth
and recognition (1987) 236

Appendices 239

Bibliography 303

Map sources 331

List of maps

Map 1 – Archaeological sites in Maliseet territory 12
Map 2 – French settlements in America, sixteenth to early seventeenth century 17
Map 3 – Location of Tadoussac in present-day Québec 27
Map 4 – New France, 1609 38
Map 5 – Meeting places, 1604 46
Map 6 – Indigenous Nations occupying the territory of present-day Québec, around 1600 53
Map 7 – The King's Domain, about 1650 66
Map 8 – Indigenous Nations and confederacies of northeastern Turtle Island, 1585 68
Map 9 – Travel routes in New Brunswick, 1895 72
Map 10 – Boundaries of Maliseet traditional territory in New Brunswick, 1946 72
Map 11 – Traditional territory of the Maliseet, 1978 73
Map 12 – Portages and rivers between the Saint John and St. Lawrence Rivers, 2001 74
Map 13 – Extract from a map by Lescarbot, 1609 77
Map 14 – Extract from a map by Champlain, 1632 78
Map 15 – Denonville's map, 1685 79
Map 16 – Extract from a map by De Rozier, 1699 80
Map 17 – Extract from a map of Acadia, 1702 81
Map 18 – Extract from a map by Aubry, 1715 82
Map 19 – Extract from a map by Bellin, 1744 83
Map 20 – Extract from a map by Morris, 1749 84
Map 21 – Extract from a map by Mitchell, 1756 85
Map 22 – Extract from a map by Mitchell, 1757 86

Map 23 – Extract from a map by Delarochette, 1763 87
Map 24 – Extract from a map by Jefferys, 1775 88
Map 25 – Extract from a map by Franquelin, 1686 91
Map 26 – Extract from a map by De Rozier, 1699 92
Map 27 – Extract from a map by Delisle, 1703 93
Map 28 – Extract from a map by Aubry, 1713 94
Map 29 – Extract from a map of New France, early eighteenth century 95
Map 30 – Extract from a map by Aubry, 1715 96
Map 31 – Extract from a map by Moll, 1720 97
Map 32 – Extract from a map by the Royal Academy of Sciences, 1729 98
Map 33 – Extract from a map by Bellin, 1744 99
Map 34 – Extract from a map by Morris, 1749 100
Map 35 – Extract from a map by d'Anville, 1755 101
Map 36 – Extract from a map by Le Rouge, 1755 102
Map 37 – Extract from a map by Jefferys, 1755 103
Map 38 – Extract from a map by Bellin, 1757 104
Map 39 – Extract from a map by Bellin, 1764 105
Map 40 – Traditional territory of the Maliseet 108
Map 41 – Territory of the Wabanaki Confederacy 115
Map 42 – Seigneuries granted by 1663 137
Map 43 – Seigneuries granted by 1674 140
Map 44 – Seigneuries granted by 1745 143
Map 45 – Grants of rights for commercial exploitation 148
Map 46 – The province of Québec, as specified in the Royal
          Proclamation of 1763 153
Map 47 – Territory claimed in 1765 161
Map 48 – Map by Champlain, 1632 166
Map 49 – Map of the village of Viger, 1847 184
Map 50 – Evolution of municipalization, 1831 188
Map 51 – Evolution of municipalization, 1851 192
Map 52 – Evolution of municipalization, 1871 199
Map 53 – Location of members of the Wolastoqiyik Wahsipekuk
          First Nation living in Québec 225
Map 54 – Evolution of municipalization, 2019 226
Map 55 – Land ownership, 2019 227
Map 56 – Ancestral lands covered by the 2019 declaration 230

List of figures

Figure 1 – Cover page of a history of the takeover of Indigenous governments of the state of Tlaxcala by Indigenous Peoples allied with the Spanish.. 19

Figure 2 – Re-enactment of the meeting on 27 May 1603 at Pointe Saint-Mathieu, (now Pointe aux Alouettes, municipality of Baie-Sainte-Catherine)... 31

Figure 3 – Celebrating the 1603–2003 alliance: Chapel located on the heritage site 32

Figure 4 – Mural depicting the history of alliances in the state of Tlaxcala, Mexico... 44

Figure 5 – France-Iroquois treaties, 1666 110

Figure 6 – Wampum belts 116

Figure 7 – The signatories to the Grande Paix de Montréal (1701) 119

Figure 8 – Plaque commemorating the Treaty of 1726..................................... 126

Figure 9 – Plaque commemorating the signing of the Treaty of 1725 by the Maliseet Nations 131

Figure 10 – Petition for land by St. John River Indians (1826)...................... 186

Figure 11 – Document: "Indian Reserve no. 4, Viger, Québec" 197

List of tables

Table 1 – Portages and rivers mentioned in maps or text 75

Table 2 – Camp or village names mentioned on maps 90

Table 3 – Grant submitting *aveux et dénombrement*, 1663 138

Table 4 – Population of New France (St. Lawrence Lowlands), 1663 138

Table 5 – Grants submitting *aveux et dénombrement*, 1674 141

Table 6 – Population of New France (St. Lawrence Lowlands), 1681 142

Table 7 – Grants submitting *aveux et dénombrement*, 1723–1745 144

Table 8 – Population of New France (St. Lawrence Lowlands), 1739 146

Table 9 – Grants of rights to hunting, fishing, and trade with Savages 149

Table 10 – Population in 1831 187

Table 11 – Population in 1851 191

Table 12 – Maliseet affected by the sale of the Viger reserve, 1870 198

Table 13 – Population in 1871 200

Table 14 – Families involved in claims by and the recognition
of the Maliseet Nation 220

Table 15 – Distribution of registered members by place of residence, 2019 223

List of appendices

Appendix 1 – Commission of the King to the Sieur de Monts, for the habitation of the lands of the Cadie, Canada and other places in New France (November 8, 1603) 241

Appendix 2 – Treaties signed by New France with the Iroquois in 1666 249

Appendix 3 – La Grande Paix de Montréal, 1701 263

Appendix 4 – Indigenous Peoples' treaties, Mi'kmaq, Maliseet, etc., 1725-1776 269

Appendix 5 – Maliseet claim, 1765, and the Governor's reply. Letter of January 19, 1765 and the Governor's reply published as an official document in The Quebec Gazette 291

Appendix 6 – Manuscript document, Maliseet and the loss of the Viger territory, August 4, 1869 295

Appendix 7 – Solemn Declaration of Mutual Respect and Inter-nation Alliance among Indigenous Peoples in Québec, May 16, 2019, in Québec City 299

Appendix 8 – Timeline 301

Preface

Kévin Morais

Chief Councillor, Culture, Education, Health, and Finance (2016–2020), Wolastoqiyik Wahsipekuk First Nation
8 July 2020

We, the Etchemin/Amaliseet/Maliseet/Wolastoqiyik, were the first, along with the Montagnais/Innu and the Algonquin/Anishinabe, to seal treaties of alliance with the French between 1603 and 1605. These treaties originated in the French policy of making and maintaining alliances with the Indigenous Peoples in New France to claim control over the territory and to stimulate immigration, trade, and the expansion of the colony. The Etchemin/Maliseet, our People, along with two other First Nations, the Mi'kmaq and the Abenaki, co-founded the Wabanaki Confederacy (1680) to strengthen the defence of our common claims and rights. With the Treaty of Utrecht in 1713, New France lost Acadia. The Maliseet, with their Indigenous allies, subsequently signed various treaties with the English between 1725–1726 and 1760. These treaties, which essentially continued French policy, recognized our Indigenous Nations and territories.

After Confederation (1867), our Nation lost its lands (1869). As with other Indigenous Nations, our status as "ally" was downgraded to that of "Indians" on "reserves." By creating reserves (1850), the United Province of Canada and the Canadian federation eliminated the traditional territories that we, the Indigenous Peoples, had occupied and possessed since time immemorial, territories that had been recognized as ours under previous regimes. The legal status attached to us changed our political status from that of "allied Nations" to that of numbered "bands" comprised of generic "Indians." By means of these discriminatory laws, we were excluded from the new Canadian nation-state that was being constructed.

In 1987, our Nation was reborn. The federal and provincial governments recognized our Nation (in 1987 and 1989, respectively), after it had been scattered and forgotten following the loss of the Viger lands in 1869. Thanks to the sustained work of families and community leaders, our resurgence began with the creation of the Maliseet of Viger First Nation government. In 2019, the Nation adopted a more representative name in its own language: Wolastoqiyik Wahsipekuk First Nation.

This book focuses on the socio-political evolution of our members from their first contacts with Europeans until today. It demonstrates the resilience of our Nation since the occupation of our ancestral territory. Today, access to our territory, cultural reappropriation, and the development of economic and political autonomy are the challenges that must be met to ensure the continuity of our Nation for generations to come. Knowing our history, making it accessible to our members and to the non-Indigenous population, is an important step towards us being recognized.

Amsqahsewey

Kévin Morais

Sakom Kinuwehtasit 'ciw Eleyimok, Ekehkitasik, Wolomolsuwey naka Maney (2016-2020). 8 July 2020.

Nilun, Wolastoqiyik, tomk, wiciw Muhtani naka Algonquin/Anishinabe, kisihtuweq lakutuwakonol 'ci mawesultiyeq wiciw Polecomonok 'ci-maciw 1603 tokkiw 1605. Yuhtol lakutuwakonol wittetul wici Polecomoney kisitahatasik 'ci elihtutit naka petoqonomuhtit mawesultikonol wiciw Skicinuwok nit Pili-Polecomonihkuk, weci pompawotuhtit ktahkomiq naka kiniluwetomuhtit petuthotimok, esunikhotimok naka mawi punomuhtit wikultimok. Wolastoqiyik, kilunweyak pomawsuwinuwok, wiciw nisonul piluweyak Skicinuwok, Mi'kmaq naka Aponahki, wici-pskomuhtit Kci-Lakutuwakon (1680) weci piyemi kisi ihkatomeq nilunuweyal eyyeq naka weckuhusaminomok. Wiciw Lakutuwakon 'cey Utrecht neke 1713, Pili-Polecomonihkuk 'koskahtuniya Ankatihk. Wolastoqiyik, wiciw Skicinu mawluhkamahtit, malom-ote wisuwonhomoniya milikil lakutuwakonol wiciw Ikolisomanok 'ci-maciw 1725-26 tokkiw 1760. Yuhtol lakutuwakonol nihtol piyemi pittokahkil kisi wisuwonhomeqpon wici Polecomonok naka cuwitpot wewinuwaniya Skicinu naka nkitahkomikumon.

Wiciw kisitposultitit nanakiw Confederation 'cey Kanata (1867), nilun Wolastoqiyik Wahsipekuk koskahtunen nkihtahkomikumon (1869). Tahalu piluweyak Skicinuwok, elitposultiyeqpon tahalu mawlukhoticik poneqehtasu tokkiw *Skicinuwok wikultitit skicinuwihkul*, kisihtasik skicinuwihkul (1850), pilitposuwinuwok 'ci Mawiw naka Confederate Kanata monehtuniya eleyimok kihtahkomikumon nilun, Skicinuwi pomawsu-winuwok, wikultiyeqpon naka tepinomeqpon tuciw askomiw, ktahkomiqol eli nomihtuhtitpon tahalu nilunuweyal piluweyak litposuwinuwok. Wiciw elitposultiyeq, kisi acelokepon 'ci-maciw litposuwey ekimqok 'ci "mawuhkacik neqtuhkomikahk" tokkiw "skicinuwihkul" wiciw kehseweyak naka kat qinte "Skicinuwok"... Nilun sesolahkiw, musqitahatuweyal tpaskuwakonol, mate wiciyemtunewin Kanatiyesuwey neqtuhkomikahk etolihtasik.

Neke 1987, nilunuwey neqtuhkomikahk minuwawsuwiw. Nit federal (1987) naka provincial (1989) litposuwinuwok wewinomoniya nilunuwey Neqtuhkomikahk, sissessu naka unitahatasu kisi Viger ktahkomiq ksihkatasik neke 1869. Woliwon 'ciw sikoluhkewakon 'ci neqtakutomucik naka skicinuwi nihkanatpahticik, mace enuwessu kisihtasik Wolastoqey 'ci Viger Amsqahsewey Neqtuhkomikahk Litposuwinuwey. Neke 2019, yut Neqtuhkomikahk 'kisi acehtuniya wisuwonuwa nekomaw ote 't-olatuwewakonuwa piyemi 'tawtaqok: *Wolastoqiyik toleyak St. Lawrence* Amsqahsewey Neqtuhkomikahk.

Yut nucikhahsik sapi-tpinasu elawsultitit kehsi acessik 'ciw yut toleyak 'ci-maciw amsqhats assihkuwahtit Okamonuhkewi tokkiw pemkiskahk. 'Sotumasu eci sakolawsuwik Neqtuhkomikahk tuciw kisi wihqehtutit kansuhsuwey ktahkomiq, **Wolastokuk**. Eli siktek nkihtakomikumon, eleyimok minuwowehkasik naka elihtasik weci kisawsultitit nihtol, pemkiskahk, qecehtasikil cuwi kisuwehkasik weci nankomawsuwik nilunuwey neqtuhkomikahk 'ciw yukt weckuwapasicik... Kecicihtuweq mecimiw eleyikpon, kisi psonomuhtit yut wikulticik naka skat-Skicinuwok, wisokokimqot weci nonaqsultiyeq.

Acknowledgements

This research on which this book is based was conducted in partnership with the Grand Council of the Wolastoqiyik Wahsipekuk First Nation (WWFN) (Maliseet of Viger), the Université du Québec à Chicoutimi (UQAC), and the Groupe de recherche sur l'histoire (GRH-UQAC) under the direction of Camil Girard, associate professor–researcher at UQAC, and Carl Brisson, researcher associated with the GRH-UQAC. Other contributors were Kévin Morais, chief councillor (education) for WWFN; Pierre Morais and Isabelle Losier, WWFN; Jacques Kurtness, Innu leader; Mashteuiatsh, researcher with the GRH-UQAC; Laura Villasana Anta, Mexican sociologist associated with the GRH-UQAC. Thanks are also due to Paul and Andrée Charest, who were the first to introduce us to the culture of the Maliseet Nation. We would also like to thank the Université du Québec à Chicoutimi (Comité de perfectionnement long and Comité de liaison institutionnel), which granted the authors leaves of absence, thus enabling them to conduct further research that led to the final publication "of the original French-language version" book by Les Presses de l'Université Laval. Many thanks also to the reviewers and to those who supported us in finalizing this volume.

In publishing this book, my thoughts are with Daniel, our son, as well as my adopted family, the Williams-Wood, in particular, Kenneth James William, his daughter, Wendy Lee, mother of Daniel, our dear Timothy Scott as well as their grandfather, Scott N. Williams, a Tuscarora.

Camil Girard, GRH-UQAC

FOREWORD
The history of the Maliseet of Viger First Nation in Québec: Research orientation and methodology

Following up on the recognition of the Maliseet of Viger First Nation (now Wolastoqiyik Wahsipekuk First Nation) by Canada in 1987 and Québec in 1989, we examine how and why this Nation was forgotten. The story, which encompasses events that occurred over a lengthy period, is set in the broader context of the official recognition of Indigenous Peoples in Canada (1982), of the recognition of the Indigenous Nations in Québec (1985 and 2000), and of the United Nations Declaration on the Rights of Indigenous Peoples (2007).

The analysis focuses on *cross-cultural encounters and alliances* with both the French and the English. We hypothesize that in New France, alliances were at the heart of the colonial relationship between Indigenous Peoples and France or England. These alliances with Indigenous Peoples were necessary so that Europeans could claim rights to lands in North America. The alliances were equally strategic for Indigenous Nations seeking to defeat their enemies and to strengthen their hold on their traditional lands.

Our historical research has focused on three elements: (a) the management and mapping of Maliseet territories, (b) the resources of the traditional territory of the Maliseet, and (c) the continued presence of the Maliseet of the St. Lawrence / Wolastoqiyik Wahsipekuk over the long term.

This approach has made it possible to describe the reality of the Maliseet of Québec, a Nation that was party to the first treaty of alliance with the Innu, the Algonquin, and France in 1603 (Girard and Brisson 2014, 2018). This third volume on the theme of treaties and alliances completes a cycle of research on the history of Indigenous Peoples of Québec, who are no longer considered to have had a conqueror–conquered relationship with the French in New France but rather one between partners and allies. The historiography of Québec and Canada has attached little importance to the concept of nation-to-nation alliances except in the context of the Conquest of 1760 and of the creation of the Canadian nation-state. It is as if the Conquest had obliterated the importance of the French regime in collective memory, just as Confederation in 1867 forced Indigenous Peoples to choose between assimilation in *reserves* and, at best, treaties that extinguished their rights.

Research into the foundations of Indigenous recognition in the province of Québec has shown that the original land title of Indigenous Peoples, including that of the Maliseet of Québec, had never been extinguished, except for the Cree, Inuit, and Naskapi. This last happened only recently and in specific circumstances (James Bay and Northern Quebec Agreement 1975; Northeastern Quebec Agreement 1978 [Naskapi]).

France preferred occupying territory in a way that required neither cession nor sale of land but rather alliances. The English continued this policy with the Royal Proclamation of 1763 but, by inserting new concepts related to the occupation and development of Indian lands and territory, the British Crown established a policy that encouraged a restrictive interpretation of the Proclamation. For the Maliseet of Québec, who lived in a border area in southeastern Québec, the issue was complex: they were bound both by alliances with the French and by treaties that they had signed with the British beginning in 1725–1726 while still maintaining their ties to the French. The Maliseet continued to assert their fundamental rights in all alliances they made, and they still claim them today.

Despite recognizing Indigenous rights in 1982, the Canadian nation-state has continued the discriminatory institutional policies toward Indigenous Peoples that began with the government of the United Province of Canada in the 1850s and persisted after Confederation (1867) and the adoption of the Indian Act (1876): termination of nation-to-nation relationships, non-compliance with the Royal Proclamation of 1763, denial of the existence of Indigenous traditional Indian Territory as recognized in that agreement; mandatory registration with a *band* managed by an agent of the federal government, and creation of *reserves*. Those who could not register or did not agree to do so, including the Maliseet, automatically lost their status and their cultural identity, becoming dispossessed of their land and limited in their practice of traditional activities on traditional Indigenous territories.

It was not until the 1970s that a gradual change in attitude began to kindle a resurgence in Indigenous Peoples and a reaffirmation of their political and cultural identity. In 1987, some 130 representatives of the Maliseet Nation of Québec succeeded in obtaining recognition by the federal government. Québec followed suit two years later.

From a historiographical perspective, Todorov (1982), on the difficulty of contemplating the *Other* in the clash of the *Americas*, and Gruzinski (2004), on the history of discoveries considered as a "globalization," facilitated our reflection on the very difficult undertaking of changing the way we viewed the Other. Both Todorov and Gruzinski favoured deconstructing colonial thought through various sources (codices, murals, paintings, sculptures, and legends), which they analyzed by trying to view the world from the perspective of the Other. Through such a lens, Indigenous Peoples appear as actors expressing their own critical points of view and resisting conquest and colonialism in their own way.

In recent decades, Mexican historiography has focused on the history of conquerors and conquered, with the aim of deconstructing colonial thinking (Florescano 2004; Matamoros 2007). Yet history shows that the Spanish also allied themselves with various Indigenous Peoples to conquer Mexico City (Levaggi 1993). The Tlaxcaltecas, Cortez's allies in 1519, have been considered either partners of the Spaniards or traitors, depending on the point of view adopted in the historiography of the nation concerned.

In English Canada, the work of John Leslie (1985), among the many authors consulted, has revealed the changes in Canadian policy that took place in the mid-nineteenth century, as the status of Indigenous Peoples shifted from *political recognition* to mere *administrative recognition*. In Canadian legislation, they were no longer recognized as Nations but were defined as "Indians to be civilized" and who belonged to "bands." Richard White (2009) discussed the dynamics of alliances and Indigenous diplomacy in the area around the Great Lakes. In some ways, this analysis has called into question the Numbered Treaties of extinguishment signed after Confederation.

In Canada, and in Québec in particular, pioneering authors of modern history—Marcel Trudel (1960); Jacques Mathieu, Serge Courville, and Rénald Lessard (1987); and Denys Delâge (2007)—laid the foundations for a historical and geographical reading of the presence of New France on North American soil. The concept of alliance was absent, except for Delâge, who questioned the fate reserved for Indigenous Peoples by the European empires that had colonized North America. These authors produced historical and geographical syntheses based on meticulous and detailed inventories that were intended to demonstrate the legitimacy of the European empires that had settled and colonized the Americas, and which had resulted in the establishment of the nation-states that we know today. Our emphasis is on demonstrating that the construction of the Canadian nation-state was to the detriment of Indigenous Nations in general and of the Wolastoqiyik Wahsipekuk, the Maliseet Nation of Québec in particular.

Before undertaking our discussion of the three elements mentioned earlier, the spatial limits of the territory under study must be defined. As Courville (1995, 54) stated, "To approach the past geographically is also to define the scale on which we intend to observe it." In our research, the area under study has been defined in two different scales of observation. The first enabled us to delineate the Maliseet presence in the Saint John River basin, which flows into the Bay of Fundy, and the smaller watersheds adjacent to it, which flow into the St. Lawrence River. These watersheds constituted the original territory of the Maliseet. The second way of defining the area under study has been based on the definition of traditional territory adopted in 2013 by the Maliseet Nation of Québec (Wolastokuk). This territory is the subject of the comprehensive land claim under negotiation between the Maliseet Nation of Québec and the governments of Canada and Québec.

Our historical and geographical reading of the presence of the Maliseet Nation of Québec required that we

(a) establish the extent of the original traditional territory of the Maliseet using existing research, including works by Ganong (1895), Erickson (1978), Speck and Hadlock (1946), and Burke (2001). To these we added an inventory and analysis of maps of New France and Acadia created between 1603 and 1760, in which we looked for clues (portages, meeting places, settlements, place names) that revealed the extent of the territory in which this Indigenous Nation was present.

(b) present available spatial and demographic data about seigneuries in an analysis that traced the geographical and demographic evolution of French colonization in the traditional territory of the Maliseet of Québec, following up on the work of Trudel (1960, 1998), Courville et al. (1988), Mathieu et al. (1987); and Mathieu et al. (1991). We further developed our portrait of the territory by analyzing the impact of the Royal Proclamation of 1763 on the Maliseet under the British regime and discussing what happened to their traditional territory following the claims they made in 1765.

(c) conduct a historical assessment, modelled on Saint-Pierre (1994), of the impact of European settlement on the traditional territory of the

Maliseet in the nineteenth and twentieth centuries and the resulting near disappearance of the Maliseet Nation in Québec.

(d) draw on current data to analyze the dispersal of this Nation throughout Québec and the area that the Nation occupies in comparison to the municipalities currently located on the traditional territory of the Maliseet (Wolastokuk).

Regarding the concept of *alliance*, it was through the exchange and movement of goods and people that reciprocal obligations were created, and these obligations formed the basis of economic and intercultural relations at the time of first contact. These early alliances bound both Indigenous Peoples and Europeans (Girard and Brisson 2014, 46; Mauss 1923–1924, 49–52; Girard and Gagné 1995).

Thinking in terms of treaties and alliances means constructing a discourse about the nation-to-nation political and economic relationships that Indigenous Peoples had with each other, their Indigenous allies, and their French or English allies. It also means trying to deconstruct a colonial and *endocolonial* (internal colonialism) history that embeds the concepts of conquest, Christianization, civilization, and assimilation in our memories. The authors of this book are aware of the risks they have taken, and they humbly assumed them, knowing full well that they are the product of a colonialism that is difficult to eradicate.

Reflecting on alliances means re-evaluating the treaties of the French regime as the foundational texts of a nation-to-nation relationship between Indigenous Peoples and colonizers. Prior to the Conquest of 1760 and the Royal Proclamation of 1763, the British regime had enshrined the recognition of allied Indigenous Nations and their traditional territory in treaties with Indigenous Peoples, but this occurred against a backdrop of the "cession or sale" of lands to the Crown.

After Confederation, the relationship with *Indians* in *bands* on *reserves* became an administrative one. Indigenous treaties were reduced to treaties of extinguishment, surrender of lands, and the submission of Indigenous Peoples, who had to lose their identity and land to become full citizens of the newly created nation-state (1867). The French regime had drawn up treaties in a nation-to-nation relationship, whereas the Canadian federation prioritized treaties of transfer and submission (extinguishment/surrender/extinction in french).

By analyzing the history of the Maliseet Nation; its participation in treaties and trade; its claims, protests, and cultural manifestations (handicrafts, language, and others); and its ties to lands and resources, we have attempted to uncover how this Nation was forgotten and, above all, how it was reborn after the dispersal of its members following the loss of their land in 1869. What emerges through the history of the Maliseet of the St. Lawrence / Wolastoqiyik Wahsipekuk is the story of all Indigenous Peoples: their relationship to their land, *Wolastokuk*, to their culture, and to their dispersal caused by discriminatory legislation. This history remains entangled in an *endocolonialism* (internal colonialism) that we have analyzed, to the best of our abilities, so as to better critique it and show its negative aspects.

Regarding the history of the Maliseet Nation in particular, Laurence Johnson's numerous research papers (1994, 1995, 1996, 2001, 2003) have proven useful in our own research. They have provided a better understanding of family dynamics, relationships to the land, and issues related to the loss of Viger in 1869 that led to the dispersal of the Nation. The work of Ghislain Michaud (2003), the only synthesis of the history of this Nation, allowed us to understand how the Maliseet evolved over an extended period.

The Etchemin/Maliseet were party to the first treaty of 1603, and they concluded alliances with Champlain in 1604–1605. Because of their geographical location (south of the St. Lawrence River between Matane and Lévis), they occupy a territory that we consider to be a *border* zone. In this term, we include the lands bordering the provinces of New Brunswick (Saint John River) and Nova Scotia, where the Maliseet and their Mi'kmaq allies are found, and the western slopes of the Appalachians, where the Abenaki are located, not forgetting the proximity of these Nations to the United States. This makes the analysis of issues and influences multiple and complex, especially over the long term. The concept of "border" also implies a multiplicity of exchanges, a movement of goods and people, thus creating numerous intercultural relationships between close neighbours. A border is, in a way, a place that favours encounters, a place of resistance and affirmation in a context of exchange.

The Maliseet of the St. Lawrence / Wolastoqiyik Wahsipekuk have tried to protect their distinct culture, not only as fishers and hunter-gatherers but also as farmers and, above all, as inhabitants of their traditional territory around the Saint John River and its tributaries, along with their traditional allies and neighbours, including the Innu, Abenaki, Mi'kmaq, and even the Iroquois, who were regarded as enemies but with whom negotiation was also necessary to resolve conflicts. The many archaeological sites (pre- and post-contact) and the current presence of the Maliseet are a testament to the resilience of a People who are trying to revitalize the Nation through various empowerment projects. The Maliseet, a People forgotten, scattered, suppressed in collective memory, seek to break the silence, to resist despite a history of being forgotten, to regain their voice, that of the Wolastoqiyik Wahsipekuk, the People of the Great River.

The contents of this volume demonstrate the importance of the alliances and treaties between the Maliseet/Wolastoqiyik Wahsipekuk and the French and then the British, even with other Indigenous Nations. The text of treaty documents is found in the appendices. In addition to maps, various images, stories, and photographs have been added to show how Indigenous Peoples have constructed their own modes of expression, resistance, and affirmation. (Several sources listed in the bibliography have been passed to the Nation for its archives.)

TERMS OF REFERENCE

In this volume, the terms *Indigenous, Peoples, Nations,* and *First Nations* are generally used. Wherever possible, we try to identify Nations either in English or in the language of that Nation. The Canadian Constitution of 1982 use the word "Aboriginal" which therefore complicate the uniformization of the appellation when we treat documentation produced after that period. For example, Québec recognize the Indigenous *Nations* of Québec in 1985 and 2001 (Loi 99), but Article 35 of 1982 Constitution relate to *aboriginal peoples*. We keep using "Indigenous Peoples" in that context. This appellation is used in the Declaration of the ONU of 2007 but with "people" without capital. As a general rule, we use **Indigenous Peoples** in reference with "Peuples autochtones." These choices have been made in consultation with different members of indigenous communities, although the application of the rule in historical context is not always clear. We hope the lector will understand that the endeavour we took, as for decolonizing our intercultural history with so many different documents of different languages produced in more than four centuries is not as easy as it may seems.

Thus, the Maliseet Nation exists as a cultural entity independently of the countries or provinces in which it is found today. Champlain often talked about *nations* (nations) or *sauvages* (savages), and he carefully identified each one with its name in his encounters. In his official texts, Henri IV normally used the term *peuples* (peoples); the term *sauvages* (savages) was seldom used by the king. They are "barbaric peoples" when it comes to conversion, of course, but they are considered above all as *Peoples* with whom to form alliances. The term *Amerindian* has been used by several authors and refers to the concept of "American Indian" (Indigenous persons who live in the Americas). Except for references, we never used this term. Indigenous Peoples currently question this usage.

Capital letters are used to refer to a specific Nation, to the Maliseet of Viger First Nation, to conform with original spelling in a quotation, or to refer to Indigenous Peoples, Nations, or person.

According to Moreau (1866, 5–6), the Etchemin were identified by the Abenaki as the Etemankiaks, or "those of the Earth." Their territory, Etemânki was located on the St. Croix and Saint John Rivers in present-day New Brunswick. The French called these people *Eteminquois* and later *Etchemin*.

In the contemporary context of self-identification, the Maliseet call themselves *Wolastoqiyik*, which means "humans" or "people" in the Passamaquoddy-Maliseet language. *Wu-as-tuk-wi-uk* means "People of the Wulstukw" or "People of the Great Saint John River' (Wicken and Read 1996, 88ff.). (The standardization of the written language is not yet complete.) The term *Maliseet* is still used today.

At the time of writing (2019), the Maliseet First Nation of Viger had changed its name to the *Wolastoqiyik Wahsipekuk First Nation*, which means the "humans, the People of the great Saint John River," who live on the banks of the St. Lawrence River. The form *Wolastoqey* is also used in some documents.

The term *Status Indian* is used when referring to the Indian Act (1876), which still defines the status of Indigenous Peoples in Canada. This law has been known by different names of varying lengths since it was introduced.

If not otherwise specified, *Québec* with an accent refers to the territory, the government, the state, and the province (except for in the Proclamation of 1763). The *Grande Paix de Montréal* also retains its French name.

INTRODUCTION
The context of research with the Maliseet of Viger First Nation

The history of the Maliseet (Etchemin) of Québec, a People who were, along with the Innu (Montagnais), the Anishinabe (Algonquin), the Mi'kmaq and the Wendat (Huron), among the first allies of France in North America, poses a challenge for research. Canadian and Québec history has been attempting to appropriately recognize the Indigenous Peoples of Canada and of Québec since they were recognized in the Constitution of 1982.

The Maliseet Nation has been scattered since the loss of their village in 1869 and also has been repressed from collective memory, so reconstruction their history poses a major challenge for researchers who have been shaped by the influence of our colonialist Canadian history. The challenge is to reconstruct, between the past and the present, the historical background of the continuous presence of the Maliseet Nation in Québec, a Nation that has expressed and asserted itself in its own way and has been part of the history of the Indigenous Peoples of Québec and Canada.

THE GENERAL CONTEXT OF THE RECOGNITION OF INDIGENOUS PEOPLES AND THE CLAIMS OF THE MALISEET PEOPLE OF QUÉBEC

The recognition of Indigenous Peoples in the Constitution Act of 1982 advanced the affirmation and the claims of Indigenous Peoples in Canada. The Maliseet of Viger First Nation has been part of this movement, with the Nation being recognized by the federal government in 1987 and the Québec government in 1989. Since then, the Maliseet of Québec have been negotiating with governments to gain recognition of their rights, based on historical treaties they intend to have recognized in their claims (for more about the Maliseet Nation in Québec, see Michaud 2003; Johnson 1995; Calderhead 2011).

Since the official recognition of Indigenous rights—by Canada in 1982 and Québec in 1985 and 2000—contemporary Canadian and Québec policy toward Indigenous Peoples has merged. Even so, governments are still looking for "certainty" by suppressing the rights of Indigenous Peoples. In 1985, the last major amendment to the Indian Act of Canada added what might be termed an obligation of "absolute surrender" or "cession à titre absolu" in French, despite the recognition of rights in the Constitution of 1982. How can one recognize the Indigenous Peoples of Canada (Constitution Act, 1982, sec. 35) and their fundamental rights, while upholding the requirement to surrender land rights while maintaining the Indian status under the Indian Act? Is this not a contradiction?

Indeed, can Indigenous Peoples truly be recognized if they must submit and continue to sign treaties that *extinguish* their rights and treat them like minors under the guardianship of the state?

The forces that led to the guardianship under which the *Indian Act* (1876) confines Indigenous Peoples have contributed to the construction of a history of Canada and Québec that has denied our colonial past in order to exclude Indigenous Peoples from the founding of the contemporary Canadian nation-state. In view of this, can we not place the concepts of alliances and treaties with Indigenous Nations in a history of nation-to-nation relations that began with the treaty concluded near Tadoussac in May 1603 and those that followed it, made with, for example, the Maliseet? It is no longer a matter of writing a history of conquerors and conquered but of revisiting our common history, a history that is composed of conflicts, inequalities, and misinterpretations, it is true, but also of meetings and formal agreements that established a nation-to-nation *relationship* and a distinct status for Indigenous Peoples, who allied themselves with various partners. Recognizing Indigenous Peoples as *actors* in and *co-founders* of Québec and Canada means revisiting the relationship based on alliances and treaties, whereby Indigenous Peoples were, and continue to be, key political, economic, and cultural actors in a collective history of the Americas (D'Avignon and Girard, 2009; Stavenhagen and d'Avignon 2010).

The values surrounding the treaty of 1603—respect, hospitality, and a relationship of equals—were the basis on which the Innu prepared their draft comprehensive negotiation of an agreement-in-principle of general nature (APGN), known as the Common Approach/ Approche commune, see Agreement 2004; Chevrette 2003; Mamit Innuat 2003). This draft comprised the first modern treaty recognizing Indigenous title to the traditional lands of the Innu, Nitassinan, and aligning with the values implicit in early alliances with the French (Girard and Brisson 2018, 36–37; for Nitassinan and land use, 102-106). In one of the first articles of the Common Approach (Agreement 2004), the Innu, in agreement with federal and Québec signatories and participating Innu Nations, stated that:

> the Parties agree that the recognition, affirmation and continuation of the aboriginal rights, including aboriginal title, of the First Nations of Mamuitun and of the First Nation of Nutashkuan, on the one hand, and the suspension of the exercise by these First Nations of these rights according to the effects and manner in which these rights are exercised other than those provided for in the Treaty, on the other hand, shall only come into force upon the signing of the Treaty and the adoption of the implementation legislation, because it is only then that the beneficiaries of the Treaty, the scope and location of the lands covered by the Treaty, the effects and manner in which aboriginal rights are to be exercised, including aboriginal title, which are to be recognized, affirmed and continued by the Treaty as well as the treaty rights agreed upon by the Parties, shall be determined with certainty; (Agreement 2004, 9; Appendix 2004;

The phrase "*recognized, affirmed and continued*" encompasses the concept of *Innu-aitun*, which, founded on appreciation of the value of Innu practices and culture, frames the various elements related to the governance and the economic, social, and cultural development of the Innu People. Thus, the Innu government of each community that is a party to the treaty would assume the responsibilities defined therein.

In their land-use plans of each Innu community would define the practices associated with *use values* for Innu territory (Nitassinan and Innu-aitun, or activities related to culture) and for natural resources, and for the shared management of those resources, which would make it possible to recognize, affirm, and ensure the sustainability of the distinctive culture of the Innu People. This approach, developed by the Innu as part of their assertion of self-governmental affirmation project, would constitute effective recognition of the rights of Indigenous Peoples (Girard and Brisson 2014). Thus, it could become a source of inspiration for future land-claim negotiations between the Maliseet of Québec and the two levels of government. (Agreement 2004; Approche commune (EPOG), 2004); Assemblée nationale du Québec, 2003)

Revisiting the traditional territory of Indigenous Peoples in Canada or in Québec means re-examining Canadian territory in its complex reality: an immense northern territory with a scattered population. From first contact in the sixteenth and seventeenth centuries, Europeans who came to New France were faced with a vast expanse of land and a difficult climate. Because of low immigration, both under the French (1600–1760) and the British (1760–1847), settlers were obliged to ally themselves with, and recognize the territories of, Indigenous Peoples, which made up more than 95 per cent of the land being claimed. It is doubtful that Europeans could even claim to have ever actually occupied it.

The *traditional lands* of Indigenous Peoples and the title to their *land title* disappeared when the government of the United Province of Canada created reserves, a form of *internal deportation*, in 1850. Governments forced Indigenous Peoples to migrate to reserved micro-territories, stripping them of, and causing them to leave their traditional lands. Indigenous Peoples lost their rights to their traditional territory after Canadian governments confined them on reserves with the status of minors, wards of the Canadian federation from 1867 onward. The construction of the modern Canadian nation-state negated the colonial history of treaties and alliances that was proof, albeit imperfect, of nation-to-nation relations between Indigenous Peoples and the Crown.

METHODOLOGY AND NEW QUESTIONS OF THE RESEARCH

This work was produced by a historian and a geographer at the Université du Québec à Chicoutimi. From a methodological point of view, it is important to remember that the purpose of consulting the maps and documents included, many of which have been passed to the Maliseet Nation, is for the advancement of knowledge.

A list of the maps included is found at the end of the book, along bibliographical reference(s) for each. The appendices given as documentation to the community are listed in the bibliography with the year of their publication, unless otherwise specified.

Attention was also paid to the evolution over time of vocabulary used to designate Indigenous persons and Peoples, their Chiefs, and their Nations, either traditional names or "Christian" or "French" names assigned by the colonizer. The family aspects of genealogy have not been touched upon. For the purposes of this study, we relied on lists provided in specialized reports and in the official lists of the Registry of the Maliseet Nation.

The authors chose to translate most of the works used under the French regime. In several cases, a copy of the original works in French (PDF format) has been listed in the list of appendices which appears in the bibliography and given to the community. For one exception, we use the d'Avignon (2018) transcription of all the works of Champlain in modern French (the first to our knowledge by a Canadian researcher). This transcription by this specialist of Champlain is done with precautions (names, toponymy, etc.) and help the understand the contribution of Champlain.

This editorial choice, not always to return to existing English translations, is linked to the fact that we wanted to stay as close as possible to contemporary French terms. Thus, "*sauvages*" is translated as "savages" and not as "Indians" or "tribes" or "band" as we have seen in many English translations. Nation is translated as nation, not "tribes" during the French regime. Generally, the original names of the Indigenous Nations identified by Champlain were left in its original forms. The important legal texts of the French regime (*Commission of 1603*, French treaties [1665-1666], English treaty [from 1726], Alliance Internations [16 mai 2019]) are presented in their original form in the appendices at the end of the book. To the best of our knowledge, in the post 1760 texts, the English versions, when they existed, were used. In Girard and Thibeault (2001) (*Rapports sur les questions autochtones*, Canada 1828-1870, 3 vol, Chicoutimi, GRH-UQAC, paper and pdf), these documents regroup, in most cases, the French and English version of original investigation commission produced in these years. For this document, we give our own pagination. This became necessary since most of the documents published at that time had no pagination and no clear authors.

Besides the most important documents which are presented at the end of the volume, another *Appendix section* appears before the bibliography. It contains all the documents that were provided to the community in support of research (PDF and Word documents).

We know that decolonizing our own respective French and English history is a challenge. As to deconstruct for re-writing an inclusive history of Indigenous Peoples is very complex for all of us.

Can we speak of genocide?

The creation of the Canadian federation has always been presented as an alliance between francophones and anglophones. Once the nation-state came into being with Confederation in 1867, Indigenous Peoples and their rights to their lands were excluded through a system of discriminatory laws, as is shown in our analysis.

Without the research carried out by the Royal Commission on Indigenous Peoples (1996; 1:274-359; Appendix 1996 Royal Commission on Aboriginal Peoples) and the Truth and Reconciliation Commission of Canada (2015; Appendix 2015 Truth and Reconciliation Commission), it would have been difficult to question and critique our colonial and national history.

Apart from a few rare interventions made by Indigenous persons, historical discourse has rarely questioned the foundations of discriminatory legislation (loss of traditional lands, undermining of the identity of Indigenous Nations) enacted by the United Province of Canada and then the Canadian federation from the 1850s onward.

To our knowledge, aside from private conversations, the term *cultural genocide* has seldom been used. Even national inquiries, such as the 1993–1997 royal commission, have seemed to regard the use of the expression very rarely if so, to our knowledge. Those who used the term were rapidly discredited, and such comments were labelled as exaggeration stemming from lack of objectivity.

It was not until Chief Justice Beverly McLachlin of the Supreme Court of Canada used the phrase, obviously outside the court, in a speech at the Global Centre for Pluralism in 2015 that a shift in discourse began:

> The objective was to "take the Indian out of the child," and thus to solve what John A. Macdonald referred to as the "Indian problem." "Indianness" was not to be tolerated; rather it must be eliminated. In the buzz-word of the day, "assimilation"; in the language of the twenty-first century, "cultural genocide." (McLachlin, 2015; <https://www.akdn.org/speech/rt-hon-beverley-mclachlin/2015-annual-pluralism-lecture-global-centre-pluralism>).

It is as if researchers had to pass through the filter of justice to challenge their own vision of a history that has often been silent and, at best, complacent about Indigenous Peoples. Canadian law has helped to create a narrative that marginalizes Indigenous Peoples in the history of Québec and Canada. Only a representative of the highest court in the land seemed capable of breaking the taboo surrounding this shadowy part of our past. Researchers could now critique the system using the words of a justice as their justification.

The National Inquiry into Missing and Murdered Indigenous Women and Girls also used the term *genocide* in its final report (2019, 199; Appendix 2019).

The Truth and Reconciliation Commission of Canada calls for change in doctrines of discovery and conquest (2015)

By 2015, the Truth and Reconciliation Commission of Canada was already emphasizing the importance of changing our perceptions and representations of history by modifying doctrines related to discovery and conquest, reflected in common law by the concept of *terra nullius* (territory without an owner). According to this concept, "nomadic" or "primitive" populations are not entitled to land or citizenship. The mere fact of being "civilized" justifies seizing land and imposing the law of the conqueror. The commission called these concepts into question and requested a new and updated royal proclamation (of 1763), as well as the signature of an agreement that reconciles Indigenous legal traditions with Canadian law:

Royal Proclamation and Covenant of Reconciliation

We call upon the Government of Canada, on behalf of all Canadians, to jointly develop with Aboriginal Peoples a Royal Proclamation of Reconciliation to be issued by the Crown. The proclamation would build on the Royal Proclamation of 1763 and the Treaty of Niagara of 1764 and re-affirm the nation-to-nation relationship between Aboriginal peoples and the Crown. The proclamation would include, but not be limited to, the following commitments:

i. Repudiate concepts used to justify European sovereignty over Indigenous lands and peoples such as the Doctrine of Discovery and terra nullius. [italics in original; territory belonging to no one].

ii. Adopt and implement the *United Nations Declaration on the Rights of Indigenous Peoples* as the framework for reconciliation [italics in the original].

iii. *Renew or establish Treaty relationships* based on principles of mutual recognition, mutual respect, and shared responsibility for *maintaining those relationships into the future* [italics added].

iv. Reconcile Aboriginal and Crown constitutional and legal orders to ensure that Aboriginal peoples are full partners in Confederation, including the recognition and integration of Indigenous laws and legal traditions in negotiation and implementation processes involving Treaties, land claims, and other constructive agreements.

FEDERAL MEMBER OF PARLIAMENT ROMÉO SAGANASH'S INITIATIVE TO RECONCILE THE UNITED NATIONS DECLARATION ON THE RIGHTS OF INDIGENOUS PEOPLES (2007) WITH CANADIAN LAW (APPENDIX 2016 SAGANASH - BILL C-262).

Other recent initiatives include a bill introduced in Parliament by New Democratic Party MP Roméo Saganash, a leader of the Cree Nation (Eeyou Istchee / James Bay). The purpose of Bill C-262 was to harmonize federal legislation with the United Nations Declaration on the Rights of Indigenous Peoples (2007). Bill C-15, an Act respecting the United Nations Declaration on the Rights of Indigenous Peoples, was passed on 20 April 2021.

Major challenges to the passing of this bill

The bill applied only to federal legislation, whereas recognition involves reconciling the traditional rights of Indigenous Peoples (more than fifty of Canada and eleven in Québec) and their distinctive cultures with those exercised by the French and British colonial regimes before Confederation and by the Canadian nation-state after 1867. The Confederation Act of 1867 assigned to the federal government "Indians, and Lands reserved for the Indians" (sec. 91.24; see also 1982, sec. 35), while the provinces were assigned rights relating to property, natural resources, and other matters (sec. 92) concerning ancestral Indigenous territories. By ceding ownership of lands and resources to the provinces and reducing Indian Territory to reserves, the Canadian nation-state had become judge and jury, asserting, in discriminatory legislation, that these rights had been abrogated or simply forgotten. This usurpation of the traditional territories of Indigenous Peoples was left unresolved in the Confederation Act of 1867. The Indian Act of 1876 completed the legal framework for the exclusion of Indigenous Peoples from the Canadian nation-state by confining them in the reserve system.

Deconstructing the Indian Act and recognizing the fundamental rights of Indigenous Peoples in Québec and Canada

Like the United Nations, Indigenous Peoples themselves have long questioned the Doctrine of Discovery and the legal theories behind it. Yet in all legal cases in which they are interested parties, governments have continued to invoke the theory of terra nullius despite the recognition of the rights of Indigenous Peoples in Canada. The Royal Commission on Indigenous Peoples saw in this situation, contradictions that are difficult to reconcile with official discourse and objectives of the Crown (Royal Commission on Aboriginal Peoples 1994; Appendix 1994 *How to Make Treaties in Canada*, the report that inspired the Innu Common Approach; 2004; on the inherent rights of Indigenous governments, see McNeil 2007).

The Assembly of First Nations of Québec reiterated before the United Nations in 2012 that the 2007 Declaration on the Rights of Indigenous Peoples should put an end to the colonial model of "discovery" and the concepts of extinguishment linked to terra nullius, which have continued to feature in the Crown's arguments in most cases brought by Indigenous Peoples before the courts of Québec and Canada, where *total submission* is demanded:

As with the discredited notion of "terra nullius," the doctrine of "discovery" was used to legitimize the colonization of Indigenous peoples in different regions of the world. It was used to dehumanize, exploit and subjugate Indigenous peoples and dispossesses them of their most basic rights.

Central to the survival of Indigenous peoples everywhere is the issue of land and resources. Bases on such fictitious and racist doctrines as "discovery" and "terra nullius," European nations were relentless in their determination to seize and control Indigenous lands. Papal bulls, such as *Dum Diversas* (1452) and *Romanus Pontifex* (1455) called for non-Christian peoples to be invaded, captured, vanquished, subdued, reduced to perpetual slavery, and have their possessions and property seized by Christian monarchs. Such ideology led to practices that continue unabated in the form of modern-day laws and policies of successor States (United Nations, 2012, Shawn A-in-chut Atleo Gran Chief, 1-2).

The United Nations Declaration on the Rights of Indigenous Peoples (2007), part of the Universal Declaration of Human Rights, called for a paradigm shift toward recognizing, within nation-states, the individual and collective rights of Indigenous Peoples. Certain articles of the Universal Declaration of Human Rights emphasize the importance of changing the way we look at Indigenous Peoples:

Article 1
Indigenous peoples have the right to the full enjoyment, as a collective or as individuals, of all human rights and fundamental freedoms as recognized in the *Charter of the United Nations, the Universal Declaration of Human Rights and international human rights law. (To which Canada is a signatory* [our italics])

Article 2
Indigenous peoples and individuals are free and equal to all other peoples and individuals and have the right to be free from any kind of discrimination, in the exercise of their rights, in particular that based on their indigenous origin or identity.

Article 3
Indigenous peoples have the right to self-determination. By virtue of that right they freely determine their political status and freely pursue their economic, social and cultural development.

Article 4
Indigenous peoples, in exercising their right to self-determination, have the right to autonomy or self-government in matters relating to their internal and local affairs, as well as ways and means for financing their autonomous functions.

Article 5
Indigenous peoples have the right to maintain and strengthen their distinct political, legal, economic, social and cultural institutions, while retaining their

right to participate fully, if they so choose, in the political, economic, social and cultural life of the State.

Article 46 establishes the context and intranational limits of Indigenous Peoples' rights. The territorial integrity and political unity of nation-states may not be called into question by Indigenous Peoples who demand recognition of their rights. This constraint leaves states a great deal of room for manoeuvre; some would say too much.

> Article 46
> 1. Nothing in this Declaration may be interpreted as implying for any State, people, group or person any right to engage in any activity or to perform any act contrary to the Charter of the United Nations or construed as authorizing or encouraging any action which would dismember or impair, totally or in part, the territorial integrity or political unity of sovereign and independent States.

In consideration of these principles, Canada and Québec have sought to establish a new relationship with Indigenous Peoples by changing discriminatory laws to recognize, through formal nation-to-nation treaties, the status of Indigenous Peoples as both distinct Peoples and as individuals.

As the Truth and Reconciliation Commission reminded us in 2015, reconciliation will take a long time and will require all of us to bid farewell to the past and change our perceptions and attitudes:

> Getting to the truth was hard, but getting to reconciliation will be harder. It requires that the paternalistic and racist foundations of the residential school system be rejected as the basis for an ongoing relationship. Reconciliation requires that a new vision, based on a commitment to mutual respect, be developed. It also requires an understanding that the most harmful impacts of residential schools have been the loss of pride and self-respect of Aboriginal people, and the lack of respect that non-Aboriginal people have been raised to have for their Indigenous neighbours. Reconciliation is not an Aboriginal problem; it is a Canadian one. Virtually all aspects of Canadian society may need to be reconsidered. This summary is intended to be the initial reference point in that important discussion. Reconciliation will take some time. (vi)

It is in this global context of recognition and affirmation, of complex historical realities, that the recognition of the fundamental rights of Indigenous Peoples in Canada and Québec is evolving.

CHAPTER 1
From pre-contact to the first coastal meetings

Chronicling the history of the Indigenous Peoples of Québec, and of the Maliseet Nation in particular, means highlighting the many diverse sources—archaeological, written, and traditional—that will enable the Maliseet Nation in Québec to be legally recognized.

The Maliseet have occupied their traditional territory since time immemorial (see map 1). Researchers estimate this occupation to date back over 7,000 years.

Archaeology has established that occupants of the upper and middle Saint John River valley interacted with groups along the St. Lawrence River, the lower Saint John River valley, and the Bay of Fundy throughout recent pre-contact history (Burke 2001; Chalifoux and Burke 1995; Chalifoux et al. 1998). These interactions were secured by a vast social network based on trade and on family ties that enabled the movement of people, materials and goods between the Laurentians and the Atlantic coast (Burke 2000).[1]

Burke (2000) and Sanger (2008) suggested that Late Archaic Peoples (specifically those of the Terminal Archaic, beginning nearly four thousand years ago [3,800 BP]) may have been the ancestors of historical Peoples such as the Penobscot, Passamaquoddy, Maliseet, and Mi'kmaq. But continuity, cultural or otherwise, is often difficult to prove using archaeology. In fact, the archaeological record is sprinkled with gaps, and temporal marking is not always up to the task. We believe, however, that breaks or discontinuities in the archaeological record are easier to distinguish than continuities. We therefore suggest that the archaeological data fron the Saint John River valley (Maine, Québec, and New Brunswick) support a hypothesis of continuity of occupation for at least the last three millennia (Chalifoux et al. 1998, quoted in Burke 2009).

---

1. Quoted in Burke (2009).

MAP 1 – Archaeological sites in Maliseet territory

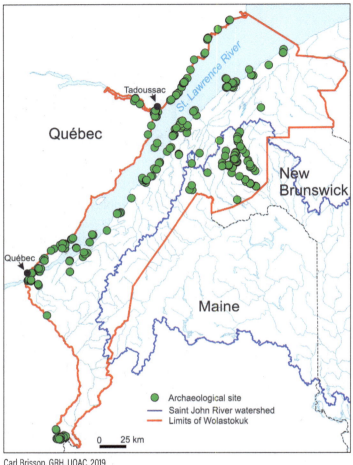

Carl Brisson, GRH, UQAC, 2019

THE ETCHEMIN/MALISEET: HUNTERS AND FISHERS

Champlain identified the Etchemin (Maliseet) as one of the Nations that had joined in the May 1603 alliance at Tadoussac. A place of meetings and traditional gatherings that became a trading post with the arrival of the French, Tadoussac had always been visited frequently by the Maliseet who only had to cross the river to reach the north shore opposite Cacouna or Bic (Erickson, 1978; for the native peoples of the northeast, see Sturtevant 1978).

Champlain stated that the Etchemin (Maliseet) lived on the Saint John River down to its mouth, as well as on the St. Croix River and Island, where he hoped to establish a colony. In this territory in southern Maine, he identified various Maliseet Nations, including the Armouchiquois (Penobscot). The Kennebec and Norembègue Rivers (Penobscot, Maine) and Passamaquoddy Bay were also mentioned as being territories of the Armouchiquois or Etchemin.

Today, the Maliseet and Passamaquoddy are associated with Eastern Algonquian culture. Erikson (1978, 123) believed that they were differentiated primarily by their adaptation to the territory. The Maliseet were more likely to favour hunting and fishing along the Saint John River while the Armouchiquois (Passamaquoddy), who lived by the sea, preferred resources from along the coasts of New Brunswick and Maine on the Bay of Fundy.

THE MALISEET: HUNTERS, FISHERS, AND ALSO FARMERS

Champlain's narratives added further nuance to Erickson's (1978) comments on the Maliseet People as he was establishing a colony on St. Croix Island with permission from his new Maliseet-Passamaquoddy allies. He stated that the Peoples he identified as living in what are now Maine (Passamaquoddy) and Canada (Maliseet, Mi'kmaq, Abenaki) followed the same lifestyle. He told of cod and other fish being caught in abundance in the fishing areas of the Bay of Fundy and Maine (D'Avignon, 2018, 117). He also noted that the Indigenous Nation grew corn, squash, beans, pumpkins, and tobacco. He stated that the Armouchiquois, with whom he has formed an alliance, occupied villages where they cultivated enough land to ensure that everybody has enough for their needs: "As we were there, we saw this rather spacious space three to four leagues around, surrounded by houses, each one having as much land as is necessary for his food" (our translation: D'Avignon 2018, 120).

These farming practices have been described in a Maliseet legend that shows how corn came to the Nation. This crop began to be cultivated following the marriage of a Maliseet woman to a foreigner, who introduced the new plant to the Nation.

Maliseet legend on the origin of corn

In ancient times, things were very different from what they are now. A very long time ago, long before the white man arrived, the Wolastoqey, the people of the Saint John or beautiful River had no corn or other crops. They lived entirely by hunting and fishing. Men lived to be 100, but women lived only to 50.

At that time there was an old chief who had several daughters. They were very beautiful girls with sparkling eyes and silky black hair. One of them was very different from the others; in fact, she was different from all the other Wolastoqey. She was also beautiful, but her hair was blond like the inside of birch bark in summer.

One day, a young warrior arrived, who was a stranger to the village. As was the custom in those days, every time a foreigner came, there were organized competitions. From these competitions, the young warrior always emerged victorious. He was brave when he was with men, but, in the presence of women, he was reserved and silent. In fact, he paid them little attention.

One day, however, he saw the chief's daughter, Sagamaskwesis, the one with the golden hair. He immediately felt attracted to her. The feeling was mutual. So, the two young people decided to get married. The warrior told the old chief that he wanted to marry his daughter and arrangements were made for a great feast and dance.

After the wedding, they did not stay in the village, but went far away to trap alone. Time passed and they were still in love with each other. So, when the woman was approaching 50, and according to custom, would soon die, her husband told her how sad he was at the thought of being separated from her. The woman said, "You know, we dont have to leave each other. You can keep me with you forever if you wish. Just follow my instructions." The man was delighted and immediately agreed.

Their wigwam [traditional conical dwelling] stood in the middle of half an acre of young forest. She told him to cut down all the trees and burn them. Then she added: "Tie my hands with cedar bark and drag me on the ground seven times around this clearing youve just made and, no matter what, don't turn around!"

Once he had cut down and burned all the trees, the forest was dotted with burned and pointed stumps. As a result, once he had dragged his wife seven times through this scenery, all that remained of her was her skeleton, everything else having been shredded by the sharp, protruding stumps.

1. FROM PRE-CONTACT TO THE FIRST COASTAL MEETINGS 15

> When he saw this, the man felt really sad and wondered why his wife could have asked him to do such a thing. He then left his wigwam and the region once and for all, he thought, completely depressed. It was springtime.
>
> When it was fall again, he felt an urge to see his old camp once more, so he returned. To his great surprise, the place was no longer black and covered with pointed stumps. Instead, the space was filled with beautiful corn plants that were waving in the wind The yellow colour he saw there reminded him of his wife's golden hair. He then thought about what she had said to him "If you want me to be with you always, do as I say. (Bélanger 2019, 52)

As commented by Bélanger (2019, 52): *This legend refers to an aspect of our ancestors' life that is rarely mentioned in historical documents: the cultivation of corn. Although the Wolastoqey were a nomadic people, they had nevertheless learned mainly along the Saint John River, to cultivate some crops, including corn.*

What is interesting is that this story also provides additional information about this practice by suggesting that it comes from another nation. In fact, the cultivation of maize was most likely influenced by contact with the Iroquois, which is symbolized in this story by the appearance of the unknown young warrior.

We can also see in this legend the theme of intermarriage, first between tribes, with the arrival of the young warrior, but also with Europeans, illustrated by the blond hair of the Chiefs daughter. The fact that the newlyweds find themselves outside the village is perhaps an indication that intermarriage sometimes led to exclusion (Bélanger 2019, 52).

The language

The Maliseet-Passamaquoddy language is a variant of the Algonquian language and is understood by speakers of either Maliseet or Passamaquoddy.[2]

FIRST CONTACTS WITH INDIGENOUS PEOPLES (1500-1603)

The formation of alliances with Indigenous Peoples appears to have been central to a particular form of French colonization in the New World, especially from the seventeenth century onward (Girard and Brisson 2014;

---

2. See the Maliseet-Passamaquoddy online dictionary, Passamaquoddy-Maliseet Language Portal, <https://pmportal.org/browse-dictionary>. See also Sturtevant 1978, "Eastern Algonquian Languages."

D'Avignon and Girard 2009; Correa and Girard 2006; Girard 2006; Girard and Gagné 1995; Girard and d'Avignon 2005; D'Avignon 2008; Beaulieu 2003; Girard and Perron 1995; Vincent and Bacon 1997, 2002; Havard 1992; Jaenan 1975, 1986; Trigger 1971, 1992).

These early alliances seem to have been at the core of relationships established by French merchants in the Americas during their first contacts in Brazil and Florida in the sixteenth century (see map 2). These alliances made by *private entrepreneurs* laid the groundwork for the official alliance policy of the French King Henry IV that was applied with Indigenous Nations in New France upon the signing of the first treaty of alliance in 1603 (Girard and Brisson 2014, 25–40): a formal alliance to ensure peace, settlement, and the expansion of trade.

This historical reality of Indigenous Nations welcoming and forming alliances with Europeans was not unique to the Innu, Maliseet, Algonquin, Mi'kmaq and Huron who were the first allies of the French in New France.

The alliance policy of the Spaniards: Alliances for conquest

Champlain likely lived in Mexico some time before he arrived at Tadoussac in 1603. He was able to see the strategies used by the Spaniards, who had formed an alliance with the Tlaxcaltecas to conquer Mexico City. The numerous publications in Europe of works by Cortés illustrate the competition between several key players in the quest for the resources of the Americas, with Spain being the major player from the sixteenth century onward.

The model began to take hold in Mexico as early as 1519. Hernán Cortés recalled, in works distributed in Europe under the patronage of the king of Spain, that he could not, with the handful of soldiers that accompanied him, defeat Moctezuma's troops and subdue Mexico. To help him overcome an overwhelming number of enemies, his main Tlaxcaltec allies, as well as their allies, raised large armies. Without these alliances, Cortés could never have conquered this new territory (Ricard 1925, app.; Cortés [c. 1520] 1996).

After the 1520s, shared management of territories, populations, and resources were the main responsibilities and concerns of the Spanish Crown, which took on the role of protector and guardian of the *Indios* (Indigenous Peoples) while granting special statutes of self-government to the Peoples that were its first allies (de Zurita [1553] 1840; Encinas 1596, quoted in Garcia Gallo 1945; Florescan 2004; International Court of Justice 1991; Cuena Boy 1998; Zavala 1990; Beltrán 1992, 2009).

MAP 2 – French settlements in America, sixteenth to early seventeenth century

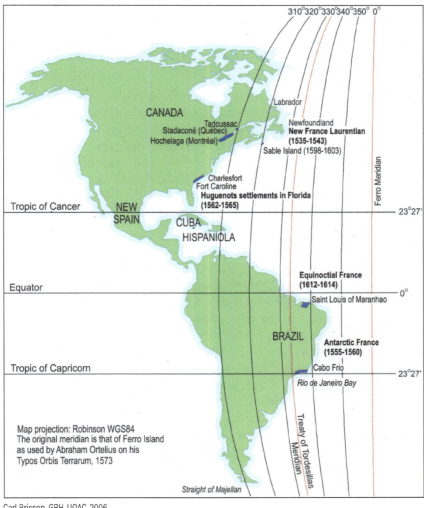

Carl Brisson, GRH, UQAC, 2006

These alliances ensured political recognition for the Tlaxcaltecas and special status in Mexico, a status that the state of Tlaxcala still claims today. The autonomy enjoyed by the Tlaxcaltecas remains a fine example of the forms of self-government that have developed outside colonial and collective histories of conquest (Garcini 1996).

The establishment of a policy of allying with Indigenous Peoples shows the adaptability of France, which was carving out a place for itself in North America mainly through merchants and private entrepreneurs, which compensated for the lack of immigration and local resources. By forming alliances with Indigenous Peoples occupying territory in New France, France sought to justify and legitimize its presence in unfamiliar territory over which it had, in fact, little control.

These trading alliances marked the first intercultural encounters in America. The recognition of the rights of Indigenous Peoples of the Americas requires us to look at the first contacts with Europeans in a new light, to move away from the concept of "one-way discovery and conquest." Reflecting on the merchant alliances that were first formed in the seventeenth century in the context of political recognition of Indigenous Peoples can help us re-evaluate our colonial or collective histories. (For the role of conquistadors and missionaries in discovery–conquests, see Matamoros Ponce 2007.)

From an anthropological and historical point of view, and from economic, political and legal perspectives, these alliances occurred in a context of giving and exchanging, as evidenced by the movement of people and the exchange of goods. Trading alliances preceded more formal political alliances, which sought to establish administrative and legal ways of managing territories. In the case of the alliances between France and Indigenous Nations, the way in which the meetings were prepared, the role of each actor, the interpreters (spokespersons), the Chiefs or representatives of the Indigenous Nations (some of whom travelled to Europe), the actions of the European nations, the alliance rituals that were preceded by feasts and other rituals (baptisms in Mexico; smoking pipes of peace, making speeches, exchanging gifts, dancing, singing, and feasting on the territory of the welcoming Indigenous Nations) all contributed to concluding alliances (Girard and Gagné, 1995; on the free movement of people within the framework of alliances, see Correa and Girard 2006).

The written records of these encounters—travel journals, missionary accounts, maps, and place names, not to mention the king's commissions and the letters patent that established the nature of the relationship with local Peoples and the management of territory and resources—are all sources through which the words of Indigenous Peoples can be heard. From the history of the conquerors, from the forgotten or rejected history of the conquered, and from the lesser-known history of their allies emerges a history of encounters. These encounters were, it is true, unequal, and they involved their share of misunderstandings and conflicts. They were, nevertheless, encounters during which trade was influenced by intercultural relationships: the "customs of the country" produced hybrid practices in a northern environment, an immense territory with a scattered population where Indigenous Peoples continued to occupy their traditional territory, far removed from the contemporary system of reserves.

FIGURE 1 – Cover page of a history of the takeover of Indigenous governments of the state of Tlaxcala by Indigenous Peoples allied with the Spanish

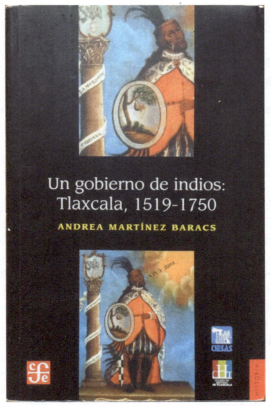

Source: Andrea Martinez Baracs. (2014). *Un gobierno de indios: Tlaxcala 1519–1750*. Mexico City: Fondo de Cultura Económica. (For further details of the history of the Indigenous governments of the state of Tlaxcala, see Garcini 1996; Oswald Spring 2004.)

For Europeans, in this case the French, alliances with the Peoples who occupied and owned the territories were necessary if France was to make any claim to New France, either in Europe or locally. It goes without saying that, for Indigenous Peoples, these alliances were part of a culture of giving and receiving, in which the free movement of people was an important element. In northern Indigenous cultures, giving was inseparable from making alliances because alliances were founded on reciprocity. In such cultures, exchange and mutual respect were at the heart of an alliance. It was this exchange, both symbolic and material, that allowed the alliance to be concluded and to endure; without alliances, it would have been difficult to secure such exchanges (Correa and Girard 2006; Havard 1992, 12ff; 2003,166, 212, 215; Thierry 2001,155; 2010).

In the case of the French, alliances allowed Indigenous Peoples to share land with the newcomers, while ensuring that their territory and culture would be respected.

The sixteenth century: Free movement of persons and exchange of goods

Recent research has revealed a multitude of actors in the history of French discoveries in New France: Indigenous Chiefs and allied, coalition, or enemy Nations; businessmen, shipowners, navigators, and sailors, fishers; and traders; coureurs des bois, and translators who participated in their own way in the great adventure of the first contacts and first alliances in North America. From the study of exchanges between the two continents emerges, a history of the movement of people, of navigation, maritime trade, and exchange of products, in what Gruzinski called "global history" (1999, 2004; See also Matamoros Ponce 2007). This perspective shows how the colonization of local cultures was structured in a global economy. Indigenous Peoples were culturally different actors, but they participated in an economy that was being established as newcomers arrived. This history, centred on economic exchange, of material culture, through a relationship of exchange, helps us to understand the influential historical structures that marked the initial phase of the development of New France. The nature of the relationship between Indigenous Peoples and Europeans was due to this underlying economic and intercultural reality, which makes it possible to review the foundations of the fundamental rights of Indigenous Peoples in North America.

This history also reveals the role of private entrepreneurs, who set sail from certain coastal regions in Europe before sovereigns became interested. These merchants and fishers played a vital role by befriending Indigenous Peoples, with whom they engaged in local and international trade. Sailors from ports on the Atlantic coast, such as Saint-Malo, Rouen, Le Havre, Granville, Nantes, Bordeaux, and La Rochelle, as well as French and Spanish Basques, Normans, and Bretons, enabled France to carry out its plan for colonizing New France. In the second half of the sixteenth century, fishing attracted attention. Biggar (1965, 19), an authority on the topic, estimated that more than fifty French, Portuguese, and English ships plied coastal waters in search of cod, turbot, and sturgeon as early as 1527. More recent surveys of later periods have confirmed that, between 1570 and 1580, European vessels coming to *terreneufve* for the cod fishery numbered 350 to 380, of which 150 were French, one hundred Spanish, fifty Portuguese, and thirty to fifty English; there were also twenty to thirty Basque whalers. This European fleet had a deadweight of approximately 28,000 to 30,400 tons and employed no less than eight to ten thousand persons (Girard, Perron, 1995, 56ff). The volume of shipping shows the importance that Newfoundland, and probably the St. Lawrence River, already represented for Europe in the sixteenth century. From the outset. the North Atlantic route was developed by merchant capital that sought to profit from fishing.

Numerous ships crossed the Atlantic in the sixteenth century. They were mainly private vessels that sought to ensure their safety by associating themselves with a Crown that would, in theory, protect them. According to statements collected by Father Lalemant, Indigenous Peoples would have seen up to twenty ships at Tadoussac in 1560 (Girard and Perron 1995, 62). Other sources show that between 1574 and 1603 more than 160 Norman ships were contracted, mainly for the *Terres neuves* and *Canada*. During the same period, Le Havre would have equipped half that number (80) to Brazil (Bréard and Bréard 1889, 12ff; Dionne 1891, 53n11; Dickason 1984, 134–5; Turgeon 1982, 2004, 108; Biggar 1965, 23; on New France in Brazil and the search for Brazilian wood, see Jean de Léry 1994, 306ff; Dickason 1993a, 1993b, 1996).

Despite England's claim to control the seas, in 1591 fishermen from the Channel Islands were still coming to Saint-Malo to obtain fishing passports for Newfoundland. These permits were sometimes denied (Harrisse 1968, v, n4).

In exchanges between the French and Indigenous Peoples, various objects and goods were used as currency. According to the account of Jacques Cartier's second voyage, the Iroquois used a currency that greatly surprised the French. It was a type of seashell, which they used as the French did gold and silver (*de l'or et de l'argent*) and which they considered to be the most precious thing in the world. Jacques Cartier and his crew had little interest in these *esnoguy* necklaces, preferring precious metals (Correa and Girard 2006; Bideaux 1986, 180, 152–3).

To communicate to other European powers his official alliance policy with Indigenous Peoples, Henri IV commissioned Marc Lescarbot to produce a lengthy work on New France, which was published in 1609 (There were five editions by 1618, including a partial one in English in 1609 and one in German in 1614). Lescarbot noted that mariners from La Rochelle also used goods from the forest to repair their ships. Gum and the bark of fir trees were prepared in large ovens on the beaches. He added that the Savages, who undoubtedly took part in the work, were surprised to see the French using resources from the forest in this way. The Indigenous Peoples called these sailors *Normans*, the term they used for all the Frenchmen they had long been encountering along the coastline (Lescarbot [1609] 2007, 211, 217; Lescarbot, in Thierry 2001; Lestringant 2007, 1999).

The Spanish also had traded a wide variety of goods with the Indigenous Peoples that they encountered in Mexico in the mid-sixteenth century. An investigator commissioned by the Spanish king to examine trade rights and taxation of the Indios in Mexico in the 1550s reported "that at that time all trade was through exchange; the use of money not being known, one conducted business by giving one object for another, which is the oldest, most respectable, safest, and most natural way of trading" (de Zurita, [circa 1553] 1840, 239; on the goods traded by the sixty Indigenous persons who frequented the Mexico City market daily in the mid-sixteenth century, see 170ff).

Property and freedom of trade

For Francisco Vittoria (1486–1546), a Dominican from the University of Salamanca, who is for the Spanish the founder of international public law (*law of nations*), commercial exchanges were central to colonization. Exchanges were at the heart of first contacts between Indigenous Peoples and Europeans; they were unequal certainly, but they nonetheless became. Vittoria set out what he considered to be the elements that justified barbarians (non-Christians) falling under the domination of *superior European powers*. He drew up fourteen principles that justified this domination, and the main ones are still used by courts to justify colonization and even some forms of suppression of Indigenous Peoples' rights.

For Vittoria, *the* <u>Indigènes</u> *possessed their territory and would truly be the owners of both public and private property until the Spaniards proved that they themselves did not own it*. Another principle maintained that *Indigenous peoples had an obligation to trade with Europeans* (Malaurie 2000, 56 ff; Morin 1997, 32ff; 2004).

The *droit des gens* was a set of legal principles that the European powers had devised to justify their ascendancy over Indigenous populations and over the territories that they were claiming. In practice, the *Savages* had to welcome Europeans, which they usually did so long as no harm was done to them. *Europeans could bring good that Indigenous persons* (indigènes) *did not have and exchange them for gold, silver, or any other product.* Vittoria stated that *"their princes cannot prevent them from trading ... and neither can kings ... prevent their subjects from trading with the Barbarians ... if the Barbarians allow the Spaniards to trade peacefully with them, the Spaniards cannot legitimately seize their goods, any more than if they were Christians"* (our translation; Malaurie 2000, 60; Morin 1997, 35).

Thus, for Vittoria, other than dividing territories between European powers, discoveries and papal bulls did not confer any rights over Indigenous Peoples and their territory. Indigenous Peoples had governed themselves, their domains and their resources before the arrival of the Europeans, and they should continue to do so. In this context, Spain and France considered that they were dealing with organized Peoples that did not have to cede or sell their land to exercise their property rights over their traditional territories.

Whalers and cod fishers in northeastern Québec: Sixteenth and seventeenth centuries

The territorial divisions associated with some of the more familiar Indigenous Nations should not obscure the fact that the concept of *exclusive territories and fixed boundaries* did not correspond to land-management practices in Algonquian cultures, with which the Maliseet are associated (Frenette 1996, quoted in Charest et al. 2004, 20ff). Over the long term and as the need arose, the movements of Indigenous Peoples depended on the resource requirements of families or the group. Along the St. Lawrence River where the facing banks are close to one another—for example, between Tadoussac, a traditional gathering place, and the south shore, Cacouna, Trois-Pistoles, Le Bic, and Rimouski—the river and its banks seem to have been border zones or locations for ongoing exchanges among Indigenous Peoples. Their travels followed the rhythm of the seasons, the need for natural resources, or the availability of meeting places such as those in Tadoussac, Le Bic, and other villages or gathering places (Fortin et al. 1993; Desjardins et al, 1999).

Despite its claims, France could not assert control over this northern New France in the seventeenth century. The French fishers who came, most often on their own initiative, had to tolerate the presence of the Spanish (Basques), the English, the Dutch, and even the Danes. As late as 1644, the French faced fierce competition, as can be seen from a reproach made to the French parliament (Parlement) by the Compagnie française du Nord

(French company of the north): "The said Basques, and other French individuals with them, claimed to have the same rights as other nations, and wanted to continue the said fishing and to send vessels, but they were chased away, their ships taken, and their people imprisoned by the English, Danes, and Dutch, who through their companies had become the strongest in the region" (our translation; Bélanger 1971,78).

Historically, certain natural harbours such as Blanc-Sablon, Sept-Îles, Tadoussac, Le Bic, and very likely Cacouna appear to have been preferred places for ships to anchor and trade with Indigenous populations. The coasts of Newfoundland, as well as the banks of the St. Lawrence up to the mouth of the Saguenay, were frequently visited from the sixteenth century on. The French, Spanish, Portuguese, English, and Dutch left ports on the Atlantic coast of Europe to fish off North America. They were merchants, traders, sailors, and fishers who had discovered in their seasonal voyages, through hard work, that fish was an important resource that found takers in the vast markets of Europe.

In these encounters, connections must have been forged with Indigenous Peoples, though these remain little known. It is highly likely that these Indigenous Peoples would have traded and participated in various activities linked to fishing. The Mi'kmaq and Maliseet, traditionally fishers, would surely have been among the first to make contact with these European fishermen.

CHAPTER 2
The Etchemin and the alliance of Indigenous Nations with France

Rethinking our colonial and collective histories and reconsidering the place occupied by Indigenous Peoples in intercultural exchanges is a major research challenge. It is as if Europeans arriving in America created colonial (sixteenth century) and then collective (nineteenth century) foundational myths based on the cities they had settled (founding of Québec city, 1608; Montréal, 1642) or "conquered" (Mexico City, 1523), with European heroes writing, publishing, and *creating* French, English, Spanish, Portuguese, and Dutch Americas (Girard and Kurtness 2012). Yet a more complex reality has emerged that goes beyond these foundational myths. The works of Todorov on the European invention of America (1982; Baudot and Todorov 2009) and those by Gruzinski (1999, 2004) on the first forms of globalization and interethnic blending that sucked all local cultures into civilizing matrices and discourses constructed by Europeans seeking to physically and symbolically appropriate all space, invite revision of our colonial and collective histories around notions related to alliances and treaties as a foundation for the recognition of Indigenous Peoples (D'Avignon and Girard 2009; D'Avignon 2008, 475ff; Delâge 2007; on Mexico and colonial thought, Matamoros Ponce 2007; on Mexican historiography, Florescano 2004).

THE FIRST TREATY OF ALLIANCE BETWEEN FRANCE AND INDIGENOUS NATIONS (1603)

Various interests underlay the nature of the alliance that was concluded between Indigenous Nations and France in May 1603 near Tadoussac. The host Peoples appear to have been establishing new forms of alliance with France. These intercultural alliances were recognized in an official policy proclaimed by Henri IV, who specified in new commissions and letters patent (8 November 1603) the importance that France placed on alliances agreed with Indigenous Nations in New France (on Henri IV's policies toward Indigenous Peoples, Thierry 2010; Bayrou 1994).

The accounts of Champlain and his contemporaries, as well as the texts of early-seventeenth-century commissions and letters patent, testify to the importance of the Indigenous Peoples of North America to making colonization and trade in New France a reality. Henri IV's policy concerning New France and its Indigenous Peoples was based on a desire to form alliances with the local population. This policy of alliance with Indigenous Nations was decisive for the birth and for the future of the colony. It was an extension of various experiments that France had carried out during the sixteenth century in Brazil, Florida, and elsewhere in the Americas (Lestringant 1999, 289ff; Havard 2003, 27ff; Dickason 1993a, 103; 1993b, chap. 9, 220–2; 1996). France had been having difficulty participating in the colonization of the Americas, constantly being pushed northward, either by the Portuguese or the Spanish in Brazil, the Spaniards in Florida, or the English and the Dutch in New England or even in New France (Davenport 1917; Cumming and Mickenberg 1980).

Therefore, from the beginning of the seventeenth century, France afforded a certain degree of autonomy to the Indigenous Peoples with whom it formed alliances for colonization, trade, and peace (D'Avignon 2008; Girard and Gagné 1995; Girard 2002, 2003a, 2003b, 2003c, 2004; Morin 1997, 2004; Girard and d'Avignon 2005; Lajoie et al. 1996; Grammond 1995; Havard 1992; Dionne 1984).

The meeting of 27 May 1603

In his famous *Des Sauvages*, which he published with the support of the king in the fall of 1603, Samuel de Champlain described the course of his voyage to New France in that year. He often used the terms *nation* or *peuple* to refer to the groups he encountered during the expedition. On 27 May 1603,

2. THE ETCHEMIN AND THE ALLIANCE OF INDIGENOUS NATIONS

Champlain and Gravé Du Pont, the latter as leader of the expedition, went to Pointe Saint-Mathieu (now Pointe aux Alouettes) near the port of Tadoussac, where they met a group of Montagnais who had set up camp there (see map 3). This meeting led to first documented alliance between France and Indigenous Nations (Girard and Brisson 2014, 26ff; 2018, 10ff; Girard and Gagné 1995, 3–14; D'Avignon 2008; for documentary records, Appendix 2002, Alliance… and French Regime, Treaties, Charters, Letters Patent; see also Battiste 2016).[1]

This site of Pointe Saint-Mathieu has potential since it is of historical interest as the location of the meeting that led to the the first treaties of alliance between First Nations and France, including the Innu of Essipit, the Maliseet of Viger, the Algonquins, and the Hurons, in collaboration with the actual municipality of Baie-Sainte-Catherine and various stakeholders.

MAP 3 – Location of Tadoussac in present-day Québec

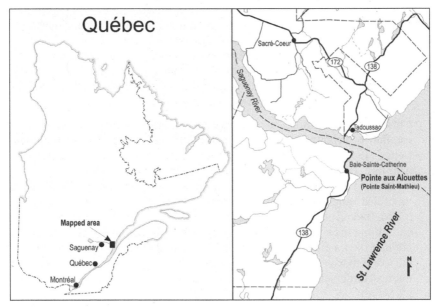

---

1. On the archaeological and heritage potential of the site, see: Archéologie, 2015, <https://www.notrepanorama.com/uploads/Pointe-aux-Alouettes.pdf>.

First treaty of alliance between the Etchemin (now known as Maliseet), Algonquin (or Anishinabe) and Montagnais (now Innu): Champlain's description of the meeting at Pointe Saint-Mathieu, 27 May 1603 – Carl Brisson, GRH, UQAC, 2006

The pleasant welcome offered to the French by the great sagamo of the savages (sauvages) of Canada, their feasts and dances, the war they have with the Iroquois, how and with what their canoes and cabins are made. With a description of Pointe Saint-Mathieu.

On the 27th day [of May] (1603), we went to find the savages at Pointe Saint-Mathieu, which is one league from Tadoussac, with the two savages led by the sieur [François Gravé] du Pont, to report on what they had seen in France and the warm welcome they had received from the king. Having set foot on land, we went to the hut of their great sagamo (utshimau, Chief, in Innu), whose name is Anadabijou, where we found him with some eighty or a hundred of his companions who were having a tabagie (which means feast), who received us very well according to the custom of the country and made us sit next to him and all the savages arranged one next to the other on both sides of the said hut. One of the savages whom we had brought with us began to make his report of the good reception that the king had given them and the good treatment they had received in France. And that they were sure that his said Majesty wished them well and wanted to populate their land, and make peace with their enemies, who are the Iroquois, or send them forces to defeat them. [...]

Now, after he had finished his speech, the said great sagamo Anadabijou having carefully heard him began to take petun [tobacco] and give some to the said sieur du Pont-Gravé of Saint-Malo, to me and to some other sagamos who were near him. Having smoked well, he began to make his speech to all, speaking positively, pausing a little a few times, and then resuming his speech by telling them that truly they must be very happy to have his said Majesty for a great friend. They all answered with one voice: "Ho, ho, ho, which means yes, yes. He, continuing his speech, said that he was very happy that his Majesty would populate their land and wage war on their enemies, that there was no nation in the world to which they wished more good than the French. Finally, he made them all understand the good and the usefulness that they could receive from his Majesty.

[...] They rejoiced the victory they had obtained over the Iroquois, of whom they had killed some hundreds, whose heads they cut off and had brought with them for their ceremony. There were three nations when they went to war, the Etchemin [now called Malecite/Walastoqiyik], Algonquin [Anishinaabe] and Montagnais [Innu], numbering a thousand, who went to war against the said

2. THE ETCHEMIN AND THE ALLIANCE OF INDIGENOUS NATIONS

Iroquois, whom they met at the entrance to the river of the said Iroquois [Richelieu River], and brought down a hundred of them. They make war only by surprise, for otherwise they would be too afraid and fearful of the said Iroquois, who are greater in number than the said Montagnais, Etchemin and Algonquin (our translation from the modern French edition by D'Avignon, 2018, 18–21; for other editions, Appendix, 1973, Champlain... Laverdière: 70ff; for the complete transcription from Champlain [1603] 1978, see Appendix, 1603, Champlain, Des Sauvages in PDF version; Girard and Gagné 1995, 3–14; Girard and Brisson 2014, 2018; Beaulieu and Ouellet 1993).

An analysis of the historical context of this first formal alliance sheds light on the beginning of diplomatic relations between France and the Montagnais (Innu), Maliseet and, Algonquin Nations and provides information about the motives behind the alliance concluded near Tadoussac. First, we should mention that the French were welcomed by their hosts with respect and deference. Champlain specified that he and Gravé Du Pont adapted to "the customs of the country" (coutume du pays), which in no way prevented him from identifying the groups encountered as three *nations*. The first to speak were "Savages" who had been taken to France by Chauvin in 1602 and had had the opportunity to meet King Henri IV (Morley, 1966). Indigenous leaders had sent some of their relatives to France on earlier voyages, indicating the importance placed on preparing for the 1603 alliance. Cartier had taken a dozen representatives of Indigenous Peoples to France on his three voyages in 1534–1540, including Donnacona, Chief of Stadacona, whom Cartier identified as "king of Canada" (Bideaux 1986, 193, 410n7; Dionne 1891, 102; on Donnacona's refusal to cede the territory, Bideaux 1986, 116; Leacock 1981).

During the formal gathering in May 1603, the French followed protocol by smoking pipes of peace and letting their hosts take turns speaking, while the Grand Chief Anadabijou led the celebrations. Champlain stated in his account that France had three objectives: (a) to have the Indigenous Peoples' best interests at heart, (b) to populate their land, and (c) to make peace with their enemies. If necessary, France could help defeat their enemies. For the Montagnais, the alliance allowed them to become close allies of the French in the fur trade. They even came to dominate the anti-Iroquois coalition for a time while limiting French access to communities within their ancestral lands (Girard and Gagné, 1995; Girard, 2003a; Royal Commission on Aboriginal Peoples 1996, 129ff).

A few days later, on 9 June 1603, the Algonquins and the Etchemin, Nations allied with the Innu (Montagnais) in the war against the Iroquois (Laurentian coalition), met with Gravé Du Pont and Champlain. The celebrations that had begun at Pointe Saint-Mathieu continued at Tadoussac, and it was the Algonquin Grand Chief Tessouat (Besouat) who this time was at the centre of the formal ceremonies.

Returning to France, Champlain was accompanied by six representatives of the Indigenous Nations, which confirmed for the allied and coalition Nations as well as for the French that a formal alliance had been agreed and was beginning to take shape. One of the persons whom Champlain took with him was the son of Tessouat, the Grand Chief of the Algonquin Nation who controlled the fur trade around the Ottawa River and Île aux Allumettes (Savard 1996; McLeod 1966). Another was a captive Iroquois woman who symbolized the common enemy; at that time, females were taken from an enemy Nation and integrated into their captors' culture. Among the representatives of an Indigenous Nation identified as "Canadian" were a female and two children, probably Mi'kmaq or Maliseet. An Indigenous person *from Acadia*, probably a Mi'kmaq or a Maliseet, was also taken to Europe. Placing these people under the protection of the French king undoubtedly prepared the way for the alliances that France concluded with the Maliseet in 1604 and 1605 and with the Mi'kmaq of Membertou in Acadia (1607). With such gestures, Indigenous Peoples and Europeans made commitments to each other (D'Avignon 2018, 51; Champlain, [1603] 1978, chap. 13).

With their new allies in New France, the French began a system of land management based on exploring the territory to find land suitable for agriculture (seigneuries) or containing natural resources (concessions). Land outside seigneuries and concessions was designated as territory reserved for the *Sauvages*. Champlain and Gravé Du Pont were central in the process. They concluded and carefully maintained the first alliances and then created new ones with the Maliseet and Armouchiquois of Acadia in 1604–1607 (Lescarbot 2007, 216; Thierry 2001; Morrison 1974); the Algonquins and Hurons in 1609; the Nepissingue, the Outaouais, and the Petun in 1615–1616; and the Iroquois in 1624.

2. THE ETCHEMIN AND THE ALLIANCE OF INDIGENOUS NATIONS

FIGURE 2 – Re-enactment of the meeting on 27 May 1603 at Pointe Saint-Mathieu, (now Pointe aux Alouettes, municipality of Baie-Sainte-Catherine)

Re-enactment of the meeting of 27 May 1603. Celebration of the four-hundredth anniversary of the 1603 alliance, Pointe Saint-Mathieu, Baie-Sainte-Catherine near Tadoussac. Anadabijou, the Innu Grand Chief, leads the talks in the company of other coalition members, a Maliseet Chief (unidentified) and Tessouat, Chief of the Algonquins. They welcomed Champlain to the alliance on 27 May 1603. Photo: Pierre Lepage. Reproduced with permission.

FIGURE 3 – Celebrating the 1603–2003 alliance:
Chapel located on the heritage site

Celebration of the four-hundredth anniversary, 27 May 2003, Pointe Saint-Mathieu (Baie-Sainte-Catherine near Tadoussac). Photo: Pierre Lepage collection.

France and Henri IV's commission of 8 November 1603: The beginning of an official policy of treaties and alliances with Indigenous Peoples in New France

Before presenting and analyzing the contents of the royal commission, let us specify that King Henri IV had announced an official policy earlier in 1603 that became clearer as the year proceeded.

The king had already stated in his letter to de Monts of 8 January 1603 (Brown 1966) that the representative of France had the mandate to *"treat and contract to the same effect, peace alliance, confederation, and good friendship, correspondence and Communication with the said Peoples and their Princes or others having power and Command over Them, maintain and keep and carefully observe the Treaties and alliances which you will agree with Them, provided that they satisfy it on their part"* (our translation;

2. THE ETCHEMIN AND THE ALLIANCE OF INDIGENOUS NATIONS

Archives nationales du Québec, C11D, vol. 1, fol. 19; D'Avignon 2006, 32; on French law, Isambert, 1829).

The mandate is clear and explains why Champlain and Gravé Du Pont set about concluding a first alliance on 27 May 1603, shortly after their arrival in North America.

In the aftermath of their voyage, Henri IV drew up a new commission on 8 November 1603, and he revised the letters patent on 18 December to specify the activities that would be undertaken on territories of the *Sauvages*. With these documents, he structured the fur trade, both in Acadia, a territory set aside for new immigrants, and elsewhere, along the St. Lawrence River and its banks.

COMMISSION OF 8 NOVEMBER 1603[2]

Commission of the King to Sieur de Monts, for the habitation of the lands of La Cadie, Canada, and other places in New France.

Together, the prohibitions to all others to trade with the Savages of the said lands.

– Expand French territory, preferably in a "legitimate" way

Henry, by the grace of God King of France and Navarre, to our dear and beloved Sieur de Monts, Gentleman Ordinary of our House, Greetings.

As our greatest care and work is and has always been, since our accession to this Crown, to maintain and preserve it in its ancient dignity, grandeur, and splendor, *to extend and amplify as much as legitimately can be done, the limits and boundaries of it.*[...]

– The king states that he has been well informed

Having been informed for a long time of the situation and condition of the country and territory of Cadie, (Acadia), moved on all things by a singular zeal and a devout and firm resolution that we have taken, with the help and assistance of God, author, distributor and protector of all kingdoms and states.

---

2. Appendix 1, Commission of the King..., original in French, including the letters patent granting a monopoly on the fur trade in certain regions. (Our headings, paragraphing, punctuation, italics, and underlining; Lescarbot [1603] 1911, 2: 490-494).

– Description of the Peoples who inhabit these lands

To convert, bring, and instruct the peoples (our emphasis) who live in this region, present barbaric people, atheists, without faith or religion, to Christianity, and to the belief and profession of our faith and religion: and to remove them from the ignorance and infidelity in which they live.

– Importance for King Henri IV of consultation before drawing up a new commission

Having also recognized for a long time on the report of the Captains of ships, pilots, merchants and others who of long hand have haunted, frequented, and traded with what is found of peoples in the aforementioned places, how much can be fruitful, convenient and useful to us, to our States and subjects, the residence, possession and dwelling of the aforementioned ones for the great and apparent profit which will be withdrawn by the great frequentation and habit which one will have with the peoples who are there, and the traffic and trade which will be able by this means to treat and negotiate surely.

– Act with prudence using knowledge and experience

We, for these causes fully confident of your great prudence, and in the knowledge and experience that you have of the quality, condition and situation of the said country of la Cadie: for the various navigations, journeys, and frequentations that you have made in these lands, and other close and surrounding ones:

– The king designates de Monts, Lieutenant General of la Cadie […], which he delineates as between the fortieth and forty-sixth parallels (see map 4)

We assure you that it is our resolution and intention, being committed to you, you will know how to attentively, diligently and not less courageously, and valiantly *execute and lead to the perfection that we desire, have expressly committed and established you, and by these presents signed by our hand, commit, order, make, constitute and establish our Lieutenant General, to represent our person in the countries, territories, coasts and confines of la Cadie:* To begin from the *fortieth degree, until the forty-sixth*. And in this extent or part of it, as much and as soon as it is possible, to establish, extend, and make known our name, power, and authority.

– One objective: Subjugate all Peoples

And by this means to *subjugate, subject and make obey all the peoples of the said land, and their neighbors*: and by means of these and all other lawful ways, to call them, to have them instructed, provoked and moved to the knowledge of God, and to the light of the Faith and Christian religion, to establish it there:

– Maintain peace and our authority

And in the exercise and profession of the aforesaid to *maintain, guard and preserve the aforesaid peoples, and all other inhabitants of the aforesaid places, and in peace, rest,* and tranquility to command them as much by sea as by land: to order, decide, and cause to be carried out all that you will judge to be due and able to do, to maintain, guard, and preserve the aforesaid places under our power and authority, by the forms, ways, and means prescribed by our ordinances.

– Appoint prudent and capable officials to enforce our laws

And to have regard to it with you, to commission, establish and constitute all the Officers, as well for matters of war as of Justice and police for the first time, and from there in front to us to name them and present them, to be disposed of by us and to give the letters, titles and provisions such as they will be necessary. And according to the occurrences of the business, *you yourselves with the opinion of prudent and capable people, to prescribe under our good pleasure, laws, statutes, and ordinances as much as it will be able to conform to ours*, in particular the things and matters to which is not provided by these:

– Policy toward Indigenous Peoples: Negotiation and alliance

To treat and contract for the same purpose peace, alliance, and confederation, good friendship, correspondence, and communication with the said peoples and their Princes, or others having power and command over them: to maintain, keep, and carefully observe the treaties and alliances which you will agree with them: provided that they satisfy it on their part.

– Go to war if treaties and alliances are not respected

And, failing that, to make open war on them to compel them and bring them to such reason as you shall deem necessary for the honour, obedience, and service of God, and the establishment, maintenance, and preservation of our said authority among them: at least to haunt and frequent by you, and all our subjects with them in all assurance, liberty, frequentation, and communication, to negotiate and trade therein amicably and peaceably. To give and grant them graces and privileges, offices, and honours.

– Reserve the necessary resources, including land, for settlers

Which full power above, we also want and order that you have over all our said subjects and others who will move and want to live, trade, negotiate, and reside in the said places; to hold, take, reserve, and appropriate to you what you will want and will see to be more convenient and suitable to your charge, quality and use of the aforementioned lands, to allocate such parts and portions of them, to give them and attribute to them such titles, honours, rights, powers and faculties as you will see need to be, according to the qualities, conditions, and merits of the people of the country or others. Overall populate, cultivate, and habituate the said lands as quickly, carefully, and dexterously as time, place, and convenience will allow:

– Continue to explore coasts and other land areas and the resources found there

To make or have made for this purpose the discovery and reconnaissance of the extent of the maritime coasts and other regions of the mainland, which you will order and prescribe in the above-mentioned space from the fortieth degree to the forty-sixth, or otherwise as much and as far as it is possible along the said coasts, and on the mainland. To carefully search and recognize all kinds of mines of gold and silver, copper and other metals and minerals, to have them excavated, drawn, purged and refined, to be converted into use, to dispose of according to what we have prescribed by the Edicts and regulations that we have made in this Kingdom of the profit and emolument of the same, by you or those whom you will have established for this purpose, *reserving* to *us* only the tenth denarius of what will come from those of gold, silver, and copper, assigning to you what we could take from the aforementioned other metals and minerals, to help you and relieve you of the great expenses that the aforementioned charge could bring you.

– Construct the buildings needed for settlement

Wanting however, that your safety and convenience, and of all those of our subjects who will go to, inhabit, and trade in the said lands: as generally of all others who will accommodate themselves there under our power and authority, *you can build and construct one or more forts, places, cities and all other houses, dwellings and habitations, harbors, havens, retreats, dwellings that you will know proper, useful and necessary for the execution of the said enterprise. To establish garrisons and men of war to guard them.* To assist and avail yourselves of the aforementioned effects of vagrants, idle persons and those without a confession, both in the cities and in the fields, and of those condemned to perpetual banishment, or to at least three years outside (of) our Kingdom, provided that it is by the advice and consent and by the authority of our Officers.

– Conquest and settlement ... under the authority of the king

In addition to the above, and which is moreover prescribed, mandated, and ordered to you by the commissions and powers given to you by our dearest cousin, the Sieur d'Anville, Admiral of France, for what concerns the fact and the charge of the Admiralty, in the exploit, expedition, and execution of the aforementioned things, to do in general for the *conquest, settlement, habitation and conservation of the said land of La Cadie, and of the coasts, surrounding territories and their belongings and dependencies under our name and authority*, which we ourselves would do and could do if we were present in person, although I know that the case requires a more special mandate than we prescribe to you in these presents: To the content of which, we mandate, order, and very expressly enjoin all our justiciars, officers and subjects, to comply: And to obey and hear you in each and every one of the above-mentioned things, their circumstances and dependencies.

– The king revokes all previous commissions and mandates to explore, conquer, settle, and inhabit lands located between forty and forty-six degrees of latitude

(To) You, also give in the execution of the same all the help and comfort, strength, and assistance that you will need, and will be required by you, the whole under penalty of rebellion and disobedience. And to the end that no one pretends to be ignorant of [...] our intention, and wants to interfere in all or part of the office, dignity and authority that we give you by these presents: *we have of our certain sciences, full power and Royal authority, revoked, suppressed and declared null and void hereafter and from now on, all other powers and Commissions, Letters and expeditions given and delivered to any person whatsoever, to discover, conquer, populate and inhabit in the aforesaid extent of the said lands situated from the said fortieth degree, up to the forty-sixth whatever they may be.* And furthermore, we mandate and order all our said Officers of whatever quality and condition they may be, that these presents, or *Vidimus* duly collated of them by one of our friends and false Councillors, Notaries and Secretaries, or other Royal Notary, it is done at your request, pursuit, and diligence, or of our Procurators, to read, publish and register the registers of their jurisdictions, powers and straits, ceasing as far as they are concerned, all troubles and impediments to the contrary. For such is our pleasure.

– Signature

Given in Fontainebleau the eighth day of November, the year of our Lord one thousand six hundred and three: And of our reign the fifteenth. Signed, HENRI and lower, By the King, POTIER. And sealed on simple yellow wax tail.

To the commission, the king added a monopoly on the fur trade. He specified the places to be favoured for this trade with the *Savages* already there (see map 4).

– Extract from the letters patent regarding the fur monopoly

to trade and barter furs and other things with the Savages, to frequent, negotiate and communicate during the said period of ten years, from the Cape of Raze to the fortieth degree, including all the coast of Acadia, land

> *and Cape Breton, bay of Saint-Cler, of Chaleur, the Percées islands, Gaspé, Chichedec, Miramichi, Les Escoumins, Tadoussac and the river of Canada (St. Lawrence river), as well on one side as on the other, & all the bays and rivers which enter into the said costes*, under penalty of disobedience, and complete confiscation of their vessels, supplies, weapons and merchandise, for the benefit of the aforementioned Sieur de Monts and his associates, and a fine of thirty thousand pounds.

MAP 4 – New France, 1609

ANALYSIS OF THE COMMISSION OF 8 NOVEMBER 1603

After Champlain's return to France at the end of September 1603, King Henri IV modified the general commission regarding the new territory (8 November 1603).

Henri IV detailed for the first time in a general commission what he had explicitly refused to do in previous commissions (Cartier, 17 October 1540; Roberval, 15 January 1541 in Bideaux 1986, 233, 247; Édit et Commission de la Roche, 12 January 1598, in Lescarbot 1911, 196). He had placed himself under an obligation to consult the local Peoples and conclude an agreement on friendship and alliance before writing to the commission of 8 November, only a few days after the publication of Champlain's account in *Les Sauvages* of his numerous meetings with these Nations between May and September. Champlain's subsequent works followed the same pattern.

This gesture by Henri IV shows that the 1603 voyage aligned with the king's desire to plan and assert his control over the territory through a policy of alliances with local Peoples, in this case the Innu (Montagnais) and their allies, the Algonquin and Etchemin (Maliseet). This foundational text dealing with the rights of Indigenous peoples seems to constitute a first recognition and confirmation of the fundamental rights of the Indigenous Peoples in New France.

The king affirmed in the commission of 8 November 1603 that he needed to be well informed and to consult those who knew the country and the local Peoples, who also had to be consulted in order to establish lasting treaties and alliances.

Henry IV insisted on abolishing all previous commissions, which, incidentally, had had little effect on the territory. The king could not claim to have a clear agreement with Indigenous Peoples on an alliance or treaty "according to the custom of the country" by relying on the general commissions accorded to Cartier, Roberval, or la Roche. In the commission given to la Roche in 1598, Henry IV had stated that he would wait for more information before specifying the powers that would be exercised in New France.

The king stipulated that management of the territory had to be respectful of the first occupants and the different uses of the available land and resources. Beyond this equitable management of territories and resources, the king frequently reiterated that, for him, alliances and treaties allowed for the most diverse exchanges, using the terms "traffic," "trade," and "commerce," without limiting these activities to one group in particular.

The king believed that, to retain the lands under his authority, he had to deploy the necessary resources to discover, conquer, populate, settle, and protect territories either known or yet to be discovered. In the paragraph on the obligation to conclude and to respect alliances with Indigenous Peoples occupying the territory, the king restated the importance of negotiating and getting along with them and of respecting their rights, to ensure the free movement of goods and persons for the purposes of trade, settlement, and development of the land.

Although what he set down in writing was addressed primarily to people in Europe in an attempt to confirm his authority, the king was relying on the Indigenous Peoples who occupied the new territories. He wanted to manage the land so as to earn money from it, mainly by organizing exchanges of every description. Trade was not limited to the fur monopoly, important as that was.

With this commission and the accompanying letters patent, King Henri IV established a system for managing territory. The letters patent identified parts of their traditional territory that, with the agreement of Indigenous Peoples, were reserved for settlement. Where territory was to be shared between Indigenous Peoples and the eventual settlers in *"Cadie"* and elsewhere, local Indigenous Peoples and those who held the monopoly were to come to an agreement on how the fur trade and other activities would be shared.

The commission shows that Indigenous Peoples were considered actors—different, it is true, but full-fledged actors nonetheless—in the system of land, resource, and trade management that was being established. For the king of France, it was important above all to trade and to structure different ways of using the territory so that both local Peoples and future settlers would profit from the development of its resources.

The French policy of alliance with Indigenous Peoples: A policy of recognition and pacification influenced by Spain

The recognition of Indigenous Peoples by France followed a trend that was prevalent in Europe at the end of the sixteenth century. Spain, which remained a major player in the Conquest of the Americas, had had to adapt after the Villadolid debate of 1550 and was forced to deal with a legal statute by which the *Indios*, or local Peoples were recognized as actors who could not be ignored legally or politically. Spain was trying to free itself from a well-established feudal mentality (Humeres 1995, 27). The Ordinances of the Spanish King Philip II of 15 July 1573 had serious consequences for the management of lands and Indigenous Peoples in New Spain. Henri IV's commission for New France bears the imprint of classical writing regarding the conquest and taking of land in the name of Christianity or a king. By insisting on notions associated with an obligation to form alliances and secure friendship with local Peoples, the French king also recognized that they were "free and independent" (Encinas 1946, 232–46; see especially Levaggi (1993) on Spain's treaties with Indigenous Peoples; Milagros Del Vas Mingo 1985; on Spanish alliance policy in Mexico, Ricard, 1925).

The Tlaxcaltecas, an Indigenous People that lived about 100 kilometres from Mexico City, had formed an alliance with the Spaniards against Moctezuma beginning in 1519. They considered themselves not vassals of the Spanish but allies and did not feel that their lands were handed over to or taken by the king when they became his allies (Velasco 2003, 324–5; Encinas 1945, 1: 60–1; Martinez Baracs 2008).

Philip II's ordinances of pacification, 13 July 1573

A careful reading of the ordinances of King Philip II, especially the articles referring to the policy of pacification, reveals an obligation to consult local Peoples and establish alliances.

The text of the commission of 8 November 1603 is quite similar to these articles, expressing a willingness to negotiate and form proceed to conquest. Henri IV's phrase—*traiter, contracter à même effet paix, alliance et confédération avec les peuples et leurs Princes*—in his commission of 8 November 1603 regarding New France undoubtedly finds its source there.

The notion of consulting and making concessions to local Indigenous Peoples and their representatives in order to peacefully colonize those who agreed to negotiate an alliance was founded on Spanish policy implemented beginning in 1573. The king's mandate was clear: "discoveries" were no longer to be called "conquests." Conquest was no longer to be used as a pretext for using force or harming Indigenous Peoples. The king of Spain wanted to be well informed about the diversity of the Nations and of the languages they spoke while also making sure he was well acquainted with the overlords they obeyed. In the commissions of 1598 and 1603, Henri IV imposed the same obligations on himself with regard to New France. Philip II specified that:

> by trade and rescues, treat friendship with them, showing them much love and showing love to them, and giving them certain things of rescue to which they are attached (gifts), without showing covetousness for their goods, regulate friendship and alliance with the lords who seem most able in the *pacification* [our italics] of the earth (our translation; Levaggi 1993, 81–82; de Encinas [1596] 1945, 244–5; Todorov 1982, 219).

Article 140

140

> *Por via de comercio y rescates, traten amistad con ellos, mostrandolos mucho amor y acariciàndolos, y dandolos algunas cosas de rescates a que ellos se aficionaren, y no mostrado codicia de sus cosas, asientese amistad y alianza con los señores y principales que pareciere se mas parte para la pacificación de la tierra* (Levaggi, 1993: 81–2; de Encinas [1596] 1945, 244–5).

Levaggi (1993), a specialist in these matters, believed that, in the Spanish world, from the sixteenth century onwards and especially after the ordinances of 1573, a policy of concluding treaties with Indigenous Peoples was considered essential. Regarding the ordinances on pacification and on the obligation to secure peace and friendship through alliances, he stated that:

the truth is that the treaty was the instrument chosen by Spain to regulate its peaceful relations with Indigenous Peoples that it was trying to bring under its jurisdiction, or with whom it simply wanted to be in peace and friendship. The custom of celebrating peace treaties extended to all frontiers of the Indies and throughout the Hispanic period until its expansion, in some cases, to the era of independence (our translation; Levaggi 1993, 90; Encinas [1596] 1945, 244-6).

The model implemented by Philip II appeared ideal. It established principles that involved several values, including the obligation to respect, consult, and make concessions to local Indigenous Peoples. In practice, the application of such principles may have left a lot to be desired.

When a legislator ruler enters into an alliance, they assume the obligation to respect and recognize the other party, not as a primitive to be converted or civilized but as a full partner. The ruler is obliged to establish a special relationship with Indigenous Peoples, and establishing such a relationship should precede any consideration of conquest or submission (Todorov 1982, 190).

It was this model that was adopted in 1603 near Tadoussac and after, with Henri IV requiring that his representatives be well informed about and on good terms with the local Chiefs with whom France was concluding alliances. The Spanish model of pacification became, in France, a policy of alliance with Indigenous Peoples.

The commission of 8 November 1603 used terms such as "barbarians to be Christianized," "conquest" and "discovery," even "submission." Politically, the principles of consultation and respect for the rights of Indigenous Peoples were embedded in the foundational texts that were the product of intercultural encounters. These hybrid texts, often contradictory in their vocabulary, were an attempt to integrate these principles into official policies of alliance with Indigenous Peoples. The king wished to assert his ascendancy over the territories of New France and to make this known to his European competitors, while at the same time ensuring that he had loyal partners and allies on the ground to protect settlement of the territory and regulate trade in the colony. Even so, the discovery of the *Other*, which is always defined in relation to oneself and one's European, Christian, civilizing worldview, continued to inspire fear, as it had in the Middle Ages. The spirit of the Crusades and of wars of religion permeates all texts from the beginning of the seventeenth century related to the Indigenous Peoples of the sixteenth and seventeenth centuries.

The treaty of alliance of 1603 and its aftermath for the Maliseet

The Etchemin, a people allied with the Montagnais and Algonquin, were also present at the celebrations in May and on 9 June 1603, but the identity of their Chief is unknown. In the seventeenth century, *Etchemin* referred to both the Maliseet and the Passamaquoddy, two Nations related through language and culture, whose territory covered the watersheds of the Saint John and Saint Croix Rivers. In the Penobscot region, this territory is now associated with the Abenaki Nation. During his first contacts with the Etchemin, Champlain did not identify this Nation, merely recalling on several occasions that these Peoples were close culturally. We will return to this topic.

According to ethnohistorian Laurence Johnson, the Etchemin present at Tadoussac "were at the northern limit of their territory [...]" (Johnson 1995, 23). They also went to the mouth of the Saguenay to trade with other Indigenous Nations or with the French. In 1604 and 1605, Champlain concluded other alliances on Etchemin territory with Bessabez (from the Penobscot River also called Norembègue), with whom he became close, Secoudon (from the Saint John River), Cabahis, and several others (Giguère 1973, 1:35; Michaud 2003).

Champlain and the September 1604 alliance with the Maliseet Nation – Norembègue (Pentagouet, Penobscot) River[3]

On his return from France, Champlain met with various Maliseet Chiefs, whom he identified as Etchemin and Armouchiquois (Pentagouet or Passamaquoddy). The gatherings always proceeded in the same manner. First, he befriended leaders and then met with various Chiefs and their representatives to agree on alliances that would secure peace, trade, and settlement in the territories occupied by the Maliseet Nations.

---

3. Appendix, 1973. Giguère 1973; for a version in Modern French, see D'Avignon (2018).

FIGURE 4 – Mural depicting the history of alliances
in the state of Tlaxcala, Mexico

Source: Private collection in Tlaxcala, 2013.

Murals, a means of expressing, contesting, and recofding the history of alliances, in the National Palace of the state of Tlaxcala in Mexico. Three large murals represent a critical vision of Mexican national history. The Malinche, a female interpreter, and the Indigenous Chiefs who were allies of Spain are central to this visual depiction of history. The murals were inspired by codices that chronicled the history of Indigenous Peoples before the arrival of the Europeans. Alliance with the Chiefs of Tlaxcala, a state near Mexico City. Cortés with his interpreter, the Malinche, the daughter of one of the kings of Tlaxcala in April 1519.

In his account of his 1604 voyage, Champlain began by describing his encounter with Secoudon, the Chief of the Saint John River, which is called Ouygoudy.

> On 20 June 1604, Champlain met with Chief Secoudon [...] that [we] named the Saint John River [New Brunswick] because it was on that day that we arrived there. By the savages it is called Ouygoudy. This river is dangerous if one does not recognize certain points and rocks which are on both sides. [...] However Ralleau, secretary to the sieur de Mons, went there some time later to find a savage [Maliseet] called Secoudon [Secondon], chief of the said river, who reported to us that it was beautiful, large and spacious, having a quantitý of

meadows and beautiful woods, such as oaks, beeches, walnut trees, and thickets of wild vines. *The inhabitants of the country go by this river to Tadoussac, which is on the great river of St. Lawrence, and cross only a little land to get there. From the Saint-Jean River to Tadoussac, [it] is sixty-five leagues.* At its entrance, which measures 45 degrees two thirds, [there] is an iron mine (our translation; D'Avignon, 2018: 86–7).

The meeting of 6 September 1604 was with Chief Bessabez, an Armouchiquois Chief (Pentagouets) from the Penobscot River, also called the Norembègue, and the goal was to conclude an alliance.

The next day, the sixth day of the month (September 1604), [we] covered two leagues and saw smoke in a cove, which was at the foot of the above mountains, and saw two canoes led by savages [Armouchiquois] who came to look us over at musket range. I sent our two in a canoe to assure them of our friendship. The fear they had of us made them run away. The next morning, they returned to the edge of our boat and parleyed with our savages. I had them given ship's biscuit, petun [tobacco] and some other small trifles. These savages had come to hunt beaver and catch fish, of which they gave us some. Having made an alliance with them, they guided us to their river of Pentagouet [Penobscot River] so called by them, where they told us that it was their captain named Bessabez who was chief of it. I believe that this river is the one that several pilots and historians call Norembègue and that most say is large and spacious, with several islands, its entrance at a latitude of 43 [degrees] and 43 and a half and others say at more or less 44 degrees latitude (D'Avignon 2018, 96).

The alliance of 16 September 1604 with Bessabez and Cabahis (Etchemin)

Champlain followed his customary protocol in these meetings, taking necessary precautions with certain Chiefs and intermediaries (interpreters)) with whom he had confidence. He continued his journey and, with the support of Chief Bessabez, he went to the Norembègue River (Penobscot) to conclude another alliance (see map 5). Although this meeting, which is described in detail, did not have the pomp and ceremony of the May 1603 meeting at Tadoussac, it was described in the same way and in the same terms. The protocals were followed by both sides, and Champlain adapted to "local customs". He showed his readers and King Henri IV that he was applying, as required by the commission of 8 November 1603, the policy of alliance with the Indigenous Peoples he was encountering in New France, in this case the Etchemin Nations (Maliseet and Passamaquoddy).

MAP 5 – Meeting places, 1604

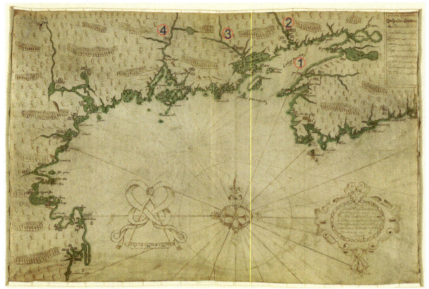

This portolan-style map on vellum, designed and drawn by Samuel de Champlain, was originally intended to be presented to the king of France. The map provides the first comprehensive delineation of the New England and Canadian coastline from Cape Sable to Cape Cod, showing Port Royal, Labaye française (1) (the Bay of Fundy) and the Saint John (2), St. Croix (3), and Penobscot (4) Rivers, as well as the islands of Kennebec and Mount Desert, which Champlain himself had named. The place names and coastline correspond very closely to Champlain's account in his *Voyages*, published in 1613. Most maps of the time were made by cartographers who depended on information from explorers and navigators. Champlain based this map entirely on his own exploration and observations, including his interviews with native Americans, as well as and his own mathematical calculations. The map shows French settlements and Indian villages along the coast. Forests are represented by stylized drawings of trees. Hill symbols indicate elevations visible from the coast. Dangerous shoals are indicated as groups of small dots, and anchors represent places where Champlain himself had dropped anchor.

Champlain continued by describing his meeting with Bessabez and Cabahis. This meeting was probably planned during the gathering at Pointe Saint-Mathieu between 27 May and 9 June 1603. He used the same narratives and the same terms to describe this more formal alliance with the Maliseet Chiefs Bessabez and Cabahis.

To ensure that the gathering of a larger number of persons would proceed without incident, Champlain made initial contact and had a discussion with the Chiefs (excerpts from D'Avignon, 2018: 98–100).

> Now, I will leave this discourse to return to the savages who had led me to the falls of the Norembègue River, who were to inform Bessabez, their chief, and other savages who went to another small river to inform their chief, named

2. THE ETCHEMIN AND THE ALLIANCE OF INDIGENOUS NATIONS

Cabahis, and give him notice of our arrival. On the 16th of the month [of September 1604], there came to us some thirty savages on the assurance given to them by those who had served us as guides. The said Bessabez also came to find us that same day with six canoes. As soon as the savages who were on land saw him arrive, they all began to sing, dance, and jump until he had set foot on land, then afterwards [they] all sat down in a circle on the ground, according to their custom when they want to make some speech or feast. Cabahis, the other chief, arrived shortly afterwards also with twenty or thirty of his companions, who withdrew separately and were very happy to see us, especially since it was the first time, they had seen Christians. Sometime later, I went ashore with two of my companions and two of our savages, who served us as interpreters and instructed those in our boat to approach the savages and keep their weapons ready to do their duty if they saw any emotion from these peoples against us.

The Chiefs began the speech-making and exchange of gifts. For their part, the French wanted to befriend them, fight their enemies, settle on their lands, and show them how to grow crops.

Bessabez seeing us on land made us sit down and began to smoke with his companions, as they usually do before making a speech. They made us a present of venison and game. I told our interpreter to tell our savages that they should make Bessabez, Cabahis, and their companions understand that Sieur de Mons had sent me to see them and their country too, that he wanted to keep them in friendship and to put them in agreement with the Souriquois and [the] Canadians their enemies. And further that he wished to dwell in their land and show them how to cultivate it, so that they would no longer live out such a miserable existence as they were doing, and some other words on this subject.

Champlain stated that, as had been the case in 1603, Indigenous Peoples welcomed the French for the purposes he reiterated. However, he made it clear that they wanted their traditional land protected to ensure trade with France.

What our savages made them hear, with which they seemed greatly pleased, saying that no greater good could befall them than to have our friendship, [that they] desired that we should inhabit their land and make peace with their enemies, *so that in the future they could go hunting for beaver more than they had ever done in order to share them with us* [italics added] while we provided them with things necessary for their use.

To celebrate the alliance, Champlain gave gifts to the Indigenous persons he had just met before the parties separated:

After he had finished his speech, I gave them a present of axes, hats, knives, and other little trinkets. Afterward, we separated from each other. All the rest of that day and the following night, they did nothing but dance, sing, and make good cheer, waiting for daylight when we traded some beaver. And then each of us went back, Bessabez with his companions on the one hand, and we on the other, very satisfied to have gotten to know these peoples (D'Avignon 2018, 98-100).

Champlain concluded his narrative by describing, after crossing the Kennebec River, the route that leads to the Etchemin River and then the St. Lawrence. While he had identified the Peoples of these territories as Armouchiquois, he specified that they were Etchemin (Maliseet) who lived on the Kennebec River and the Norembègue River. He concluded that all these Peoples followed the same lifestyle.

> On the 17th of the month [of September 1604], I took measurements and found 45 degrees and 25 minutes of latitude. Having done this, we left to go to another river called the Kennebec, thirty-five leagues distant from this place, and nearly twenty from Bedabedec. *This nation of savages from the Kennebec is called Etchemin, as well as those from the Norembègue.* On the 18th of the month, we passed near a small river where Cabahis was, who came with us in our boat some twelve leagues. And having asked him where the river Norembègue came from, he told me that past the Falls of which I made mention above and that travelling some way on it, one entered a lake by which they go to *the river Sainte-Croix*, from where they go a little by land then enter *the river of the Etchemin*. Further down the lake is another river on which they travel for a few days, then enter another lake and pass through the middle. Then having arrived at the end, they still go some way by land, then enter *another small river* [the current Etchemin River] which comes to discharge itself at one league from Québec, which is on the great Saint Lawrence River. *All these Norembègue peoples are very swarthy, dressed in beaver skins and other furs like the savage Canadians and Souriquois, and* [they] *have* [the] *same way of life* (italics added; D'Avignon 2018, 98-101; Appendix, 1973, Champlain…, Laverdière: 179 ff).

Champlain and the alliance of 5 July 1605[4]

Champlain continued his meetings with the Chiefs of the Kennebec River, Manthoumermer, Machim, and Sazinou. He concluded new alliances and formed friendships with the help of his guides, who led him to the Chiefs of the Nations, who were accompanied by about thirty members in welcoming the representatives of France.

> And [we] left for this purpose on the 5th of the month (July 1605). Having covered a few leagues, our boat was nearly lost on a rock which we grazed in passing. Further on [we] met two canoes which had come to hunt birds, which for the most part moult in this time and cannot fly. We accosted these savages by means of ours who went to them with his wife, who made them understand the subject of our coming. We made friendship with them and the savages of this river, who

---

4. Modern French edition, D'Avignon (2018).

2. THE ETCHEMIN AND THE ALLIANCE OF INDIGENOUS NATIONS

served as our guides. And going further to see their captain called Manthoumermer, as we had covered seven or eight leagues, we passed by some islands, straits, and streams which spread along the river, where we saw beautiful meadows. And skirting an island which is some four leagues long, they led us to where their chief was with twenty-five or thirty savages, who as soon as we had anchored came to us in a canoe a little separated from ten others, who were those accompanying him. Approaching near our boat, he made a speech, in which he made known the ease he had in seeing us and that he wished to have our alliance and to make peace with their enemies by our means, saying that the next day he would send [a dispatch] to two other savage captains who were inland, one called Marchim and the other Sazinou, chief of the Kennebec River (D'Avignon 2018, 107; Appendix, 1973, Champlain... Laverdière: 195–6).

Bessabez was the Chief of a Penobscot Nation that lived near present-day Bangor, Maine. Although it is not known who represented the Maliseet (Etchemin) Nation at the May 1603 meetings near Tadoussac, this Grand Chief, with whom Champlain had a special relationship, was certainly well informed about the meetings and the intentions of the French with regard to the Maliseet. This also seems to have been the case with Chief Cabahis, whose name was used by Champlain. Bessabez had been central to the 1604 negotiations. A favoured mediator, he was respected by Champlain, who chose him over other Chiefs. He was the first to speak. He ensured the smooth running of the ceremony, which made it possible to conclude the alliance along the same lines as the one adopted during the May and June 1603 meetings in Tadoussac (for his biography, see Campeau [1602–1616] 1967, 662). Along with the Chiefs with whom he had already concluded alliances, he encouraged other meetings that allowed Champlain to continue the work with which he had been tasked by King Henry IV, that is, to form alliances that would ensure peace and trade with the Indigenous Nations around the Norembègue River (Pentagouet, Penobscot).

The other Chiefs identified were Cabahis, Manthoumermer, Marchin, and Sazinou, Chief of the Kennebec River. Campeau (1967, 678) identified another Maliseet Chief, Oagimont (Oagimou), representing an Etchemin Nation living in Passamaquoddy Bay along the St. Croix River. The latter would have facilitated alliances between the French and other Nations, namely the Souriquois and the Armouchiquois (Passamaquoddy). He accompanied Membertou, the great Souriquois chief, a great ally of the French, who converted to the Catholic religion and had exceptional influence over his peers (Campeau [1602–1616] 1967, 677).

Most of these Chiefs were well known to Champlain, who identified them by name on several occasions throughout his works. He associated them most often with the rivers or other places they came from and referred to various Indigenous Nations that were culturally close and that are recognized today as Indigenous Nations: Maliseet/Passamaquoddy, Mi'kmaq, and Abenaki. They occupy New Brunswick, Maine, and the region south of the St. Lawrence River in Québec.

RECENT READINGS OF THE 1603 ALLIANCE

Although the 1603 alliance has not received, until now, any particular attention in Québec and Canadian historiography, it has been mentioned in several historical works. Authors have tended to note that a meeting was held at Pointe Saint-Mathieu without, however, elaborating on its consequences for the French or the Montagnais, allies in the Laurentian coalition.

To our knowledge, Canadian historiography has never considered the commission of 8 November 1603 as a treaty recognizing the fundamental rights of the Indigenous Peoples of New France. We refer the reader to D'Avignon (2006, 2008), who focused on the historiography of foundations and alliances over the long term. These more recent works which were written to celebrate the founding of Québec (1608–2008) focused on the concept of foundational alliances. It has helped show the predominance of a traditional history that rejects any idea of meaningful alliances while perpetuating the notion of a nascent and conquering French America (Girard 2006; D'Avignon and Girard 2009; Tremblay 1959, 1963; Trigger 1971, 1992; Trudel 1963, 1966, 1967; on alliances, see also Brisson and al.,1993).

Alliances and the recognition of the rights of Indigenous Peoples in Canada (1982) and in Québec (1973 and 1985)

Judge Albert Malouf, in his famed decision of 15 November 1973 that led to the 1975 James Bay and Northern Quebec Agreement, repeated several times that the Royal Proclamation of 1763 had little bearing on the rights of the Indigenous Peoples of Québec because "no treaty was ever made with the Indians of the Province of Québec [...] for the cession to the Crown of the land comprised in that province" (Malouf 1973, 42, 56–7; Girard and Thibeault 2001, 2:48; app. T, 152).[5]

---

5. Girard, Camil, and Jessica Thibeault. 2001. *Rapports sur les questions autochtones: Canada 1828–1870*, 3 vol. Chicoutimi, QC: Alliance de recherche universités-communautés (ARUC); monts Valin-monts Otish (CRSH); Groupe recherche sur l'histoire – Université du Québec à Chicoutimi. These documents include French and English versions with our pagination to facilitate referencing (most documents

In Québec, prior to this agreement, which had forced negotiations, no "cession" or "extinguishment" of title to the lands of Indigenous Peoples had occurred.

The Royal Commission on Arboriginal Peoples recognized that the official text from 1603 serves as an embryonic doctrine of the rights of Indigenous Peoples in Canada. Commissioners René Dussault and Georges Erasmus stated at the outset of their work in 1993 that historians and legal scholars needed to study more closely the commissions and letters patent that were used to establish French Indigenous policy in the early seventeenth century. This policy established nation-to-nation rights between Indigenous Peoples and the representatives of France in New France.

According to the Royal Commission, treaties were the best means of extending the influence of the king of France in America, and the possibility of forming a "confederation" with Indigenous Peoples was mentioned. De Monts was ordered to scrupulously maintain and respect these treaties, provided that the Indigenous Peoples and their leaders did the same.

> From the early stages of French settlement, we find harbingers of the doctrine of Aboriginal rights. For example, in 1603 the French Crown issued a Royal Commission to the Sieur de Monts, giving him the authority to represent the King within a huge territory extending along the Atlantic coast from modern New Jersey north to Cape Breton Island and indefinitely westward within the fortieth and forty-sixth parallels. The document makes no attempt to disguise its imperial ambitions: it empowers De Monts to extend the King's authority as far as possible within these limits and to subdue the local inhabitants. Nevertheless, in the same breath, it acknowledges the independent status of the Indigenous peoples of America and recognizes their capacity to conclude treaties of peace and friendship. De Monts is given the following instructions: "*traiter & contracter à même effet paix, alliance &: confederation, bonne amitié, ajustercorrespondance & communication avec lesdits peuples & leurs Princes, ou autres ayans pouvoir & commandement sur eux...*"
>
> De Monts' Commission portrays treaties as a principal means for enlarging the King's influence in America and mentions the possibility of "confederation" with the Aboriginal peoples. De Monts is told to uphold and observe such treaties scrupulously, provided the Indigenous peoples and their rulers do likewise. If they default on their treaty obligations, De Monts is authorized to resort to war in order to gain at least enough authority among the Indigenous peoples to enable the French to settle in their vicinity and trade with them in peace and security. (Royal Commission on Aboriginal Peoples 1993, 10; D'Avignon 2006,

---

had no pagination). A pdf version has been given to the community: See, *Les Classiques des Sciences sociales*, Université du Québec à Chicoutimi.

445ss; on alliances and entering into treaties, Royal Commission on Aboriginal Peoples 1993, vol. .2.1; 1994, 1996; Lajoie et al. 1996).

For Indigenous Peoples, their occupation of their territory for thousands of years and the welcome they had extended to Europeans implied treaties of alliance, friendship, and trade (see map 6). There was in these alliances no question of ceding territory. As the Royal Commission on Aboriginal Peoples pointed out, this original policy established nation-to-nation rights between Indigenous Peoples and French representatives in New France.

The French became members of an alliance of independent nations and relied, from an economic and military point of view, on a relationship of cooperation. They had no sovereign power beyond the limits of French settlements (Royal Commission on Aboriginal Rights 1996, 1:127).

According to Olive Patricia Dickason, a historian of Indigenous origin, France had developed a practice of instituting special protocols with Indigenous Peoples in Brazil in the sixteenth century (Dickason, 1984). French mariners and merchants encouraged trade and commerce by adopting the customs and rituals of the Indigenous Peoples they encountered. These protocols were part of numerous processes of commercial and intercultural exchange that had to be maintained. Feasts, speeches, and exchanges of gifts helped formalize and perpetuate alliances. It is useful to recall the importance of the movement of people (women, children, Chiefs) and the presence of interpreters or Indigenous ambassadors who had visited France and learned the language (Correa and Girard 2006, 2007; Girard and D'Avignon 2005; Dickason 1993a, 1996; D'Avignon 2001; Lestringant 1999, 2007; on Florida, Dionne 1891).

For Brian Slattery (1979), a specialist in the history of the rights of Indigenous Peoples in Canada, it is important to recognize that 1603 marked a turning point for France, which wished to restructure its activities in New France on a more solid basis. It appears that these treaties of peace and friendship were part of an official policy of recognizing Indigenous Peoples as independent and capable of entering into treaties of alliance—treaties of peace and friendship, of course, but above all formal alliances, with legal and political values of recognition that the Crown and the Indigenous Peoples mutually agreed to respect. Slattery recognized the importance for France of establishing treaty alliances with "the said peoples," beginning with Henri IV's commission of 8 November 1603.

> Treaties with the indigenous peoples are viewed as a principal means for extending French influence and authority. Significantly, the Crown acknowledges the present independent status of these peoples and the capacity of their rulers and leaders to conclude not only treaties of peace and friendship but also

2. THE ETCHEMIN AND THE ALLIANCE OF INDIGENOUS NATIONS

alliances. De Monts is instructed to observe scrupulously such treaties, provided that the Indians [*sic*] do likewise (Slattery 1979, 84).

French texts mostly use the terms *peuple*, *nation*, and *sauvage* rather than *indien* or *Indian* to refer to Indigenous persons. In the commission of 8 November 1603, in addition to referring to barbarians and atheists without faith or religion, Henri IV used the term *peuple*. Champlain used the terms *peuples* and *nations*, which he came to identify either by the name of their Nation (Etchemin, or by the traditional territory that they occupied, Saint John River, Kennebec, or their watersheds). As Elders of Indigenous communities often remind us, "Lakes and rivers are our papers." Champlain was fully cognizant of that that and relied on the detailed descriptions provided by the Chiefs who accompanied him in their respective territories. Maliseet descriptions of the Saint John River and its tributaries enabled Champlain the cartographer to determine how to map different parts of the Maliseet lands during the first decades of meetings between the French and the Indigenous Nations of New France (see especially Champlain's post-1612 maps).

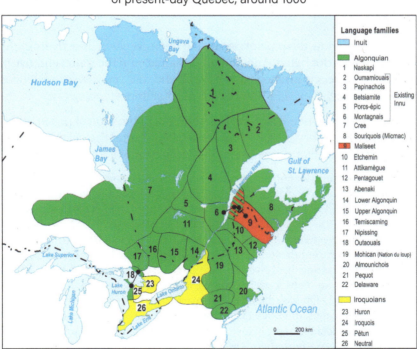

MAP 6 – Indigenous Nations occupying the territory of present-day Québec, around 1600

Cartographic reprint: Carl Brisson, Groupe de recherche sur l'histoire, Université du Québec à Chicoutimi, 2019

Interpreting the 1603 alliance: Cross-cultural narratives

In reporting on the meetings of 27 May and 9 June 1603, Champlain recorded the words of the great *sagamo* Chief of the Savages Canada, Anadabijou. In addition to describing the ritual of feasts, Champlain recounted two brief *atalukan* (Innu story or legend) that the Chiefs had wished to transmit to him (Boucher 2005, 103, 149, 174). For the Indigenous Peoples who had joined the alliances, the free movement of persons was guaranteed both by alliances made on earth and by covenants with higher beings. Covenants with the gods were a prerequisite, an inseparable condition for alliances between humans and their allies on earth.

Champlain presented a new intercultural narrative that showed, on the one hand, that for the Indigenous Peoples who were part of the covenant, the true possessor and protector of the land and its resources was God or the deities. In Champlain's account, which was intended for European readers, the Chiefs emphasized the importance they attached to higher values, which contradicted some of what Champlain said.

In one of the stories, the Chief described how the calumet (pipe of peace) was considered a sacred object that confirmed both heavenly and earthly alliances.

By relating how the pipe of peace had been received directly from the hands of a superior being, Anadabijou, Tessouat, and the representative of the Maliseet (Etchemin) showed that the alliance between these Indigenous Peoples and their new ally, France, was of great importance.

The sacred alliance... and the transmission of the pipe of peace by the Superior Being. Story recorded by Champlain during the celebrations of 27 May to 9 June 1603 at Pointe Sainte-Mathieu and Tadoussac:

> He also told me that another time there was a man who had a quantity of tobacco (which is an herb from which they take the smoke), that God came to this man and asked him where his pétunoir (pipe) was. The man took his pipe and gave it to God, who smoked it a lot. After he had smoked, God broke the said pipe into several pieces and the man asked him: "Why did you break my pipe? You see, I don't have another one." And God took one that he had and gave it to him, saying: "Here is one that I give you, take it to your great *sagamo* (Chief): let him keep it, and if he keeps it well, he will not lack anything, nor any of his companions." The said man took the pipe and gave it to his great *sagamo*, who while he had it, the savages did not lack anything in the world. But that since the said *sagamo* had lost this pipe, [which] is the occasion of the great famine that they sometimes have among them. I asked him if he believed all this. He told me that he did and that it was the truth (our translation; D'Avignon 2018, 26; Appendix, 1973, Champlain... Laverdière: 79–80).

For these Indigenous Peoples, smoking the pipe of peace in the traditional way at gatherings and accompanying celebrations formalized an alliance. Champlain was aware of this as he was recording these words. He certainly understood that all these rituals were essential to conclude alliances with the Indigenous Peoples he met, to make peace, and to ensure a welcome for the French on Indigenous lands. In a certain way, a covenant that was both spiritual and sacred was created by the ceremony of the pipe of peace, which influenced the dynamics of earthly exchanges, both exchanges between persons, since the covenant also created kinship, and exchanges of commercial goods (Correa and Girard 2006; 2007).

If we think about the notion of gift (le don) as understood by Marcel Mauss (1923), it is certain that the gift of objects of wood and stone to humans who meet God, as well as the gift of the pipe of peace, which comes directly from God, confer on such exchanges the fundamental character of covenants of the highest importance. When Chief Anadabijou, acting as the representative of the group that had gathered, entered into the alliance, he represented and embodied the ancestors, the gods, and those present at the celebrations. He had an obligation to receive, to give, and to give back (Mauss 1923, 58, 59ff, 84ff, 93, 97–8). And the things given, goods as well as persons, bound the parties legally because objects and persons have *souls*; and through their souls they were bound to the gods and to humans (on the sacred aspect of treaties and alliances, Borrows 2010, 24–28).

Under the French regime (about 1700), the ceremony of the pipe of peace was used to finalize alliances. It was therefore an integral part of a conscious process of facilitating peace, alliances, exchanges, and freedom of movement throughout the region. By ending hostilities, the pipe of peace initiated a truce during which negotiations could take place. When these negotiations were successful, the ceremony of the pipe ratified the peace and established a fictitious but obligatory kinship between the one offering the sacred pipe and the one receiving it (Havard 2003, 166–73; White 2009, 59).

Within the current framework of the recognition of Indigenous Peoples in Canada, leaders maintain that sovereignty comes directly from the Creator. Sovereignty, as a gift from the Creator, cannot be surrendered or taken away. Thus, the concepts of sovereignty and self-government have spiritual dimensions in contemporary Indigenous thought as was the case with early alliances.

Contemporary oral tradition

The oral tradition of the Innu has preserved the memory of these first contacts with the Europeans. Testimony collected in Natashquan, Unamen Shipu (La Romaine), and Betsiamites (Pessamit) in the last thirty years gives a lesser known, but equally important, picture of the first encounters between Indigenous Nations and France. These narratives mention the nature of the first contacts between Indigenous Peoples and Europeans in the sixteenth and seventeenth centuries. The words of the Elders do not refer directly to 1603 as oral tradition does not allow for such precision. Many believe that the first contacts took place in Québec (city), which was Montagnais territory at the time (Vincent and Bacon 1997, 2; on Innu history and oral tradition, Vincent 1982, 1991, 1992; Girard 1997).

These accounts most often state that the lands were truly those of the Innu. The Elders affirm that they had never given up their ancestral land:

> We never heard that the Innu had given up their land, we never heard that [...] and they never signed anything to that effect. [...] The Innu never gave up their land; on the contrary, they want to hold on to it, and it's the same with the Elders. They want to keep their land. Every time I hear them talk about it, they talk about keeping the land, not giving it up. They are doing today what the Elders used to do in the past (our translation; words of Joseph Bellefleur, Innu from the North Shore of the Saint Lawrence River, quoted in Vincent and Bacon 1997, 35).

These accounts show that, according to oral tradition, the Montagnais welcomed the French to their land. Attracted by the possibility of a better supply of food and various objects for everyday use, they followed their tradition of welcoming and sharing resources for the benefit of the community. This Indigenous concept of land and relationships with human beings is based on a notion of collective ownership of land, which can be developed if the balance between humans, animals, and nature is maintained. In this context, the sacred tree appears as an important metaphor for understanding the culture of Indigenous Peoples, including the Maliseet/Wolastoqiyik Wahsipekuk. Among the Maya, the ceiba tree plays the same role, with the branches and leaves representing the present, the trunk the recent past, and the roots the distant past, that of the Elders and the dead (Hernández 2009, 68–9; Matamoros Ponce 2007, 173). The tree and the space that surrounds it are sacred, for they connect worlds.

Maliseet oral tradition and the birth of the Saint John River territory, Wolastoqey

The Saint John River is at the heart of the territory of the Maliseet of Viger First Nation. The creation of the river is told in the following Maliseet story.

> **THE EMPOUNDED WATER, MALISEET LEGEND**
>
> Aglabem kept back all the water in the world, so that the rivers stopped flowing, the lakes dried up, and the people everywhere began dying of thirst. As a last resort, they sent a messenger to him to ask him to give the people water; but he refused and gave the messenger only a drink from the water in which he washed. But this was not enough to satisfy even the thirst of one. Then the people began complaining, some saying, "I'm as dry as a fish," "I am dry as a frog," "I'm as dry as a turtle," "I'm as dry as a beaver," and the like, as they were on the verge of dying of thirst.
>
> At last, a great man was sent to Aglabem to beg him to release water for the people. Aglabem refused, saying that he needed it for himself to lie in. Then the messenger felled a tree so that it fell on the monster and killed him. The body of this tree became the main river (Saint John's River), and the branches became the tributary branches of the river, while the leaves became the ponds at the heads of these streams. As the waters flowed down to the villages of the people again, they plunged in to drink and became transformed into the animals to which they had likened themselves to when formerly complaining of their thirst (other version, Bélanger 2019, 38–9).
>
> Speck, Frank, G., 1917, "Malecites Tales," *Journal of American Folk-Lore*, XXX, no. 118, 480-481. <https://www.jstor.org/stable/534497>

Water and river networks were indispensable elements of the identities and affiliations of Indigenous Peoples, hunters, fishers, who, during the seasons, criss-crossed the land and, in so doing, gave it meaning and substance. Defining or redefining territory by creating a mythical narrative about it meant taking possession of it, giving it a name. As territory was mapped, Indigenous and French names mingled, which for Champlain and the Maliseet constituted a negotiation, an intercultural exchange. During these exchanges, unequal but accepted by Champlain, the Etchemin perpetuated their myths and legends. They fashioned a discourse of reappropriation and resistance based on the Saint John River, their ancestral territory from time immemorial, bearer of their identity and their culture.

The legend shows that, in the end, the Maliseet lands originated in a tree that had both killed the enemy and created the river. In the real and symbolic universe of Algonquian cultures, this was not trivial. Barriault (1971, available online at the site *Classiques des sciences sociales, Université du Québec à Chicoutimi*) showed the importance of the tree among the Innu as a link to life and as an indispensable intermediary between the world above (gods, elements, the sacred) and the world below (roots, water, earth, enemy gods). It was through the tree, sacred in a way, that movement could occur among the worlds of animals, humans, and gods. The sacrifice of the tree to give life and the river that was at the heart of their identity made possible links between humans, animals, and gods. In the Algonquian world, where animals had preceded humans in the construction of the Earth, it was normal for the Maliseet to transform themselves into animals during celebrations.

Barriault (1971, 26–7) showed the importance of comparing the symbols of verticality linked to trees among the Innu with those of certain other Indigenous Peoples, including, one might suppose, the Maliseet. Does not every people have their sacred mountain and universally, the tree would be:

> a mystery of verticalization, of prodigious growth towards the sky, of perpetual regeneration; it is not only the expansion of life, but also the constant victory over death; it is the perfect expression of the mystery of life that is the sacred reality of the cosmos (our translation; Sterckx 1966, 298, quoted by Barriault 1971, 27).

Barriault concluded that there is no more widespread concept than that of the living cosmos *symbolized by a tree* (27).

Maliseet origin myths are important for other reasons. These myths speak of the origin of life, of the cosmos, of the creation of a sacred territory in which animals and humans must live in harmony and in respect for the gods that watch over the world from above and that control the elements.

Beyond the imperatives of conquest, and beyond alliances that have been forgotten, denied, and ignored by colonial and collective historiographies, and even by Indigenous Peoples themselves, these "stories," situated outside time and space, make mockery of political and economic ideologies. They tell of a world, a culture beyond rationality and chronological time. They are myths that are the "receptacle and synthesis of unconscious and symbolic constructions of the history of a people, a key to understanding passivity or rebellion" (our translation; Matamoros Ponce 2007, 176). Myths act as a manifestation of a culture that is both real and symbolic. These "parallel histories" to colonial and collective histories are both manifestation and contestation, enabling the Maliseet and other Indigenous Peoples to reshape their resistance movements.

Such a story is located outside the historical time and space from which the Maliseet have been excluded. The community still finds meaning in this story today, evidence of an affirmation of identity and resistance that opposes European historical linear time to a time of all time, a sacred time, the time of origins. The legend that tells of the creation of the world from the sacred tree that spread out to create the Saint John River and its tributaries shows the importance of the territory, "a sacred territory" for the Tree-River-People, the Wolastoqiyik Wahsipekuk (on the importance of the symbolic conquest of the tree during the Conquest in Mexico, Matamoros Ponce 2007, 173–4; on Indigenous Peoples' resistance movements, 277).

The Maliseet confirm, through their legends, the foundational myths of their identity that are linked to their territory, in other words, to a sacred land to which they are, with the animals, the trees, and the rivers that run through it, fused in a natural universe where the search for balance between an animal world, a plant world, humans, and gods is central. It is obvious that conquest and discovery had major consequences for these worlds, which entered into competition with the worlds of the Europeans and their gods. This clash of cultures resulted in the disappearance of the Maliseet until their rebirth in 1987.

Through these legends-stories outside chronological time, the Maliseet signify that they are part of their territory. They manifest their defiance, their presence, and their refusal to be forgotten and denied by those who wrote history without consulting them. The Maliseet are reconstructing a memory that is timeless, one that releases them from their oblivion to contest, protest, and reaffirm their place in a historical discourse that had made them disappear. The loss of land and the dispersal of the Maliseet had favoured the construction of a memory that institutionalized amnesia. But, despite this, history continues to let not only the dead speak but also the silent protagonists (on memory and forgetting, Ricoeur 2000, 447, 576ff).

Contemporary Maliseet leaders' views on the first encounters with Champlain

In the draft claim they submitted to the Government of Québec in 2010, the Maliseet of Viger First Nation mentioned the 1603 meeting with Champlain to which they were party. They explained that their territory is close to Tadoussac since the Saint John River is only sixty-five leagues from the facing shore of the St. Lawrence.

Identifying themselves as the *Wulust'agooga'wiks*, "the people of the beautiful river," the Wolastoq River, they reminded the government that it was they, the Maliseet, who had given Champlain a description of the routes and portages between the Bay of Fundy to the south and the St. Lawrence River to the north, which showed that they had occupied the territory (Malecite of Viger First Nation 2010, 3.)

For the Maliseet Nation, their ancestral lands are centred in, but are not limited to, the Saint John River valley. This territory includes part of present-day New Brunswick and Maine, to which would be added the land located between Lévis and Rimouski in Québec (Fortin et al. 1993, 95, quoted in Malecite of Viger First Nation, 2010, 12).

In their brief, the Maliseet vigorously opposed any claim by governments to abrogate treaties concluded with the British. They did not refer to treaties with the French (Maliseet of Viger First Nation 2010, 10).

To our knowledge, after the Conquest in 1763, England did not abrogate treaties concluded by either the French or themselves with Indigenous Nations. The obligation to issue a Royal Proclamation in 1763 was part of an obligation to continue a policy of trade and alliances with Indigenous Peoples. We will return to this question later.

Contemporary Innu leaders' views on the 1603 alliance

In a presentation to the Assemblée nationale du Québec in 2003 during the public hearings on the Common Approach (Entente de principe et d'ordre général) the representatives of the Conseil Mamit Innuat, representing the Innu Nations of the North Shore of the St. Lawrence River, stressed the importance of returning to the spirit of the 1603 alliances. For these Innu leaders, those first alliances had established principles for a relationship rather than a rigid and definitive mode of making laws.

> On the contrary, the Innu, Québec, and Canada have chosen to focus the Mamuitun-Nutashkuan agreement-in-principle and the Mamit Innuat draft agreement-in-principle on the notion of partnership. This means that the treaty, in addition to recognizing rights, also creates processes of continuous discussion, by means of which the partners can arrive at a common vision of the terms of the sharing of the territory. The treaty is no longer conceived as a document that rigidly and definitively establishes the rights of the parties, but rather as the definition of principles that should guide the evolution of a cooperative relationship. This approach is reminiscent of the spirit of the alliance treaties concluded by the Innu and the French at the beginning of the colony, whose essential characteristic was the establishment of a relationship rather than the definition of rights (our translation; Mamit Innuat 2003, 42).

During a conference that celebrated 400 years of Tadoussac's history (13-14 October 2000), the negotiator for the Mamuitun Tribal Council (now the Regroupement Petapan), Rémy Kurtness, also spoke about the importance of reviving the spirit of the 1603 alliance within the framework of the then ongoing negotiations on the Common Approach:

> When we refer to the 1603 alliance between the Innu and the French, we must remember that there were also the Algonquins and the Maliseet, who were later joined by the Abenakis and some other Nations. I do not want to go into details. [...] What I think is important to explain is the symbolism behind the 1603 alliance. It is exactly the same *symbolism that we want to find in our treaty. At that time, we negotiated nation to nation, people to people, government to government. It is in this spirit and with the same symbols that we are negotiating today with the governments of Canada and Québec* [our italics]. Of course, this notion of equals irritates some sensitivities, but this is really how we behave at the central negotiating table, just as Chief Anadabijou behaved when he made an alliance with Champlain and Pont Gravé. The word "treaty" is a big word. It was in a context of oral tradition. The people who preceded me spoke about it at length. The ceremonies that surrounded the covenant confirm that it was a treaty. The dances, the smoking, the formal speeches, the smoking of the pipe, all of these ceremonies that are quite formal in the Innu culture and tradition confirm that when you do that, when you do all of that, you are marking an event in an official way (our translation: Actes de colloque 2000; Kurtness 2000, 132-3; Kurtness, Assemblée nationale du Québec, 2003).[6]

At the end of his reflection, the representative of the Mamuitun Tribal Council reminded those present that the 1603 alliance had made it possible to initiate lasting relationships in a climate of mutual respect and as equals. The then ongoing negotiations were in keeping with the spirit that the original architects of the 1603 alliance had passed on:

---

6. On the General consultation of the Government of Québec on the new Treaty with the Innu Nations which recognize the *aboriginal title* without *cession or sale* to the crown, see online, Assemblée Nationale du Québec, 21 January 2003, « Consultation générale sur le document intitulé *Entente de principe et d'ordre général entre les premières nations de Mamuitun et Nutashkuan et le gouvernement du Québec et le gouvernement du Canada*», *Journal des débats de la Commission permanente des institutions*, vol. 37, no. 194. On the Alliance/Treaty of 1603 with the French, recognition of aboriginal title, legal certitude, territorial integrity, objection to the creation of a third order of government and self-government: Louis Bernard, negotiator for Government of Québec, 17-18; Guy Chevrette, adviser for the Government of Québec, 26-31; André Maltais, for the Canadian Government: 15, 16 ff; for the Innus Nations, Kurtness, Remy Kak'wa: 18-19, 22; Sylvain Ross, 42; Clifford Moar, 2003, 44. <https://www.assnat.qc.ca/Media/Process.aspx?MediaId=ANQ. Vigie.Bll.DocumentGenerique_167135&process=Original&token=ZyMoxNwUn8 ikQ+TRKYwPCjWrKwg+vIv9rjij7p3xLGTZDmLVSmJLoqe/vG7/YWzz>

In our negotiation process [...], we want the same relationship, the same essence that was present in the 1603 treaty, that is, a relationship of friendship, of peace, of alliance, and this in the context of a relationship of equals. That's why [...] I started with the 1603 treaty and came to our negotiation process to say that the same principles, the same values, and the same concepts had to be the basis of our treaty (our translation; Kurtness 2000, 139; 2003, Assemblée nationale du Québec).

Another Innu leader from Mashteuiatsh, Clifford Moar, who played a central role in the negotiations for the new Treaty, *L'Approche commune* (31 March 2004), expressed himself in similar terms when he stated that his Nation had demonstrated in the past, that it could cohabit in a harmonious and peaceful manner with all the citizens of Québec (Girard, Brisson, 2018, 37-38; Moar 2002; 2003).[7]

Conclusions regarding Champlain's first alliances

Various interests underlay the nature of an alliance established between specific Indigenous Peoples and the French. Matters covered could include colonizing, populating, evangelizing, trading, and forming alliances to defend themselves against a common enemy. Initially, the host Indigenous Peoples, composed of Nations, determined the content of the alliances that were concluded. These alliances were made in the Indigenous way, as confirmed in Champlain's account. The details contained in the revised commission and letters patent signed near the end of 1603 show the importance that France placed on alliances and treaties with Indigenous Nations in the policy it was implementing in New France.

The purpose of the meeting in the spring of 1603 was to conclude alliances with the Indigenous Peoples of New France. The letter of 8 January 1603 signed by King Henri IV provided the framework for an official policy for New France and the Americas (Thierry 2010). Over a year full of new developments, the commander of the expedition, Gravé Du Pont, was able take full advantage of the meeting with Indigenous Nations near Tadoussac on 27 May. He had direct and formal contact with the representatives of the Indigenous Nations, whose main spokesman was Grand Chief Anadabijou, and traditional ceremonies and rules took precedence

---

7. On the Treaty, 31 March 2004, Agreement, 2004; Approche commune/ EPOG, 2004, the recognition of "aboriginal title", the territorial regime of each community, the concept "innu aitun" see Agreement, 2004, *Agreement-in-Principle of General Nature between the First Nations of Mamuitun and Nutashkuan and the Government of Quebec and the Government of Canada*, Ottawa, Québec. (Girard, Brisson, 2014, 99-114). <https://www.rcaanc-cirnac.gc.ca/eng/1100100031951/1539797054964>

2. THE ETCHEMIN AND THE ALLIANCE OF INDIGENOUS NATIONS

(McLeod 1966). The prolonged stay by the French in the area around Tadoussac and along the Saguenay, further confirms that this encounter established a first intercultural alliance, from the perspective of both the French and the Indigenous Peoples.

With several Indigenous persons accompanying him on his return to France, Champlain was able to emphasize the importance of the actions taken to form alliances with the local Peoples. The speed with which the king ensured that the monopoly would not be left vacant following the death of Aymar de Chaste; the ease with which Champlain himself managed, with the king's permission, to publish his work *Des Sauvages* (15 November); the king's eagerness to renew the general commission that specified the importance of concluding and respecting the alliances (8 November 1603); and the letters patent relating to trade (18 December 1603): all these events were all connected. They confirmed that France wanted to adopt a policy of alliance with the Indigenous Peoples in New France.

After Champlain returned to France in 1604 and 1605, he again published works with the permission of the king. As he had done in his first book (1603), he told of his meetings and the alliances he had made with the Etchemin and the Armouchiquois, as well as with various other Indigenous Nations that had formed alliances to fight their common enemies. He had visited several Chiefs, including Bessabez, Secoudon, and Cabahis, with whom he had concluded alliances. Preparations for meetings in locations identified by Indigenous Nations (mainly rivers), meetings with representatives of each Nation, the exchange of gifts, and celebrations: this is what constituted the "customs of the country." As a representative of the king, Champlain showed in his writings that he had applied the alliance policy specified in the king's commission. He would continue to conclude and maintain these alliances throughout his career.

Formal signed treaties with the Iroquois (1666) and with the many Nations recognized in the Grande Paix de Montréal (Great Peace of Montréal) in 1701 were not yet in place. In these later treaties, traditional ceremonies took place, including speeches, exchanges of captives and gifts (symbolic pipes of peace, wampum [symbolic belts that confirmed the alliance]), and celebrations. The French added to these later formal celebrations a recognition of each Indigenous Nation. Following each formal gathering, Champlain included the text of the agreement, with signatures, and of the formal speeches in official documents that would be published by the king. The English also included formal meetings and official texts in the treaties they concluded, for example, with the Maliseet in 1725–1726 and up until 1776. We will return to these points in our analysis of the treaties signed by the French and English with Indigenous Nations.

THE INNU PRESENCE ON THE ANCESTRAL LANDS OF THE MALISEET

According to the history of Saguenay-Lac-Saint-Jean (Girard and Perron 1995, 87; Girard and Brisson 2014, 37, 57), in about 1650 the boundaries of the King's Domain (Domaine du roi) or the Traite de Tadoussac extended to the south shore of the St. Lawrence. The authors noted that the south bank of the St. Lawrence was an area that the Innu (Montagnais) considered to be hunting or fishing territory that they used according to need and season, even though these lands were primarily occupied by neighbours and close allies, in this case the Etchemin or Maliseet and Mi'kmaq (areas further east). Similarly, the Maliseet were undoubtedly welcome to collect certain resources on the north shore if needed, as was the case during the 27 May to 9 June gathering at Pointe Saint-Mathieu near Tadoussac, at which the Etchemin (Maliseet) were made welcome.

The King's Domain, recognized Innu territory

It is generally accepted that present-day Saguenay-Lac-Saint-Jean, part of the North Shore (Côte-Nord), and the Lower St. Lawrence (Bas-Saint-Laurent) were occupied by the Indigenous Peoples of the King's Domain (created in 1652) and by the Montagnais or Ilnu (central group, Innu) in particular.

The King's Domain, or the King's Posts (Traite de Tadoussac), was territory reserved for the Indigenous Peoples who occupied it, holding the land and resources under the express protection of the king of France (see map 7). The Royal Proclamation of 1763, and the British king himself in 1767, recognized these lands as exclusive Innu territory. The only way for France or England to claim control on this territory was to agree on an alliance and recognize the territory as Indigenous land. This recognition later enabled England to lay claim to the territory of the Hudson's Bay Company since trading posts were really the only places where the Crowns could claim any control of the lands of Indigenous Peoples.

In the Innu territory associated with the King's Domain, or the Traite de Tadoussac under the French regime and the King's Posts under the British regime, selling land to non-Indigenous persons was forbidden until 1842. European settlement was also forbidden in the territory (until 1842), except in trading posts, where merchants traded with the Indigenous Peoples of the King's Domain. From the territory that they possessed and exploited to the exclusion of others, Indigenous Peoples harvested furs that they exchanged for various goods. The Innu acted as middlemen in this trade from 1600 to 1652. Thereafter, the territory was leased to a tenant who set up posts throughout the Traite de Tadoussac or King's Domain.

Before 1733, the boundaries of the King's Domain were imprecise. Officially, the territory extended along both sides of the St. Lawrence, but its boundaries were most often limited to points on the river from Sept-Îles to Île aux Coudres (Frénette 1996, 183, app. I). After 1685, the south bank of the river was detached from the King's Domain since several seigneuries had been granted there. This did not prevent smuggling or trading to meet food needs (Frénette 1996, 184).

The territory was occupied exclusively by the Indigenous Peoples of the King's Domain who, according to their activities and the season, the resources available, and their needs, ensured a supply of furs or other goods (Girard and Perron 1995, 83ff). The Conquest of 1760 did not change the management of the Traite de Tadoussac, which became known as the King's Posts. In practice, the British had to continue to recognize the entire King's Domain as "Indian lands" (Schulze 1997).

Human occupation of this vast territory in northern Québec dates back some 6,000 years. The occupants were mainly hunter-gatherers, primarily nomads related to the Indigenous Nations identified at the time of first contact as Algonquian Nations, which included the Ilnus or Montagnais. Around 1600, several Algonquian Nations inhabited the territory of present-day Saguenay-Lac-Saint-Jean, as well as a large part of the North Shore and even part of the Lower St. Lawrence. These were the Oumamiouais, the Papinachois, the Betsiamites, the Porc-Épics and the Innu/Montagnais (Girard et Perro 1995, 87). It can be seen in map 7 that the Innu or Montagnais occasionally visited the southern shore of the St. Lawrence River, an area that corresponds to the present-day Lower St. Lawrence, which corresponds to the territory of the Etchemin and the Maliseet.

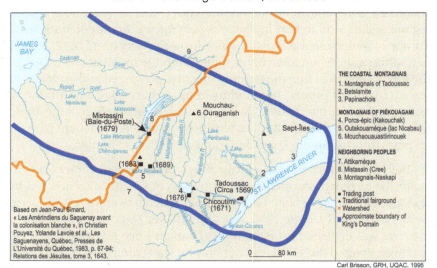

MAP 7 – The King's Domain, about 1650

Obviously, this map does not consider the movements of these Nations or of the numerous conflicts that could exist between neighbouring Indigenous Peoples (Attikamek, Naskapi, Maliseet, Etchemin, and Mi'kmaq). Depending on the need for food or goods, particularly in border areas, families from neighbouring Nations might venture onto territories usually occupied by a different Nation during a given season. This explains the presence of objects from Iroquoian, Maliseet, and other sources in archaeological sites of the region, especially along the most easily accessible waterways. An Indigenous People occupied and exploited one main territory, the borders of which were extended as needed to meet their needs for wildlife (hunting, fishing), plants (bark, wood), or other resources (stones) Langevin 2000, 12). Gathering places such as Tadoussac encouraged the exchange of all types of goods between Indigenous Nations. A traditional meeting place and trading post, it is a few kilometres from the south shore of the St. Lawrence River where the Maliseet lived, so it was easy for them to cross the river in winter and summer to trade and exchange goods at the nearby post.

The south bank of the St. Lawrence...

While the presence of Iroquois was noted during the voyages of Cartier, who met the first Canadiens (probably Maliseet or Mi'kmaq) near Tadoussac, Montagnais Nations were present there when Champlain arrived in 1600. Theories suggest that Iroquoian Peoples were limited to the shores of the St. Lawrence in the sixteenth century, while the Algonquians occupied the interior (Parent 1985, 3ff).

According to Parent (1985, 8, app. IV, V, VI), the Montagnais viewed their homeland as beginning in the present-day Québec city area. Tadoussac remained one of the main meeting places where the Ilnus held traditional gatherings throughout the seasons with various Indigenous Nations, including the Maliseet, Mi'kmaq, and other Nations familiar with the area. It was here in May 1603 that they concluded the first alliance with the French (Girard and Gagné 1995a, 3-14), which became the approach used from then on, as the Montagnais became, along with the Maliseet and Algonquins and then the Hurons, the preferred political, commercial, and military intermediaries for the French in the Franco-Laurentian alliance, especially in the early days of the colony. This group, known as the Laurentian alliance, brought together in addition to the Ilnu Nations the Mi'kmaq, Etchemin, and Abenaki, as well as the Mistassin, Papinachois, and Attikamek (Parent 1985, 165-6). These networks of allies also existed among the Wabanaki confederacies, which included the Etchemin, Mi'kmaq, Abenaki, the Haudesaunee (Great Lakes Iroquois), and Kanatian (St. Lawrence Iroquois, see map 8).

On the south bank of the St. Lawrence, the Innu frequented the Rivière du Loup watershed up to and including Matane (Parent 1985, 8). The Innu or Montagnais inhabited both the Laurentians on the northern shore and the Appalachians on the southern bank. On the north bank, hunts were organized from present-day Québec city to Rivière aux Outardes. On the other bank, they were organized from Rivière-du-Loup to Matane (Parent, quoted in Hamelin 1981; Parent 1985, 1:66-70, app. VII). Certain old maps confirm the presence of Montagnais on both sides of the St. Lawrence from 1609 (Lescarbot 1866, 287). Other early maps confirm their presence on the south bank in the seventeenth century (Castonguay 1980; 14; Lescarbot (1609) 1991, map of 1609, 37-39; Jean de Laet 1640, 43; Barthélémy Vimont 1642-1643, 73; Hendrick Donker 1669, 77; Frederick De Witt 1670, 132; Guillaume Delisle 1696).

MAP 8 – Indigenous Nations and confederacies of northeastern Turtle Island, 1585

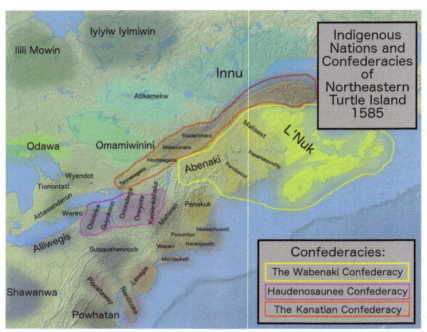

In their *Histoire du Bas-Saint-Laurent*, Fortin et al. (1993, 88–91, app. VIII) confirmed the presence of Montagnais on the southern shore of the St. Lawrence and theorized that hunting lands were reserved there for the Montagnais of Tadoussac (see Simard, quoted in Pouyez 1983, 69). The Montagnais (Innus) and especially the Porc-Épics or Kakouchakis who lived in Lac-Saint-Jean region would have exercised control over subordinate Nations. Fortin et al. considered that, at that time, Innu territory on the southern bank included almost all the Lower St. Lawrence, stating that the Mi'kmaq and the Maliseet, who also lived in the Lower St. Lawrence and the Gaspé, "seemed to belong to the group of Nations that were 'vassals' of the Innu" (our translation; Fortin et al.1993, 89).

Interesting as it may seem, this theory does not stand up to an in-depth analysis. Let us remember that the Innu occupied a huge territory and that they were few. Even after a conflict with a neighbouring group, how could effective control over the defeated be maintained when there was no governance structure? Even if the concept of Innu territory, the Nitassinan, has been borrowed from Indigenous cultural reality, it is important to consider it in the empirical and historical context in which it functioned. Otherwise, pan-European conceptualizations of territory, whereby everything is reduced to the concept of "reserve," distort observed reality.

The reality of a nomadic or semi-nomadic society consists of building a social, economic, cultural, and political system around structures that require minimal management; hence, the importance of reaching consensus, of opinions shared by the group and their allies, especially in border areas. Good relations with neighbours, whether the Maliseet across from Tadoussac, the Mi'kmaq to the east, the Abenaki to the west, or other Nations within the border areas, were essential for each of the Nations. In border areas where there were also fairs and trading posts, the free movement of persons from different Indigenous Nations was necessary and dependent on need, the season, and the occasion. In this respect, the King's Domain, or Traite de Tadoussac, was included in a conceptualization of borders around places like Tadoussac that created spaces for movement between Nations rather than closing off areas.

In conclusion, the thesis of reserved hunting lands for the Innu must be more nuanced. It is derived from a capitalist concept that has little to do with Indigenous cultures (Girard and Perron 1995, 64–65). Moreover, in border areas, there was more movement of people and resources according to need (hunting, fishing, war) or gatherings (locations of fairs and trading posts: Tadoussac, Le Bic). The St. Lawrence River, at least where its banks were accessible both winter and summer, did not really represent an obstacle but rather a navigable route that favoured exchanges.

Conclusion: Border areas as territories for meeting and sharing

In the current historiographical context, Indigenous Peoples and Nations, whether Innu or Maliseet/Wolastoqiyik, were guardians of the land. They were also guardians of resources that were first shared with the clan and the nearby community. If needed, a Nation could move to hunting or fishing areas at a distance from their usual territory. This depended on the season and the needs of the group. When groups were culturally related, Indigenous persons could be welcomed by neighbouring Nations who would share resources when these were available and sufficient. This did not prevent wars from breaking out or conflicts from arising for many reasons that remain to be clarified historically. Wars to right wrongs? Wars over the sharing of resources? In this respect, field studies of Innu culture should reflect the perception of Indigenous Peoples that they are guardians or, in more contemporary terms, managers of a territory to be shared by all (Lacasse 1996, 189; Lajoie et al. 1996: 122, 196ff). This land is to be cared for and looked after. Archaeological research has also confirmed that territory was shared around parcels of land that were easier to protect from incursion, as well as around buffer zones such as the St. Lawrence, where movement was easier and there was less control over the presence of various communities throughout the year (Langevin 2000). It should be remembered that the system of land management in nomadic Indigenous cultures consisted of a central core with areas at the margins being available for shared occupation. The next section discusses the central core of the traditional territory of the Maliseet.

PRESENCE OF THE MALISEET ON THEIR TRADITIONAL LANDS

If in Maine and New Brunswick, the Saint John River and its tributaries defined the traditional territory of the Maliseet, in Québec several rivers and, consequently, several smaller watersheds were used by the Maliseet to reach the shores of the St. Lawrence.

The strategic position of the upper and middle Saint John River valley, which linked by portage and river the St. Lawrence River and its estuary on the one hand and the Saint John River valley, Bay of Fundy, Gulf of Maine, and the Atlantic coast on the other, was long ago described by historians (Caron 1980; Ganong 1906; Marie-Victorin 1918). The portage system of the upper valley was closely associated with the Maliseet, and the portage from Les Sept Lacs to Témiscouata is still called the Maliseet portage. Furthermore, the discovery and use of portages by the French and English during the colonial period was made possible by knowledge acquired from the Maliseet (Campbell 1937).

Despite the growing presence of non-Indigenous persons on Maliseet lands in the seventeenth century, particularly in the Lower St. Lawrence, most of the Maliseet continued to use and occupy the territory as before, even though posts and missions had been established at Rivière du Loup (Michaud, 2003).

In this section, we portray the Maliseet presence on the territory under study. The synthesis of available cartographic documents includes the places where first meetings with the French took place, villages and camps, and portages and rivers. The focus is on detecting in maps published between 1603 and 1776 the items that indicate the presence of the Maliseet, their arrival, their return, and their expansion. All these pieces of information contribute to defining the traditional lands of the Maliseet and enable the creation of an original contemporary map that combines the elements mentioned above in the same cartographic document. The map is presented at the end of this section, preceded by a demonstration how each document contributed to it.

Watersheds

Waterways played an essential role in the occupation of the traditional territory of the Maliseet. They enabled travel by canoe, so that persons and goods could be transported over great distances when possible. Travelling by water was faster and required less physical effort than travelling long distances on foot. Combined with trails and portages, this means of transportation enabled all territory within the boundaries of a watershed to be covered. The Saint John River was the main route, and its tributaries the secondary routes, of a network that allowed travel from the mouth of the river in the south to the highlands in the north. In addition, from the highlands (the boundary of the Saint John River watershed), it was possible to use trails (portages) to bypass obstacles to navigation and reach waterways leading to Chaleur Bay in the east, to the St. Croix, Penobscot, Kennebec and Chaudière Rivers in the west, and the St. Lawrence in the north. As early as 1604, Champlain learned that it was possible to travel between the mouth of the Saint John River and the south shore of the St. Lawrence.

Among researchers who studied the territory occupied by the Maliseet, let us mention the work of William F. Ganong who, after studying maps of the travel routes of pre-contact Indigenous Peoples in New Brunswick and the north of Maine, published a map in 1895 showing the extent of the river system they had used (see map 9). In addition, the map showe the limits of the traditional lands of the Maliseet surrounded by the lands of the Mi'kmaq and Penobscot. Ganong even suggested using watershed boundaries to determine the limits of traditional lands. On his map, boundaries of territory are indicated by a line of double dashes. This map influenced other researchers interested in the Maliseet presence in eastern Canada.

In 1946, Frank G. Speck and Wendell S. Hadlock proposed revised boundaries for the traditional lands of the Maliseet in New Brunswick (see map 10). These were based on the Ganong map and on information gathered from Maliseet persons born and raised near the Saint John River in New Brunswick, and they correspond to the boundaries of a portion of the Saint John River watershed in New Brunswick.

MAP 9 – Travel routes in New Brunswick, 1895

MAP 10 – Boundaries of Maliseet traditional territory in New Brunswick, 1946

2. THE ETCHEMIN AND THE ALLIANCE OF INDIGENOUS NATIONS

Vincent O. Erickson went a step further in mapping the traditional lands of the Maliseet. In 1978, he published a map that shows the traditional territory of the Maliseet as corresponding to the portion of the Saint John River watershed that is found in Québec, as well as portions of the watersheds that flow into the St. Lawrence (see map 11). The map does not, however, specify the boundaries of the traditional territory of the Maliseet of Québec.

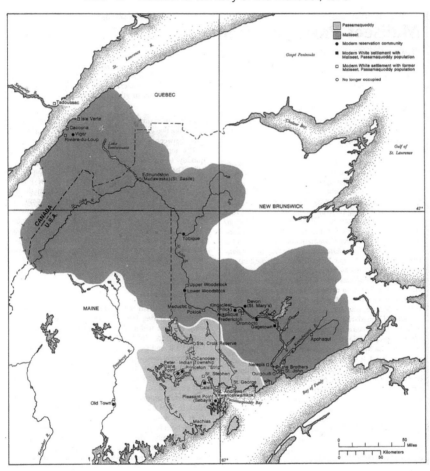

MAP 11 – Traditional territory of the Maliseet, 1978

Finally, Adrian L. Burke, in a 2001 map, did not define territorial boundaries but marked portages that connect the Saint John River and the St. Lawrence (see map 12). Ghislain Michaud used some of Burke's cartographic information in his book, *Les gardiens des portages: l'histoire des Malécites du Québec*, published in 2003.

MAP 12 – Portages and rivers between the Saint John and St. Lawrence Rivers, 2001

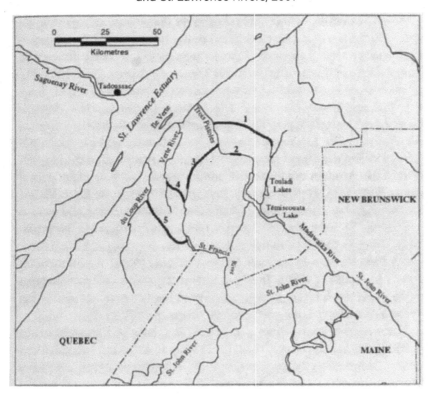

Portages and rivers

Although the Maliseet visited the banks of the St. Lawrence to the north and the shores of the *baie Française* (Bay of Fundy) in the south, they lived primarily inland. They inhabited and criss-crossed a territory dotted with waterways that enabled travel by canoe between villages and various seasonal campsites. Moreover, the discovery and use of portages by the French and the English during the colonial period were made possible by the knowledge shared with them by the Maliseet.

2. THE ETCHEMIN AND THE ALLIANCE OF INDIGENOUS NATIONS

The information about travel routes has been mapped from west to east. The Maliseet used eleven routes, of which at least seven appeared on maps we inventoried that covered the period from 1603 to 1776 (see table 1). Among the routes indicated, the Rivière Daaquam ("Achiganaré-Chogué" on Denonville's map) to the Rivière du Sud and the Pohénégamook to the Rivière du Loup appear on maps most often and over time. Next are the routes using the Petite and Grande rivières Noire toward the Rivière Ouelle, as well as that from the Saint John River to the Rivière des Sauvages. This last route no longer appeared on maps as of 1662. From 1699 on, Lake Témiscouata became part of this route. Finally, the route to Chaleur Bay and the route to the Rivière Chaudière appear on only two of the maps consulted. The first is mentioned by Champlain in 1603. Is this a route that was quickly abandoned afterwards, or was it too far east since trips in the direction of the Rivière du Loup were more frequent? The route to the Rivière Chaudière River only appears on a map from 1776. Is this a route that was discovered later, or was it too far west in relation to Rivière du Loup? These questions remain open.

TABLE 1 – Portages and rivers mentioned in maps or text

PORTAGE AND RIVER	MAP OR TEXT
Saint John River via Rivière des Sauvages	Champlain 1604; Lescarbot 1609; Champlain 1632; Boisseau 1643; Bleau 1662
Via the Daaquam River to the South River	Denonville 1685; Author unknown 1702; Bellin 1744; Bowen 1747; De Vaugondy 1753; Jefferys 1755; Mitchel, 1756; Seale 1757; Delarochette 1763
Via Lake Pohénégamook and the Saint-François River to the Rivière du Loup	De Rosier 1699; Aubry 1713; Aubry 1715; Bellin 1744; Bowen 1747; De Vaugondy 1753; De Vaugondy 1755; Jefferys 1755; Mitchell 1756
Via the Petite and Grande Rivières Noire to the Ouelle River	Aubry 1713, 1715; Morris 1749; Jefferys 1755; Mitchell 1756
Via the Madawaska River and Lake Témiscouata to the Trois-Pistoles River	De Rosier 1699; Belli, 1744; Bowen 1747; Mitchell 1756
Chaleur Bay to Lac-Matapédia or the Saint John River?	Champlain 1603
Saint John River to Rivière Chaudière	Jefferys 1775

According to Champlain, "in 1603, the Savages say that in the said great Chaleur Bay there is a river (Restigouche) which is some twenty leagues inland, at the end of which is a lake which may be some twenty leagues,[8] where there is very little water" (Champlain 1603, 52). The distance of twenty leagues makes it possible to reach Lake Matapédia via the river of the same name. From there, it is possible to reach the Rivière Matane. This distance also indicates that the Restigouche River route is close to the eastern boundary of the Saint John River watershed. From there, it is possible to reach the Saint John River via the Grande Rivière, for example.

In his history of New France, Lescarbot mentioned additional details about the link between the Saint John River and Chaleur Bay: "In addition, this river extending far inland, the Savages wonderfully abbreviate great voyages by means of it. For in six days, they go to Gachepé reaching the bay or gulf of Chaleur when they are at the end, carrying their canoes for a few leagues" (Lescarbot, 1609: 487).

> In 1604, Ralleau, secretary to the Sieur de Monts, learns from Secoudon, chief of the said river, that the inhabitants of the country go by the said river to Tadoussac, which is in the great river of Sainct Laurens: and pass only a little land to get there. From the Sainct Jean River to Tadoussac there are 65 leagues (Champlain 1604, 23).[9] And by the same river, in eight days, they go to Tadoussac by an arm of which comes towards the northwest. So that in Port Royal one can have, in fifteen or eighteen days, news of Frenchmen accustomed to the great river of Canada by such ways which could not be done by sea in a month, nor without hazard (Lescarbot 1609, 487).

On Lescarbot's map, the course of the Saint John River is virtually contiguous with that of another river that flows into the St. Lawrence (see map 13). Number 65 on the map corresponds to "the Saint John islets that we take to be Le Pic." This is not certain. The position of the waterway seems to correspond to the location of the Rivière des Sauvages, which Champlain identified on his 1632 map as number 12 (see map 14). Champlain was unsure of the name of this river: it could have been the Rivière Verte.

---

8. This is an estimate, as there are no lakes of this size in the area studied.
9. This distance does not correspond exactly to the distance from the mouth of the Saint John River to the mouth of Rivière des Trois Pistoles – as the crow flies (395 km or eighty leagues). The difference can be explained by the less precise means of measurement at the time or by inaccurate positioning of cartographic items on maps.

2. THE ETCHEMIN AND THE ALLIANCE OF INDIGENOUS NATIONS 77

According to the Commission de toponymie du Québec, it would be the Rivière des Trois-Pistoles. In any case, Champlain labelled this river with the name *Sauvages*, most likely because Indigenous Peoples used it. The information he had collected on the location and extent of the Rivière des Sauvages and the Saint John River, which was supported by oral evidence, seemed to indicate to him that the two rivers formed a travel link between the *baie Française* (Bay of Fundy) and the St. Lawrence that minimized portages, as noted by the Chief Secoudon.

MAP 13 – Extract from a map by Lescarbot, 1609

65 Les Îlots Saint-Jean que je prens pour Le Pic (Le Bic)

MAP 14 – Extract from a map by Champlain, 1632

12 Rivière des Sauvages ou de l'île Verte

Jacques-René de Brisay de Denonville was governor of New France from 1685 to 1689. From the beginning of his mandate, he was interested in the state of society in New France, which he found disorganized. Among the many tasks that fell to him, he had a map made of the route from Québec City to the *baie Française* in Acadia (see map 15). This map is based on information from a man from Médocté (Médoctec), a known Maliseet village along the Saint John River. According to the maps consulted, Denonville's map was the first to describe this route, and it appeared in several subsequent maps that are presented below. This route was used until the end of the French regime and the beginning of the British. Please note that on this map north is at the bottom.

2. THE ETCHEMIN AND THE ALLIANCE OF INDIGENOUS NATIONS

MAP 15 – Denonville's map, 1685

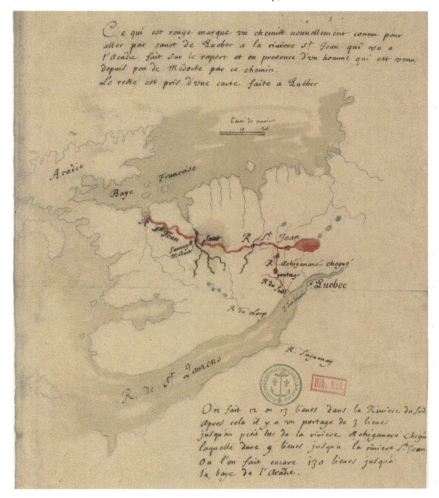

At the end of the seventeenth century, Guillaume De Rozier travelled through New France, leaving a detailed map of the Saint John River, which he followed during his journey (see map 16). According to William F. Ganong (1906, 60), "while containing some curious errors, it is at the same time wonderfully accurate, far more accurate indeed than any other map for nearly a century thereafter. The map produced no effect upon any other later maps that I have been able to trace, and it seems itself to have entirely [sic] from the personal observation of its author." During his journey up the Saint John River in 1699, De Rozier identified two portages. The first connected the Saint John River via the Rivière Noire to the Rivière du Loup. The second portage was between the Saint John River and Rivière des Trois-Pistoles via Rivière Saint-François. De Rozier explained that that, using this route, it was necessary to travel a distance of 154 to 155 leagues (756 to 761 kilometres) from the mouth of the Rivière du Sud to the *Baie de l'Acadie*.

MAP 16 – Extract from a map by De Rozier, 1699

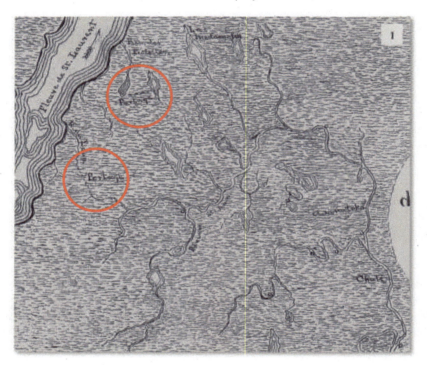

The next map (author unknown) adds a nuance regarding the portage located between the Rivière du Sud and the Achiganaré-Chegué River (Rivière Daaquam). This portage was divided into a long and a short portage (see map 17).

2. THE ETCHEMIN AND THE ALLIANCE OF INDIGENOUS NATIONS 81

MAP 17 – Extract from a map of Acadia, 1702

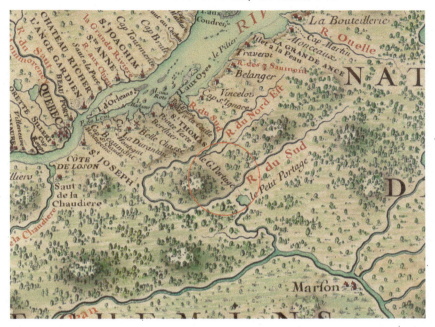

Joseph Jacques Aubry was a Jesuit missionary priest who settled in New France in 1694. The Treaty of Utrecht, signed in 1713, created a difficult situation for the Abenaki of the Atlantic coast, who now found themselves on lands claimed by both the French and British Crowns after Acadia had been ceded to England "according to its ancient boundaries." Aware of the danger, Aubry sent a memorandum to the French court that same year, along with a map proposing clear boundaries between the two territories, so as not to let "the English, in peacetime, to spread out, advance, and settle on our lands, and in that way become masters of Canada" (Johnson 1974).

Aubry's map, dating from 1713, shows two routes connecting the Saint John River to the St. Lawrence (see map 18). The first connects the Saint John River to the Rivière Ouelle. The second route includes Lake Pohénégamook and follows the Saint-François River toward the Rivière du Loup. It allowed the Maliseet to reach the mission and trading post established in 1674 at the mouth of the Rivière du Loup.

MAP 18 – Extract from a map by Aubry, 1715

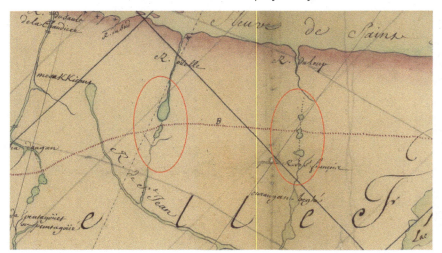

Jacques-Nicolas Bellin was a French cartographer and hydrographer who essentially worked from information collected by mariners, travellers, or explorers, which was the case for his maps of New France. In the detail from Bellin's map, published in 1744, three routes are indicated (see map 19). In the southwestern part of the map detail are the portages that lead to the Rivière du Sud, a route similar to the one shown on Aubry's 1702 map. The second route, in the centre, connects to the Rivière du Loup, but not by using the Rivière Saint-François. The third route follows the Madawaska River and Lake Témiscouata to the Rivière des Trois-Pistoles.

In addition, on Bellin's 1744 map from the St. Lawrence River and the Grande rivière Noire, Indigenous Peoples could follow the deep valley of the Rivière Saint-Roch, a natural route to Lac Sainte-Anne, a tributary (via the Grande rivière Noire and the Rivière Sainte-Anne) of the Rivière Ouelle (Picard et al. 2005, 26). This portage is indicated by a blue circle on the map.

MAP 19 – Extract from a map by Bellin, 1744

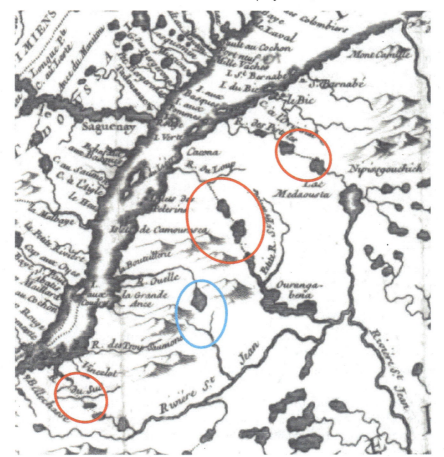

The map by Morris (surveyor general of Nova Scotia), dating from 1749, shows only one route (see map 20), from the Saint John River to the Rivière Ouelle. Morris stated that it took seven days to travel from Chignecto (at the head of the Bay of Fundy) to Québec (city).

MAP 20 – Extract from a map by Morris, 1749

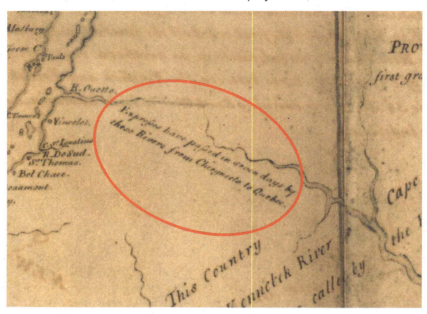

The map by John Mitchell (an English physician and botanist) shows the same three routes as Bellin's 1744 map (see map 21). To the southwest are the portages that lead to the Rivière du Sud. This route is like that shown on the 1702 map. Furthermore, Mitchell indicated that this route was a portage on the way to Québec. The second route, in the centre of the map, connects to the Rivière du Loup but without using the Rivière Saint-François. The third route follows the Madawaska River and Lake Témiscouata to the Rivière des Trois-Pistoles.

MAP 21 – Extract from a map by Mitchell, 1756

On Mitchell's 1757 map, we find the three routes present on the previous map (see map 22). In addition, he indicated the routes to the Rivière du Loup and the Rivière des Trois-Pistoles as being portages on the way to "Canada."

MAP 22 – Extract from a map by Mitchell, 1757

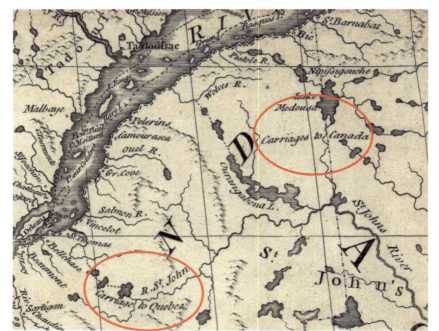

Although possibly of French origin, Louis Stanislas d'Arcy Delarochette was an English cartographer who produced a map of English possessions in North America following the Treaty of Paris in 1763 (see map 23). On his map, he indicated two already well-known routes: the route to the Rivière du Sud, with the note "carriage to Quebec," and the route to the Rivière du Loup.

MAP 23 – Extract from a map by Delarochette, 1763

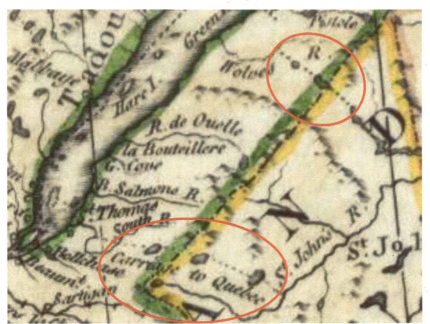

Even though this last map extends beyond the period of New France, which ended in 1763, we have included it because it shows a route not appearing in the other maps analyzed. The map by Jefferys (King George III's geographer), prepared in 1776, mentions a portage between the Saint John River and the Rivière Chaudière (see map 24). It is indicated that this portage was used by Indigenous Peoples of the Saint John River.

MAP 24 – Extract from a map by Jefferys, 1775

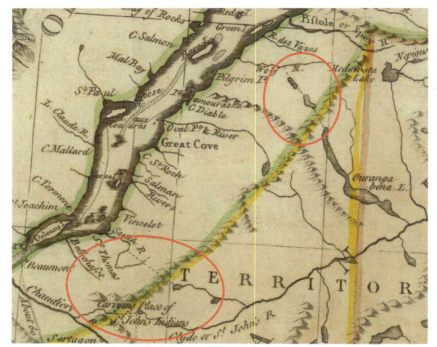

Meeting places

Mapping the sites of the first meetings between the Maliseet and the French helps to delineate the traditional lands of the Maliseet. These first encounters took place near the coasts, either along the St. Lawrence River (Tadoussac) or in the *baie* Française (mouth of the Saint John River). These sites were important because alliances were concluded there.

Missions and trading posts

Missions and trading posts were located on the banks of waterways on sites that were already being used by Indigenous Peoples for fishing in summer. The addition of trading posts prolonged the life of such locations since they allowed Indigenous People to exchange goods for necessities.

In 1652, the governor of New France created the King's Domain, or Traite de Tadoussac, where the Innu and the Maliseet (in Tadoussac) traded furs. On the south bank of the St. Lawrence, however, the king granted seigneuries, and he also granted to several seigneurs the right to trade with the *Sauvages*.

2. THE ETCHEMIN AND THE ALLIANCE OF INDIGENOUS NATIONS

Among these seigneurs, Charles Aubert de La Chesnaye, who was granted a seigneury on the Rivière du Loup in 1673, had a trading post built at the mouth of the river in 1674. As new seigneurial concessions were granted, many in fact to Charles Aubert de La Chesnaye through intermediaries, they gradually took over all trading activities. Despite regulations that forbade trading outside of Tadoussac, these activities continued.

In 1684, following complaints from farmers (leaseholders) in the Traite de Tadoussac, a report was drawn up by M. Joseph-Antoine Le Febvre de La Barre, then governor of New France (CDB online), who went to the Rivière du Loup to observe trading going on with the *Sauvages* from the Saint John River. During the summer, these same Savages engaged in "the fishing of salmon and sea bass and would return in the middle of the fall to their country, taking with them the sea bass skins and oils that they got from them, and the salmon that remained salted" (our translation; Appendix 1684).

M. de La Barre also went to Le Bic. There he found "five cabins of savages from the Baye des Chaleurs and towards Acadia who were prepared to fish for wolffish and salmon, which kept the said savages alive throughout the summer and part of the autumn, and in the winter they withdrew inland to the south where they hunted marten, otters, and moose, of which they made little as well as beaver." It is not known by which rivers the Indigenous persons reached Le Bic (our translation; Appendix 1684).

Villages or encampments

Between 1603 and 1760, many mapmakers identified sites of Maliseet encampments or villages (see table 2). Of the twenty-one locations mapped, some are named, and these are places that were likely occupied regularly by the Maliseet. According to our calculations, the village of Jemseq is mentioned on thirteen of the fifty-five maps. This name appears on Franquelin's map of 1686 and on Mitchell's map of 1757. Next is the village of Medoctec, which is mentioned on twelve maps. It appears on Denonville's map of 1685 and on Bellin's map of 1764. According to Ghislain Michaud (2003, 58), Medoctec was the chief settlement of the Maliseet on the Saint John River. It was one of the major centres for the Indigenous Nations of Acadia, located at the eastern end of the portage route linking the Saint John, Saint Croix, Pentegouet, and even Kennebec Rivers. In 1715, Intendant Bégon estimated that it had about 400 inhabitants, including some 100 warriors. The village of Naxouat appears on eight maps by Bellin between 1686 and 1764, and the village of Nacohonac on three maps between 1703 and 1729. Arassatuk and Ougpauk are each mentioned only once.

TABLE 2 – Camp or village names mentioned on maps

VILLAGE OR CAMP	MAP
Jemseq, Gemseq, Jenseq	Franquelin 1686, 1689; De Rozier 1699; Author unknown 1702; Delisle 1703; Moll 1720; Académie des sciences 1729; Bellin 1744; Laurie 1749; Jefferys 1755; Le Rouge 1755; Bowen 1747; Mitchell 1757
Nantchouac, Nachouac, Narantsouak, Naxouat	Franquelin 1686, 1689; De Rozier 1699; D'Anville 1755; Jefferys 1755; Chambon 1756; Bellin 1757; Bellin 1764
Nacohonac, Nakohonac	Delisle 1703; Moll 1720; Académie des sciences 1729
Medoctec, Medoktek, Medoctek, Medocti, Medostec	Denonville 1685; De Rozier 1699; Aubry 1713, 1715; Bellin 1744; Bowen 1747; Laurie 1749; Le Rouge 1755; Chambon 1756; Mitchell 1756; Bellin 1764
Arassatuk	De Rozier 1699
Ougpauk	Jefferys 1755

We now present, in chronological order, examples of maps that contain Maliseet place names. This allows us to visualize these locations on a map and to note the various ways of spelling their names.

In 1671, Jean-Baptiste-Louis Franquelin came to New France as a trader. In 1674, Governor Frontenac persuaded him to abandon trade and devote himself entirely to cartography. Thus, from 1674 to 1693, Franquelin produced maps that the governors and intendants attached to the dispatches they sent to France (CDB). In particular, in 1686 he drew a map "ge[ne]rale X [sic] of the journey that Monsieur De Meulles, intendant responsible for justice, police, and finances for New France, had made by order of the king" (our translation; see map 25). The trip included all the lands of Acadia with all the bays, islands, harbours, ports, and rivers to be found there, according to the remarks and observations that were made during the said voyage. This map shows one encampment called Nachouac and another called Jemsec along the Saint John River.

2. THE ETCHEMIN AND THE ALLIANCE OF INDIGENOUS NATIONS 91

MAP 25 – Extract from a map by Franquelin, 1686

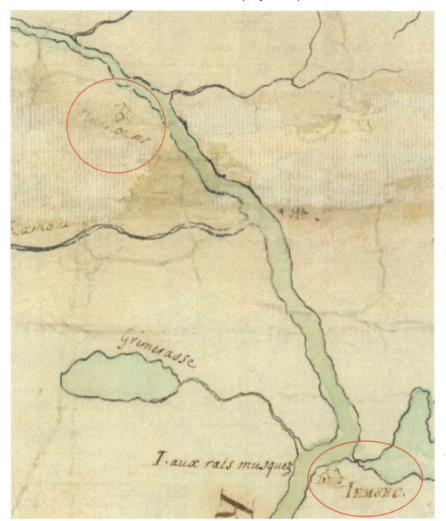

At the end of the seventeenth century, Guillaume de Rozier travelled through New France, leaving a detailed map of the Maliseet camps or villages he came across during his journey (see map 26). On this map, four Maliseet sites can be seen: Nanxouat, Jemsec, Arassatuk, and Medoctec.

MAP 26 – Extract from a map by De Rozier, 1699

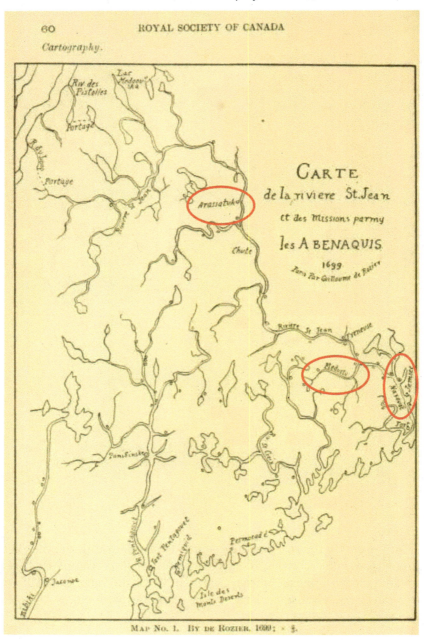

Guillaume Delisle was a cartographer who studied astronomy at the Academy of Sciences in 1702; he became a member in 1718. He taught geography to the young Louis XV and was became the first geographer to the king. He produced some one hundred maps that he edited himself, some of which are of New France. In 1703, he produced a map of New France on which two Maliseet sites, Nacohomac and Jemsec, are labelled (see map 27).

MAP 27 – Extract from a map by Delisle, 1703

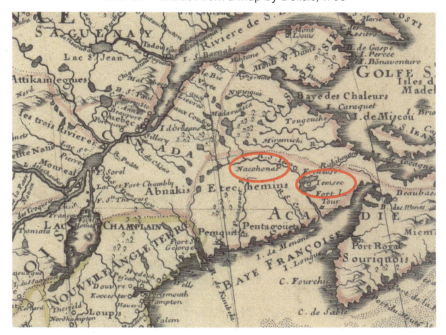

In 1713, Jacques Aubry produced a map that focused on Abenaki lands (see map 28). He labelled the village of Medoctec, which he described as being the village of the Savages of the Saint John River.

MAP 28 – Extract from a map by Aubry, 1713

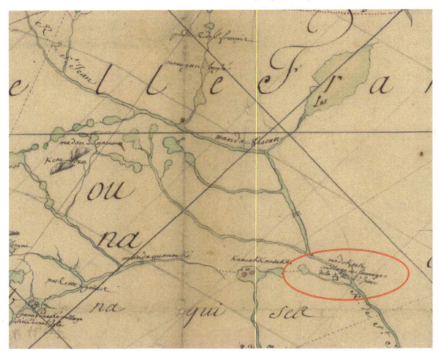

The next map shows the location of a village belonging to the Indigenous People of the Saint John River or Maliseets (Village des Sauvages de la Rivière de St-Jean ou Malécites; see map 29). The location of this village corresponds to that of Medoctec. Of all the maps consulted, this is the only mention of a Maliseet village. Unfortunately, the name of the author of this map is unknown.

2. THE ETCHEMIN AND THE ALLIANCE OF INDIGENOUS NATIONS

MAP 29 – Extract from a map of New France, early eighteenth century

In 1715, two years after the signing of the Treaty of Utrecht, which transferred part of Acadia to the British Crown, Aubry still took an interest in the fate of Acadia, particularly the Indigenous communities, including the Maliseet, who remained allies of New France against the English conqueror. He produced a map that again shows the village of Medoctec, which he identified as Abenaki (see map 30).

MAP 30 – Extract from a map by Aubry, 1715

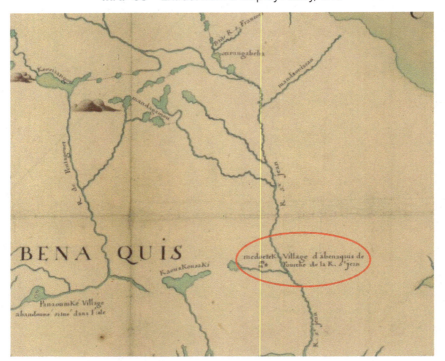

After the Treaty of Utrecht in 1713, the British Crown laid claim to present-day New Brunswick and Maine which include much of the Saint John River watershed. As a result, English geographers and cartographers produced maps that included all of Maine, New Brunswick, and the Gaspé and Lower St. Lawrence regions, which were part of Nova Scotia at that time. The same place names as those on previous French maps continued in use. The first map in English was produced by Herman Moll, and it shows the location of the villages of Nakohonac and Jemsec (see map 31).

MAP 31 – Extract from a map by Moll, 1720

In 1729, a map "made by the gentlemen of the Royal Academy of Sciences according to new observations" used the same two place names as the previous map with a small variation in the spelling of "Nakohonac": the *k* in the second syllable was replaced by a *c* (see map 32).

MAP 32 – Extract from a map by the Royal Academy of Sciences, 1729

The next map, produced by Nicolas Bellin and dated 1744, shows the location of Medoctec and Jemsec along the Saint John River (see map 33).

MAP 33 – Extract from a map by Bellin, 1744

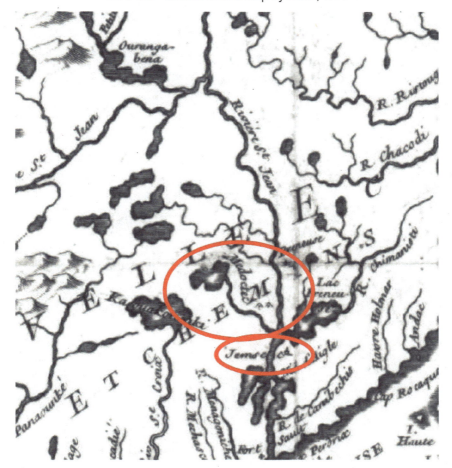

Charles Morris was originally from Boston. In 1747, he was commissioned to carry out a survey in Acadia, and he also recorded his observations of Nova Scotia and the Indians living there (CDB). On this map, Morris indicates Indigenous settlements along the Saint John River (see map 34).

MAP 34 – Extract from a map by Morris, 1749

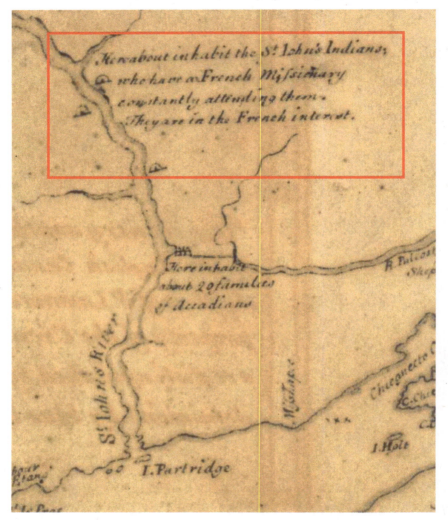

Jean-Baptiste Bouguignon d'Anville was a French geographer and cartographer. He was appointed geographer to the king in 1718 and produced 211 maps. As the king's geographer, d'Anville had access to information sent to the French authorities from New France. Among his maps, we find one entitled "Canada, Louisiane et terres anglaises" (Canada. Louisiana, and English lands). On this map, there is mention of Narantsouak and various French settlements along the Saint John River (see map 35).

MAP 35 – Extract from a map by d'Anville, 1755

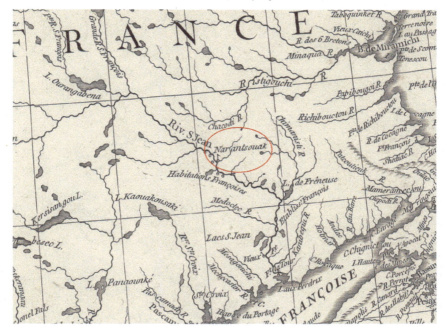

Georges-Louis Le Rouge was the king's geographer and engineer. Like d'Anville, he had access to information sent to the French authorities from New France. On the map entitled "Canada et Louisiane," we find the settlements of Medoctec and Jensec (see map 36).

MAP 36 – Extract from a map by Le Rouge, 1755

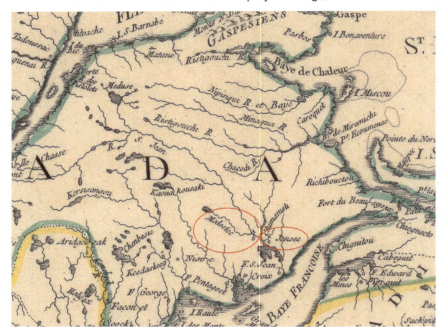

Thomas Jefferys was King George III's geographer. As such, he had access to information from New England, which enabled him to produce maps for the government. In his 1755 map, like d'Anville, he indicates the French settlements along the Saint John River and labels the names of two of them, Naxoqat and Ougpauk. Jemseq is also included (see map 37).

MAP 37 – Extract from a map by Jefferys, 1755

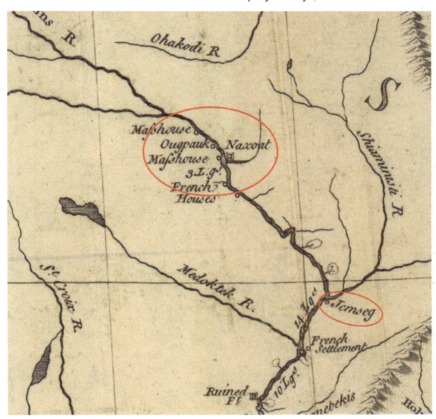

Bellin produced a map of Acadia and neighbouring regions in 1757, a contribution to the general history of travel. On this map, he labelled Nantchouat and Medoctec (Abenaki village; see map 38).

MAP 38 – Extract from a map by Bellin, 1757

On this 1764 map, Bellin again showed Nantchouat and Medoctec but reversed their locations (see map 39).

2. THE ETCHEMIN AND THE ALLIANCE OF INDIGENOUS NATIONS

MAP 39 – Extract from a map by Bellin, 1764

The occupation of the Saint John River by the Maliseet and their defence against their enemies

The occupation of the traditional lands of the Maliseet has also been revealed through tales and legends. The legend of Malobiannah is a good example. At the time of the treaty known as the Grande Paix de Montréal (1701), Mehtaqtek, now Meductic in New Brunswick, was the principal gathering place of the Maliseet of the Saint John River.

MALOBIANNAH AND GRAND FALLS

A long time ago, a young woman named Malobiannah was on a visit with her father, Sacobie, on an island in the Saint John River near the mouth of the Porcupine River (Madawaska). They were to meet Grand Chief Pemmyhaouet whose son was to marry Malobiannah. As the young woman and her father prepared to return to their village, Mehtaqtek, they heard screams coming from the area where people lived. They rushed to see what was happening and were terrified when they saw a horde of Mohawk warriors setting fire to the camp. More than two hundred men were determined not to leave any survivors. Despite the resistance offered by Pemmyhaouet and his bravest warriors, all wikuwams were set on fire and men, women, and children fell, one after the other, under Mohawk attacks.

Malobiannah and her father tried to escape, but they were quickly spotted. Sacobie was killed, and the young woman taken prisoner. The leader of the attackers said to Malobiannah, "At nightfall, we leave. If you take us to your village, we'll let you live."

Once darkness came, the warriors boarded their canoes with their prisoner. They let themselves drift, carried by the current of the river. Malobiannah did not understand everything they said to each other, but she knew that they intended to eliminate all the Maliseet they encountered, to exterminate them. Nevertheless, she never showed them her fear or anger. She remained impassive.

In a short time, rocked by the waves, the Mohawks fell asleep while continuing to let themselves be carried along by the water. Malobiannah, on the other hand, was not asleep. She knew the river well and knew what was to come. A deep rumble was heard. At first far away, the noise became louder and louder, so much so that some warriors woke up and turned to Malobiannah. She reassured them by explaining that it was the sound of the Aroostook, another river that flows into the Saint John River. As she kept perfectly calm and sat quietly, no one questioned her words.

The noise grew louder and louder and louder and, before they had time to manoeuvre, the flotilla of warriors saw a torrent of immense strength appear before it: Grand Falls. They did not have time to react and were all thrown into the falls that swallowed them and smashed them all on against the rocks. The village of Mehtaqtek had just been saved.

Some still say that without the intervention of this brave young woman, there would be no Maliseet today along the Saint John River. It is also said that sometimes, above Grand Falls, when a bird hovers high in the sky, it is the spirit of Malobiannah that is always there.

This legend evokes a rather dark period in Wolastoqey/Maliseet history, that of repeated attacks on villages by different enemy. In this version of the story, the attackers are Mohawks; however, there are other versions of the story that make the Mi'kmaq bear the blame for this attack. Some interpretations suggest that it is an attack by the Stadacona Iroquoians. In any case, although this story seems to have become distorted over time, it appears to be based on actual fact. It gives us a glimpse of the strike force of these warriors who were engaging in a campaign of destruction, two hundred men at a time. Maliseet villages downstream of the Saint John River were more often subjected to attacks by enemies arriving by sea. In this case, the attackers came from the upper reaches of the river, which makes this story so special. This was also what caused the loss of the flotilla because it was only because they were going downstream that they were flung into Grand Falls. The history of Malobiannah also evokes an important character trait that was frequently attributed to our ancestors by the chroniclers of the time: self-control. The heroine who is heading straight for death to save her people does so with courage and composure, without arousing suspicion. Isn't this an essential feature of a great warrior? (Collection of Maliseet Legends including analyses, Maliseet of Viger First Nation, internal document; Bélanger 2019, 64–65).

Contemporary mapping of traditional Maliseet lands

Geomatics has made it possible to link a contemporary map database to one derived from an analysis of primary-source historical documents. Although aware of the difficulty involved in synchronizing historical maps with those of today, we nevertheless endeavoured to create a map that incorporates, as accurately as possible, the information derived from our analysis. Such a map makes it possible to see at a glance the extent of the traditional territory of the Maliseet and the various historical elements that define it.

There was already sufficient cartographic documentation from the seventeenth and eighteenth centuries to create such a map. All that was required was to collect as many maps as possible from that period and to read and analyze them carefully in conjunction with more recent historical studies.

On the map below (map 40), we see that Maliseet territory corresponds to the Saint John River watershed and, from east to west, to those of the Saint-Claude, Beaumont, Bellechasse, du Sud, Vincelotte, Tortue, Trois-Saumons, Port Joli, Ferrée, Ouelle, Saint-Jean, Le Bras, Kamouraska, Fouquette, du Loup, Verte, des Vases, Trois-Pistoles, Bic, Rimouski, and Mitis Rivers. The boundaries drawn by Ganong in 1895 corresponded to the watershed of the Saint John River. The extent of traditional Maliseet lands in the present-day province of Québec are defined by travel routes and trading posts.

Our map shows the complexity of the traditional lands of the Maliseet. It highlights the presence of a border zone with its multiple exchanges, free movement of persons and goods, and numerous essential intercultural relationships with close neighbours. The border zone is a place of resistance and affirmation in a context of exchange.

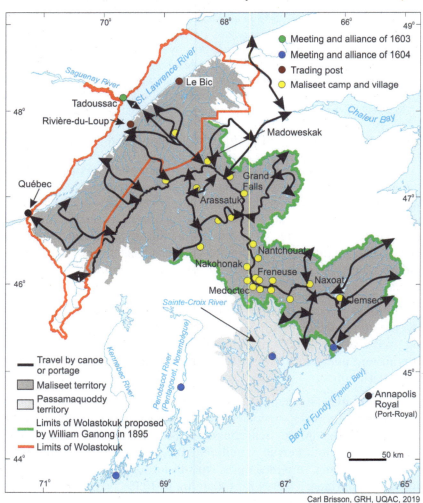

MAP 40 – Traditional territory of the Maliseet

THE FRENCH POLICY REGARDING ALLIANCES AND TREATIES

As traditional modes of alliance that had been concluded according to the "custom of the country" shifted to hybrid modes, writing and mapping became more and more important.

All of Champlain's work was devoted to creating and strengthening alliances in meetings during which the exchange of gifts, discussion, and management of conflict ensured peace, trading relationships, and settlement of the colony.

By analyzing the phrasing used in the many treaties, we have shown that the French policy of alliance, which began in 1603, had a major impact throughout the seventeenth century as France worked to implement their alliance policy, a process that was completed by the Grande Paix de Montréal (1701).

The treaties with the Iroquois in the mid-1660s are formal texts that show a change in the negotiation and dissemination of alliances. These written treaties were part of France's desire to implement a formal policy of alliance with local Indigenous Peoples, and the peace treaties with the Iroquois allowed France to sign the Grande Paix de Montréal. These treaties paved the way for the Grande Paix de Montréal (1701), which crowned nearly 100 years of a French policy of trading and forming alliances with Indigenous Peoples and their allies in New France. This approach was also used by the English until 1760. The Maliseet were active participants in this policy to ensure trade and settlement in New France through freedom of movement in a context of peace and mutual respect. The strategy was essential for a northern colony with a scattered population, a colony that could only be settled and developed in conjunction with the Indigenous Peoples who had occupied the land since time immemorial.

FIGURE 5 – France-Iroquois treaties, 1666

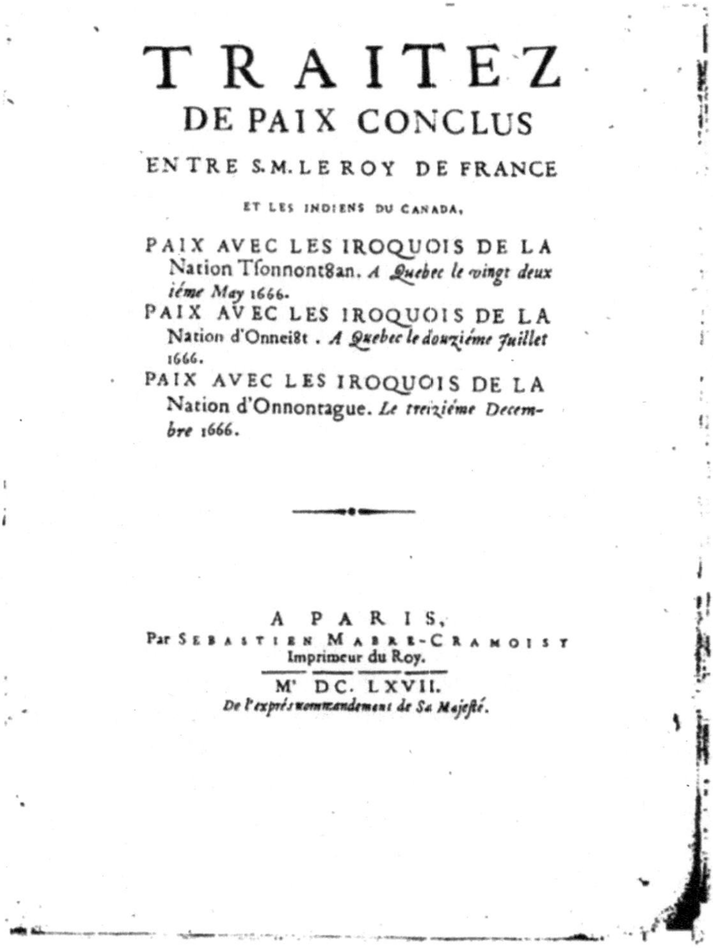

TRAITEZ
DE PAIX CONCLUS
ENTRE S.M. LE ROY DE FRANCE
ET LES INDIENS DU CANADA.

PAIX AVEC LES IROQUOIS DE LA Nation Tfonnont8an. *A Quebec le vingt deux iéme May 1666.*
PAIX AVEC LES IROQUOIS DE LA Nation d'Onnei8t. *A Quebec le douziéme Juillet 1666.*
PAIX AVEC LES IROQUOIS DE LA Nation d'Onnontague. *Le treiziéme Decembre 1666.*

A PARIS,
Par SEBASTIEN MABRE-CRAMOISY
Imprimeur du Roy.
M' DC. LXVII.
De l'exprés commandement de Sa Majefté.

See Appendix 2 for the complete version.[10]

---

10. For the Treaty of 22 May 1666, a meeting at Québec with 10 ambassadors and the treaty of 12 July, Onnei8t, Oneidas and Mohawk Nations, see Archives nationales de France, ser. C11A, vol. 2, fol. 234–5. On the peace Treaty of 13 December 1666, articles proposed by six ambassadors of the Onontague Nation (Iroquois) to the French, see Archives nationales de France, ser. C11A, vol. 2, fol. 187–90.

Peace with the Iroquois in 1666: France and the Onondagas, Cayugas, Senecas, and Oneidas

The Third Peace was signed on 13 December 1666. It involved *six Iroquois ambassadors* and *two Grand Chiefs*, Goiouen and Tionnontouan. The Iroquois Nations represented were the Onondaga, Cayuga, Seneca and Oneida. The king was represented by Alexandre de Prouville, seigneur de Tracy (Appendix 2, 1666, Treaties between New France and the Iroquois).

The king's difficulties in subjugating the territory beyond the Island of Montréal

The king recalled the trouble he had had in "discovering" unknown countries occupied by barbarous, non-Christian Indigenous Nations, stating that the Third Peace was the result of attempts to meet with the Indigenous Peoples living west of Montréal on the shores of Lake Ontario. Through force of arms, it had become possible to bring Indigenous Peoples under French domination (*d'assujettir à la domination française les Peuples sauvages*).

Continuation of the first peace between the Iroquois and the French

Representatives of the Indigenous Peoples and Nations stated that they had not come to ask for a new peace. They claimed that peace with the French had never been broken. The date of this first peace was not specified. Iroquois Chiefs asked the continuation of this peace, which would include being protected from their enemies by the king.

Ensuring peace between the Indigenous Peoples and the French

Article 2 stipulates that the four Iroquois Nations could no longer harass other Indigenous Nations trading in Montréal, Trois-Rivières, and Québec. In particular, the hunting by long-time French allies was not to be impeded, namely that of the Hurons and Algonquins who lived north of the St. Lawrence River, and the "Esquimaux (*"Eskimos"*) & Bertiamites" (Inuit and Innus of the North Shore) as far as Lakes Huron and Ontario. Each had to treat the other with respect and provide mutual assistance in times of need: "[T]here shall be friendship and mutual aid between all the said Nations, who shall unite as brothers for their common defence, under the protection of the said Lord King" (our translation).

This article protects the free movement of persons to enable peace and commerce in the colony around three poles of economic activity.

Article 3 deals with the return of prisoners and giving of gifts, essential ceremonies in such circumstances.

The king also undertook to guarantee respect for the treaty by placing two Jesuit priests among the Iroquois Nations. An armourer and a surgeon were to be sent the following spring to the Nations concerned (article 4).

Occupation of lands by the French and the Iroquois

Article 5 provides for the safe passage of French families, who would be able to live in peace on Iroquois territory, practise agriculture on good arable land, and share hunting and fishing rights with the original inhabitants:

That hunting and fishing will be common to the French families, who will moreover receive from the Iroquois all the help and assistance, that true Brothers must render to each other [our italics and translation].

In article 6, the king specifies that Iroquois families who wished to practise agriculture might do so and that they would be given fields and seeds. This would be in addition to shared rights to hunting and fishing:

[*T*]*here shall be sent from each of the four Superior Nations to Montréal, Trois-Rivières, and Québec, two persons from the main Iroquois families, to whom shall be given fields, and corn* [blé d'inde] *and wheat* [blé français], *in addition to the common benefit of hunting and fishing which will be granted to them* (our italics and translation).

Article 9, the last, states that the treaty would be made ready and signed by all parties after it has been read out in the Iroquois language.

France reconfirmed its commitment to a policy of "pacification" by consulting and trading with Indigenous Nations to ensure peace, shared occupation of the territory, and development of resources, while specifying special protection for hunting and fishing (traditional activities), which were to be practised by and for both parties.

Despite armed conflict, despite the shortcomings of past alliances that the respective parties had noted, nation-to-nation treaties remained at the core of a relationship of mutual respect and trust that ensured peace, freedom of movement, and trade in the lands of Indigenous Peoples in New France.

The shared occupation of the territory and the use of its resources for the benefit of all, including Indigenous Peoples and Nations, was a foundational element of the relationship, which was to be one of *brothers and sisters*.

2. THE ETCHEMIN AND THE ALLIANCE OF INDIGENOUS NATIONS

The division of land for agriculture was to depend on whether French or Indigenous families wanted to engage in such activity. Hunting and fishing rights were to be shared.

The Royal Commission on Indigenous Peoples commented on the concept of ownership by Indigenous Peoples in this treaty between the Iroquois Nations and France:

> These provisions acknowledge the Iroquois title to their territories and recognize their power to grant (or not to grant) lands and hunting rights to incoming French settlers. The reciprocal nature of the articles is revealing. It undercuts the exaggerated claims of the French Crown in earlier articles and places them in a more realistic context. Overall, the treaty portrays Aboriginal nations as autonomous, self-governing nations in possession of their territories, within an asserted frame-work of French suzerainty and protection. (Royal Commission on Aboriginal Peoples 1993, 12; Appendix 1993).

Under the French regime, there was no cession or sale of land to the Crown, as was proposed in the Royal Proclamation of 1763 under the British regime. The territory and its resources were to be developed concurrently with the agreement of everyone and with respect for the nation-to-nation rights that the Iroquois had established with France. Iroquois families who wished to farm would receive fields or properties that they could develop.

The text is a product of its time, with the king assuming a "conquering" stance while displaying a true desire to ensure by treaty that France, in alliance with local Indigenous Peoples, would have a permanent presence in New France. To support his claims in Europe, the king relied on both the French population and the Indigenous Peoples of New France to claim and to ensure an effective occupation of the territory of New France, the territory of the Indigenous Peoples.

The French policy of treaties and nation-to-nation relationships has, for the most part, been lost from our collective history. It is as if the Royal Proclamation of 1763, with the Conquest, became the primary, if not the only real text that recognized the relationship between the Crown and Indigenous Peoples. The British continued in many ways the French policy, as they would often point out in texts they published about the Royal Proclamation of 1763 and its application. This was the case in their recognition of the hunting lands of the Maliseet (1765) and of the King's Domain (1767), where the Innu Nation was located.

Several elements of the Royal Proclamation of 1763 made their way into the relationship with Indigenous Peoples, notably the protection of *Indian territories for "hunting"* and the requirement that Indigenous Peoples who "wished" to occupy a settlement could *cede or sell* these lands only to the Crown. With time and the establishment of the Canadian federation, this possibility became a requirement, which resulted in the seizure of *Indian territories* as to restrict it the notion of *Hunting Grounds*. These traditional lands disappeared with the passage of numerous pieces of legislation concerning laws concerning *Indians* in the United Province of Canada from the 1850s onward that reduced the Indian Territory to mere pieces of reserved land. Thus, the *Indian Territory* with its limitation to *Hunting Grounds* by the governments, forced Indigenous persons, who had become generic individuals, to live on small parcels of land. We will return to the Royal Proclamation of 1763 and the implementation of the various Indian Acts (1850–1876) in following chapters.

The Maliseet and the Wabanaki Confederacy

As previously mentioned, when he arrived in New France, Champlain set up a system of alliances with the Nations he encountered, based on networks that already existed in Indigenous lands. His own alliances and the diplomatic policy for settling the colony were designed to fit into these existing networks. He sought to influence issues that were dealt with by Chiefs, and he tried to influence the appointment of certain leaders. He participated in decisions to begin or terminate conflicts and in trials that involved French or Indigenous persons.

Like the Laurentian alliance referred to earlier, the Wabanaki Confederacy was made up of various Nations that negotiated as one with either the French or the English. The Wabanaki Confederacy consisted of four major Algonquian Nations in the northeast: the Abenaki, Maliseet-Passamaquoddy, Penobscot, and Mi'kmaq (see map 41). Speck estimated that the confederacy formed about 1680 and continued until the early 1860s (Speck 1915; Appendix, 1915). The Wabanaki Confederacy had been built on long-standing relationships, and physical and cultural proximity fostered these political and strategic ties. During the 1680s the confederacy would have adapted to the conflicts between the French and the English, as well as the wars against the Nations associated with the Haudenosaunee (Iroquois) Confederacy. The Wabanaki Confederacy maintained diplomatic relations with the Mohawk through the Ottawa Nation, which acted as mediator (Speck 1915, 496). Among the Maliseet, it was the Penobscot who seemed to play this mediating and unifying role over time.

2. THE ETCHEMIN AND THE ALLIANCE OF INDIGENOUS NATIONS

MAP 41 – Territory of the Wabanaki Confederacy

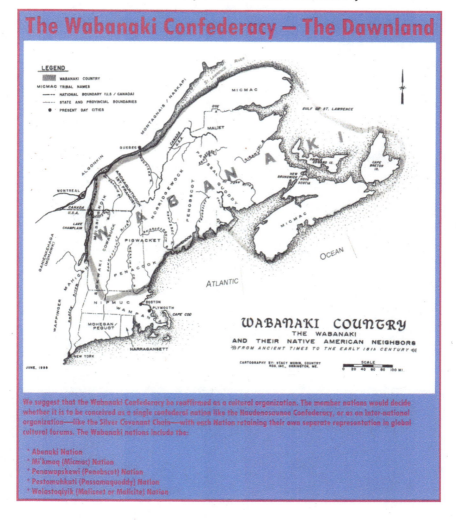

Wampum had an important symbolic value for the members of the Wabanaki Confederacy, including the Maliseet. Wampum carried sacred codes that embodied a Nation's values: the importance of each of the parts that make up a whole, solidarity around common objectives, alliance, and respect. Only Elders, who were entrusted with it and who transported it, were authorized to decode the messages that wampum contained and to transmit these during meetings or celebrations. The role of these messengers was to translate into speech the timeless symbols and values represented in the wampum (Speck 1915, 500ff).

FIGURE 6 – Wampum belts

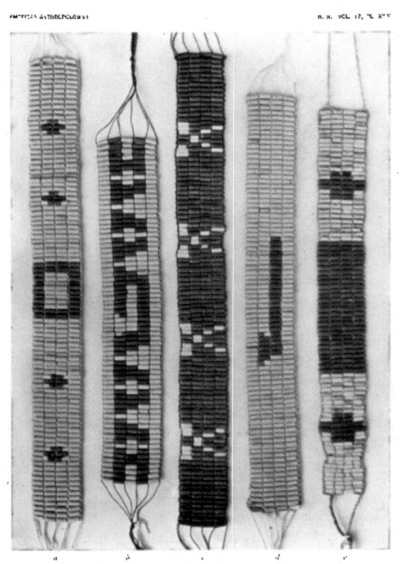

Although interpreting the signs in wampum is difficult, their ongoing value as heritage objects shows that they were used to mark and to immortalize events of the utmost importance, such as alliances with other Nations or with Europeans. In the wampums presented in figure 6, from photographs collected by the anthropologist Speck (1915), appear the symbols of the four or five Nations that were part of the Wabanaki Confederacy. Another wampum represents the pipe of peace, which can be offered to finalize an alliance or shared to reinforce it or to mark an important ceremony. In his account of the alliance of 1603, Champlain retold the story of the sacred pipe that he had been told by the Chiefs. The pipe of peace came from the gods and was used to ratify alliances and to end conflict.

THE GRANDE PAIX DE MONTRÉAL OF 1701[11]

The French alliance policy that began in 1603 and culminated in the Grande Paix de Montréal (1701) has not received its due in Québec and Canadian historiography. As Havard (1992) argued, the Grande Paix de Montréal and the concept of alliance show that Indigenous Peoples participated in this treaty as sovereign Nations. The number of participants, the scope of the negotiations, the formal and public celebrations surrounding the signing, all serve to confirm that the written records that have come down to us captured the proceedings. Since there was no question of ceding land, there was no question of deception or of texts subject to interpretations that could mislead one or other of the parties. The French knew that they had to have the support of all to ensure peace, an essential condition for the continued settlement of the colony and for trade.

> One thing is certain. By negotiating treaties with Indigenous Nations, the Europeans, even if this was not their vision, were in fact recognizing the sovereignty of these Nations. Forty sovereign, politically independent actors participated in the 1701 conference, and the treaty of Montréal carried a historical reality that the events of the summer of 1990 in Kanesatake brought home to us with a vengeance: we cannot speak in contemporary Canada of "two founding peoples"—the English and the French—and ignore this Indigenous past and present. Indigenous Peoples are a fundamental part of the Canadian reality, and they assert this today with the confidence of a People aware of his historical role (our translation; Havard 1992, 188).

---

11. See Appendix 3 for the french version.

In Québec historiography, the concepts of alliance and treaty have led to Indigenous Peoples being acknowledged historically as full-fledged actors. French colonial reality and the political and diplomatic issues associated with it created a space in which they have taken up a more "realistic" place than Canadian history has attributed to them.

Champlain and France understood that the northern reality forced pragmatism upon those managing the territories and the Indigenous Peoples in them. Developing trade and commerce could only be accomplished by ensuring peace and the free movement of all the actors in the territory, both Indigenous Peoples and new migrants from France. Conflicts with the English—the Hudson's Bay Company in the north and the British colonies in the south—had serious consequences for the nature of the relationship between Indigenous Peoples and the Crowns.

Among the participants and in signatories of the Grande Paix de Montréal, to whom must be added allies who were in some way involved in the process, we find the following Nations mentioned by name:

> It is an extreme joy to see here at this time all my children assembled, you Hurons, Sand Outaouais [Akonapi], Kiskakons, Sinago Outaouais, Fork Nation [Odawas Nassawaketons], Saulteurs [Ojibwe], Potawatomi, Sauks, Puants [Ho-Chunk], Folles-Avoines [Menominees], Renards [Meskwaki], Mascoutens, Miamis, Illinois, Amikwas, Népissingues, Algonquins, Témiskamingues, Cristinaux [Cris], people of the Lands, Kickapous, people of the Sault [Mohawks of Kahnawake], of the Mountain, Abenakis, and you Iroquois Nations, and that having placed your interests in my hands, I may allow you all to live in tranquillity (our translation; Grande Paix de Montréal in modern French, Appendix 3).

The first five signatories to the peace treaty included, in order, the Kiskakons, the Iroquois, the Hurons, and two Nations of the Outaouais, the Outaouais du Sable and the Outaouais Sinago. The second signatories, the Iroquois, confirmed their adherence to the treaty in these terms:

> Here we are assembled, Father, as you wished. Last year, you planted a tree of peace and put roots and leaves on it so that we would be safe. Now we hope that everyone hears what you say that this tree will not be touched. For us, we assure you, by these four collars, that we will follow all that you have regulated. We present you with two prisoners, and we will give you back the others that we have. We also hope, now that the doors are open for peace, that the rest of our people will be returned to us (our translation).

The Iroquois spokesman referred to the tree as a symbol of a living alliance that must be consolidated and strengthened over the course of time, the tree symbolizing the relationship between the worlds, above and below, and the earth with its life cycles.

2. THE ETCHEMIN AND THE ALLIANCE OF INDIGENOUS NATIONS   119

FIGURE 7 – The signatories to the Grande Paix de Montréal (1701)

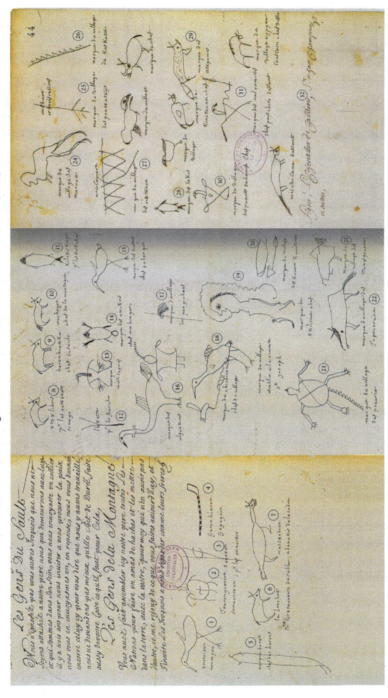

Source: <https://www.fondationlionelgroulx.org/IMG/jpg/traite-grande-paix-de-montreal-1701.jpg>.

The Maliseet were represented by the Abenaki at the meetings. According to Havard (1992), the Abenaki Chief Meskouadoue, Chief of the Rivière Saint-François, was a signatory of the treaty. He had already initialled the treaty of September 1700 that had preceded and paved the way for the Grande Paix de Montréal.

Havard stated that Meskouadoue was probably speaking on behalf of the Wabanaki Confederacy, "namely for the Pentagouets, the Pesmocodys (Passamaquoddys), the Maliseet and the Micmacs" (Havard 1992, 138).

Speaking third from last, the Abenaki representative said, "*The Abenaki*: Even though I speak among the last, I am no less yours, Father. You know that I have always been attached to you. I no longer have an axe; you put it in a pit last year, and I will not take it out until you order me to" (our translation).

Conclusion: The Grande Paix de Montréal

The Grande Paix de Montréal of 1701 crowned a century of politics by France that finally resulted in a formal peace covering a vast territory. This peace, which was concluded in Montréal with numerous Indigenous Nations, allowed France to complete its network of alliances for trade and settlement while hoping to ensure the loyalty of allied Indigenous Peoples in the event of conflict with the English.

The Grande Paix de Montréal was concluded in an environment of festivities and formal diplomatic celebrations that revealed to the population the role and place of Indigenous Peoples in the city. The exchanges that took place in French, the diplomatic language of exchange, with numerous interpreters participating with Indigenous Chiefs in the celebrations, testified to the nation-to-nation relationships that were essential to ensuring a strong presence for France in New France. The French spoke of Indigenous Nations, each with its own identity. *Brotherly* relationships had become *fatherly* relationships, but it is certain that, for the Indigenous Nations, being under the protection of a father or a Crown did not mean losing their identity or giving up their territory. It meant entering into a relationship of co-operation and mutual respect as they shared the land and its resources.

CHAPTER 3
Maliseet Nations' treaties with the British, 1725-1760

Both historically and legally, Canadian and Québec historians—and governments—have refused to recognize treaties concluded under the French regime. It is as if the model imposed by the British were the only valid one. The treaties of the French regime have been forgotten; the Conquest of 1760 and subsequent history became the cornerstones of Canadian and Québec history.

Yet the English signed several treaties during the French regime with various Indigenous Nations that live in present-day Canada. These treaties, to which the Maliseet and their allies were parties, are well known in the regional historiography of the Atlantic Provinces (Battiste 2016; Wicken and Reid 1996). To the federal government, they are known as "treaties of peace and friendship." Pre-Conquest treaties (before 1760) provide important historical evidence that throws light on the nature of the relationship established by the French and British, who sought to forge lasting ties with local Indigenous Peoples through formal agreements, particularly in border zones.

The Conquest of 1760, despite the Royal Proclamation, encouraged the construction of a history in which only the English had made treaties with Indigenous Peoples. This negation of the French policy of making alliances with Indigenous Peoples indicates that the Conquest and the British conceptualization of treaties have been internalized by both francophone and anglophone historians (for historian Marcel Trudel's restricted vision of treaties, Trudel *in* d'Avignon 2009).

THE TREATY OF 1725-1726: NEUTRALITY AND RIGHTS OF INDIGENOUS PEOPLES CONFIRMED AND CONTINUED

The series of treaties between the English and Indigenous Nations between 1725 and 1760 were part of the larger context of the wars that France and England waged in North America to secure control of territory.[1] If the Treaty of Ryswick in 1696 allowed France to recover territory lost to the English, the Treaty of Utrecht in 1713 saw the first real concessions made by France, which ceded Acadia, which would become the province of Nova Scotia.

One of the most important treaties to be negotiated, the Treaty of 1725 (signed in 1726) had, like the Grand Paix de Montréal signed by the French in 1701, as its objective ensuring the neutrality of the *tribes* or *Indian tribes* (terms generally used by the English, as opposed to *sauvages* (used by the French) in British-held territory. Recovering territory in Acadia had been advantageous from a strategic point of view; however, the government in place had little affinity with or control over this territory. The local Peoples were long-time allies of the French, with whom they had been connected from the time of first contact, and they included the Maliseet of the St. Lawrence and Saint John Rivers, those of the Penobscot and Kennebec Rivers and of St. Croix Island (1604–1605), as well as the Mi'kmaq from 1605, 1607 on Membertou (*Dictionary of Canadian Biography* online).

Peace and friendship with their majesties

The Treaty of 1725 was similar to that signed between the French and the Iroquois Nations in 1666. The first few articles stated that its purpose was to consult legitimate Indigenous representatives who could sign statutes of "pacification" with their various majesties, in this case, Nova Scotia, Massachusetts, New York, Connecticut, and Rhode Island. This is the only treaty we know of that used the term *pacification* (Wicken and Reid 1996).

The text states that the treaty would allow everyone to enjoy, under the protection of the British, the right to land and resources in the former English colonies. Penobscot, Narrigewalk, and other Indigenous Peoples in the region and their descendants would have their *liberties and landed property*

---

1. See the text of the treaties in Appendix 4, Appendix: Indigenous peoples' treaties, Mi'kmaq, Maliseet, etc., 1725–1776; Cape Breton University, "Treaties 1725-1761, Treaty of Watertown", <https://www.cbu.ca/indigenous-initiatives/lnu-resource-centre/treaties/>; New Brunswick Aboriginal Peoples Council (NBAPC), "Treaty of 1726", <https://nbapc.org/treaty-of-1725/>.

safeguarded. The treaty specifies that no land would be sold or transferred to any English persons.

The rights to fishing and hunting are guaranteed as before.

Trade between British and the "Indians" would be regulated by the Government of Massachusetts:

> Saving unto the Penobscot, Narridgewalk And other Tribes within His Majesties Province aforesaid and their Natural descendants respectively All their Lands liberties & properties not by them Conveyed or sold to, or possess'd by any of the English Subjects or aforesaid as also the Privilege of Fishing, Hunting & Fowling as formerly. That all Trade and Commerce which hereafter may be allowed betwixt the English & Indians shall be under such Management & Regulation, as the Government of the Massachusetts Province shall direct (Appendix 4, Indigenous Peoples treaties, Mi'kmaq, Maliseet, etc., 1725-1776).

Indigenous Peoples living in French territory were party to the treaty

The treaty specifies that delegates from various Indigenous Peoples inhabiting French territory had also participated in wars waged by the British.

The treaty states that the Crown was entitled to negotiate with representatives of the "tribes of Indians," who agreed to keep peace with the English.

Finally, it notes that the Penobscot would act as intermediaries to ensure that other Peoples signed the treaty at a later date:

> We do further in behalf of the Tribe of the Penobscot Indians Promise & Engage That if any of the other Tribes Intended to be included in this Treaty, shall not withstanding refuse to Confirm & Ratify this present Treaty Entered into on their behalf & Continue or renew Acts of Hostility against the English in such case the said Penobscot Tribe shall Join their Young Men with the English in reducing them to reason.

The Penobscot, Champlain's former allies under the French regime, seemed to be continuing to play the role of mediator among the Maliseet Nation and the allied or member Nations of the Wabanaki Confederacy.

The signing of the Treaty of 1725, 4 June 1726

The Crown had recalled that, following the signing of the Treaty of Utrecht (1713), it was entitled to trade with the Indian tribes. By this treaty, the king took possession of part of Acadia (Nova Scotia), a territory that had been ceded by France.

The treaty contained provisions that affected commercial activity, which were now regulated. As in most of the previous treaties concluded by France, there was a reminder concerning the management of conflict, which were to be judged "in accordance with the laws of His Majesty."

After mention of the exchange of a few prisoners, as was customary among Indigenous Peoples, the various dignitaries, Grand Chiefs, and representatives of various communities, signed either with an X next to their names or with their signatures. Based on the transcription available, some Chiefs affixed their eponymous animal, which was translated as "Chief of" (see Appendix 4, 1725).

Among the first three dignitaries to sign were Chief Nicholas of Saint Johns (Saint John River) and those of Cape Sable, Paul Tecumart and Joseph Ounaginitish. These signatures were followed by the marks of the twenty or so representatives from Saint Johns.

Among the places identified are Saint Johns (Saint John) with the largest number of signatories. More than twenty signed, all with an X, only one of whom had a French first name. There were no surnames or first names of Indigenous origin among the Saint John River signatories. The remaining signatures were associated, in order, with the following locations: Cap de Sable (five signatures), "Chichabenady" (three), "Rethiboucto," now Richibucto (six), "Chokanicto" (seven), Grand Glode and a Grand Totem (three) from Pentaquit, or Penobscot (twelve), Passamaquoddy (eight), the "Coast" (13 signatures), and, finally, one signature from "Breton," possibly Cape Breton Island. Many signed by referring to their clan or family, and some appeared to have drawn the animal associated with their community. The titles of Chiefs were associated with their totem (probably drawn by hand), Pon, Chief, or Grand Glode.

Some seventy representatives of Indigenous Nations signed this treaty, which confirmed and renewed recognition of the rights of Indigenous Peoples.

Several Maliseet surnames are still found among the present-day Maliseet of Viger First Nation. For example, Obins (Aubin, St-Aubin), Athanas, Nicolas, Joseph, Denis, and Bernard. Other names appear in the history of Indigenous families in Québec: Reny/René, Jermain (Germain),

Pisnett (Pinet), Baptiste, Étienne, Philippe, Benoit, Piuze, Mark, and Lavoint (Lavoie). Several first names have become Indigenous surnames in certain communities.

Among the signatories who had kept their Indigenous names were the following:

- Nipimoit, Tecumart, and Ounaginitish (from Cape Sable)
- Attanas, Gidark, Armquarett, and Eargomot (Richibucto)
- Eargamet, (Chicanicto), Muse, Miductuk, and Pemeriot (Cape Sable)
- Pemeroit, Nimquarett, Chegau, Nextabau, Nimcharrett, and Shomitt (Pentaquit, Penobscot)
- Nimcharrett, Chegau, Chikarett, Tecumart, St Aboqmadin, Outine, Eastern, and Egidish (Passamaquoddy)
- from the coast: Quaret, Nelanoit, Spugonoit, Nughquit, Begamonit, Penall, Migaton, Chigaguist, and Chegan and Chegan (Breton / Cape Breton)

A study of these names and the territories they are associated with would probably connect these names and their families with the same name in contemporary Indigenous communities. It appears that the Maliseet of the Saint John River did not use names linked to their Nation of origin when signing the treaty. French first names appear to have become surnames over time.

The British confirmed that signatories to the treaty would maintain their rights to their land and resources and their right to trade, subject to regulations. With this treaty, the Indigenous Nations came under the protection of both the French and the English and were confirmed in their rights as allies as well as in their right to possess their lands and resources (Johnson 2003; Competing Sovereignties Brief...; Appendix, 2003; see figure 8 on the Commemoration of Treaty. Ratification of 1725 Treaty).

FIGURE 8 – Plaque commemorating the Treaty of 1726

TREATY

Ratification of 1725 Treaty

Whereas by the Articles of Peace and agreement Made & concluded upon at Boston in New England the Fifteenth Day of Decr: One Thousand Seven Hundred & twenty five by our Delegates & Representatives Sanguaum (allias Laronn) Alexis Francois Xavier & Megumonbe as appears by the Instruments then Sign'd Seal'd & Exchanged in the Presence of the Great & Gen'll Court or Assembly of y.e Massachusetts Bay by our Said Delegates in behalf of us the Said Indians of Penobscot, Norridgewolk, S.t Johns, Cape Sable, and the other Indian Tribes belonging to & inhabiting within these His Majesty of Great Brittains Territories [of] Nova Scotia & New England & by Maj.r Paul Mascarene Comissioner from this said Province in behalf of His Majesty by which Agreem.t its being required that the Said Articles Should be ratified [?] at His Majesty's Fort of Annapolis Royall We'e the Chiefs & Representatives of the Said Indians with Full Power & Authority by Unanimous Consent & desire of the Said Indian Tribes are Come in Complyance with y.e Articles Stipulated by our Delegates as aforesaid and so in Obedience thereunto Solemnly Confirm & ratifie y.e Same & in Testimony thereof with Hearts full of Sincerity. We have Sign'd & seal'd the following Articles being Conform to what was requir'd by the Said Maj.r Paul Mascarene & Promile to be performed by our Said Delegates.

Whereas His Majesty King George; by the Concep{s}ion of the Most Christian King made at the Treaty of Utrecht; is become y.e Rightfull Pos{s}es{s}or of the Province of Nova Scotia or Acadia According to its ancient Boundaries we'e the Said Chiefs & Representatives of y.e Penobscott, Norridgewolk S.t Johns, Cape Sables & of the Other Indian Tribes Belonging to & inhabiting within This His Majesties Province of Nova Scotia or Acadia & New England do for our Selves & the Said Tribes We'e represent acknowledge His Said Majesty King George's Juri{s}diction & Dominion Over the Territories of the Said Province of Nova Scotia or Acadia & make our Submi{s}sion to His Said Majesty in as ample a Manner as we have formerly done to the Most Christian King.

That the Indians shall nott molest any of His Majesty's Subjects or their Dependants in their Settlements already made or Lawfully to be made or in their carrying on Their Trade or Other Affaires within the Said Province.

That If there Happen any robbery or outrage Comitted by any of Our Indians the Tribe or Tribes they belong to Shall Cause Satisfaction to be made to y.e partys Injur'd.

That the Indians Shall nott help to convey away any Soldiers belonging to His Majesty's Forts butt on the Contrary Shall bring back any Souldier they Shall find Endeavouring to run away.

That in Case of any Misunderstanding Quarrell or Injury between the English & the Indians no Private revenge Shall be taken, butt Application Shall be made for relief According to His Majesty Laws.

That if there any English Prisoners amongst any of our aforesaid Tribes wee faithfuly promi{s} that the Said Prisoners shall be released & Carefully Conducted & Deliver'd up to this Govern.nt, or that of New England.

That in Testimony of our Sincerity wee have for our Selves & in behalf of Our Said Indian Tribes Confirmes to what was Stipulated by our Delegates att Boston as aforesaid this day Solemnly Confirm'd & ratified each & ratified each & every One of the aforegoing Articles which Shall be Punctually observ'd & duly perform'd by Each & all of us the Said Indians. In Witne{s} Whereof wee have before the [?] [?] John Doucett & Council'l for this His Majesty Said Province & the Deputies of the ffrench Inhabitants of Sd Province hereunto Sett our Hands & Seals at Annapolis Royall this 4th Day of June 1726 & in the Twelveth Year of His Majesty Reign.

THE TREATIES OF 1749 CONFIRM THE TREATY OF 1725 AND REITERATE THE PARTIES' COMMITMENT

On 15 August and 14 September 1749, other, brief treaties were ratified. The Chiefs and captains of the Saint John River and adjacent communities were signatories (Appendix 4).

THE TREATY OF 16 SEPTEMBER 1752

War with New France was raging and, for both Indigenous Nations and the British, treaties that provided a measure of neutrality and a commitment to peace or at least to non-aggression by Indigenous Peoples were of the utmost diplomatic and strategic importance in a time of armed conflict.

The Treaty of 1752 reiterates that Indigenous Peoples could continue to hunt and fish freely "as usual." They were entitled to a trading post. They could sell skins, feathers, birds, fish, or any other goods, and they were to be free to dispose of these goods to their best advantage:

> 4. It is agreed that the said Tribe of Indians shall not be hindered from, but have free liberty of Hunting and Fishing as usual and that if they shall think a Truck house needful at the River Chibenaccadie, or any other place of their resort they shall have the same built and proper Merchandize, lodged therein to be exchanged for what the Indians shall have to dispose of and that in the meantime *the Indians shall have free liberty to being to Sale* to Halifax or any other Settlement within this Province, Skins, feathers, fowl, fish or any other thing they shall have to sell, where *they shall have liberty to dispose thereof to the best Advantage* (italics added; Appendix, 1725…).

The Treaty of 1725 had confirmed that Indigenous Peoples retained their hunting and fishing rights and could continue to trade and sell their goods. This recognition entailed freedom and the possibility of setting up sites where business that benefitted Indigenous Peoples could be conducted, subject to regulation by the Crown.

THE TREATY OF 1760: RENEWAL AND CONFIRMATION OF THE TREATY OF 1725

The Treaty of 1760 repeats much of the text of the Treaty of 1725, to which it refers in its opening lines: "Whereas Articles of Submission and Agreement were made and concluded at Boston in New England in the Year of Our Lord 1725."

This treaty specifies that the tribes of Nova Scotia (Acadia) are parties to the treaty. It also states that another treaty had been signed in 1749. The treaty reiterates the importance of the Indigenous Peoples of the Passamaquoddy and Saint John Rivers renewing allegiance and submission to King George II. The parties agreed to scrupulously respect the commitments made by both sides in these treaties.

The treaty restates that the Tribes must always trade and exchange their goods in trading posts established for them. To ensure the peace and commitment of the Passamaquoddy and the Saint John River *Indians* (*Sauvages* generally used by the French) a trading post is guaranteed. At least three Indigenous representatives would be sent to these posts to facilitate the smooth flow of trade and commerce:

> And We the said Mitchel Neptune and Ballomy Glode, for ourselves and in the name and behalf of the said Tribes of Passamaquody and Saint John's Indians Do respectively further promise and engage that no person or persons belonging to the said Tribes shall at any time hereafter aid or Assist any of the Enemies of His most Sacred Majesty King George the Second or of his Heirs and successors nor shall hold any Correspondence or Commerce with any such His Majestys Enemies in any way or manner whatsoever and that, for the more effectually preventing any such Correspondence and Commerce with any of His Majestys Enemies *the said Tribes shall at all times hereafter Trafic and barter and exchange Commodities with the Managers of such Truckhouses as shall be established for that purpose by* his Majesty's *Governors of this Province* at Fort Frederick or elsewhere within the Said Province and at no other place without permission from his Majestys Government of the said Province. And We do in like manner further promise and engage that for the more effectually securing and due performance of this Treaty and every part thereof a certain Number, which shall not be less than Three from each of the aforesaid tribes, shall from and after the ratification hereof constantly reside in Fort Frederick at St. Johns or at such other place or places within the Province as shall and at no other place without permission from His Majestys Government of the said Province (Appendix, 1725...).

***

Although these treaties clearly show the nature of the nation-to-nation relationship under the British regime, which included mutual respect, right to land and resources, and free but regulated trade, it was not until 1999 that the Supreme Court of Canada (1999) recognized the right of Indigenous Peoples to trade, in particular by obtaining various fishing licences on the St. Lawrence based on their treaties (1725–1760). How did the Canadian system come to deny Indigenous Peoples the right to trade or commerce, when the right to trade was the very foundation of relations under the French and British regimes?

While lower courts had tended to view trade with Indigenous Peoples only as "barter" reserved for "primitive" hunter-gatherers, the Supreme Court of Canada recognized that Indigenous Peoples have a basic right to trade. With the 1999 Marshall decision, the Supreme Court recognized the treaties concluded under the French regime (1603–1760) and redefined the nation-to-nation relationship that had been lost with Confederation (1867). Treaties signed from 1725 onward are recognized in subsequent treaties, including in the Treaty of 1760. Recognized, confirmed, and renewed, these treaties were ratified in a political and diplomatic context that rendered the French and British, as well as Indigenous Peoples, dependent on each other.

After 1999, when the Canadian system renewed the right of Indigenous Peoples to trade following the Marshall decision, which had recognized the 1725–1760 treaties, the Maliseet of Québec First Nation was able to resume commercial fishing activities. By obtaining licences that allowed them to regain their identity through commercial fishing, the Maliseet Nation of Québec was able to engage in this activity to further the development of their community (Supreme Court of Canada 1999; on contemporary commercial fishing, Michaux 2007).

MALISEET LEADERS RECOGNIZE THE TREATY OF 1725 DURING CELEBRATIONS ON 4 JUNE 2016

On 4 June 2016, the Great Chiefs of the Maliseet Nations celebrated the Treaty of 1725 in a special way, recalling in an official declaration signed by eight Maliseet Chiefs in Cacouna that this treaty perpetuated to some extent the cycle of alliances by which they had begun their nation-to-nation relationship with France as early as 1603.

The declaration recalls the importance of the Treaty of 1725 with regard to the mutual protection and friendship to which the parties had committed themselves. The statement also recalls that the Royal Proclamation of 1763 initiated a policy of treaties that allowed lands to be ceded to the Crown.

In the declaration, the Maliseet Chiefs assert that section 35 of the 1982 Constitution recognizes and affirms existing Indigenous and treaty rights of the Indigenous Peoples of Canada, *including "all treaties with First Nations" and in particular those in which there has been no cession of land.*

This statement is part of a larger history of nation-to-nation alliances in which land is not ceded but, in consultation and with the agreement of Indigenous Peoples, territory and resources are shared according to the needs of and agreements between the parties. The Treaty of 1725 and those that were signed by the English before 1760 with the Maliseet, Passamaquoddy, Penobscot, and Mi'kmaq Nations were based on a system *of no cession or sale of land*. The Nations came under the protection of the Crown but defended their rights, territory, and possessions as a People. Agreeing to put themselves under the protection of the Crown, even of several Crowns (French then British), did not mean that Indigenous Peoples were agreeing to being deprived of the right to their lands, their resources, and their culture.

DECLARATION BY MALISEET CHIEFS REGARDING A DAY TO COMMEMORATE THE TREATY OF 1725, SIGNED ON 4 JUNE 1726

This declaration was signed on 4 June 2016 by eight Chiefs of the Maliseet Nation to commemorate the treaty signed with the British by the Chiefs of the Maliseet, Mi'kmaq, Passamaquoddy, and Penobscot Nations at Annapolis on 4 June 1726 (see Appendix 4, Treaties...; figure 9).

The signatures of eight Maliseet Chiefs appear at the bottom of this commemorative plaque. Transcription of the text of the Declaration by the Maliseet Chiefs (signed 4 June 2016).

FIGURE 9 – Plaque commemorating the signing of the Treaty of 1725 by the Maliseet Nations

DECLARATION BY MALISEET CHIEFS FOR JUNE 4TH AS OFFICIAL TREATY DAY

In recognition and celebration of the Mascarene's Treaty of 1725, signed on June 4, 1726, at Annapolis Royal, and ratified by Lieutenant Governor John Doucett and by Maliseet, Mi'kmaq, Passamaquoddy and Penobscot Chiefs and headmen.

As set forth in the Treaty, that the said Nations "be afforded all marks of favour protection and Friendship and further engage and promise on behalf of the said Government that the Indians shall not be molested in their persons, hunting, fishing and planting grounds nor in any other their lawful occasions by His Majestys Subjects or their Dependants nor in the exercise of their religion";

Further set forth in the Treaty, "that if any of the Indians are injured by any of Her Majesty's aforesaid Subjects or their Dependents they shall have satisfaction and reparation made to them according to His Majesty's laws wherenl (sic/wherein) the Indians shall have the benefit equal with His Majesty's other Subjects";

Further affirmed by the Royal Proclamation of 1763, which established the process of treaty-making as the means by which title to Indigenous lands can be ceded;

Further affirmed by the Constitution of Canada, 1982, section 35, which recognizes all treaties with First Nations, this Treaty being amongst the oldest, having endured for the past 290 years;

Whereas we did not cede any land in this treaty; and

Whereas this treaty became the template for all later treaties between our nation and the Crown; and

Whereas, the Maliseet Nation has lived since time immemorial within our traditional homeland in the watershed of the Walastakw, the Beautiful River, extending all the way to the St. Lawrence River; and

Whereas this homeland is our sacred source of life; and

Whereas our tradition recognizes this treaty as the means by which we became related as brothers and sisters to all people of the immigrant society; and

Whereas the Maliseet Nation wishes to assert our sovereignty as recognized in the Treaty through our nation-to-nation relationship with the Crown; and

Whereas it is important to recognize and assert the benefits endowed in the Treaty; and

Whereas it is important to remember and celebrate the spirit of peace and friendship under which the Treaty was signed;

3. MALISEET NATIONS' TREATIES WITH THE BRITISH, 1725-1760

Henceforth, We, the Maliseet Chiefs on behalf of the Maliseet Nation, proclaim June 4 as our Treaty Day.

Signed by

Anne Archambault, Kahkona (Cacouna)
Patricia Bernard, Matoweskok (Madawaska)
Brenda Commanda, Mehtakwsenihkek (Houlton)
Candid Paul, Sakamawi Malihk (St. Mary's)
Gabriel Atwin, Pilick (Kingsclear)
Ross Perley, Nekotkok (Tobique)
Shelley Sabattis, Welamokatok (Oromocto)
Timothy Paul, Wetstak (Woodstock)

CHAPTER 4
Managing land for agriculture and settlement

Under the French regime, the process for the privatization of land was centred on seigneuries, a system of colonization designed primarily for agriculture.

FROM 1534 TO 1627

Between 1534 and 1627, France failed to establish a viable colony in North America. It did not have the means to wage war to subjugate the Indigenous Peoples that its representatives encountered. As early as 1603, these representatives were directed to make alliances with Indigenous Peoples and their leaders, and such alliances were subsequently concluded. Indeed, it was only these alliances that allowed the king to claim sovereignty, albeit fragile, over these vast territories.

In 1627, the decree that established the Compagnie des Cent-Associés (Company of one hundred associates) to manage trade in Canada also established the first seigneury in New France, in this vast territory that France obviously did not control. Recall that New France was meant to encompass the whole of the North American continent, from Spanish Florida to the far north; and this is what France claimed, in principle, for the Compagnie des Cent-Associés (Trudel 1965, 206). Cardinal Richelieu noted that colonization in New France was stagnant: "Nevertheless, those who had been entrusted with this care had been so uninterested in providing for it, that even now only one dwelling has been established, in which, although usually forty or fifty Frenchmen are maintained, rather for the interest of the merchants than for the good and advancement of the king's service in the said country" (our translation; Assemblée legislative 1854, 1: 6–8).

Faced with this distressing observation, the cardinal realized that the sovereignty of the king in New France was far from being a given: "My said lord the cardinal thought he was obliged to provide for it, and by admonishing them, to carry out the intention of the king, and to make sure that, to assist in the conversion of these Peoples, to establish a powerful colony in this province, *New France be acquired by the king with all its extent, for good, without fear that the enemies of this Crown take it away from the French, as could happen if it were not provided for*" (our translation; Assemblée legislative 1854, 1:6–8).

During this period, no seigneuries were granted within the limits of traditional Maliseet lands.

1627 TO 1663

Between 1627 and 1663, it was the king (through the *Compagnie des Cent-Associés*) who "possessed" all the land, and only an *acte de concession* (grant) signed and ratified by French authorities transferred the right to possess land, under this hierarchical system, the king—or his representatives—detached land from the royal domain and granted it to private individuals. No one could own land without a ratified acte de concession; this was a prerequisite (Boily 2006, 5).

In fact, the king, who acted as if he owned New France, granted seigneuries without worrying about the territory of the savages because he had concluded alliances with them. The text of these alliances makes no mention of the surrender of traditional lands by the Indigenous Peoples who inhabited them.

In the seigneurial system, the *acte de concession* was the written and tangible instrument by which the French authorities transferred property rights. The landowner was subject to certain conditions that had to be met, or else the king would repossess the land.

Between 1627 and 1663, the first seigneuries were granted within the limits of traditional Maliseet territory (see map 42). In his analysis of the 1663 terrier (land registry), Marcel Trudel (1993b) identified nine scattered seigneuries located in whole or in part on traditional Maliseet lands. Of this number, five seigneuries were located on the coast and the other four on islands. However, only the two largest seigneuries had *censitaires* (tenants) actually residing on their holdings. These were the seigneury of Lauzon with thirty-four holdings under cultivation (2.1 square kilometres) and the seigneury of Île-d'Orléans with 102 (7.0 square kilometres; see table 3).

4. MANAGING LAND FOR AGRICULTURE AND SETTLEMENT

The lands granted to the nine seigneuries comprises 1,526 square kilometres, or 4.6 percent of the 32,990 square kilometres of Wolastokuk (Maliseet of Viger First Nation 2013). During this thirty-six-year period, the seigneurs enticed only 382 people to come and live in one or another of the seigneuries granted on Maliseet traditional territory (see table 4). This still represented 12.5 percent of the population of the St. Lawrence Lowlands, which at that time numbered 3,035 persons.

MAP 42 – Seigneuries granted by 1663

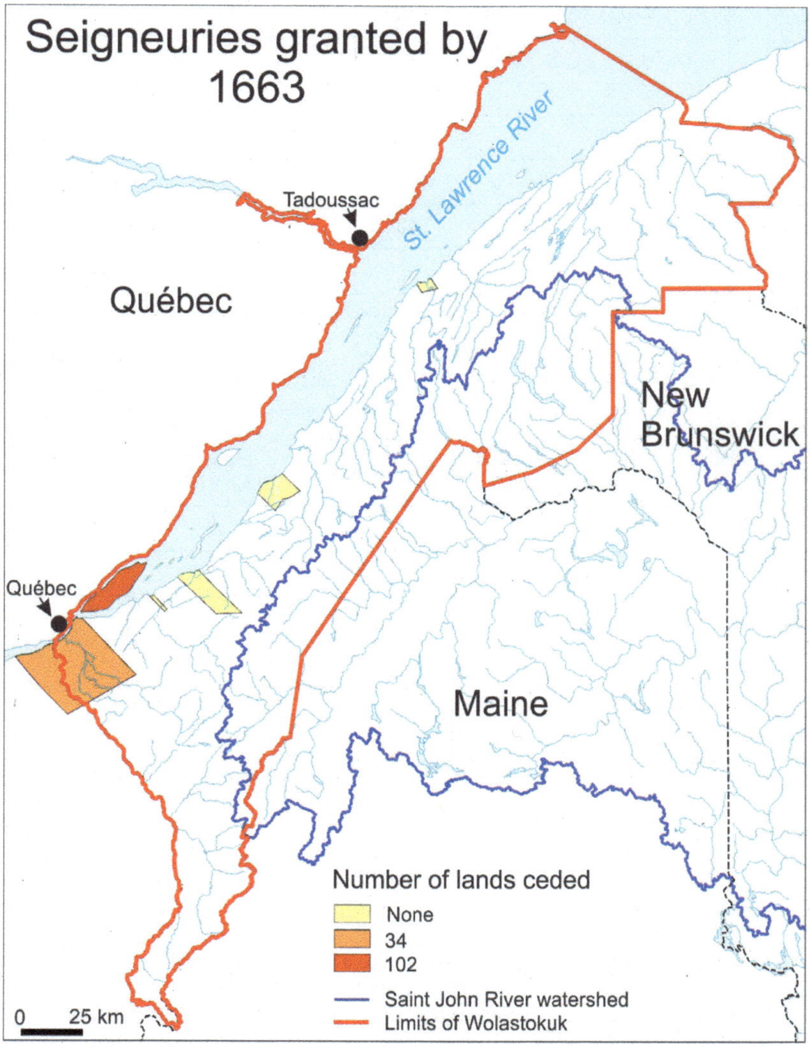

TABLE 3 – Grant submitting *aveux et dénombrement*,[1] 1663

YEAR OF CONCESSION	SEIGNEURY	TOTAL AREA (HECTARES)	NUMBER OF TENANT HOLDINGS	AREA OF TENANT HOLDINGS IN (HECTARES)	PERCENTAGE HELD BY TENANTS
SEIGNEURIES ALONG THE COAST					
1636	Lauzon	86,845	34	2,143	2.4
1637	Bellechasse	9,649	No tenants in 1663		
1646	Rivière-du-Sud	14,474	No tenants in 1663		
1656	Grande-Anse (Les Aulnaies)	14,474	No tenants in 1663		
1663	Rivière-du-Saumon	7,056	No tenants in 1663		
ISLAND SEIGNEURIES					
1636	Île-d'Orléans	19,459	102	7,018	36.0
1638	Île-au-Ruau	175	No tenants in 1663		
1662	Île-Patience	218	No tenants in 1663		
1662	Île-au-Canot	301	No tenants in 1663		

Source: Marcel Trudel 1973b *Le terrier du Canada en 1663*. Ottawa, Éditions de l'Université d'Ottawa, 618 p.

TABLE 4 – Population of New France (St. Lawrence Lowlands), 1663

SEIGNEURY	YEAR FOUNDED	POPULATION IN 1663	% OF THE TERRITORY UNDER STUDY	% OF NEW FRANCE
Île-d'Orléans	1636	278	73.2	9.2
Lauzon	1636	102	26.8	3.3
Territory under study		380	100.0	12.5
Other seigneuries		2,655		87.5
New France (St. Lawrence Lowlands)		3,035		100.0

Source: Marcel Trudel 1973a, *La population du Canada en 1663*. Montréal, Fides, p. 163–263.

---

1. *Aveux et dénombrement* is the name given to a document in which a seigneur gives an account to the king of what he has done to improve his seigneury according to the terms of the agreement signed and ratified by the king. The *seigneur* indicates if he resides in his seigneury, the number of tenants he has, the amount of land that has been cleared and is being farmed, etc.

4. MANAGING LAND FOR AGRICULTURE AND SETTLEMENT

The period from ended with the withdrawal of the Compagnie des Cent-Associés from New France. The king noted that:

> [W]e have learned with regret that not only was the number of inhabitants very small, but even that they were in daily danger of being driven out by the Iroquois. It being necessary to provide for them and considering that this company of one hundred men was nearly annihilated by the voluntary abandonment by the greatest number of those Interested in it and that the *few which remained of this number were not strong enough to support this country and to send there the forces and the men necessary to both inhabit and defend it*.[2] (our translation)

After thirty-six years of attempted colonization by the Compagnie des Cent-Associés, the king could only note the failure of the company to fulfill its obligations. The king's claim to the lands of New France remained fragile despite alliances with several Indigenous Nations. For this reason, he decided to make New France a royal province administered by a ruling council responsible for carrying out royal decrees.

1663 TO 1674

From 1663 to 1674, colonization intensified with the arrival of new settlers and soldiers and the addition of new seigneuries. However, the French authorities had reservations about the large number of seigneuries granted compared to the (low) rate of settlement. This led to an almost complete halt in the granting of seigneuries until the decade 1670–1680, which saw a spectacular resumption (90 new seigneuries), especially under Intendant Jean Talon (Grenier 2015, 143). Analysis of data from the 1674 land registry (terrier) has revealed that, within traditional Maliseet territory, this translated to the addition of fifteen seigneuries to those granted before 1663, for a total of twenty-five.

The following map shows that the seigneuries were established close to each other and formed two groups, the first located near Québec and the second centred on the Rivière du Loup (see map 43). Settlement had advanced further in the first group, mainly because of the presence of older seigneuries such as Lauzon, with 106 holdings granted to tenant farmers, and Île-d'Orléans, with 286 such holdings. The latter seigneury was by far the most successful, as 79.1 percent of its area was under cultivation. The second group was made up of seigneuries that had been more newly granted, and only in those of La Pocatière and Rivière-Ouelle had clearing and

---

2. *Édit du roi Louis XIV érigeant la Nouvelle-France en province royale*, March 1663.

cultivation of land begun. It should also be noted that no acte de concession has yet been granted inland. Seigneuries were either on the coast (18) or on islands (7). In summary, land granted by 1674 represents 2,477 square kilometres or 7.5 percent of present-day Wolastokuk, and land held by tenant farmers had an area of 238 square kilometres (see table 5).

From 1663 to 1674, the development of the seigneuries granted on Maliseet ancestral lands remained negligible. In fact, apart from the seigneury of Île-d'Orléans, which had 1,082 inhabitants in 1681, most others had modest or even non-existent populations (see table 6).

MAP 43 – Seigneuries granted by 1674

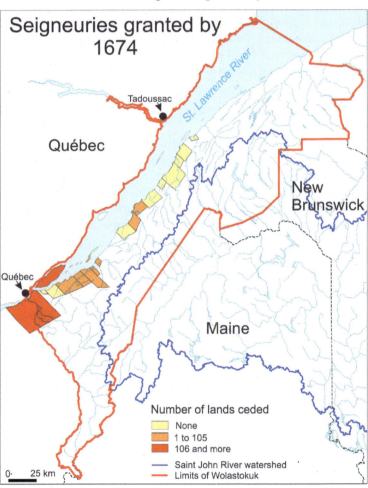

TABLE 5 – Grants submitting *aveux et dénombrement*, 1674

YEAR OF CONCESSION	SEIGNEURY	TOTAL AREA (HECTARES)	NUMBER OF TENANT HOLDINGS	AREA OF TENANT HOLDINGS IN (HECTARES)	PERCENTAGE HELD BY TENANTS
SEIGNEURIES ALONG THE COAST					
1636	Lauzon	86,845	106	5,924	6.8
1672	Vincennes	2,010	No tenants in 1674		
1672	Beaumont	7,237	No tenants in 1674		
1672	La Durantaye	14,474	9	68	0.4
1637	Bellechasse	9,649	8	307	3.1
1646	Rivière-du-Sud	14,474	20	902	6.2
1672	Fournier (Saint-Joseph)	1,723	2	82	4.7
1672	Lafrenaye	1,206	No tenants in 1674		
1672	Vincelotte	2,412	4	259	10.7
1656	Grande-Anse (Les Aulnaies)	14,474	No tenants in 1674		
1672	La Pocatière	5,427	2	150	2.7
1672	Rivière-Ouelle	7,237	7	465	6.4
1674	Kamouraska	14,598	No tenants in 1674		
1672	Islet-du-Portage	2,412	No tenants in 1674		
1673	Verbois	21,711	No tenants in 1674		
1673	Rivière-du-Loup	5,427	No tenants in 1674		
1673	Leparc	9,649	No tenants in 1674		
1663	Rivière-du-Saumon	3,530	No tenants in 1674		
ISLAND SEIGNEURIES					
1636	Île-d'Orléans	19,459	286	15,410	79.1
1672	Île-Madame	127	No tenants in 1674		
1638	Île-au-Ruau	175	1	114	65.1
1662	Île-Patience	218	No tenants in 1674		
1662	Île-au-Canot	301	No tenants in 1674		
1646	Île-aux-Grues	1,809	4	172	9.5
1668	Île-aux-Oies	1,206	No tenants in 1674		

Source: Marcel Trudel (1998). *Le terrier du Canada en 1674*, vol. 1 et 2, Montréal, Éditions du Méridien, 912 p.

TABLE 6 – Population of New France (St. Lawrence Lowlands), 1681

YEAR OF CONCESSION	SEIGNEURY	TOTAL AREA (HECTARES)	NUMBER OF TENANT HOLDINGS	AREA OF TENANT HOLDINGS IN (HECTARES)
Lauzon	1636	291	15.8	3.0
Vincennes (Cap Claude)	1672	27	1.5	0.3
Beaumont	1672	53	2.8	0.6
La Durantaye	1672	58	3.3	0.6
Bellechasse	1637	227	12.3	2.3
Saint-Denis-de-la-Bouteillerie	1679	62	3.3	0.6
Île-aux-Oies	1668	39	2.2	0.4
Île-d'Orléans	1636	1,082	58.8	11.2
Territory under study		1,839	100.0	19.0
Other seigneuries		7,838		81.0
New France (St. Lawrence Lowlands)		9,677		100.0

Source: Benjamin Sulte (1977), *Histoire des canadiens-français, 1608-1880*. Montréal, Presse Élite, vol. 5: 89.

1723 TO 1745

In 1723, Intendant Bégon issued a decree that obliged each seigneur to submit a document called an *aveu et dénombrement* (a description of the degree of development of their grant). At this time, there were fifty seigneuries on the traditional territory of the Maliseet in Québec, according to the inventory carried out by Mathieu et al. in 1991. This requirement, which ended in 1745, has enabled the calculation of the number of holdings occupied by tenant farmers. The following map shows the distribution of the seigneuries that had been granted (see map 44). The entire coastline within the boundaries of Wolastokuk had been ceded to seigneurs, and seigneuries had been granted inland. At that time, the surface area of the seigneuries amounted to 9,096 square kilometres (27.5 percent of present-day Wolastokuk). However, only 673 square kilometres of this seigneurial land had been brought under cultivation (see table 7). The seigneuries near Québec were the most developed and, the further away from Québec, the less developed they were. In addition to the seigneuries of Île-d'Orléans (310 tenant farms) and Lauzon (108 tenant farms), three other stood out: the seigneuries of Saint-Michel (173 tenant farms), Rivière-du-Sud (120 tenant farms), and Bellechasse (97 tenant farms).

4. MANAGING LAND FOR AGRICULTURE AND SETTLEMENT

According to the last census taken in New France (1739), the population of the area under study was 8,802 persons, out of a total of 42,701 living in the St. Lawrence Lowlands (see table 8). Not surprisingly, the seigneuries with the most tenant farms had the most inhabitants.

At the end of the French regime, less than half of the traditional Maliseet territory in the interior of Québec had been granted as seigneuries. Moreover, only a small part of that territory had been developed for agriculture. The lack of settlement on seigneurial land in most of Wolastokuk left the Maliseet free to move around and practise their customary activities where still possible.

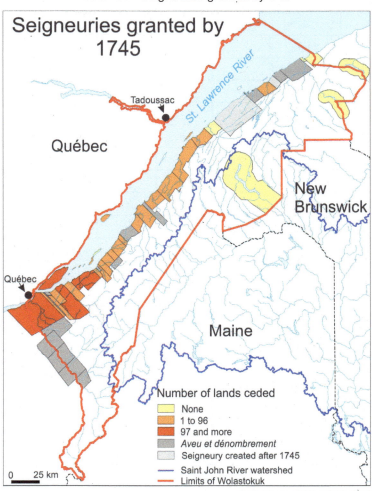

MAP 44 – Seigneuries granted by 1745

Carl Brisson, GRH, UQAC, 2019

TABLE 7 – Grants submitting *aveux et dénombrement*, 1723-1745

YEAR OF CONCESSION	SEIGNEURY	TOTAL AREA (HECTARES)	NUMBER OF TENANT HOLDINGS	AREA OF TENANT HOLDINGS IN (HECTARES)	PERCENTAGE HELD BY TENANTS
\multicolumn{6}{c}{SEIGNEURIES ALONG THE COAST}
1636	Lauzon	86,845	108	6,961	8.0
1692	La Martinière	2,894	8	246	8.5
1683	Montapeine	1,723	\multicolumn{3}{c	}{No information}
1672	Vincennes	2,010	\multicolumn{3}{c	}{No information}
1736	Livaudière	5,427	43	1,804	33.2
1672	Beaumont	12,664	66	2,803	22.1
1672	Saint-Michel	15,272	173	4,383	28.6
1672	Saint-Vallier	12,544	58	2,632	20.9
1637	Bellechasse	9,649	97	4,716	48.8
1646	Rivière-du-Sud	14,474	120	4,325	29.8
1672	Fournier (Saint-Joseph)	1,723	5	8	0.4
1672	Lafrenaye (Gagné)	603	\multicolumn{3}{c	}{No information}
1672	Gamache (Sainte-Claire)	603	3	373	61.8
1672	Vincelotte	4,824	26	1,634	33.8
1677	Bonsecours	7,237	39	3,518	48.6
1677	Islet Saint-Jean	4,824	16	1,866	38.6
1698	Lessard (L'Islet)	9,649	\multicolumn{3}{c	}{No information}
1677	Port-Joly	9,649	10	1,090	11.2
1677	Islet-à-la-Peau	2,412	1	57	2.3
1656	Grande-Anse (Les Aulnaies)	14,474	\multicolumn{3}{c	}{No information}
1672	La Pocatière	5,427	41	2,747	50.6
1672	Rivière-Ouelle	7,237	56	2,735	37.7
1679	Saint-Denis-de-la-Bouteillerie	9,649	\multicolumn{3}{c	}{No information}
1674	Kamouraska	14,598	36	3,200	21.9
1672	Islet-du-Portage	25,329	12	635	2.5
1673	Rivière-du-Loup	36,787	3	720	1.9

4. MANAGING LAND FOR AGRICULTURE AND SETTLEMENT

YEAR OF CONCESSION	SEIGNEURY	TOTAL AREA (HECTARES)	NUMBER OF TENANT HOLDINGS	AREA OF TENANT HOLDINGS IN (HECTARES)	PERCENTAGE HELD BY TENANTS
1684	Île-Verte	14,474	1	82	0.5
1687	Trois-Pistoles	9,649	No tenants in 1723		
1751	Nicolas-Riou	28,948	Conceded after 1745		
1675	Le Bic	9,649	No information		
1688	Rimouski	9,649	15	2,933	30.3
1751	Saint-Barnabé	28,948	Conceded after 1745		
1696	Lessard (Pointe-au-Père)	7,237	No aveux et dénombrement		
1696	Lepage et Thivierge	28,948	No aveux et dénombrement		
1689	Pachot (Rivière Mitis)	2,412	No tenants in 1723		
1675	Mitis (Peiras)	9,649	No tenants in 1723		
**ISLAND SEIGNEURIES**					
1636	Île-d'Orléans	19,459	310	15,410	79.1
1672	Île-Madame	127	No aveux et dénombrement		
1638	Île-au-Ruau	175	1	114	65.1
1646	Grandville	3,535	7	818	23.1
1668	Île-aux-Oies	1,206	No tenants in 1739		
1687	Île-aux-Coudres	3,010	18	1,555	51.6
**INLAND SEIGNEURIES**					
1697	Joliet (Sainte-Claire)	21,711	No aveux et dénombrement		
1736	Sainte-Marie-de-Beauce	14,474	No aveux et dénombrement		
1736	Saint-Joseph-de-Beauce	14,474	No aveux et dénombrement		
1736	Saint-François-de-Beauce	14,474	No aveux et dénombrement		
1736	Aubin-De L'Isle	9,649	No aveux et dénombrement		
1683	Madawaska	125,000	No tenants in 1723		
1693	Lac-Mitis	24,123	No tenants in 1725		
1694	Lac-Matapédia	190,145	No aveux et dénombrement		

Source: Jacques Mathieu, Alain Laberge et Lina Gouger (1991). *L'occupation des terres dans la vallée du Saint-Laurent, 1723-1745*. Sillery, Septentrion, 415 p.

TABLE 8 – Population of New France (St. Lawrence Lowlands), 1739

SEIGNEURY	POPULATION	PERCENTAGE OF THE TERRITORY UNDER STUDY	PERCENTAGE OF NEW FRANCE
Lauzon (including Saint-Nicolas)	1,237	14.4	2.9
Beaumont and Vincennes	504	5.8	1.2
La Durantaye, Saint-Vallier, and Saint-Michel	732	8.5	1.7
Bellechasse	488	5.7	1.1
Île-aux-Oies, Île-aux-Grues, Pointe-aux-Foins, Gamache, Vincelotte, Bonsecours	521	6.2	1.2
Île-d'Orléans	2,318	26.9	5.4
Islet Saint-Jean, Port-Joly, La Pocatière	554	6.4	1.3
Rivière-du-Sud	1,160	13.5	2.7
L'Islet (Lessard), Les Aulnaies, Saint-Denis	239	2.8	0.5
Islet-du-Portage, Rivière-du-Loup, Île-Verte, Trois-Pistoles, Rimouski	227	2.6	0.5
Saint-Denis-de-la-Bouteillerie	302	3.5	0.8
Kamouraska	320	3.7	0.8
Territory under study	8,602	100.0	20.1
Other seigneuries	34,099		79.9
New France (St. Lawrence Lowlands)	42,701		100.0

Source: Benjamin Sulte (1977). Histoire des canadiens-français, 1608-1880. Montréal, Presse Élite, vol. 6, p. 88.

MANAGEMENT OF LAND USED FOR COMMERCIAL PURPOSES

An analysis of the documents relating to seigneurial tenure has shown that the king granted rights to seigneurs along with the obligation to settle and cultivate the lands granted to them. They were allowed to exploit certain natural resources (hunting and fishing) and to engage in commercial activities, including trading with the *Sauvages*. However, these rights were not attached to all seigneurial grants. There are several reasons for this. First, when they obtained their grants, some seigneurs, like Charles Aubert de La Chesnaye, seigneur of Rivière-du-Loup, who were already trading with the *Sauvages*, wanted to continue this activity. Other seigneurs turned to commercial fishing and hunting because of the limited potential for the agricultural development of the lands they had been granted, as Alain Laberge showed in *Peuplements colonisateurs aux XVIIe et XVIIIe siècles* (Mathieu, Courville, 1987).

The right to trade with Indigenous peoples (*Sauvages*) was the one most often granted to the seigneurs within Wolastokuk. This right contributed to freedom of movement: specifically, the Maliseet were invited to do business with seigneurs at trading posts. This right was granted in twenty-five of the fifty seigneuries (see map 45; table 9). Most of the seigneuries granted this right were located east of Rivière-du-Loup, though some were in the interior. Many of these seigneurs also had the right to hunt and fish, which led to competition between French settlers and the Maliseet in their traditional hunting areas. In addition, seigneurs east of Rivière-du-Loup had access to two trading posts, one at Rivière-du-Loup and the other at Bic. The Maliseet could also access these trading posts. When M. Joseph-Antoine Le Febvre de La Barre travelled up the Rivière du Loup, he came to rapids located upstream from the river's mouth. These rapids forced Indigenous People to come ashore, where they traded the furs of animals they had hunted on the lands near the river, as well as other furs collected in the south toward the Saint John River and of Port Royal (Appendix 1684).

MAP 45 – Grants of rights for commercial exploitation

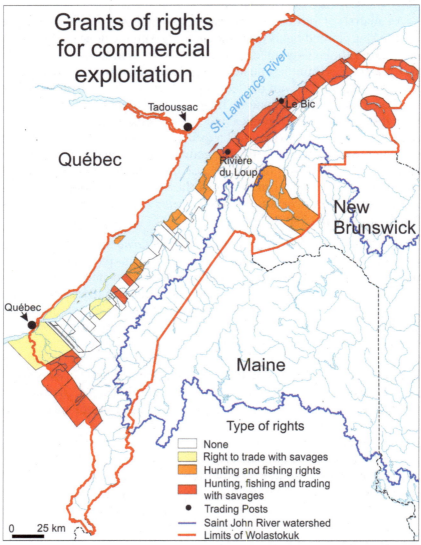

4. MANAGING LAND FOR AGRICULTURE AND SETTLEMENT 149

TABLE 9 – Grants of rights to hunting, fishing, and trade with Savages

YEAR OF CONCESSION	SEIGNEURY	HUNTING	FISHING	TRADE WITH SAVAGES
	SEIGNEURIES ALONG THE COAST				
1636	Lauzon			■
1692	La Martinière			
1683	Montapeine			
1672	Vincennes			
1736	Livaudière			
1672	Beaumont			
1672	Saint-Michel			
1672	Saint-Vallier			
1637	Bellechasse			
1646	Rivière-du-Sud			■
1672	Fournier (Saint-Joseph)			
1672	Lafrenaye (Gagné)			
1672	Gamache			
1697	Sainte-Claire (Joliet)			
1672	Vincelotte	■	■	■
1677	Bonsecours			
1677	Islet-Saint-Jean	■	■	■
1698	Lessard (L'Islet)			
1677	Port-Joly	■	■	
1677	Islet-à-la-Peau	■	■	
1656	Grande-Anse (Les Aulnaies)			
1672	La Pocatière			
1672	Rivière-Ouelle			
1679	Saint-Denis-de-la-Bouteillerie			
1674	Kamouraska	■	■	
1672	Islet-du-Portage			
1673	Rivière-du-Loup	■	■	

YEAR OF CONCESSION	SEIGNEURY	HUNTING	FISHING	TRADE WITH SAVAGES
1684	Île-Verte			
1687	Trois-Pistoles			
1751	Nicolas-Riou			
1675	Le Bic			
1688	Rimouski			
1751	Saint-Barnabé			
1696	Lessard (Pointe-au-Père)			
1696	Lepage et Thivierge			
1689	Pachot (Rivière Mitis)			
1675	Mitis (Peiras)			
ISLAND SEIGNEURIES				
1636	Île-d'Orléans			
1672	Île-Madame			
1638	Île-au-Ruau			
1646	Grandville			
1668	Île-aux-Oies			
1687	Île-aux-Coudres			
INLAND SEIGNEURIES				
1697	Joliet (Sainte-Claire)			
1736	Sainte-Marie-de-Beauce			
1736	Saint-Joseph-de-Beauce			
1736	Saint-François-de-Beauce			
1736	Aubin-de L'Isle			
1683	Madawaska (Lac Témiscouata)			
1693	Lac-Mitis			
1694	Lac-Matapédia			

Source: Assemblée législative 1852, *Pièces et documents relatifs à la tenure seigneuriale, demandée par une adresse de l'Assemblée législative*, Québec, E.R. Fréchette, printer.

CHAPTER 5
The Conquest, the Royal Proclamation, and the recognition of Indigenous Nations

THE ROYAL PROCLAMATION OF 1763[1]

We proceed with the Royal Proclamation (1763) as we did with the commission of Henri IV (8 November 1603), presenting the original text and commenting briefly on it. The proclamation is the second major constitutional text, after the 1603 commission, in which the special status of Indigenous Peoples is defined. The Constitution of 1982 refers to it explicitly.

The policy of the United Province of Canada toward Indigenous Peoples between 1840 and 1867 borrowed from various sources in French and then British colonial history and then was redefined at the time of Confederation (1867). The foundational principles of the relationship that was established, whether in the treaty of alliance of 1603 or after the Conquest of 1760, are essential to an understanding of current policy regarding the Indigenous Peoples of Canada and Québec in the federal system, a policy that encourages the extinguishment of the fundamental rights of Indigenous Peoples.

---

1. Royal Proclamation, 1763: *Revised Statutes of Canada, 1985, Appendices*, Prepared under the authority of the statute Revision Act, Appendice II, no. 1, The Royal Proclamation, 7 October 1763, Ottawa, the Queen's Printer.

By the Royal Proclamation of 7 October 1763, Britain created four governmental authorities and annexed various territories to already existing ones. We focus our analysis on the creation of the government of Québec and on text that specifically concerns Indigenous Peoples (see map 46).

The boundaries of Québec are specified in the following terms:

> First – The Government of Quebec bounded on the Labrador Coast by the River St. John, and from thence by a Line drawn from the Head of that River through the Lake St. John to the South end of the Lake Nipissim; from whence the said Line crossing the River St. Lawrence, and the Lake Champlain, in 45. Degrees of North Latitude, passes along the High Lands which divide the Rivers that empty themselves into the said River St. Lawrence from those which fall into the Sea; and also along the North Coast of the Baye des Chaleurs, and the Coast of the Gulph of St. Lawrence to Cape Rosieres, and from thence crossing the Mouth of the River St. Lawrence by the West End of the Island of Anticosti, terminates at the aforesaid River of St. John. (Appendix, 1763, Royal Proclamation…).

THE CROWN COMMITS TO PROTECTING TRADITIONAL LANDS "POSSESSED" BY "NATIONS OR TRIBES"

The Royal Proclamation of 1763 states that it was essential, for the safety of all, to clarify with the "Nations or Tribes of Indians with whom We are connected" matters relating to the management of the territory and the manner of granting land.

For the British, the objective was to secure for the "Nations or Tribes of Indians with whom we are connected" the full possession of such parts of "our dominions and territories" that had not been ceded or purchased (only the Crown could purchase or receive such lands before they could be granted elsewhere). Those lands not "ceded to or purchased by us" were therefore reserved "as their Hunting Grounds" with title to the lands underlying that of the Crown. These Hunting Grounds would be identified after the Royal Proclamation of 1763 as "Indian Territory / Lands / Hunting Grounds."

> And whereas it is *just and reasonable, and essential* to *our* Interest, and the Security of our Colonies, *that the several Nations or Tribes of* Indians, *with whom We are connected, and who live under our Protection, should not be molested or disturbed in the Possession of such Parts of Our Dominions and Territories as, not having been ceded to, or purchased by Us,* are *reserved to them, or any of them, as their Hunting Grounds* (our italics; Appendix, 1763, Royal Proclamation…).

5. THE CONQUEST, THE ROYAL PROCLAMATION 153

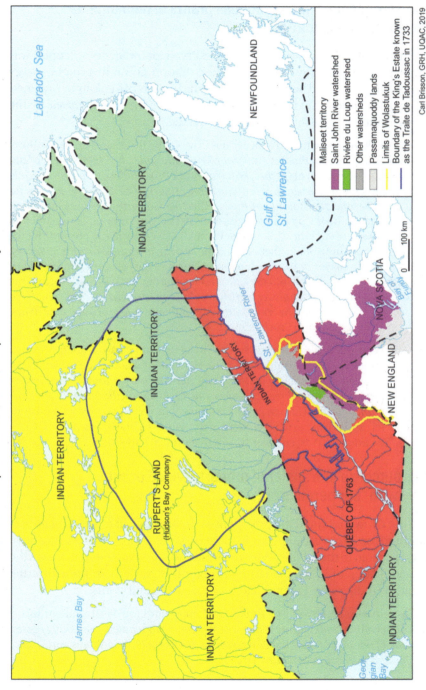

MAP 46 – The province of Québec, as specified in the Royal Proclamation of 1763

Transfer or sale of land precedes grants of land outside government boundaries

This management system for land reserved for Indigenous Peoples was important for the Crown, as it specified that on no pretext might survey permits or title to land be granted outside the borders of a colony or province. Prior to any grant, the land had to have been *ceded or purchased* by the Crown, until other instructions were provided.

> We do therefore, with the Advice of our Privy Council, declare it to be our Royal Will and Pleasure, *that no Governor or Commander in Chief in any of our Colonies* [our italics] of *Quebec, East Florida*, or *West Florida*, do presume, *upon any Pretence whatever, to grant Warrants of Survey, or pass any Patents for Lands beyond the Bounds of their respective Governments* [our italics], as described in their Commissions; as also that no Governor or Commander in Chief in any of our other Colonies or Plantations in *America* do presume for the present, and until our further Pleasure be known, *to grant Warrants of Survey, or pass Patents for any Lands* [our italics] beyond the Heads or Sources of any of the Rivers which fall into the *Atlantic* Ocean from the West and North West, or *upon any Lands whatever, which, not having been ceded to, or purchased by Us* as aforesaid, *are reserved to the said* Indians, *or any of them* (our italics; Appendix, 1763, Royal Proclamation…).

> And We do further declare it to be Our Royal Will and Pleasure, for the present as aforesaid, to reserve under our Sovereignty, Protection, and Dominion, *for the use of the said* Indians, *all the Lands and Territories not included within the Limits of Our said Three new Governments, or within the Limits of the Territory granted to the Hudson's Bay Company* [our italics], as also all the Lands and Territories lying to the Westward of the Sources of the Rivers which fall into the Sea from the West and North West as aforesaid (Appendix 1763).

Any purchase or transfer of property would occur only with "our permission"

The Crown retained the prerogative of managing all matters relating to land and resources in the territories of Indigenous Peoples that had not been ceded or sold to them. The role of the king's subjects was defined, as was the special status of lands owned by Indigenous Nations in their hunting territory. Indigenous Peoples had a special protected status.

> And, We do hereby *strictly forbid*, on Pain of our Displeasure, all our loving Subjects from *making any Purchases or Settlements whatever, or taking Possession of any of the Lands above reserved, without our especial Leave and Licence for that Purpose first obtained* [our italics].

And, We do further strictly enjoin and require all Persons whatever who have either wilfully or inadvertently *seated themselves upon any Lands within the Countries above described, or upon any other Lands which, not having been ceded to or purchased by Us* [our italics], are still reserved to the said *Indians* as aforesaid, forthwith to remove themselves from such Settlements (Appendix 1763).

Indigenous persons could cede or sell land owned in colonies

The proclamation specifies that, if they desired, Indigenous persons could dispose of their land, but exclusively "for us, on our behalf." Free and open trade was guaranteed; however, a licence was required to trade with Indigenous Peoples.

If, at any Time, any of the Said Indians *should be inclined to dispose of the said Lands, the same shall be Purchased only for Us, in our Name* [our italics], at some public Meeting or Assembly of the said *Indians*, to be held for that Purpose by the *Governor or Commander in Chief of our Colony respectively within which they shall lie* [our italics]; and in case *they* shall lie within the limits of any Proprietary Government, they shall be purchased only for the Use and in the name of such Proprietaries, conformable to such Directions and Instructions as We or they shall think proper to give for that Purpose; And we do, by the Advice of our Privy Council, declare and enjoin, that the Trade with the said *Indians* shall be free and open to all our Subjects whatever, *provided that every Person who may incline to Trade with the said Indians do take out a Licence for carrying on such Trade* [our italics] from the Governor or Commander in Chief of any of our Colonies respectively where such Person shall reside (Appendix 1763).

The Royal Proclamation concludes by reminding administrators that licences should be granted without charge or benefit and reiterating that the rights of all parties should be scrupulously respected, especially those of Indigenous Nations (they include the term tribes), including recognition of their possession of their territories, which they used as Hunting Grounds.

The new regime being established was both a continuation of and a departure from the French regime. France had placed at the core of its relationship the obligation to trade and to conclude alliances with Indigenous Peoples and their leaders to ensure peace, settlement, and trade.

With the British regime, the vocabulary changed. The Indigenous Peoples were identified from then on as "*Nations or Tribes of Indians*. They were "connected to us" and under "our protection." The word "Tribe" is used in the text of the Royal Proclamation, and this contributed to define the *Indians/ Sauvages* Peoples in the official vocabulary. The shift in was important, and the Bagot Commission (1844–1847) will reinforce this.

At the beginning of the first report of the Bagot Commission (Appendix EEE; Girard and Thibeault, 2001; Appendix 1844.2001, 2:46–48; 90–93), it is asserted that instructions issued as early as 1760–1763 by the British Crown as guidance for governors stipulated that land beyond the borders of colonies remained "Indian territory" (Appendix 1844.2001, 2: 46).[2]

According to the report, at the time of the Conquest in 1760, the fortieth article of the surrender of Montréal stated "that 'The Savage or Indian allies of His Most Christian Majesty shall be maintained in possession of the lands they inhabit'" (Girard and Thibeault, 91). The report further stated that the Royal Proclamation of 1763 had added "a fresh guarantee for the possession of their hunting grounds and the protection of the Crown."

The Crown was committed to providing Indigenous Peoples with "peaceful possession" of their lands that had not been *"ceded or purchased" and that had been "reserved"* for them as "Hunting Grounds." The term *Indian territory* carried the underlying meaning of territory also reserved for Indigenous Peoples. Great Britain recognized the importance of protecting "Indian territories" which Indigenous Peoples *would continue to own*, until they decided of their own volition to cede or sell them to the Crown.

New vocabulary and a new way of managing land and property arrived with the British regime. The notion of ceding or selling land to the Crown had not existed under the French regime. Seigneurial lands had been given to Indigenous Peoples under the guardianship of missionaries who assumed the landowner role, lands on which Indigenous persons settled, of their own volition to become "sedentary" and "Christianized." Outside seigneurial lands, under the French regime, Indigenous Nations lived freely on their traditional territory.

Reserved lands, which were to become *reserves* under the Canadian system (the fate of Hunting Grounds is not mentioned), and the post-Confederation "Numbered Treaties" signed with Indigenous Nations are all associated with the notion of *surrender*, actions that served to subjugate Indigenous Peoples and strip them of their traditional lands and the underlying title to their territory. Far from recognizing the rights of Indigenous

---

2. Girard, Camil and Jessica Thibeault, 2001. *Rapports sur les questions autochtones: Canada 1828-1870*, 3 vol. Chicoutimi, QC: Alliance de recherche universités-communautés (ARUC); monts Valin-monts Otish (CRSH); Groupe recherche sur l'histoire – Université du Québec à Chicoutimi. Include French and English versions with our pagination to facilitate referencing since most original documents had no pagination). *Charles Bagot Report* included in English, 42-87, in French, 88-132. See online, *Les Classiques des Sciences sociales*, Université du Québec à Chicoutimi.

Peoples, their status, and their lands, governments would adopt laws to create reserves while remaining silent on the topic of Indigenous territory, which would become Crown land. The "surrender" of Indian Territory ultimately would be completed by the advent of the *reserve system*. In becoming owners of these micro-territories, Indigenous Peoples lost all rights to their traditional lands. The Royal Proclamation of 1763, by inserting the notion of "cession or sale," had undermined the rights of Indigenous Peoples to their lands. The Crown recognized possession but also established procedures for dispossessing Indigenous Peoples of their territory and their identity, a mixture of conquest and colonialism that recognized Indigenous Peoples while undermining their rights.

Indigenous Peoples believe that even *surrendering* the territory of a reserve or Indigenous community, a micro-territory, does not affect their rights to their traditional lands. Through negotiation of new treaties or specific agreements, they are seeking to redefine co-ownership with the Crown of their traditional lands, which includes title to the land and a right to its resources. This possession of territory, including the resources within it, is not exclusive, and it means redefining the relationship between governments and Indigenous Nations.

In summary, the Royal Proclamation of 1763 introduced new vocabulary and revised many notions related to British colonial policy toward Indigenous Peoples. It recognized that, apart from the seigneuries and territories occupied by the French, which included towns and Indigenous missions, Indigenous Peoples occupied all the territory that had been conquered. This territory possessed by Indigenous Peoples was recognized as theirs and was under the express protection of the Crown. The Hudson Bay territory and land outside colonies were recognized as *Indian Territory* (Girard, Brisson, 2018: 131-133). In the province of Québec, the recognition of Indigenous territory would be confirmed in 1765 for the Maliseet and in 1767 for the Innu, as we show in later pages.

The British recognized that the Indian territory in the province of Québec could be ceded or sold to the Crown, which did not happen until the 1975 James Bay Agreement. However, as early as 1774 with the Quebec Act, and with the creation of the reserve system in the 1850s, the terms of the Royal Proclamation were reinterpreted to the disadvantage of Indigenous Peoples despite numerous protests, including those of the Maliseet and Innu, who advocated for the recognition of their traditional territory and a share of its resources (Girard Brisson: 2018: Quebec Act, 76-83; reserve system, 110ff).

PROTEST AND ENSUING RECOGNITION OF THE TRADITIONAL LANDS OF THE MALISEET IN THE PROVINCE OF QUÉBEC (1765)

In 1765, two years after the Royal Proclamation, the Maliseet approached the governor to demand protection of their traditional lands, which were under threat. The governor used this opportunity to establish the boundaries of Maliseet hunting territory, specifying that these *territories were their property*. He specified that *the French* were forbidden to hunt beaver at any time and *Canadian*s should be similarly constrained.

> Secretary's-Office, 19th January, 1765
>
> Whereas the Nation of Maricittes [sic] Indians, by the following Paragraph, of a petition to His Excellency the Governor of this Province, have represented that they are encroached upon by the Canadian Inhabitants, hunting Beaver on the Lands therein mentioned, which have ever belonged to, and are the Property of the said Nation: This therefore, is to give Notice, That the Privilege prayed for, by the said Indians, will be allowed and confirmed to them, unless any Person or Persons can show just Cause to the Contrary, by Memorial to His Excellency the Governor and Council, directed to the Secretary of this Province, on or before the first Day of May.
>
> By command of his Excellency.
>
> J. Goldfrap, D.Sec.
>
> "Your Petitioner also has the Honor to represent to Your Excellency, that the Brethren Indians find themselves reduced to the lowest Ebb of Misery by the unwarrantable Incroachments of the Canadian Inhabitants, hunting Beaver **on the Lands belonging to the Nation (our emphasis)** by which you Petitioner has been deputed; which Track begins **at the Great Fall of St-John's, and runs as far as Témisquata, including the Wolf-River [or Riviere du Loup/ added in the original] and the River Madawaska, which Rivers discharge themselves into the River St. John's** [na: which is inexact for Rivière du Loup**) making a Space of about Twenty Leagues, on which the Nation, whose Grievances your Petitioner has the Honor to lay before Your Excellency, always had exclusive Privilege of hunting Beaver in the Time of the French Government, therefore your Petitioner humbly request in the Name of his Nation, that Your**

Excellency will be pleased to continue their Privilege by forbidding the Inhabitants of this Province to hunt Beaver on Old Grounds[3].

[The French version]

Du Secrétariat le 19 de janvier, 1765.

Comme la nation de Sauvages *Maricittes*, [sic] a représenté par le paragraphe qui suit, d'une requête présentée à son Excellence le Gouverneur de cette Province, que les habitants Canadiens empiètent sur eux, en faisant la chasse du Castor sur les terres spécifiées dans ladite requête, qui ont toujours appartenu à la dite nation, et des quels **ils ont de tous tems été censés les propriétaires.** [our emphasis] Ceci est donc pour avertir, que le **privilège qu'ils demandent par leur requête leur sera alloué et confirmé**, à moins que quelques personnes ou personnes n'allèguent de bonnes raisons à ce contraires, en forme de mémoire au Gouverneur et au Conseil, adressé au Secrétaire de cette Province, au premier jour de Mai… … …

Par Son Excellence,

J. Goldfrap, D. Sec.

Le Suppléant a aussi l'honneur de représenter à Votre Excellence que les Sauvages de sa nation se trouvèrent réduits à la dernière misère, par la chasse illicite de castor, que font les habitans Canadiens, **sur les Terres appartenantes [sic] à sa dite nation, à prendre depuis le grand sault de la rivière de St. Jean jusques à Témisquata, ce qui fait un espace d'environ vingt lieues, y comprenant la rivière du Loup et celle de Madawaska, qui se déchargent dans la rivière de St. Jean,** [n.a. should be Rivière du Loup] où **il était de tout tems défendu aux François [sic] de faire la chasse du castor**, comme cette chasse a toujours été **réservée aux Sauvages de la nation** dont il a l'honneur de représenter les griefs à Votre Excellence, il supplie donc Votre Excellence au nom de ses frères, qu'il vous plaise de continuer leur privilège en ordonnant qu'il soit **défendu aux habitans Canadiens** de faire la chasse de castor sur ces terres.[4]

---

3. *Quebec Gazette,* 24 January 1765, 2. (Appendix 5, Maliseet Claims, 1765 and Governor's Response. Order in Council *Gazette de Québec.* <https://numerique.banq.qc.ca/patrimoine/details/52327/4265872>. For more information: <http://www.upperstjohn.com/history/natives.htm>.
4. See Appendix 5: <http://www.upperstjohn.com/history/natives.htm>.

We have mapped the geographical information contained in the 1765 Maliseet petition to show the places mentioned in the above text (see map 47): Grand Falls on the Saint John River, Madawaska, the Rivière du Loup and the Madawaska River. It should be noted that the text does not mention precise boundaries. It mentions the "space" between Grand Falls and Madawaska, which are about twenty leagues apart. The word "space" means a distance between two points, in this case, Grand Falls and Madawaska, which makes sense since this area was frequented by the Maliseet. Grand Falls was well known because travellers were forced to disembark there: as far back as 1685, the falls were identified on Denonville's map. Moreover, a legend tells the story of Malobiannah, a young Maliseet who sacrificed herself to save her people from an Iroquois attack (see chapter 2). Today, an interpretive centre is located on this spot, which is recognized as a local heritage site and is managed by the town of Grand Falls, New Brunswick. In the case of Madawaska, we do not know if it was the lake or the seigneury. In any case, when we calculate a distance of twenty leagues from Grand Falls, it brings us to the area of Lake Madawaska (now called Témiscouata) and the seigneury of the same name.

As for the Madawaska River, it fits into the twenty leagues, and it flows into the Saint John River. Rivière du Loup flows not into the Saint John River but into the Saint Lawrence. This error is undoubtedly due to insufficient knowledge of the territory on the part of the British authorities. It also makes sense that the Maliseet would mention the Rivière du Loup as part of their traditional territory. We have already mentioned the report of Monsieur de La Barre in 1684, which recorded the presence of *Sauvages* from the Saint John River on the Rivière du Loup. Moreover, according to the summary map presented earlier, many different portages were used by the Maliseet to travel between the seigneuries of Lauzon and Rivière-du-Loup.

Authors such as Speck and Hadlock (1946) and Ganong (1895, 1906) have designated the limits of the Saint John River watershed as the boundaries of the traditional territory of the Maliseet in New Brunswick. Erickson (1978) extended the boundary of traditional Maliseet territory to the south bank of the St. Lawrence, which includes the Madawaska River and the Rivière du Loup watershed.

Map 47 shows that the Rivière du Loup watershed was entirely within the province of Québec in 1763, as the edge of the Saint John River watershed served as the boundary of the province in this area at the time. In addition, the watersheds of the Rivière du Loup and the Madawaska River overlapped

5. THE CONQUEST, THE ROYAL PROCLAMATION 161

seigneurial territories. Even after 1763, the British governor protected traditional Indigenous lands within the boundaries of the province of Québec, regardless of whether seigneuries were present or not.

MAP 47 – Territory claimed in 1765

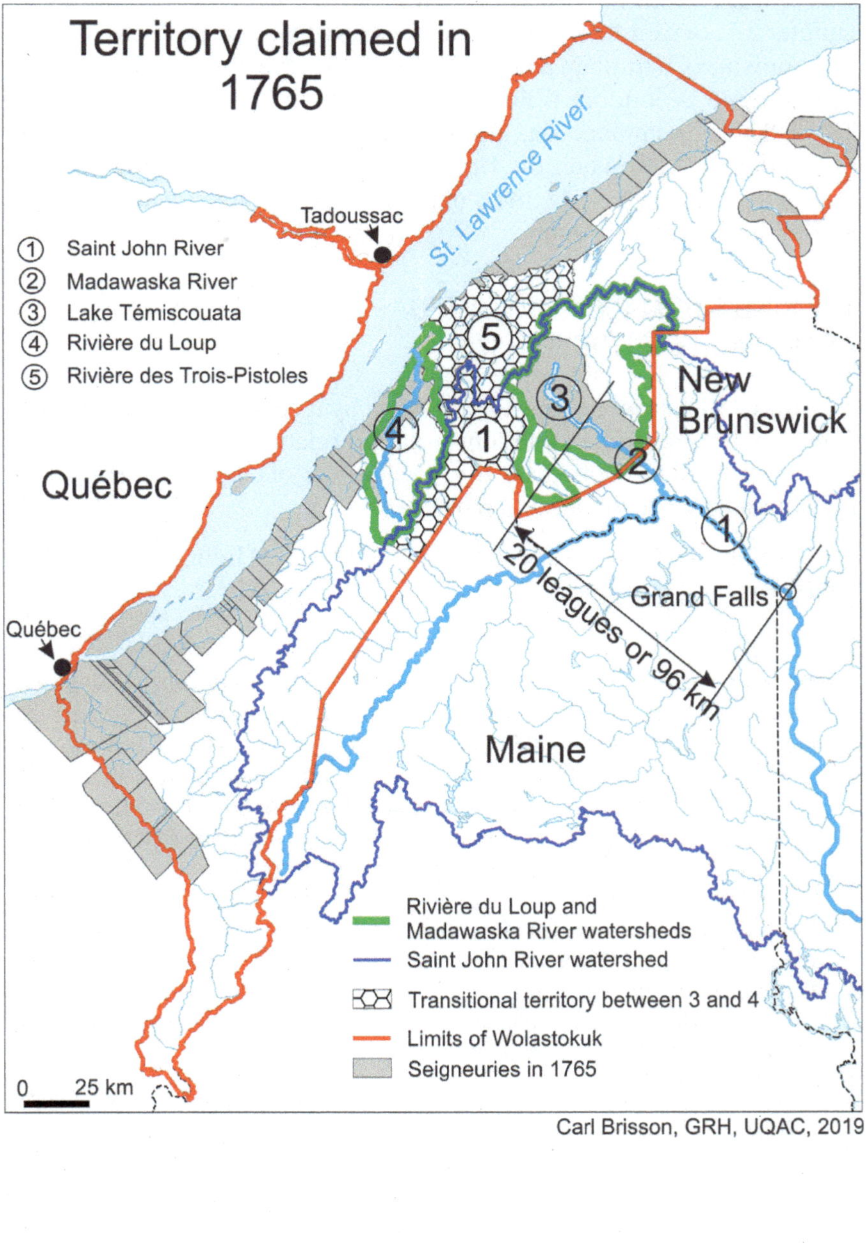

Finally, it should be noted that the traditional hunting territory agreed to in 1765 cannot be limited to the Madawaska and Rivière du Loup watersheds. Between these two river systems lies transitional territory with many rivers and portages that the Maliseet had to negotiate when travelling from one watershed to the other in the practice of their traditional activities. (These rivers and portages are indicated on the maps inventoried in chapter 2.) For example, the Rivière des Trois-Pistoles (no. 5 on map 47) was known to Champlain as early as 1604, as it gave access to Tadoussac, according to Secoudon, Chief of the Saint John River. The Rivière des Trois-Pistoles watershed was also within the boundaries of the province of Québec in 1763. When the United States and Canada agreed on the border in this area in 1842, most of the Madawaska River watershed fell within the province of Québec.

THE KING'S DOMAIN: RECOGNIZED AS "INDIAN TERRITORY" IN 1767

In 1767, Governor Murray followed suit by recognizing that the British Crown had to respect the nation-to-nation relationship it had with the *savages* of the King's Domain, with whom the king of France had concluded previous alliance without cession or sale.

The King's Domain *(Traite de Tadoussac)*, lands of Indigenous Peoples. James Murray, Governor, 1767:

> My Lords
>
> The *Lands of the King's Domain were never ceded to nor purchased by the French King, nor by his Britannic Majesty*; But, by *Compact* [italics added] with the savages inhabiting the said Lands, the particular Posts or Spots of ground, whereon the Kings buildings are erected and now stand, were ceded to the French King, for the purpose of erecting storehouses & other conveniences for the Factors Commis or Servants employed to carry on the trade; and *the Savages residing within the Limits of the Domain*, & who resort to the said Posts of His Majesty at certain seasons of the year, *were adopted as Domicile Indians under the sole & immediate protection of the King, & so remained till the reduction of the Province*, & a Missionary was sent to reside constantly among them. *The Lands of the Domain therefore, are to all intents & purposes reserved, as hunting Grounds to the Savages, of which they are ever jealous, on the least appearance of an encroachment even amongst themselves.*
>
> With what propriety therefore, could the Governor have complyd with Mr. Alsop's petition for grants of Land there, would it not have been in direct contradiction to His Maj's. Proclamation? & I flatter myself the contempt he has shown to the

5. THE CONQUEST, THE ROYAL PROCLAMATION

said Royal Proclamation, & his Maj's. Government will be far from entitling him to the favour he claims from the Kings servants here. I must further add that this man has been the author of all the disputes, factions, & jealousies which have taken place, since the establishment of civil Government in the Colony, and I firmly believe his Enterprise to these Posts was with a view to augment the same, he being the only man who attempted it corroborates this opinion.

I have the honor to be with great Truth and Regard

My Lords your Lordships most obedient, and most humble Servant

Ja. Murray

(Governor Murray to Board of Trade 1767; Girard and Brisson 2014, 133; Schulze 1997, 566)

As a result of the Royal Proclamation of 1763, Governor Murray had been asked to make a statement on the vision of the British Crown for Indigenous Peoples whose territory was threatened.

The Royal Proclamation stated that Indigenous lands were protected, and that Nations or Tribes were assured of "possession of their land." For both the Maliseet and the Innu of the King's Domain, two Nations long allied with the French (1603) and later the British (1725–1726), the requests for confirmation and protection of their traditional lands were made in a historical context whereby the principles of alliance and recognition were confirmed and renewed. There was a desire not only to protect traditional territories, which for Indigenous Peoples were not for hunting activities alone, but also and above all to avoid encroachment by settlers on lands that had not been ceded or purchased by the Crown. For Indigenous Peoples, traditional hunting territories are not limited by a title that permits only usufruct activity (linked to a few activities); traditional territory is all the territory, including that used for traditional activities, for more or less permanent settlement (including ownership), and for resource development.

The new regimen imposed by the Royal Proclamation introduced the notion of a policy of "voluntary" cession or sale of Indian lands to the British Crown. This policy was new and open to wide interpretation by administrators and legislators, both colonial and Canadian. Many Indigenous Nations, including the Maliseet Nation of Québec, were not consulted on the *cession* of their land until Canadian courts in the 1970s reminded governments of certain fiduciary obligations regarding Indian land. Indian Territory continued to belong to and be owned by the Indigenous Peoples, who occupied it to meet their needs, and Indigenous persons were considered as domiciled and under the protection of the Crown until the complete British takeover (Reduction) of the province.

French and British recognition of Indigenous Nations' title to their lands

The village or reserve of the Iroquois Nation of Saint-Régis was analyzed in 1839 during the commissions of inquiry on Indigenous Peoples leading up to the Durham Report, which would create the United Province of Canada in 1841. The Bagot Report (Appendix EEE; 1844.2001) estimated the population of this village as approximately 450 persons.

The term *village* was used in a historical context. From first contact with New France, the title of the Iroquois to lands was recognized, both to the settlements in which they adopted a sedentary lifestyle and to their traditional hunting territory. According to the report, the British regime had continued the French policy of recognizing title to Iroquois (Mohawk) lands:

> These lands form but a small portion of the hunting grounds of the once powerful Iroquois Nation and are supposed to have been occupied by this tribe since the first settlement of Canada. *Their title was originally a mere occupancy for the purpose of hunting; but it was recognized and acknowledged by the Government of France before the conquest, and was subsequently secured to them by that of England, in common with all other titles of the same nature existing at the time of the conquest* [our italics] Appendix, 1844.2001, Bagot Commission, Appendix EEE, Girard and Thibeault, 2001: 2:106).

In contrast, several other comments in the Bagot Commission's report led the charge to disqualify Indigenous Peoples as primitive and half-civilized and to justify their new status as "non-citizens" by bundling them onto reserves. As noted above, parts of the report contradicted this view of the recognition of Indigenous title to land. However, the negative view prevailed and was used to justify, in a so-called benevolent colonial spirit, dispossessing Indigenous Peoples of their traditional territories and depriving them of citizenship. Taking away, by omission, the hunting territory of Indigenous Nations meant extinguishing their culture and undermining their identity and their dignity. Excluded from "Canadian" citizenship, they became foreigners in their own country.

Indigenous territories, which the Americas were at the time of the first contact in New France, continued to be recognized under both the French and the British regimes. It was the Province of United Canada and Confederation (post-1867) that changed the nature of the relationship between the Crown and Indigenous Peoples.

In the alliances made by Champlain, who established the territory of Indigenous Nations by carefully mapping the rivers and lakes with which they identified (see map 48), and in the creation of the King's Domain (from 1652 on, *Traite de Tadoussac*), France recognized territory that was exclusive to Indigenous Peoples, under the express protection of the king. Alliances strengthened and justified co-ownership of the territory of New France.

In 1627, New France consisted of just over one hundred people, according to research by historian Marcel Trudel. France was able to justify, both in Europe and locally, its hold on New France because it had allied itself with the only true occupants and possessors of those vast northern territories, the Indigenous Peoples.

France's official treaties with the Iroquois Nations in 1665–1666 and at the time of the Grande Paix de Montréal in 1701 confirmed, well beyond the notions of peace and friendship, that the traditional lands of Indigenous Nations were shared between France and the Nations that were parties to the treaty. France had found that the only way to assert sovereignty over the Indian territories was by forming alliances with the Indigenous Peoples who had occupied and possessed their lands for millennia. The British faced the same reality in 1760, first with French Canadians, some sixty thousand people living mainly in Montréal, Québec, and Trois-Rivières, and then with Indigenous Nations, who owned and occupied all the land outside the settled seigneuries that constituted a tiny part of the whole territory.

The Maliseet, allies of the French and the British

The ownership of land by Indigenous Nations was guaranteed by treaties with the Maliseet in 1725–1726. The Royal Proclamation of 1763 also recognized Indigenous territories, continuing the obligations and the reality of the French regime. To achieve the same objective, claiming possession of territory that they did not actually occupy, the British pragmatically recognized the Indigenous Peoples that did occupy that territory, including the Maliseet, in 1760.

166 ALLIANCES AND TREATIES WITH INDIGENOUS PEOPLES OF QUÉBEC

MAP 48 – Map by Champlain, 1632

Map of Champlain's meetings with the Indigenous Nations that had described their territory to him

5. THE CONQUEST, THE ROYAL PROCLAMATION

The history of Québec and Canada until the emergence of the United Province of Canada in 1840 is the history of Indigenous Peoples and recognition of their lands by the French and British. Allies in trade, war, welcoming settlers, and the search for peace, Indigenous Peoples occupied the immense northern territories of Canada, while Europeans occupied the urban and rural south, which never represented more than 5 to 10 percent of total Indigenous territory. This history would be repudiated by Canadians, who would favour the notion of "submission" and the elimination of Indian lands, which has been reduced to the tiny confines of Indian reserves (at 1,500 square kilometres, reserves in Québec are equivalent to about one-thousandth of the territory of the province). After the Conquest, Britain was faced with the same reality as the French had been. In 1760, the Indian territories owned by the Indigenous Peoples outside the seigneuries and the few missions constituted almost 98 to 99 percent of the territory of present-day Québec.

To assert and claim sovereignty over this territory without recognition of those who inhabited and occupied it since time immemorial, become a creation of a national history that is still prevalent in Québec and Canada.

CHAPTER 6
The Maliseet: From recognition (1763) to oblivion and dispersal (1869)

ESTABLISHING THE POLICIES AND LEGISLATION THAT EXCLUDED INDIGENOUS PEOPLES FROM CONFEDERATION (1774-1876)

In 1774, the Quebec Act was approved by King George III (Appendix 1774, Quebec Act). The act seemed to offer a pragmatic plan for the administration of the province of Québec. The free exercise of the Catholic religion and the use of French civil law in the justice system became legal, and the seigneurial system of French origin would continue. The disproportionate number of settlers of French origin living in the province compared with those of British origin made these provisions necessary to guarantee their neutrality in face of the possible secession of the New England colonies.

The Quebec Act was silent on the fate of Indigenous Peoples. It contained no clauses dealing with Indian rights. Did this mean that the rights stated in the Royal Proclamation of 1763 were still in force, since the Quebec Act had important territorial repercussions for Indigenous Peoples and their lands? The act annexed part of the *Indian territories* to Québec without any cession or sale by the Indigenous Peoples living there, as had been specified in the royal proclamation.

At that time, despite the annexation to the province of Québec in 1774 of Indian territories that had been recognized in 1763, there was still no settlement outside seigneuries. Only the Indigenous Nations who had been living on their lands for thousands of years were still present, continuing to live independently, maintaining their traditional way of life, and preserving their customs (Girard, Brisson, 2018: 76ff).

Less than twenty years later, the British authorities passed the Constitutional Act (1791) to satisfy the demands of Loyalist subjects who had left the United States following the American War of Independence (1775–1783; Appendix, 1791, Constitutional Act of 1791).

This act makes no mention of the rights of Indigenous Peoples, who still lived on their traditional lands. However, the Constitutional Act of 1791 split *Indian* territory into two provinces with different legal systems. In the province of Upper Canada (Ontario), common law and English criminal law had been applied since 1763 while, in Lower Canada (Québec), the English criminal code and the French civil code coexisted.

The Constitutional Act of 1791 focuses on the process of municipalization (creation of cities, towns, and other municipal entities). Article 14 divides the province of Lower Canada into counties for the purpose of electing representatives to the new legislative assembly. The process was hampered by economic difficulties afflicting the province that affected the population's ability to pay taxes. It was not until 1841 that twenty-two municipal districts were created that covered the entire province. We will see later the spatial impact of dividing territory into municipalities and its effect on the alienation of the traditional territory of the Maliseet (Girard, Brisson, 2018: 78ff).

Investigating the Indigenous question: From Nations or Peoples on shared territory to "Indians" to be "civilized" on reserves

Beginning in the 1820s, immigrants from England, Ireland, and Scotland began to arrive in Canada in greater numbers. At the same time, the creation of Upper and Lower Canada left members of the legislative assembly in disarray because a governor's clique effectively dictated public policy, ignoring those who had been elected. This "representation without responsibility" led to the rebellions of 1837–1838 in both present-day Québec and Ontario.

The Durham Report (February 1839) on the causes of those political upheavals led to the creation of the United Province of Canada (1840–1867), which brought together Upper Canada and Lower Canada, the two provinces created in 1791, under a single government. Following on from Durham's work, the Bagot Commission focused on land management and Indians. The commission reports, published between 1844 and 1847 set out rules for a new Indigenous policy, which was implemented after 1847. The seigneurial system was abolished in 1854. The United Province of Canada achieved responsible government; in other words, elected representatives with a majority in the legislative assembly could finally vote for the legislation they wanted without having to answer to the governor's clique. It was in this context that preparations for Confederation began in the province. Concurrently, legislation was being drawn up that would deprive Indigenous Peoples of their traditional lands and define their legal status as needing to be "civilized," which would be achieved by relegating them to *reserves*.

As early as 1850, the first of these discriminatory laws was passed with the objective of eliminating traditional Indian territories and isolating "Indians" on reserves, while legally defining their status. The lands designated for the *Indians* became the future "reserves" that, with Confederation in 1867, came under the exclusive jurisdiction of the federal government. Indigenous territory no longer was recognized.

On the economic front, reciprocity with the United States (1854) brought economic expansion, which was characterized, after Confederation in 1867, by policies to expand Canadian territory. The construction of the coast-to-coast railroad and the National Policy of 1879 were aimed at strengthening the Canadian economy through protective tariffs. These initiatives were undertaken without any consultation with or agreement by Indigenous Peoples. The development of local economies occurred with the assistance of provincial and federal governments. The opening up of lands further north was intended to encourage the settlement of persons who might otherwise migrate to the United States. Occupying these northern lands was also part of the French-Canadian national project, which was based on three key principles: preserving the Catholic faith, building a French-speaking nation, and advancing agriculture. Québec could ensure its future within Canada. The development of agriculture and forestry also meant that Indigenous lands and former Hunting Grounds of Indigenous Peoples were encroached upon and even seized by French Canadians (Girard and Perron 1995).

According to John Leslie, a researcher with the Department of Indian Affairs, during the forty years prior to Confederation numerous commissions of inquiry formulated policies that transformed Indigenous Peoples from Nations or Peoples allied with each other in occupation, trade, or war into a group that governments would "administer" to suit their interests:

> The central philosophical assumptions and policies of modern Canadian Indian administration were shaped in the Canadas during the four decades prior to Confederation. Instrumental in this process were six government commissions of inquiry which devised, evaluated, and modified a programme for Indian advancement and civilization based on treaties, reserves, religious conversion,

and agricultural instruction. Though not apparent at the time, the series of investigative reports *created a corporate memory* [our italics] for the Indian department and established a policy framework for dealing with Native peoples and issues. The approach became entrenched, like the department itself, and remained virtually unchanged and unchallenged until 1969, when the federal government issued its white paper on Indian policy (Leslie 1985, 185).

This "corporate memory" ignored alliances and treaties as well as the recognition of the status of Indigenous Peoples and Nations that had prevailed under the French and British regimes. That recognition was imperfect, of course, because the colonial authorities also acted like conquerors. But both the French and the British worked to resolve differences and share territory and resources, recognizing Indigenous Peoples as having distinct and fundamental rights to their lands that they had agreed to share, sometimes unwillingly, with the newcomers.

Public inquiries and new vocabulary that created a collective memory: The return of the "primitive Indian" needing to be "civilized"

In the following pages, we show how public inquiries into Indigenous issues (1828–1858) justified and structured a system of exclusion of Indigenous Peoples in the policies enacted in the United Province of Canada. These inquiries were integral to the construction of a collective memory that, under the guise of apparent good intentions, encouraged contempt and disregard in "nation builders" who wanted to assimilate the Other, the "primitive Indian" (Appendix, 1844.2001, Bagot, PDF, Girard and Thibeault, 2001).[1]

Who was consulted? Were Indigenous Peoples consulted during these inquiries? Which Indigenous persons were invited to participate? Were they invited to participate in the implementation of the policies that affected them? Certainly not, despite several protests (see Girard and Brisson 2018,

---

1. Girard, Camil and Jessica Thibeault. 2001. *Rapports sur les questions autochtones: Canada 1828–1870*, 3 vol. Chicoutimi, QC: Alliance de recherche universités-communautés (ARUC); monts Valin-monts Otish (CRSH); Groupe recherche sur l'histoire - Université du Québec à Chicoutimi. These documents include French and English versions with our pagination to facilitate referencing (most documents had no pagination). A pdf version has been given to the community: See, *Les Classiques des Sciences sociales*, Université du Québec à Chicoutimi. See, Bagot, 1844, *Les Classiques des Sciences sociales*, Université du Québec à Chicoutimi.

110-15, for protests by the Montagnais [Innu]). Were they included in Confederation? They had been excluded long before the Fathers of Confederation finalized their planning. Were they excluded from the drawing up of discriminatory legislation that changed their status and took away their traditional lands? Legislators acted as judge and jury as they passed legislation to create a Canadian federation that would suit them.

In the following pages, we describe the context underpinning the expansion of settlements and the creation of Indigenous reserves. The report of the Bagot Commission is analyzed briefly, as well as how the Maliseet of Viger First Nation experienced at the local level the implementation of a policy that, beginning in the 1820s, reinforced a colonizing vision. Finally, we show how the Maliseet obtained and then lost their territory of Cacouna, remaining in exile until the rebirth of their Nation in 1987.

UNITED PROVINCE OF CANADA AND THE IMPLEMENTATION OF A POLICY OF MUNICIPALIZATION

Between 1840 and 1867, the expansion of settlement and the opening of former *Indian territory* to colonization and to exploitation of natural resources began. From then on, Indigenous Peoples were strongly encouraged to leave their ancestral lands and traditional way of life and to move to districts reserved for them, where they could settle down and take up farming (Girard and Brisson 2018, 98-104).

The rebellions of 1837-1838 plunged the provinces of Upper and Lower Canada into a forced unification. The purpose was to reduce the representation of French Canadians and to prohibit the use of French in debates and in the drafting of legislation. The traditional territories of Indigenous Peoples were coveted for agriculture and for their natural resources. More specifically, article 58 of the Act of Union (Appendix, 1840, Act of Union, United Province of Canada) confirmed the intention to establish townships, a process that had already begun and would lead to the abolition of the seigneurial system of the French regime:

> **LVIII.** And be it enacted. That it shall be Lawful for the Governor, by an Instrument or Instruments to be issued by him for that Purpose under the Great Seal of the Province, to constitute Townships in those Parts of the Province of Canada in which Townships are not already constituted, and to fix the Metes and Bounds thereof; and to provide for the Election and Appointment of Township Officers therein, who shall have and exercise the like Powers as are exercised by the like Officers in the Townships already constituted in that Part of the Province of Canada now called Upper Canada; and every such Instrument shall be published

by Proclamation, and shall have the Force of Law from a Day to be named in each Case in such Proclamation.[2]

Under the government of the United Province of Canada, municipalization inflicted irreversible damage on Indigenous Peoples, who were still living freely on their ancestral lands. The process was accompanied by the establishment of reserves, as we will see later.

Following an attempt to municipalize the former Lower Canada by creating twenty-two municipal districts in 1840, a first municipal law[3] (1845) introduced a new administrative division (in addition to cities and towns). From then on, in rural areas, each parish or township formed a municipal corporation represented by a council elected by the local population. However, it was not until 1855, with the adoption of the Lower Canada Municipalities and Roads Act, that the foundations of the current municipal system were laid. By 1855, Lower Canada (Québec) already had sixty-one county municipalities (*municipalités de comté*), four cities, two towns, twenty-nine village municipalities, 277 parish municipalities, 112 township municipalities, four united township municipalities, and twelve municipalities without designation (Saint-Pierre 1994, 65).

Two obstacles remained to be overcome before municipalization could be extended unimpeded to the entire territory of Lower Canada. *The savage tribes who were living freely on their ancestral lands had to be integrated into the municipalization process, and the seigneurial system had to be abolished.*

The Bagot Commission reports, 1844–1847: Qualifying to disqualify Indigenous Peoples (Girard, 2017)

The report of the Bagot Commission, named after Governor General Charles Bagot (1842–1843), was published between 1844 and 1847. This official document, published without pagination, was directed at administrators, and remained difficult to access until recently. A document of the utmost importance, it provided a comprehensive review of previous inquiries and laid the foundations for policy regarding Indigenous Peoples as plans for Confederation were being prepared (Girard 2017; Royal Commission

---

2. The Act of Union. 1840, an Act to unite the Provinces of Upper and Lower Canada and the Government of Canada, Laws of Great Britain (1840) 4 Vict, Chapter 35.
3. Parliament, Legislative Assembly, 1845, An Act to repeal certain Ordinances aforesaid and to make better provision for the establishment of local and municipal authorities in Lower Canada, 8 Victoria, chap. 40. <https://bnald.lib.unb.ca/sites/default/files/UnC.1845.ch%2040.pdf>.

1996, 1: 287 ff; Province of Canada 1845; copy English [and French] in Bagot Report 1844–1847 in Girard and Thibeault 2001, vol. 2.[4])

Against the backdrop of the "good or bad Indian," who had to be "civilized" at all costs, the notion of a new Canadian nation-state took shape, based on the policies put in place to administer the United Province of Canada (Upper and Lower Canada) in the aftermath of the Durham Report.

The Bagot Report (Appendix EEE, 1845) quickly establishes the general position that justified the actions of the administrators toward a primitive Indigenous person who survived in harmony with nature:

> In his native state the Indian is simple-minded, generous, proud and energetic; his craftiness is exhibited chiefly in the chase and war. He is generally docile and possesses a lively and happy disposition. He is very hospitable, never refusing to share his provisions with the indigent, and usually dividing the fruits of the chase with his neighbours. [...] In his half-civilised state, he is indolent to excess, intemperate, suspicious, cunning, covetous, and addicted to lying and fraud. These are not the fruits of Christianity, and therefore it is evident that in such case the mode of their treatment has been defective, and calls for alteration (Girard and Thibeault 2001, 2: 58)

These official remarks attributed to the governor general carried considerable weight. They normalized and justified disqualifying Indigenous Peoples from participating as full-fledged actors in nation-building.

The Indian territories of Lower Canada were never ceded, but...

It is acknowledged in certain sections of the Bagot Report (Appendix T, 1847) that the lands of Lower Canada had never been ceded:

> In Lower Canada, the Indians have not ceded any lands to the Crown, and consequently the Government is only required to intervene in their affairs to appoint or sanction the appointment of Agents, to receive the rents and seigneurial dues on their lands, and also to receive and examine the accounts rendered by the Agents and to control the manner in which they act (our translation; Girard and Thibeault 2001 Appendix 1844.2001, 2: 152; Appendix T of the Report, 1847).

Yet in other parts of the report, it is asserted, with all the authority conferred by the title of governor general, that the Crown, as custodian of the lands, was vested with title by the Royal Proclamation of 1763 (Girard and Thibeault 2001, 2:91 [Appendix EEE] and 2:149, 152 [Appendix T]).

---

4. Since the original documents did not have pagination, we have included our pagination in the following references.

An article of the surrender of Montréal had specified "that the Indians or Indians allied to his Majesty shall be maintained in the possession of the lands they inhabit" (Province of Canada 1845, quoted in Girard and Thibeault 2001, 2:91). This position was confirmed in the Royal Proclamation, which defined the territory of Indigenous Peoples as territory for hunting.

In view of the inability of Indigenous Peoples to protect themselves (according to its authors), the Bagot Report (Appendix EEE) recommends that the Crown become the *guardian* of the *Sauvages* on reserves that would be allocated to them (Girard and Thibeault 2001, 2:93, 99, 155).

> As the Indian lands were held in common, and the title to them was vested in the Crown, as Guardian, the Indians were excluded from all political rights, the tenure of which depended upon an extent of interest, not conferred upon them by the Crown.
>
> The inability also to compete with their white brethren debarred them, in a great measure, from the enjoyment of civil rights, while the policy of the Government led to the belief that they did not in fact posess [*sic*] them.
>
> They were thus left in a state of tutelage, which although devised for their protection and benefit, has in the event proved very detrimental to their interests by encouraging them to rely wholly upon the support and advice of the Government, and to neglect opportunities to elevate themselves from a state of dependence to the level of the surrounding population (Girard and Thibeault 2001, 2: 49).

This trusteeship policy could be implemented using the following means:

1- Create compact settlements that were separated and isolated, if possible, from European populations (the concept of reserves). The goal was to settle Indigenous Peoples in "reserved lands" that were not subject to seizure.

2- Assimilate Indigenous Peoples through agriculture, by training young people in schools, and by encouraging the appointment of priests to ensure good morals and religious supervision (for more details, see 53–54).

The report envisages the application of a uniform policy throughout the province, though agriculture was feasible in only a tiny part of the northern regions where nomadic Indigenous Peoples were found. In our opinion, the statistical data and information collected from the Indigenous Nations of Québec seems unreliable. Thus, the Crown remained poorly informed about Indigenous Peoples living far from major centres, such as the Maliseet, the Cree, the Innu, the Naskapi, and the Inuit. These Nations, which often could not be identified, were referred to as "wandering groups with no fixed abode."

6. THE MALISEET: FROM RECOGNITION TO OBLIVION AND DISPERSAL

The ultimate goal becomes clear when the authors state, quoting Lord Durham,

> Regarding the Indians that their concerns must be continued under the exclusive care and superintendence of the Crown [...] the Indians must continue to be as they have hitherto been, under the peculiar care and management of the Crown, to which, whether under French or English dominion, they have been taught exclusively to look for paternal protection, in compensation for the rights and independence which they have lost; until circumstances make it expedient that they should be turned over by the Crown to the Provincial Legislature, and receive Legislative provision and care (Girard and Thibeault 2001, 2: 54).

It is proposed that Indigenous Peoples be left in or moved to more remote lands or be "confined" within smaller boundaries, which would become reserves.

> The Government, therefore, adopted the most humane and the most just course, in inducing the Indians, by offers of compensation, to remove quietly to more distant hunting grounds, or to confine themselves within more limited reserves, instead of leaving them and the white settlers exposed to the horrors of a protracted struggle for ownership (Girard and Thibeault 2001, 2: 48).

This statement is based on Vattel (1714–1767), who in *The Law of Nations, or Principles of Natural Law, applied to the conduct and affairs of Nations and Sovereigns* reinforced the theory of terra nullius (empty lands, or lands occupied by non-Christian or uncivilized people) to justify the seizure of lands and the guardianship of Indigenous Peoples. A nomad could not have rights in the system that was being set up. Before quoting the legal specialist, the authors took care to specify the real objectives of the Crown, for whom "the habits of rapine and the vengeance of the *Indians* made their removal desirable" in view of the need for land for new immigrants.

> [Quoting Vattel, *Droit des gens* [...], 1758] "The wisdom and justice of such a procedure are strongly recommended by Vatel [*sic*], in his Law of Nations from which the following passage is taken":

> There is *another celebrated question to which the discovery of the new world* [our italics] has principally given rise. It is asked whether a nation may lawfully take possession of some part of a vast country in which they are none but *erratic nations whose scanty population is incapable of occupying the whole*. We have already observed, in *establishing the obligation to cultivate the earth*, that these *nations cannot exclusively appropriate to themselves more land than they have occupied or more than they are able to settle and cultivate. Their unsettled habitation in those immense regions cannot be accounted a true and legal possession,* [our italics] and the people of Europe, too closely pent up at home. Finding land of which the Savage stood in no particular need, and of which they

made no actual and constant use, were lawfully entitled to take possession of it and to settle it with Colonies (Girard and Thibeault 2001, 2: 48).

Such statements became the basis of the construction of a corporate memory. In pre- and post-Confederation discourse, *dispossessing Indigenous Peoples of their land and their fundamental rights became justified in law.* Indigenous Peoples were perceived as wanderers, incapable because they were few and dispersed throughout their territory.

The Europeans set the standard as *settling down in one place* and *farming* while nomadic Indigenous Peoples had their own set of values and system for managing their land. For the authors of the report, the divide between civilized and primitive led to the conclusion that Indigenous Peoples would not be in a "state to inhabit" the territory because they could not cultivate the land. Moreover, their vague occupation of these vast territories could not be considered "a true and legitimate taking of possession."

They concluded that, outside the province of Québec (1763), the Royal Proclamation, with its system of *cession and sale* that allowed the system of gifts and compensation to continue, showed that governments treated Indigenous People even better than settlers of European descent. According to the report, it was "thanks to us" that Indigenous Peoples had acquired a certain degree of wealth:

> The Indians are now in possession of advantages which far exceed those of the surrounding white population, and which afford them the means under a proper system of mental improvement, of obtaining independence, and even opulence (Girard and Thibeault 2001, 2: 48).

Finally, the report states that both sides had complied with the arrangements they had made with each other, transforming the concept of *cession* to that of *surrender.* "These agreements have been faithfully observed by both parties. The Indians have not disputed the title of the Crown to the lands, which they have surrendered" (Girard and Thibeault 2001, 2: 48).

These statements contradict the testimony of numerous witnesses before the commissioners and recorded in the report, including in the lesser-known appendices that recorded the words of Indigenous persons.

The Bagot Reports (1844–1847) provided the justification for the establishment of an administrative framework that became embedded in the Canadian legal system in the 1850s and 1860s and served as the basis for the Constitution of 1867.

Canadian history: Shaping a collective memory by disqualifying Indigenous Peoples from the Canadian nation-state

The Bagot Report (Appendix EEE) contains a summary analysis of the Indigenous Nations of Upper and Lower Canada (Girard and Thibeault 2001, 2:57ff, 103ff, 111f).

Before reviewing that analysis, in which the authors repeatedly emphasize the uncertain nature of the information they were able to collect, let us recall the general framework underlying the new Canadian Indian policy at the time (circa 1844). French Canadian historiography of the time fit perfectly into the discourse that disqualified Indigenous Peoples from participating in the founding of the Canadian federation in 1867 (Girard and Brisson 2014, 2018; Girard, 2017; on the concept of qualifying for disqualification in the history of Canada after Confederation, Girard 2017, available online at the site *Les Classiques des sciences sociales*).

Before presenting a brief description of each Nation, the authors of the report state that Indigenous persons were usually docile. They are of "happy" and "hospitable" character. They never fail to share the fruits of the hunt with their neighbours (Girard and Thibeault 2001, 2:103). The Indigenous person is reduced to a generic individual who is either sedentary or nomadic. He is no longer a member of a distinct community or culture, a Nation, but has become an individual to be distrusted and, above all, "civilized."

This image of the "Savage" hid another that was believed to require change:

> An Indian *brave* would rather die than commit an act derogatory to his character as a warrior [...]. In his half civilised state, he is indolent to excess, intemperate, suspicious, cunning, covetous, and addicted to lying and fraud. These are not the fruits of Christianity, and therefore it is evident that in such cases the mode of their treatment has been defective, and calls for alteration. (Girard and Thibeault 2001, 2:58). Appendix 1844.2001, vol. II, p. 58 e, 103, f)

The reports commissioned by Governor General Charles Bagot contributed to determining Indian policy by describing Indigenous people them in their natural state as degenerate and decadent and in contact with a civilization that they could not manage.

The historian François-Xavier Garneau, whose work was published at the same time as the Bagot reports, authored his first history of French Canada (1845) in response to the well-known Durham Report (1839), which states that French Canadians should be *assimilated into the great British civilization*, similarly to what the Bagot Report asserts about

Indigenous Peoples. In his view of the *Indian*, Garneau, though associated with a liberal historiography, blithely mixes images of the good and bad savage who lives in the wilderness and can be an ally in trade or war. However, the *savage must be kept peaceful*. There is a *need to control and civilize* these Peoples *without laws, without property, so fragile and incapable*. Ultimately, Garneau also disqualifies these persons who hide within themselves a warlike, dangerous, even abnormal creature, a barbarian who is close to being an animal. His perspective seems to have been inspired by the Bagot Report:

> But the art of these barbarians consisted of surprising their enemies [...] in a sudden attack when the warrior knocked out his sleeping antagonist with a single blow. The very word "war" aroused in the young warrior a sort of delightful quiver, the fruit of a deep enthusiasm. *The sound of combat, the sight of enemies pulsating with blood, intoxicated them with joy; they enjoyed this spectacle in advance, the only one capable of impressing their placid souls.* [...] *It was the only one of their fibres that had been excited since they were able to feel. Their whole soul was there* (our italics and translation; Garneau [1845] 1996, 204–5; on the relationship to animals in Cartier's writings, Gagnon and Petel, 1986).

More than one hundred years later, Lionel Groulx, a conservative and Catholic historiographer, perpetuated an equally stereotyped image of Indigenous persons in his *Histoire du Canada français*, published in 1960. Although he acknowledged that, at the time of Spanish and Portuguese exploration, the population of Central and South America was estimated at more than fifty million (current estimates are seventy to one hundred million for America and sixty to sixty-five million for Europe), Groulx considered these Peoples as less-evolved races (Groulx 1960, 53; for population, Delâge 1991, 54–55).

Groulx avoided generalizing about the warrior and did not distinguish between sedentary and nomadic Peoples. In the end, he produced a series of descriptors that disqualifed this "primitive" who remained too close to warlike instincts that could lead him to "cannibalism." Presented thus, Indigenous Peoples had to assimilate or be assimilated.

> The Huron-Iroquois have reached the first phase: that whereby humans try to increase, through activity, the spontaneous productivity of nature. The Algonquins linger in the primitive phase: the phase of simple gathering, hunting, fishing, harvesting of wild fruits. Among both, political institutions remain rudimentary. [...] Established almost without matrimonial rites, the concept of family condones both the half-slavery of the woman and an almost absolute independence of the children. Strangers to the notion of individual property, the Indian is not alien to the idea of homeland, especially those living in settlements. Physically healthy and robust, the supreme deprivation of North America

6. THE MALISEET: FROM RECOGNITION TO OBLIVION AND DISPERSAL   181

lies in their spiritual poverty: a vague belief in a single God, a belief overrun and distorted by a mad belief in all sorts of subaltern and evil genies; neither temples, nor religious ceremonies of any elevation or serenity; on the other hand, a tyrannical submission to dreams and, instead of priests, jugglers, sorcerers, mixtures of charlatans and burlesque magicians. The morals are the same: natural morals, obedience to instinct. The Indian only distinguishes himself by his veneration of the dead, which is really admirable, and also by his faith in the immortality of the soul, by his spirit of hospitality towards his own, by his warrior values. *Unfortunately, war degenerates for him into a sport, a game of strength and cunning, and even into cannibalism. Not a cannibal by profession, he becomes one by passion of revenge, just as he becomes a ferocious torturer of prisoners of war* (our italics and translation; Groulx 1960, 53–54).

It is like reading Garneau again. Groulx returns to the monster of the origin, who instinctively hides a taste for war leading to *cannibalism, vengeance, and the capacity to torture*. When Indigenous People are characterized in this way, it is difficult for the reader to perceive them positively. Unlike Garneau, Groulx thinks that the *Indian* could believe in the immortality of the soul despite their great spiritual poverty. He returns to earlier tropes (Christianity/barbarism) that saw conversion to the Catholic or Christian faith as the only avenue for Indigenous Peoples.

Garneau, the liberal, and Groulx, the conservative, both contributed to reinforcing a discourse that perpetuated the stereotype and justified exclusion of Indigenous Peoples from Confederation (1867). The Canadian legal system completed the process: Indigenous Peoples did not qualify as full actors in the Canadian federation, a position that became official in the *Indian Act* of 1876.

In their analysis of history textbooks used in Québec (1979), Vincent and Arcand noted that the situation was problematic in education, to say the least, particularly at the high-school level. In most textbooks, nothing seemed to have changed, at least not by 1979. Indigenous Peoples did not behave like everyone else. They had an innate taste for war; they were hostile and threatening; cruelty was in their blood and embedded in their culture, and they could not get rid of it. At least this is what the history textbooks approved by the Québec Ministry of Education in the 1970s lead us to believe, despite a purge that had eliminated descriptions of the torture inflicted on famous Canadian martyrs (our translation; Vincent and Arcand 1979, 28; see also Groulx 1998, 377ff).

Since the middle of the nineteenth century, discourse has depicted the *Indian* in Canada as degenerate humans close to animals. A kingdom that mixes the human and the animal invites violation of human and divine rights because a human-animal mixture is a transgression that requires rectification. In fact: "There is monstrosity only where the disorder of the natural law comes to touch, to jostle, to worry the right, that is the civil right, the canonical right, the religious right. "There is monstrosity only where the disorder of the natural law comes to touch, to jostle, to worry the right, that it is the civil right, the canonical right, the religious right" (Foucault, 1999, 59, our traduction).

This historical discourse was supported by Canadian legislation: Indigenous populations could not be considered as actors in the Canadian federation, and this was made official by discriminatory laws passed from the 1850s onward and culminating in the synthesis of the Indian Act of 1876 (Numerous Appendices on Canadian laws on Indigenous Peoples, from 1850 to 1876; Girard and Brisson 2018, 121ff).

The Maliseet and the Bagot Commission: From Nation to "wandering tribes"

In the Bagot Report (Appendix EEE, 1844), the description of the Maliseet appears in the section "Unsettled Tribes" (Girard and Thibeault 2001, 2:46 for English version and 90 for the French version of the report: *History of the relation of the Government and the Indians* and *Histoire des relations entre le Gouvernement et les Sauvages.*

This adjective "unsettled" is not trivial since we have seen that the report emphasizes the fact that nomadic Indigenous Peoples could have no rights to lands and resources beyond their needs. This vocabulary *subtly introduces the justification of systematic exclusion.*

The Report recalls that, in the course of inquiries conducted in 1828, the government had made a commitment to some thirty "Amalacite" families to establish a settlement near the Rivière Verte: By an Order in Council, dated 28 May 1827, they received a grant of 3000 acres, in lots of 100 acres to each family Girard and Thibeault, 2011, 2, 64 and 111 for the french). The government had provided seeds and other items necessary for planting for two years. Highligting the expenses of 138 pounds, the authors pointed out that 44 pounds were used for surveying and 11, for paying the surintendant expenses. The report states that, "despite good harvests, unfortunately no further notice of the settlement was taken by the Government. From 1829 up to the present time [1845], *it has not been visited by any officer of the Indian Department and it is supposed that it is now abandoned*" (our italics, Girard and Thibeault, 2001, 64).

The authors of the report reiterated that

The Committee of the Executive Council, in noticing this settlement in their Report, justly observe, that "from the circumstance of these Indians having been left very much to themselves, without sufficient superintendence, and from the fact that some families still remain on the land, the Committee do not see reason to think that a fair chance of success was offered to the settlement in its progress, or its apparent failure would justify the entire abandonment of it. [...] No steps, however, have been taken to carry out this suggestion (Girard and Thibeault 2001, 2: 64-65).

The section concludes with a reminder that the *Amalacites* who abandoned the Rivière Verte settlement are wanderers, as are the Mi'kmaq and Abenaki. their brothers. Their number was estimated at 180. These wandering "Indians" were for the most part "perfectly destitute" and lived off hunting, fishing, and from the sale of articles made by the women. (Girard and Thibeault, 2001, 111 and 65).

In 1854, when lands reserved for Indigenous Peoples were distributed in Lower Canada, the Maliseet of Viger, in the county of Rimouski, were allotted not 3,000 but 3,650 acres. This tract of land behind L'Isle-Verte (see map 49) was bounded on the southwest by the third range and by lot 33, in the first and second ranges and the range marked *A* of the township (Appendix, 1851, Fortin and Frenette 1989, 35). On this map, it is possible to see several buildings constructed along the Rivière La Fourche.

In the following section, we learn how the Maliseet managed their territory from 1827 onward and how they lost the rights to their land and were forced to disperse in 1869.

The seizure of the traditional territory of the Maliseet

When the Maliseet (1765) and the Innu (1767) complained to government officials following the British Conquest, they always requested protection of their traditional land, which was recognized by the Crown as "unceded" territory that assured the continuation of their traditional cultural practice as "Indian" Nations or Tribes.

In 1765, when the governor responded to the Maliseet request for protection from encroachment on their hunting, he was quick to point out that Maliseet territory was officially recognized as *traditional Indian territory*, belonging to Indigenous Peoples and set aside as "Hunting Grounds" for "Nations or Tribes" as stated by the Royal Proclamation of 1763.

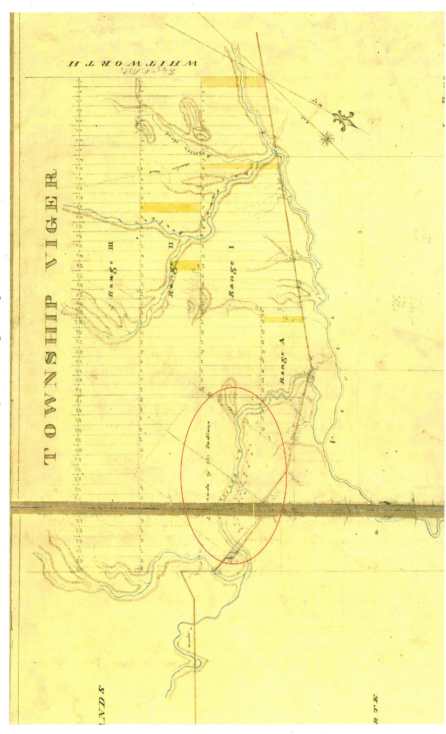

MAP 49 – Map of the village of Viger, 1847

Governor Murray returned to the charge in 1767 following a request by the Innu to protect their traditional lands. He confirmed that, as an extension of the *pacts* that the French had agreed with the Innu, the King's Domain, or Traite de Tadoussac, created by royal decree in 1652, was to be considered Indigenous traditional territory. Further, occupying it was prohibited without the express permission of the Crown, which was to ensure that these lands were ceded or sold as specified in the Proclamation of 1763.

The Crown's response to these requests recognized and confirmed the traditional territory of the Innu and the Maliseet, Nitassinan Innu and Wolastokuk respectively. These lands were not limited to "reserved lands" but included all "Hunting Grounds or Traditional Territories." They comprised territories both within and outside the borders of the province of Québec as established in 1763, along with the resources therein.

The Maliseet and their request to settle in a village (1826)[5]

The petition of 11 January 1826, led to the creation of Viger. This request was signed by two Chiefs who identified themselves as belonging to the Abenaki Nation. They represented ninety-six or ninety-eight individuals of the "same tribe" who resided along the Meduxnekeag River, a tributary of the Saint John River in present-day New Brunswick (see figure 10).

The handwritten document signed at the time states that "*the Lands which has formerly been Your Excellency Petitioner Hunting Grounds*" were increasingly being settled by a large population and that Indigenous persons no longer had the wherewithal to support themselves.

The available data from the 1831 census (see table 10) confirms this statement: non-Indigenous persons present on traditional Maliseet lands numbered 78,074, a significant increase given that the total population of the seigneuries located in the territory under study was only 8,602 in 1739.

The petitioners and the hundred or so people involved in the official request said they wanted to "emigrate to Lower Canada."

---

5. Appendix, 1826, Viger Creation Land Request; article by Laurence Johnson, Appendix, 1996, Origin Reserve Request.

FIGURE 10 – Petition for land by St. John River Indians (1826)[6]

Source: Library and Archives Canada. 1826. Land Papers of Lower Canada fonds, no. RGI, L3L, 29: 15234-8.

---

6. For the French translation, see Johnson 1996, 78; manuscript, Appendix, 1826.

TABLE 10 – Population in 1831

COUNTY	POPULATION IN 1831
Beauce	12,527
Bellechasse	13,486
Dorchester	14,041
Kamouraska	14,495
L'Islet	13,464
Rimouski	10,061
Total	**78,074**

Source: Canadian Census. 1874. Canada Statistics, vol. IV. Ottawa: I.B. Taylor, 1876.
* These data do not include the The populations of Île d'Orléans and Île aux Coudres.

The Chiefs are identified in the text as Abenaki. On 11 January 1826, Luis Tomas and Joseph X Thomas signed documents prepared in the name of Lord Dalhousie, the governor of Lower Canada. They requested access to a *"village near the Isle-Verte lands"* (see map 49). They were not asking for a reserve because no legislation yet governed the creation of this type of territory. Nor were they asking to cede or sell anything to the Crown or to give up their rights to their traditional lands.

The request for a village could be associated with a settlement, a territory to be occupied as owners or residents. It was a place where Indigenous persons would be able to settle down in a community connected to their Indigenous culture, as was the case for seigneuries and for villages in parishes. In this respect, the creation of a Maliseet village was part of the movement to municipalize Crown lands. In the petition of 11 January 1826, the surveyor Joseph Bouchette "certifies that all the lands behind the seigneury of Île-Verte (a seigneury which is only two leagues inland from the St. Lawrence) are uncleared [*non défrichées*] Crown lands not surveyed and consequently are free and grantable, according to the books in his office." For Bouchette, acting surveyor general for the Government of Lower Canada, the traditional lands of the Maliseet in this case appeared to be the de facto property of the Crown, which could dispose of them as the need arose without traditional lands having been formally ceded or sold as specified in the Royal Proclamation of 1763.

In map 50, it can be seen that settlement on the traditional lands of the Maliseet continued with the addition of seven townships to the already existing seigneuries, without any consultation taking place or compensation being granted to the Maliseet for this encroachment on their traditional territory. Thus, the government of Lower Canada was continuing to claim that the traditional territory of Indigenous People was made up of "free lands" that it could grant without the consent of its inhabitants, the Maliseet, even though the British authorities had explicitly recognized in 1765 that the Maliseet possessed traditional lands within the 1763 limits of the province of Québec.

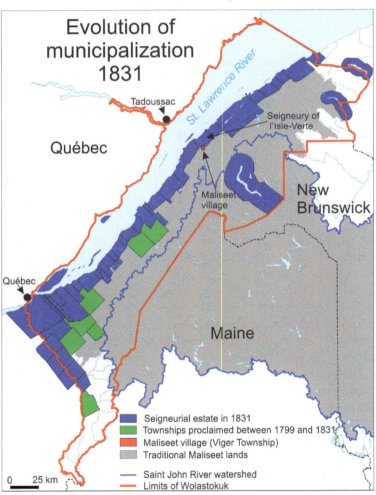

MAP 50 – Evolution of municipalization, 1831

An Abenaki or Maliseet claim

No signatures other than those of the two Abenaki Chiefs appear on the two-page handwritten document. Luis Tomas and Joseph Thomas, the signatory Chiefs, are believed to be Louis-Thomas Saint-Aubin and Joseph Thomas Saint-Aubin (Johnson 1996, 77). Their French surnames descended from Jean Serreau de Saint-Aubin, whose son Charles had married a Maliseet woman around 1690. The two brothers took responsible for the Viger settlement until its closure in 1869.

Laurence Johnson (1996, 79) pointed out that the Thomas Chiefs chose to come and settle in Lower Canada (province of Québec) and more precisely at L'Isle-Verte, where their father, Joseph-Thomas Saint-Aubin, had been buried. The Maliseet were regulars at L'Isle-Verte, which they had inhabited for a long time since they had laid claim to the territory with Governor Murray as early as 1765 (Appendix 5, Maliseet Claims, 1765).

Attached to the document is a rudimentary map of L'Isle-Verte, on which Cacouna, Rivière-du-Loup, and a southern section bearing the label of "Waste Land" are identified.

The manuscript, in English only, was signed by the governor general, Lord Dalhousie. Does it accurately reflect the wishes of the Chiefs and the persons they claimed to represent? For the moment, we can only rely on this source. We know from articles by Johnson (1996) and Antonio Lechasseur in Fortin, Lechasseur, 1993 and Appendix 1993) on the history of the Viger community that the Maliseet were given a few thousand acres (2,000 to 3,000 acres) to create a settlement at Viger. The tragedy arose from the fact that this territory was taken away from them and that, following this, they lost all claim to their traditional territory. They became an "unsettled" People.

Indigenous Peoples living on their traditional territories in then New Brunswick and Québec, no longer able to provide for themselves, sought government intervention to ensure that their traditional lands were respected.

What Lechasseur (Fortin et al. 1993 and Johnson (1994) pointed out is that Viger served as an experiment in Québec (Lower Canada), similarly to what was happening concurrently in Ontario (Upper Canada) with members of the Mississauga Nation at the mouth of the Credit River (Johnson 1994, 242) and on Manitoulin Island (1834) (Appendix, 1844.2001 vol. 2: Manitoulin: 12-13-, 99, 123); for Credit River: 5-8-19-21-39; Credit River: 5-8-19-21-39;

The government granted land to the Maliseet where they could establish a village. There was no cession or sale, as decided by Governor Dalhousie. A village was created at the request of petitioners from several families identified as members of the Maliseet Nation. However, even though land was granted for residential purposes, no mention was made of the protection of hunting territory, although the text explicitly refers to "Hunting Grounds" that were being invaded by Euro-Canadians. The text uses the same terms as those in the Royal Proclamation of 1763 but with no mention of cession or sale of Maliseet lands, with regard to neither their traditional territory nor the new lands they were requesting to found a village.

Grant of land to the Maliseet to establish a village (1827)

On 15 May 1827, the Executive Council of Lower Canada, presided over by Lord Dalhousie, confirmed a grant of territory to the Maliseet (Amalecites).

The committee said that it was "pleased that a portion of a tribe of the Indian nations is willing to *abandon its wandering life* for the purpose of settling at a point to cultivate the land, and humbly recommends, on an experimental basis, that a site of two thousand acres of land be allotted to the Amalecites" (our translation; Lechasseur 1993: 230).

The territory of the Maliseet village was to be little used, and the government took little notice of this. Shortly before the Province of United Canada began implementing its policy, of setting aside land in Lower Canada for Indigenous Peoples in the 1850s, the government more than once inventoried the territory of the Maliseet (Girard and Brisson 2018, 121–38; Moss, Gardner-O'toole, 1987, *The Indigenous People. A History of Laws Discriminating Against Them, paper prepared for the Canadian Federal Government and Law Division*; Appendix, 1991 revised edition.

The maps prepared by government ministries in 1847 and 1849 (Lechasseur 1993, 234) no longer identified the territory as *Waste Land* but as *Lands of the Indians*. In 1850, when the time came to reserve land and to identify the Nation to which it belonged, the Maliseet were among the Nations named. On official maps prepared at that time, the generic term *Indians* was used by land agents, cartographers, and government officials. The term *reserve* was not yet in use.

In 1849, farmers living around the territory allocated to the Maliseet Nation coveted Maliseet lands. This acquisitiveness was part of the mission to create a French-speaking province within an eventual Canadian federation. Three principles, three ideals, were becoming integral to the collective concept of a distinct Québec society: agriculture, the Catholic religion, and

6. THE MALISEET: FROM RECOGNITION TO OBLIVION AND DISPERSAL

the French language. These three overarching strands of French Canadian thought conveyed the message that ownership of land came from working it. Idealized values of the family and the Catholic religion reinforced this vision.

Farmers' requests to take over the Viger lands had begun in the early 1850s as the government prepared, through new legislation, to define *Indian status* and to enshrine in vocabulary the concept of *reserved lands* for *Indians* while remaining silent on the question of traditional lands as recognized in the Royal Proclamation of 1763 (Girard and Brisson 2018, 121; Appendix, 1850, Lower Canada Land Reserves).

The 1851 act set aside 230,000 acres (931 square kilometres) for all the tribes of Lower Canada. In accordance with this law, the government of United Province of Canada created several reserves, including the Viger reserve, which it established in the same location as the village granted to the Maliseet in 1827. It was a small area, 14.77 square kilometres (see map 51).

This map also shows that municipalization of the traditional territory of the Maliseet was continuing. Six new townships had been created, and new landowners were settling in them. In all, the area contained eighty-three townships in which 132,157 persons resided, according to the 1851 census (see table 11). The population of the area under study had nearly doubled since the 1831 census. These newcomers required more land for agriculture, which was still the base of economic activity for French Canadians.

TABLE 11 – Population in 1851

COUNTY	POPULATION IN 1851
Bellechasse	17,982
Dorchester	46,386
Kamouraska	20,396
L'Islet	16,853
Montmorency (Île d'Orléans)	4,416
Rimouski	25,405
Saguenay (Île aux Coudres)	719
Total	**132,157**

Source: Bureau of Registration and Statistics, *Canadian Census,1851 2Census of Persons*, vol. 1. Québec City: John Lovell, 1853.

MAP 51 – Evolution of municipalization, 1851

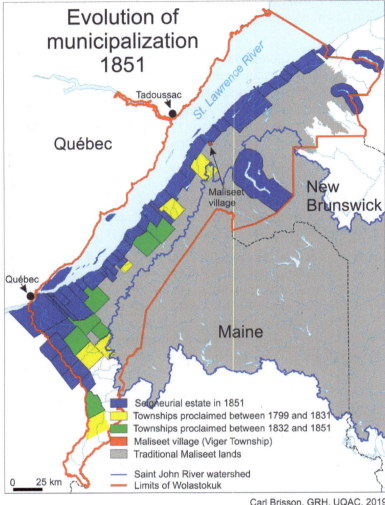

It should be noted that the status of "Indian" women was defined more precisely during this period. If a non-Indigenous female married an Indigenous male, she acquired status by marriage. An Indigenous female who married a non-Indigenous male lost her status (Schedule, 1851, Abrogation Act... and Lower Canada Land Reserves; Schedule, 1851, Article Fortin...; Girard and Brisson 2018, 124). This provision would have a significant influence on the transmission of language and culture among Indigenous Peoples. In addition, the descendants of these women swelled the ranks of non-Status Indians under this new system imposed by the United Province of Canada.

The Innu protest of 1851: Protests and claims of Indigenous Peoples in response to invasion of their traditional lands

The Indigenous Peoples of Québec took little part in consultations undertaken by the commissions of inquiry that began in the 1820s. The Innu and Maliseet were not consulted and do not appear to have participated directly in the inquiries, either as witnesses or otherwise.

This is not to say that Québec's Indigenous Peoples did not participate in the debate. They expressed their disagreement with the government in various ways, demanding the protection of their traditional lands and the resources they contained (Girard and Brisson 2018, 110ff; for the claims and numerous protests of the Innu as early as 1844).

In a protest filed in 1851 (Appendix, 1851, Protest...; Girard 2003), the Innu detailed the nature of their rights, which they reaffirmed as Indigenous Peoples. They reminded those receiving the protest that, as a "People," they had occupied and possessed their traditional lands since "time immemorial." Being allied with the Crown did not take away their right to own and possess lands.

The specific reason for this protest was to prevent the Government of the United Province of Canada from selling off traditional Innu land in new townships that had just been opened to private ownership and agriculture in the Saguenay and to the southeast of Lac St. Jean. These were the very townships that the Innu claimed as their home. They protested by arguing that:

> the said lands have been the property of the said Montagnais *Sauvages* [our italics] from time immemorial and from all time, the territory on which the said lands are situated has been their property & in their possession, serving as their residence & as hunting grounds the only means of existence for them & their families; that the government cannot, without being in contravention of all existing laws, sell their lands without having previously compromised with them for their rights of possession & ownership (Girard and Brisson 2014, 92 ff).

The Innu claimed that they owned not only the disputed land but also the larger territory in which that land was located. Their ownership therefore extended beyond the boundaries of the townships where land was being offered for sale. They condemned the sale of the lands, which, in the absence of prior arrangement with them, constituted illegal seizure. The Innu proclaimed their ownership and possession of their lands because the British conquest had not overridden their right of ownership or their title to the lands and their resources:

> The Crown of England, by conquering the country, did not conquer the right of ownership and possession of these lands that the first *Sauvage* Montagnais, the first father of them, received as a share of divine providence to feed and support the descendants of his tribe (Girard and Brisson 2014, 93).

The Innu rejected the claims of the British Crown to their territory, which had acted without consulting them. They were the owners of the land and the possessors of the soil they had inhabited since time immemorial. The term "ownership and possession" excluded any reference to a right of use alone and included what Indigenous Peoples perceived as an *inalienable title to their traditional lands*:

> Consequently, we, the said notaries [...] have summoned, required & challenged the said John Kane [...] not to make any sale, assignment or gift of the aforesaid lands to anyone unless it comes to his knowledge by authentic documents [*sic*] that the government of this Province would have compromised with the said *Sauvages* as to their aforesaid rights of ownership & possession (Girard and Brisson 2014, 93).

Without referring to it by name, this document invokes the Royal Proclamation of 1763, which obliged the Crown to negotiate with Indigenous Nations before proceeding with any sale of their lands to individuals. The Innu, like other Indigenous Peoples including the Maliseet, demanded that the colonial government negotiate with them and respect their traditional territory in accordance with their fundamental rights.

The Maliseet, like the Innu, asserted their rights and protested, as we have seen previously, requesting that the governor protect their traditional territory (1765, 1767). They repeated their demands in various ways from the 1820s onwards as municipalization proceeded.

The Gradual Civilization Act (1857): Loss of citizenship and attachment to a "band"

The Act to Encourage the Gradual Civilization of the Indian Tribes in the Province (10 June 1857) introduced a new notion, that of *gradual civilization*, and the possibility for Indigenous persons to *emancipate* themselves. This emancipation implied that from then on Indians (individuals and nations) were no longer considered full citizens by the Canadian legal system. Although this was not stated explicitly, if Indians could become citizens by becoming disenfranchised, this implied that by being enfranchised, they did not have the status of citizens. If they were not emancipated, Indigenous people could not own land. As far as we know, the obligation to belong to a band appeared clearly for the first time in a Canadian legislation.

The Maliseet and the loss of Viger (1869)

The Maliseet had to cede, or retrocede, their reserve in 1869, even though they had been granted ownership of this territory as a village for settlement (Appendix, 1857, Indian "Civilization and Emancipation" Act...; Girard and Brisson 2018, 125). Three powerful entities—federal, provincial, and religious (the Catholic Church)—ensured the success of this attempt to gain control of the territory that the Maliseet had been granted in 1827. The federal government, the prime mover, had just been granted constitutional authority over "Indians and Lands reserved for the Indians" (Constitution Act, 1867, sec. 91.24).

Provincial governments are allocated responsibility for property and resources (sec. 92, 109). However, the Government of Québec was largely absent, even though it should have taken responsibility for all off-reserve matters relating to Indigenous Peoples, that is, off-reserve Indian land and all off-reserve Indian rights. In the Constitution Act of 1867, traditional or ancestral Indian lands and the natural resources they contain are not considered or covered in the allocation of responsibilities. Each level of government has consolidated their constitutionally vested powers and passed other responsibilities on to the other level. This has left the Indian question in a constant state of flux between federal and provincial governments.

At the time of Confederation, the third powerful entity was the Catholic Church. As its priests worked on writing a new collective history, local leaders helped French Canadian families settle in northern agricultural parishes. Faith, family, agriculture, and Frenchness (francité) were the key messages embedded in the history of a people seeking their "destiny" as a French-speaking nation in North America.

For the Maliseet, this alliance between church and politics culminated in the concerted efforts of the three Langevin brothers, each working at the centre of national, provincial, or local power, which ensured the rapid resolution of the issue of the "Viger reserve" after Confederation.

This triumvirate included Sir Hector-Louis Langevin, an active politician who had participated in the preparations for Confederation and was a protégé of the first prime minister elected in 1867, Sir John A. Macdonald. Elected federally in the first post-Confederation election, Langevin was appointed secretary of state and superintendent of Indian affairs (Lechasseur 1993, 240; *Dictionary of Canadian Biography*; Johnson 1994, 1995, 2001). His brother, Jean Langevin, was the first bishop of the diocese of Rimouski (1867–1891), and Edmond Langevin was vicar general of the same diocese (1867–1889). During the negotiations preceding retrocession, which was signed 4 August 1869, Lazare Marceau, parish priest of L'Isle-Verte, was the local agent for the delicate venture of dislodging the Maliseet. Few problems were encountered. Details of the flow of information and the negotiations, assisted by the superintendent of Indian affairs, who had a front-row seat in Ottawa for the definition of the new policy, can be found in Lechasseur (1993; Appendix 1993: 240ff; Johnson 1994).

Can we speak of cession or retrocession: The fate of Viger and the dispersal of the Nation

In the following pages, we present an analysis of the manuscript text (1869) found in government archives. Our analysis highlights changes in the management of Indigenous issues after Confederation in which Minister Langevin was an important actor (Appendix 6: Manuscript document, Maliseet and the Viger cession, 1869).

The original text provided by the archives of the Department of Indian Affairs and Northern Development has a cover page with a date of 15 August 1973. The number X017354 with the stamp "Land Register, Received... approval" (see figure 11; Appendix, 1869, Land Grant...).

The template form is imprinted with "Indian Reserve No.", and "Viger," "No. 4," and "Québec" have been added by hand. Below, in handwritten capital letters, appears the term "SURRENDER" (see figure 11). Along with other handwritten notes ("oc 482," "schedule of 15565," and "Aug 9 1853"[?]), it is stated that the government allows "distribution." The pages that follow contain the handwritten text of the "cession or sale" of the lands reserved for the "Amalecites" of Viger (draft 1869).

FIGURE 11 – Document: "Indian Reserve no. 4, Viger, Québec"

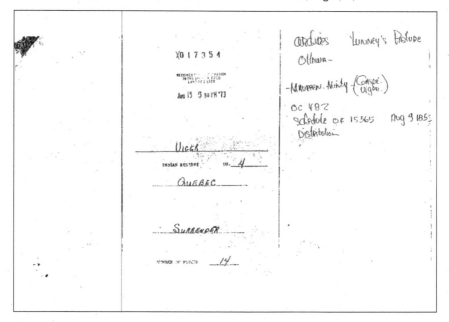

The document is written by hand in French and is followed by an English translation. The French and English versions are not written by the same person. Father Marceau acts as a witness to the preparation of the documents and to its signature by the representatives of the Maliseet. The document, dated 4 August 1869, is signed by seventeen representatives of the Maliseet Nation: François Étienne St-Aubain, first Chief; Jean Athanas, second Chief; Joseph Laurent; Jean Athanas senior; James Grey; Antoine Athanas; Joseph Nicolas; Jean Bernard; Thomas Athanas; Jean Denis; Noël Denis; Laurent Athanas; Félix Étienne St-Aubain; Baptiste Denis; François Grey; Paul Joseph; Élisabeth Terrien, widow of Paul Joseph.

The Chiefs and principals of the "Amalecite Tribe of Indians" resided in Isle-Verte, Rivière-du-Loup, Cacouna, and in the "vicinity." They acted in the name of their People and had represented them in the council meeting held on 4 August 1869.

The text states that the land agent had reserved for "our People" (our italics) lands that "we transfer and cede" (underlined in the text) to our sovereign, Queen Victoria. This cession is made in "trust to be sold for the benefit of our said people." A survey is to be completed, and the proceeds of the sale are to be paid in equal shares to the "Indians who are now residing in any of the localities above mentioned."

The auction that followed the sale of Viger brought in approximately $10,000. Lechasseur (1993, 244-5) stated that the Maliseet receiving annual funding from the sale of Viger numbered 156, "not all of whom reside in the area" (see table 12). By 1870, 25 percent of the Malecites of Viger were living in the United States.

Both the French and English versions of the document refer to *céder* in French and *cede* in English) and to sale (*vente* in French and *sale* in English). The terms *cession in trust to be sold* (Proclamation 1763) were also used in 1869. *Surrender* was not used, although the term appeared in the document given by government archives in 1973. Use of the phrase *Reserve in Viger township* became more precise with the passing of the Indian Act of 1876.

TABLE 12 – Maliseet affected by the sale of the Viger reserve, 1870

TERRITORY	NUMBER	PERCENTAGE
United States	37	25.0 %
New Brunswick (Tobique)	2	1.4 %
Wolastokuk	101	68.2 %
Rivière-du-Loup	40	
Cacouna	39	
Pointe-Lévis	12	
L'Isle-Verte	8	
Trois-Pistoles	2	
Elsewhere in Québec	8	5.4 %
La Malbaie	4	
Moisie	4	

Source: Jean-Charles Fortin, Antonio Lechasseur et al. 1993, *Histoire du Bas-Saint-Laurent*, Les Éditions de l'IQRC, Québec, Les Presses de l'Université Laval, p, 245.
Note: The authors provide the place of residence of 148 of the 156 Maliseet surveyed.

The heading "Plan of the Indian Reserve of the Township Viger" appears to have been added to the map (Crown Lands Department, Toronto dated 20 February 1858) that is appended to the handwritten document. On the detailed plan, the phrases "Indian Lands, 3,650 acres" and "Indian Reserve" appear.

At the time of the dissolution of the Viger reserve, elsewhere in Wolastokuk, municipalization was taking over a large part of the traditional lands

6. THE MALISEET: FROM RECOGNITION TO OBLIVION AND DISPERSAL

of the Maliseet (see map 52. In fact, thirty new townships were formed between 1852 and 1871. Since 1799, fifty townships had been formed on the traditional territory of the Maliseet with no agreements of cession or sale having been reached between government authorities and the Maliseet Nation. In addition, in 1854, seigneuries were incorporated as municipal districts in the same way that townships had been. This resulted in ninety-six municipalities with a population of 153,552, according to the 1871 census (see table 13).

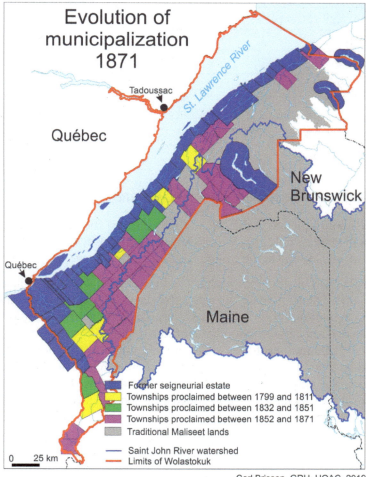

MAP 52 – Evolution of municipalization, 1871

TABLE 13 – Population in 1871

COUNTY	POPULATION IN 1871
Beauce	16,993
Bellechasse	17,697
Dorchester	13,486
Kamouraska	21,254
L'Islet	13,515
Lévis	22,475
Montmorency (île d'Orléans)	5,421
Rimouski	19,502
Témiscouata	22,491
Charlevoix (île aux Coudres)	718
Total	**153,552**

Source: Canadian Census, 1870–71, vol. 1, Ottawa, John I. B. Ottawa: John I. B. Taylor, 1878.

The Maliseet: "Unsettled" on their own land

As a consequence of the sale of their territory, the Maliseet scattered across their ancestral lands, Wolastokuk, as well as elsewhere in Québec, in New Brunswick, and in the United States.

In 1875–1876, attempts were made to obtain land for the Maliseet in Whitworth (Saint-François) but without success. The land there was unsuitable for agriculture. The Maliseet became an Indians without status or land, without rights outside the boundaries of their original Reserve no. 4, forgotten in their traditional territories and scattered. This was the model thst the Canadian federal system had imposed. A small parcel of land at the tip of Cacouna was inhabited by a few Maliseet until the early 1970s. The parcel, measuring 0.8 hectare, was purchased by the federal government on 8 July 1891 (Lechasseur 1993, 246).

The Maliseet continued to integrate into the communities where they took up residence and to practise their ancestral activities to the best of their ability, searching for their identity.

Research conducted by Laurence Johnson in 2001 on the consequences of the loss of the Viger reserve for the Maliseet confirmed the inability of both levels of government to respond adequately to the needs of the Maliseet. Fluctuating between sedentariness and mobility, the Indian Act has acted as a straitjacket from which public servants and the Maliseet themselves have had trouble escaping. The Maliseet want their ancestral territories to be respected even if they had asked for land or a village for those who wished to become landowners. The federal government's Indian Act establishes only one model, that of assimilation on micro-reserves. All references to the status of Peoples and Nations with which they had had alliances and treaties, as well as the rights to their traditional lands, are forgotten. Between *reserve* and *Indian territory*, Indigenous Peoples are caught in an administrative spiral whereby they are no longer allies but beggars, in the words of Innu leader Sylvain Ross (Girard and Brisson 2014, xiv).

In Johnson's (2001) report on the loss of Viger and the dramatic consequences it had for the Maliseet Nation in Québec, she stated that:

> thus, on the one hand, we have the Whitworth reserve whose characteristics never interested the Maliseet. However, for want of anything better, they agreed to try it. Consequently, some members lived on the reserve temporarily, mainly to cut wood; the income from the sale of wood was to be distributed to all. There were also problems of illegal cutting by Euro-Canadians [...]. On the other hand, the Cacouna reserve certainly met a need, although, at that time, it was mainly a summer encampment, while in winter the occupants scattered inland, close to their hunting grounds and wood for heating. Cacouna would, however, be used to house a few families permanently in the twentieth century [...], but the area of the reserve was insufficient to house the entire group. Thus, the Maliseet would find themselves with two inadequate reserves (our translation; Johnson 2001, 44).

The author concluded that the loss of their land led to the dissolution and dispersal of the Maliseet Nation in Québec:

> After the sale of the Viger reserve, the Whitworth and Cacouna reserves did not enable the group to stay in their communities. Scattered across the territory, intermarriage with Euro-Canadians helped families to integrate into the populations among which they lived. On the other hand, the few individuals who joined the Tobique reserve retained their "Indian ways" and were considered unfit for emancipation. Thus, it seems clear to us that the sale of the reserve caused the dispersal and dissolution of the Maliseet of Viger (our translation; Johnson 2001, 77).

The rapid action after the three Langevin brothers became involved, between 1867 (Confederation) and 1869 (the time of the sale), and the follow-up that found no solution that enabled the Maliseet to occupy land, confirms that policy and legislation discriminated against the fundamental rights of the Maliseet and, consequently, those of all Indigenous Peoples (Appendix, 2005, Viger Fiduciary Duty... on the fiduciary responsibility of governments; on post-Confederation Numbered Treaties and the concept of surrender applied to them, Krasowski 2019).

In 1987, the Maliseet Nation rose from this oblivion as a plan to revive the Nation took shape.

CHAPTER 7
From dispersal to the rebirth of the Wolastoqiyik Nation of the St. Lawrence

During the French and English colonial periods, Indigenous Peoples were allies and partners in trade and war, while welcoming and sharing territory and resources with the European conquerors.

The creation of the Canadian nation-state was an initiative of English- and French-speaking Canadian elites who decided to write a new history that excluded Indigenous Peoples from the new state they were founding. To do this, they set up commissions of inquiry with the aim of developing a discourse that would justify legislation that authorized usurping Indigenous territory and introducing the status of primitive and minor "Indian" under the guardianship of the state. The real conquest of Indigenous Peoples of Canada did not occur in 1534 with Jacques Cartier or with the Conquest of 1760 but with Confederation in 1867.

The history of Viger shows how the development of policy toward Indigenous Peoples, beginning in the 1850s in the United Province of Canada, systematically eliminated Indigenous Peoples from Confederation by alienating their rights to land and identity. In this respect, the Maliseet represented a kind of ideal, a dream come true, for those who, like Langevin and other Fathers of Confederation, saw the *Indian* as a "child" to be civilized. Hector-Louis Langevin, who had managed the Viger case with his brothers, recalled in 1876, when the Indian Act was being drafted, that Indians were not in the same position as White men. As a rule, they had no education, and they were like children to a very great extent. They, therefore, required a great deal more protection that [sic] White men (quoted in Appendix, 1994, Royal Commission...Making Treaties 1994, 29n77).

Beyond the political issues, what is surprising about the 1827 and 1869 documents is the change in vocabulary.

The 1826 text is in English only. It speaks of Indigenous persons who live on their "Hunting Grounds" and would like to found a village. No cession here, no sale, but "Waste Land." In the 1869 document, the terms *cession and sale* is clear, and the term *reserve* is used. Can there be "retrocession" (transferring back) when there had been no previous "cession"? At least, the 1827 documents of creation present as nothing other than an experiment that is an extension of the Royal Proclamation of 1763 but without "cede or sell," mirroring practice under the French regime. Could the Maliseet retrocede what they had never ceded? And by ceding this piece of village land, were they giving up their rights to their ancestral lands or hunting territory? Certainly not. Ceding or alienating rights to reserve land at no time implies that Indigenous Nations have ceded any rights to their traditional lands, no matter what governments may claim (Appendix, Malouf Decision, 1973).

WOLASTOQIYIK WAHSIPEKUK FIRST NATION (MALISEET NATION OF QUÉBEC)

During the 1960s, the Government of Québec nationalized companies that produced electricity, a process that had begun with the creation of Hydro-Québec in 1944. Government authorities saw control of this economic sector as an important vehicle for the socio-economic development of Québec society. In addition, a better knowledge of the hydraulic potential of watersheds made it possible to add new generating stations, particularly on the North Shore of the Saint Lawrence River. At the end of the 1960s, a great deal of research and planning was conducted with a view to proceeding with the hydroelectric development of James Bay, which lay in Indigenous territory.

In parallel with the intensive natural-resource development of Crown lands in Québec (former Indigenous territory) that had begun in the 1950s, the Canadian government was revisiting the rights of Indigenous Peoples and their policy toward them. The Statement of the Government of Canada on Indian Policy (White Paper) was introduced in the federal Parliament in 1969 (Indian Affairs and Northern Development, Jean Chrétien, 1968–1974).

THE 1969 WHITE PAPER AND THE CREATION OF INDIGENOUS ADVOCACY ORGANIZATIONS

Starting in the 1970s, both Québec and Canada sought to redefine their policies toward Indigenous Peoples. The resource potential of the North, which was occupied by Indigenous Nations, was attracting investors. Forced by the courts and by the efforts of various advocacy organizations, challenged by pressure from investors, both levels of government were obliged to recognize the rights of Indigenous Peoples in some fashion. With the repatriation of the Constitution in 1982, Indigenous Peoples sought to ensure that their rights were recognized and confirmed, even though the Indian Act of 1876, despite amendments, continued to apply.

Reconciling the recognition of the fundamental rights of Indigenous Peoples with a backdrop of historical and legal discrimination was becoming a major challenge for those who were re-examining public policy with the participation of Indigenous Peoples. Québec was also trying to redefine a separate policy toward Indigenous Nations by detailing, through a 1985 motion, a new relationship of equals with the Indigenous Nations on its territory that it recognized (Girard and Brisson 2014: 138–41).

At the federal level, the publication of Jean Chrétien's white paper (1969) launched the debate over a new Indian policy in Canada (Appendix, 1969, Jean Chrétien White Paper). The objectives were clear: to abolish the Indian Act and transfer to the provinces the responsibility for Indians and their territory. The desire to "fix" history by abolishing reserves and transferring everything to the provinces has been born. Easier said than done...

Indigenous Peoples opposed these changes. They insisted on being consulted and listened to on all aspects of their future before such important changes were proposed unilaterally. Without their agreement, the negation of 150 years of history through unilateral changes to a law, even if that law was hated by the *Indians*, could not be justified. A transfer of responsibility to the provinces also involved many legal and practical difficulties and would require constitutional amendments.

As the federal government and the provinces wrangled over policy toward Indigenous Peoples, several judicial decisions on claims by Indigenous Peoples were changing the views of politicians who had thought that the former had few or no rights. Governments committed themselves to various policies of recognition, and Indigenous political movements were organized as Indigenous rights to land and resources and issues related to their status became clearer.

Following the 1969 white paper, as Indigenous organizations restructured to better represent Peoples living on and off reserve, several court decisions changed the landscape by confirming that *Indigenous Peoples' rights had not been extinguished in Canada*. The Calder decision (Supreme Court of Canada, 1973) and the Malouf decision in the same year (Québec Superior Court) forced legislators to negotiate with Indigenous Peoples to re-establish new agreements based on nation-to-nation alliances. The federal government adopted a policy on Indigenous land claims. It also established a tribunal to oversee and monitor both comprehensive and specific negotiations (see *Specific Claims Tribunal of Canada*, 1973). It was because of judicial decisions that the Québec government was forced to negotiate with the Cree, Naskapi, and Inuit (James Bay and Northern Quebec Native Claims Settlement Act 1977; Northeastern Quebec Agreement 1978 [Naskapi]).

Two decisions were particularly significant for the province of Québec, where more than 90 percent of the land was First Nations or Inuit territory.

On 31 January 1973, the Supreme Court of Canada, through the *Calder decision*, confirmed the existence of Indigenous rights to land because they had occupied and used it before the Europeans. Subsequently, on 15 November 1973, the Superior Court of Québec, through the Malouf decision, recognized the rights of the Cree and Inuit and ordered the suspension of work on hydroelectric projects, which paved the way for negotiations and the conclusion, in 1975, of the James Bay and Northern Québec Agreement. In 1978, the Northeastern Québec Agreement was signed with the Naskapi (https://caid.ca/AgrNorEasQueA1974.pdf).

Judge Malouf called governments and historians to order by affirming in his decision the distinct character of Québec in matters of cession or surrender, since no treaty had alienated any rights of Indigenous Peoples in the province, as had been the case for the Robinson Treaties (1850) and the post-Confederation Numbered Treaties in other provinces.

> William McKim, a representative of the Department of Indian Affairs, produced, as exhibit P-15, fourteen treaties between the Crown, on the one hand, and certain tribes of Indians residing in different parts of Canada (west of the Province of Québec), on the other. In each of these treaties, the Indian tribes mentioned therein consented to cede, release and render to the Crown all the lands included in the territory described therein for the consideration established therein. In most of the treaties, the Crown recognized the right of the Indians to continue to pursue their hunting, trapping and fishing occupations throughout the ceded territory (p. 45). [...] The evidence also shows that the rights of the Cree and Inuit

populations were never extinguished. McKim, representing the Department of Indian Affairs, has stated that there are no treaties covering the cession of lands by the Indians in the province of Québec (our translation; Malouf 1973, 57; Appendix 1973).

In support of his subordinate, Vergette, the head of the Lands Division, Department of Indian Affairs,

> stated that the Department has no record of the extinguishment of any rights the Indians may have in the Province of Québec. There is also a reference in Order in Council P.C. 1569 dated August 1, 1907, Exhibit P-22/42 to the effect that no treaty has ever been made with the Indians of the Province of Québec for the cession to the Crown of the land comprised in that province.
>
> The Order in Council CP 1569 dated August 1, 1907 and assented to the same day (Exhibit P-22/42) states: "*That no treaty has ever been made with the Indians of the Province of Québec (formally Lower Canada) for the surrender to the Crown of the land understood in that province*; but small portions of Indian reserves have, within recent years, been surrendered to the Crown by different Bands in that province for the purpose of disposition for their benefit" (Appendix, 1973, Malouf decision, para. 77; our emphasis).

The James Bay and Northern Québec Agreement (1975) is one of these so-called modern treaties. This treaty, which became part of Canadian policy, obligated the Cree, Inuit, and Naskapi to *extinguish* (sic) their lands to the Crown (art. 2.6, *extinction* in French version).

In this context of claims by and affirmation of the Indigenous Peoples of Canada and Québec, including non-Status Indians (Girard and Brisson 2018), the repatriation of the Constitution took place in 1982. The government of Pierre Trudeau was therefore obligated to include a certain recognition of Indigenous Peoples in the new constitution.

THE CONSTITUTION ACT, 1982: REPATRIATION OF THE CONSTITUTION, ALONG WITH CONSTITUTIONAL RECOGNITION AND CONTINUING EXCLUSION OF INDIGENOUS PEOPLES

On 17 April 1982, Prime Minister Pierre Elliott Trudeau, Queen Elizabeth II, and Canada's attorney-general, Jean Chrétien, signed the Constitution Act of 1982, which includes the Charter of Rights and Freedoms and a procedure for constitutional amendments. Articles 25 and 35 refer to Indigenous Peoples and the recognition of their rights as distinct Peoples (Constitutional Act, 1982).

Article 25 states:

The guarantee in this Charter of certain rights and freedoms shall not be construed so as to abrogate or derogate from any aboriginal, treaty or other rights or freedoms that pertain to the aboriginal peoples of Canada including

(a) any rights or freedoms that have been recognized by the Royal Proclamation of October 7, 1763; and

(b) any rights or freedoms that now exist by way of land claims agreements or may be so acquired.

Article 35 states:

RIGHTS OF THE ABORIGINAL PEOPLES OF CANADA

(1) The existing aboriginal and treaty rights of the aboriginal peoples of Canada are hereby recognized and affirmed.

(2) In this Act, aboriginal peoples of Canada includes the Indian, Inuit and Métis peoples of Canada.

(3) For greater certainty, in subsection (1) treaty rights includes rights that now exist by way of land claims agreements or may be so acquired.

(4) Notwithstanding any other provision of this Act, the aboriginal and treaty rights referred to in subsection (1) are guaranteed equally to male and female persons.

The text makes explicit reference to the Royal Proclamation of 1763 and confirms the obligation to apply rights equally to males and females. It also calls for meetings to be held with the Indigenous Peoples of Canada, who are the "Indian, Inuit and Métis peoples," to discuss constitutional issues of specific concern to them.

Article 35 specifies the importance of respecting treaties: "treaty rights of the aboriginal peoples of Canada are hereby recognized and affirmed." Included are existing treaties between the parties (1603, 1666, 1701 (with France); 1725 to 1760 (with Great Britain), the Royal Proclamation of 1763, and those yet to be negotiated. The phrase "treaty rights of the aboriginal peoples of Canada are hereby recognized and affirmed" includes historical treaties (Marslall, Supreme Court of Canada 1999). At every opportunity, Maliseet Chiefs have been quick to emphasize that respect for their historical treaties and covenants is the core of the nation-to-nation relationship they wish to have with governments.

> For over 200 years, the Maliseet were important allies of the French and later the English. For more than two centuries, we were guides, trading partners and even brothers in arms. Unfortunately, these 200 years of alliance were followed

by a great period of darkness. A time when Maliseet people were shunned, ignored and even forgotten. Yet, although we have always inhabited and still inhabit this territory, Wolastokuk, for too long our rights, our traditions, and our way of life have been scorned.

I said earlier that our First Nation has a history of partnership with Canada. That partnership still exists and has evolved. Our territory, Wolastokuk, is today occupied by different forms of government authorities. Whether it is Canada, Québec, the MRCs [regional municipalities], or the municipalities, we recognize their presence and wish to work in collaboration with them.

Despite certain differences, the Maliseet of Viger First Nation and the inhabitants of this region share many issues. Whether it is economic development or the protection of our environment, the population of the region can consider us as allies (our translation; address by the Grand Chief of the Maliseet of Viger First Nation, Jacques Tremblay, Cacouna, 5 March 2019, quoted in Lebel 2019; Appendix 5 March 2019 Agreement. For the original French version).

The Province of Québec distanced itself from the federal government following the unilateral repatriation of the Constitution in 1982, meeting with the Indigenous Peoples of Québec to discuss a new relationship. The Québec government led by René Lévesque and the Parti Québécois worked with Indigenous Peoples to clarify relevant constitutional issues in preparation for the various federal-provincial meetings that followed repatriation. The government also held consultations that eventually enabled the development, for the first time in its history, of an official policy toward the Indigenous Nations in the province and toward the communities in which they lived. The Alliance autochtone du Québec (non-Status Indians) was invited to all consultations, and its representatives participated actively in all meetings. In 1985, the *Assemblée nationale* (provincial legislature) adopted a motion recognizing the fundamental rights of Indigenous Peoples (*Débats de l'Assemblée nationale*, 19 March 1985; Girard and Brisson 2014, 2018).

In January 1978, facing difficulty in applying the terms of the James Bay and Northern Québec Agreement, the Québec government created the *Secrétariat des activités gouvernementales en milieu autochtone (amérindien) et inuit* (secretariat for government activities in Indigenous and Inuit regions). The new secretariat assumed the responsibilities of both the *Direction générale du Nouveau-Québec* (agency that administered northern Québec) and the *Bureau de coordination de l'Entente de la Baie-James* (office that coordinated the James Bay agreement), created in the meantime. Its mandate was to coordinate government activities with Indigenous Peoples and to develop a comprehensive policy for Indigenous and Inuit regions (Appendix, 2013, J.-Y. Morin on René Lévesque and the fundamental rights of Indigenous Peoples in Québec).

A first meeting with Québec Indigenous leaders, including the *Alliance autochtone du Québec*, was held in December 1978. For the first time since the Grande Paix de Montréal of 1701, said Jacques-Yvan Morin (2013)—since the first treaty of alliance of 1603 near Tadoussac, we might add—the government was having fruitful discussions with Indigenous Peoples about the recognition of Indigenous Nations in Québec. These discussions dealt with issues of nation-to-nation recognition and economic, social (education, health, communications), and cultural development. The meetings set the stage for subsequent discussions surrounding the repatriation of the constitution in 1982 and Québec's actions at that time. Premier René Lévesque convened various Indigenous leaders to prepare a plan that they would find satisfactory. These consultations led, with the 1985 motion and Bill 99, An Act respecting the exercise of the fundamental rights and prerogatives of the people of Québec and the Québec State (Bill 99, November 2000), to the first official policy of recognition of Indigenous Peoples and Nations by the State of Québec. Expressing its will in motions and laws, Québec changed *Status Indians under the Indian Act* to Indigenous Peoples and Nations identified by name, with specific rights regarding *self-government, their rights to own and control land, and their cultural rights (languages, traditions), including rights to participate in economic development within Québec* (copy of the Bill 99: Girard and Brisson 2014: 142–7).

AMENDMENT OF THE INDIAN ACT (1985): THE FEDERAL GOVERNMENT'S OBSESSION WITH EXTINGUISHMENT (ABSOLUTE SURRENDER)

In the 1985 amendment of the Indian Act, the term "surrender" was further clarified by prioritizing the concept of *absolute surrender (cession à titre absolu)*. The term *band* was still used to refer to Indigenous Peoples who remained Status Indians within the meaning of the act.

The 1951 Act had earlier made several changes to sections 37 and 38, which dealt with surrender, stating that "a band may surrender to His Majesty any right or interest of the band and its members in a reserve." The term "surrender" was defined as follows (sec. 38.2): "A surrender may be absolute or qualified, conditional or unconditional."

Amendments to the act in 1985 changed this definition:

37. (1) Lands in a reserve shall not be sold nor title to them conveyed until they have been absolutely surrendered to Her Majesty pursuant to subsection 38(1) by the band for whose use and benefit in common the reserve was set apart.

38. (1) A band may absolutely surrender to Her Majesty, conditionally or unconditionally, all of the rights and interests of the band and its members in all or part of a reserve. (L.R. (1985), ch. I-5, art. 38; L.R. (1985), ch. 17 (4^e suppl.), art. 2.)

The amendment cited above clarified the concept of surrender, which was now "absolute," which contradicted the Constitution Act of 1982 (sec. 35). How could constitutional rights be recognized and the *Indian Act*, which continued to exist, require as "absolute" the extinguishment of those rights? The word *band* was still being used to designate an Indigenous People. Thus, in 1987, the Maliseet, like all Indigenous Peoples in Canada, were designated not as a People or a Nation but as an *Indian band*—from *tribe* in the Proclamation of 1763 to *band* in Canada in 1867—in order to obtain recognition, in spite of the fact that they did not have a "reserve."

However, if the law specified that "bands may ... surrender," this also meant that Indigenous Nations *did not have to surrender*, if this required extinguishing and subjugating their rights, and could find other ways to manage their members, lands, and resources that were more closely related to their cultural identity. The Agreement-in-Principle of General Nature signed by the Innu Nations of Québec with the federal and provincial governments is emblematic of this desire to conclude modern nation-to-nation treaties of recognition without extinguishing the fundamental rights of Indigenous Peoples (Agreement, 2004).

REBIRTH OF THE MALISEET OF VIGER FIRST NATION, 27 AND 28 JUNE 1987 IN RIVIÈRE-DU-LOUP

After the debates over the repatriation of the Canadian constitution in 1982 and the recognition of Indigenous Nations by Québec, the Maliseet Nation was not one of the Nations recognized. Jean-Marie Aubin took it upon himself to reassemble and refound the Maliseet of Viger First Nation. He wrote repeatedly to federal and provincial governments, asking either the premier, the minister responsible for Indigenous affairs, or public servants to organize a formal election in 1987 to elect the first band council since 1869 (see Appendices 1986 and 1987).

He succeeded in gathering 132 members and an interim council, and they refounded the Maliseet of Viger First Nation. These members were from thirty families (spouses, brothers, and sisters) that were mainly from three extended families: the Aubins, the Launières, and the Nicolas/Nicholas, the last being the most numerous.

The elections for the first *band* council were held on 27 and 28 June 1987, with sixty-two registered members voting in the city of Rivière-du-Loup. The election was held according to traditional practice because, since the 1951 amendments to the Indian Act, only residents of a reserve could vote in the election of a "band" council. Using the traditional method of appointing the Band Council circumvented this problem.

First elected council of the Maliseet Nation of Québec

MINUTES OF THE GENERAL MEETING, 27–28 JULY 1987 (56 VOTERS; 62 REGISTERED)
Traditional method of election (Source: Appendix, 1987. Foundation Assembly, 4)
Jean-Marie Aubin, Grand Chief Other elected Chiefs Johanne Aubin Claude Aubin Guy Launière Léandre Nicolas

The federal government was made aware of the event and recognized the Maliseet, who had previously established conditions for membership of the Nation, which governments had been calling "a group of Indians" associated with a "band" since 1985.

A resolution (n.d., about 1986–1987) of the Chiefs of the Assembly of First Nations of Québec (AFNQ) also recognized the Maliseet of Viger First Nation as a full member of the First Nations of Québec (Appendix, 1986, Application for Funding…, 186ff).

The AFNQ resolution confirmed that Grand Chief Jean-Marie Aubin had been acting as interim Chief since his appointment by a majority of members in April 1986. The AFNQ also stated that Minister David Crombie, federal minister of Indian Affairs, had recognized this distinct First Nation and that the federal government must financially support the Maliseet Nation in the future.

> The AFNQ also stated that the Waban-Aki Council had recognized the Maliseet Nation. Created in 1979, the council represented the Abenaki communities of Odanak and Wolinak. The Assembly of First Nations of Québec encouraged communication between closely related nations, in this case the Abenaki.
>
> On 30 May 1989, the Assemblée nationale (Québec legislature) also recognized the Maliseet Nation by resolution, just as it had the ten other Indigenous Nations on 20 March 1985. The Province of Québec confirmed that the Maliseet could sign agreements to ensure the exercise of their
>
> - right to autonomy within Québec;
> - right to their culture, language, and traditions;
> - right to own and control land;
> - right to hunt, fish, trap, harvest, and participate in the management of wildlife resources;
> - right to participate in and benefit from the economic development of Québec to enable them to develop as a distinct Nation with its own identity and to exercise their rights within Québec.
>
> (our translation; Appendix, 1989, Québec reconnaissance nation malécite; Girard and Brisson 2018, 187–8)

List of members of Maliseet of Viger First Nation as of 30 November 1986

The 132 founding members of the Maliseet First Nation of Viger comprises thirty families (spouses and siblings totalling seventy persons) and sixty-two individuals.

The Nation consists mainly of persons belonging to the Aubin, Launière, and Nicolas/Nicholas families.

LIST OF MEMBERS COMPRISING THE MALISEET FIRST NATION OF VIGER AS OF 30 NOVEMBER 1986[1]

AUBIN, Louis, and AUBIN, Marie-Luce; AUBIN, Jean-Marie, and AUBIN, Gaétane; AUBIN, Caroline; AUBIN, Roland; AUBIN, (Desormeaux) Jeannette; AUBIN, Philippe, and AUBIN, Gabrielle; AUBIN, Emeline (Carle); AUBIN, Denise; AUBIN, Nicole (Plante); AUBIN, Marcel, and AUBIN, Helene; AUBIN, Suzanne (Forster); AUBIN, France (Simard); AUBIN, Jean-François, and AUBIN, Nicole; AUBIN, Ginette (Dubois); AUBIN, Richard; AUBIN, Marie-Claude; AUBIN, Christian; AUBIN, Joel; AUBIN, Louise (Fahmi); BRIÈRE, André, and BRIÈRE, Monique; BRIÈRE, Régent, and BRIÈRE, Denise; LAUNIÈRE, Gertrude (Durand); LAUNIÈRE, Albert; LAUNIÈRE, Antoine; LAUNIÈRE, Éva (Lauzon); LAUNIÈRE, Marie (Gauthier); LAUNIÈRE, Lucienne; LAUNIÈRE, Marcel; LAUNIÈRE, Guy; LAUNIÈRE, Diane; LAUNIÈRE, Guylaine; NICHOLAS, Carmelle; NICHOLAS, Raymonde (Edgar); NICHOLAS, John Scott, and NICHOLAS, Rose Marie, NICHOLAS, Deanna Fay; NICHOLAS, Leopold, and NICHOLAS, Diana; NICHOLAS, Joseph (Laur); NICHOLAS, Evelyn (Allen); NICHOLAS, Maurice, and NICHOLAS, Yvette; NICHOLAS, Angéline; NICHOLAS, Aurile, and NICHOLAS, Dolores Ève; NICOLAS, Reginald; NICOLAS, Anita (Mullen); NICOLAS, Ninette (Dubois); NICOLAS, Léandre, and NICOLAS, Odette, NICOLAS, Stéphane, and NICOLAS, Frédérick; NICOLAS, Jean-Guy, and NICOLAS, Ida Dolores, NICOLAS, Guy Raymond; NICOLAS, Rose Délima; NICOLAS, Gaétane; NICOLAS, Denise; NICOLAS, Paul Régent; NICOLAS, Yvon Léo Paul; NICOLAS, Raymond; NICOLAS, Stella; NICOLAS, Julie Ann; NICOLAS, Ernest Daniel, and NICOLAS, Naomi, NICOLAS, Jason Alex, NICOLAS, Ryan Dennis, and NICOLAS, Peter Daniel; NICOLAS, Nikki Jo Victoria; NICOLAS, Gérald Louis; NICOLAS, Martin Gérald; NICOLAS, Elise Claudelle; NICOLAS, David Raymond; NICOLAS, David Brian; NICOLAS, Michael.

REGULAR REGISTRANTS

AUBIN, Lori Ann; AUBIN, Yan, and AUBIN, Edith; AUBIN, Céline; AUBIN, Maria, AUBIN, Julie; AUBIN, Claude; AUBIN, François; AUBIN, Marlène (Girardot), and AUBIN, Richard; BRIÈRE, Claude, and BRIÈRE, Diane; BRIÈRE, Elaine; BRIÈRE, Stéphane; BRIÈRE, Rémi; FAHMI, Moad, Naima; GLASGOW, Paula AUBIN, GLASGOW, James, and GLASGOW, Christopher; LAUNIÈRE, Jacqueline; LAUNIÈRE, Gaston, and COMEAU, Lorraine; LEVESQUE, Nicole, and LEVESQUE, Jean-Claude; NICOLAS,

---

1. Source: Appendix, 1986, Nation Malécite de Viger, 1986, *Première assemblée de la Nation Malécite du Québec depuis 1869*, document interne, WWFN).

Laurentienne; NICOLAS, Michael; NICOLAS, Jerry; NICOLAS, Guylaine, and NICOLAS, Sylvain; NICOLAS, Marie-Paule; NICOLAS, Jean, NICOLAS, Marie-Reine, NICOLAS, Lise, NICOLAS, Danny, and NICOLAS, Sandra; NICOLAS, Roger;

REGISTERED. Bill C-31

CAPISTAN, #, Jean-Paul, CAPISTAN, Caroll, CAPISTAN, Nancy, and CAPISTAN, Line; CAPISTAN, Jean-Claude, #, CAPISTAN, Ginette, CAPISTAN Germain, CAPISTAN, Serge (age 12), and CAPISTAN, Chantale (aged 10); CAPISTAN, Jacques; DESORMEAUX, Michel, #011701; DESORMEAUX, Jean-Paul, #011701; DESORMEAUX, Lise; DESORMEAUX, Thérèse; LEBLANC, Édouard, and LEBLANC, Linda, and LEBLANC, Jason Édouard; LEBLANC, Maurice; LEBLANC, Donald.

FROM THE FRENCH REGIME TO THE PRESENT: MALISEET FAMILIES THAT HAVE MADE CLAIMS OR AND AFFIRMED THE CULTURE OF THE WOLASTOQIYIK

Signatories in 1725-1726[2]

A quick scan of the signatures on the Treaty of 1725 and ratified in 1726 reveals several surnames found among members of the present Wolastoqiyik Wahsipekuk First Nation or in other Indigenous Nations of Québec. It is not always obvious to distinguish first names and surnames; for example, *Joseph, Paul, Denis, Baptiste, Jean-Baptiste, and Germain* are first names that have become surnames and can be found among Indigenous Nations in Québec. For 1726, we have listed surnames that are common in present-day Québec and, where relevant, names associated with a totem or a grand globe (Chief, Grand Chief), that have also become surnames. Additional research would further clarify the links between the families of the past and those of the present.

The same surnames have been in use over a long period of time, which testifies to a desire, for the Maliseet, to claim, affirm, and perpetuate their identity as an Indigenous Nation. It is through family dynamics that issues related to affirmation and transmission of identity seem to play out.

---

2. See Appendix 4 at the end of the book.

Surnames in 1726 ratification

Among the original signatories to the treaty were several Indigenous representatives who had French names. Some names indicated where a person came from, particularly "St John."

Chiefs *Nicholas* Nipimoit, St. John, was first to sign, with *Paul* Tecumart and *Joseph* Ounaginitish of Cape Sable. Following, below another group of signatures from St. John, *Obin* was the first signatory, *Pierre X Benoît* was the second, and *Denis* the third, all of whom were well known among the Maliseet Nation. Pierre Benoît took part in several other signings, including the Treaty of 1760. In addition to the many first names that followed (*Louis, Joseph, François*) were *St Obin* and *Joseph* (three times as totem, or head of family) and *Jean Baptist* (totem). The surname *Attanas* also appeared in the Treaty of 1726. *Jirome son of was* the representative from Richibucto.

The families *Joseph* (totem le grand), *Claude*, *René* (also *Reny*) *François* (grand globe), *Étienne, Noël, Philippe, Bernard, Tomus* and *Tomas*, and *Denis* also appear. Several of these same surnames were found among the Maliseet in 1869 (Appendix, 1869; Appendix, 2001, Johnson 2001, 16–17; Appendix, 2001…).

Like Johnson, we think it reasonable that, in the course of time, French first names became more prevalent and Indigenous names were no longer used. These first names sometimes took over, becoming well-known surnames in Québec.

Among the signatories to the Treaty of 1726 was a certain *Petit Jermain*, a *François Jermain* (*Germain* among the Innu) and *Pisnett* (*Pinet*).

There were also *Pierre Paul* (there are many Paul families among the Innu Nation) in 1749 and 1760–1761, *François* Gorman in 1749, and *François Germain* in 1760–1761, (surnames also found in Mashteuiatsh among the Innu), as well as *Pierre Bennoit* in 1749 and 1760–1761. (Pierre Benoît was the second signatory to the Treaty of 1726, part of a group representing Saint John.)

The Maliseet, the American War of Independence, and the Treaty of 1776: *St-Aubin, Thomas, Jenniss…*

During the American War of Independence, in September 1775, Pierre Tomah and Ambroise St Aubin were identified as Chiefs of the Saint John River. They went to the Penobscot trading post to meet with their long-time faithful allies to prepare for negotiations with the Americans on behalf of their Nation.

> We heartily join with our brethren the Penobscot Indians in all that they have or shall agree with our brethren in the Massachusetts colony and are resolved to stand together and oppose the people of Old England that are endeavoring to take your's and our lands and liberties from us. [...] We have nowhere to look to for assistance but to you and we desire that you will help us to a priest that he may pray with us to God Almighty. We have no place to go but Penobscot for support, and we desire you would provide us with ammunition, provisions and goods for us there, and we will come in there and give you our furs and skins and take our support from you in return and will be thankful to you for your kindness (quoted in Raymond [1895] n.d.).

In February 1776, General Washington wrote a letter to the Chiefs of the Mi'kmaq and Maliseet. His letter was accompanied by wampum, according to Indigenous tradition with respect to alliances. In the letter, Washington presents the advantages of joining the Americans in the conflict against the British government (Raymond [1895] n.d.).

In accordance with the tradition of exchanges and of support during armed conflict, talks continued with the Maliseet Chief, Pierre Tomah, who went to Washington's headquarters on the Delaware River with a group of warriors. During this meeting, Washington reminded them of the *long friendship that linked the parties and had led to the signing of treaties* (Raymond, [1895] n.d.). This alliance was formalized in the Treaty of Watertown (1776), which bound the Maliseet of the Saint John River to the Americans (Appendix: Treaty of 1776, known as the Treaty of Watertown).

During the formal exchanges that preceded the signing of the treaty, on 19 July 1776, Chief Ambroise St. Aubin acted on behalf of the Maliseet. He presented the letter sent by Washington the preceding February. He then showed the Americans a copy of the treaty signed in Halifax in 1760, in which his Nation had pledged allegiance to the king of England, just as they had done previously with the king of France (Raymond [1895] n.d.; on the Treaty of 1760–1761, Supreme Court of Canada 1999, Marshall decision, 467–69).

One outcome of this alliance was that on 16 November 1776, during the American siege of Fort Cumberland at the head of the Bay of Fundy, a group of 140 Maliseet warriors from the Saint John and Passamaquoddy Rivers joined the troops. A certain number of them were from the eighty Maliseet families then living in the "Maliseet capital of Aukpaque." Aukpaque, now Springhill, is located six kilometres west of present-day Fredericton in New Brunswick (Clarke 1995, 217).

Among the list of combatants are the names of sixteen Maliseet, including Jean and Michel Baptiste as well as three Tomahs: Joseph, Joseph junior, and Pierre, the latter not being the Grand Chief of the same name.

The name Antoine Tuennis (Att. Juennis), living near Woodstock, New Brunswick, in 1788, appears among the Maliseet combatants (Clarke 1995, 217). It is undoubtedly the same JUENNIS, ATT. identified as a "St. John's Indian" who was associated with the territory of Maine (Grundset 2008, 23).

W. O. Raymond ([1895] n.d.) stated that, of the sixteen Malecite combatants at Fort Cumberland, at least five were living near Woodstock in 1788, namely Att. Juennis, Tomo Squatapan, Pierre Tomer, Joseph Tomer, and one named Bazil. Both Tomers [sic] and Tomo Squatapan / Thomas Quodpan (written in both forms in the text) lived, in 1790, at the mouth of the Becaquimec River in present-day Hartland, New Brunswick (Raymond [1895] n.d.).

Maliseet families from 1869 to 1987: St-Aubin, Athanas, Nicolas, Denis...

The surname Aubin (St-Aubin) continued to be associated with claims made by the Maliseet Nation of Québec. Chief François Étienne St-Aubin signed the document of the sale as the first Chief of the Maliseet Nation of Viger (4 August 1869). Félix Étienne St-Aubin signed as the thirteenth of seventeen signatories. Among the other signatories were five Athanas, one Nicolas, three Denis, two Joseph, and one Bernard. The signature of Joseph Laurent also appears (Paul Laurent had signed the Treaty of 1760–1761).

During the negotiations to refound the Maliseet Nation in 1986, Jean-Marie, the leader of the Aubin family, was elected Grand Chief of the new council during the elections of 27 and 28 June 1987. Two other elected Chiefs were Aubins, and the others were a Launière and a Nicolas. The Aubin, Launière, Nicolas, and Nicholas families were highly involved in the creation of the council in 1987 and in the revitalization of the Maliseet Nation.

Maliseet families in 1869

The surname Atanas (Jirome Attanas, Chief and first signatory from Richibucto in 1726) is still well known to Maliseet today. The Athanas/Atanas families were present in 1869, and five of them signed the act: Jean, the second Chief of the Nation; Jean senior; and Antoine, Thomas, and Laurent.

In the lists drawn up by Johnson (2001), the Thomas and Aubin, Laurent and St-Aubin, and Athanas and Thomas families, for example, are connected by several marriages.

Among the families associated with the Maliseet of Viger Nation in 1869 were the following:

- eight Thomas families (including one associated with Thomas St-Aubin)
- six Athanase families (Tanase, Athanas)
- six Denis families
- six Nicolas families
- four Launière families
- surnames appearing three times: St-Aubin, Bernard, Étienne (Thomas/St-Aubin), Joseph, Lesourd (Paul), and Laporte
- surnames appearing twice only: Noël and Reny (René)
- surnames appearing only once: Francis, Grey (two signatories to the act, James and Francis), Laurent (St. Aubin)

(Appendix, 2001, Johnson 2001, 79–89).

From signatories to the 1726 treaties to the present day: Families involved in cultural transmission and in claims

Among the signatures to Maliseet treaties in 1726 were more than sixty persons with the names Obin, St Obin, Denis and Athanas. In 1775–1776, during the American War of Independence, the St-Aubin, Baptiste, Thomas, and Jenniss families either participated in treaty negotiations or as combatants. In 1826, at the time of the request for land that would enable them to leave New Brunswick and settle in Québec, the hundred or so Maliseet were represented by Thomas or Tamas, who were in fact Maliseet of the St-Aubin clan. Later, in 1869, at the time of the sale of the Viger lands, the list of the Maliseet Nation included some fifty-five families, among which were typical surnames like St-Aubin, Thomas, Athanas, Denis, Nicolas, Nicholas, Launière, Noël, Reny, and Grey.

At the time of the refounding of the Maliseet Nation in 1987, the 132 members of the list consisted of thirty families (seventy persons) and sixty-two individuals. The Aubins, the Nicolas/Nicholas, and the Launières played an important part in the Maliseet Nation's revival.

For nearly three centuries, certain surnames have stood out in the Nation's affairs (see table 14). Among the members of the current Nation in Québec, the Nicolas/Nicholas, Jenniss, Aubin, Brière, Launière, Athanase, Denis, Thomas, and many other families are ensuring the continuity of the Maliseet culture in Québec (Chopin n.d-a, n.d-b; Clarke 1995; Grundset 2008; Raymond 1895).

TABLE 14 – Families involved in claims by and the recognition of the Maliseet Nation

TREATY OF 1725-1726	TREATY OF 1776 AND THE AMERICAN WAR OF INDEPENDENCE	CLAIMS OF 1826		MALISEET FAMILIES 1869	REBUILDING THE MALISEET NATION 1987	WOLASTOQEY NATION 2019
St Johns: Nicholas (chief) (1st signatory)	St-Aubin, Ambroise/ Ambrose 2nd Chief of the Maliseet Nation	Louis Tomas (Louis Thomas St-Aubin)	Louis Tomas (Louis Thomas St-Aubin)	François Étienne St-Aubin (1st chief)	Nicolas and Nicholas	Nicolas and Nicholas
St John's – X mark: Obin (1st signatory)	Baptiste, Jean and Michel	Joseph Thomas (Joseph Thomas St-Aubin)	Joseph Thomas (Joseph Thomas St-Aubin)	Jean Athanas (2nd chief)	Aubin	Jennis
St John's – X mark: Pierre Benoit (2nd signatory)	Tomer, Peter and Joseph/ Tomah/ Tommah/			Antoine Athanas (senior)	Launière	Aubin
	Tuennis, Antoine/Att. Juennis (Jennis)					Brière
St John's – X mark: Denis (3rd signatory)				Joseph Nicolas		Launière
St John's – X mark: Piuse Paul				Thomas Athanas		Athanase
St John's – X mark: Jofeph St-Obin				Laurent Athanas		Denis
Refhiboucto/ Ritchibucto: Jiron of Athanas (chief) (1st signatory)				Félix Etienne St-Aubin		
Chikanicto/Chignecto: René Grand Glode (5th signatory)				MAIN FAMILIES		

7. FROM DISPERSAL TO THE REBIRTH OF THE WOLASTOQIYIK NATION

TREATY OF 1725-1726	TREATY OF 1776 AND THE AMERICAN WAR OF INDEPENDENCE	CLAIMS OF 1826	MALISEET FAMILIES 1869	REBUILDING THE MALISEET NATION 1987	WOLASTOQEY NATION 2019
Pentaquit: Petit Jermain (1st signatory)			8 Thomas families		
Pentaquit: Pierre Pisnett (2nd signatory)			6 Athanas families (Atanas, Tamas, Athenas)		
Pentaquit: Rény Nectabau			6 Denis families		**LEGEND**
Annapolis Royal: Baptist Thomas (chief) (1st signatory)			5 Nicolas (Nicholas) families		ATHANAS, ATONAS, ATHÉNAS
Annapolis Royal: Jean Pisnett (2nd signatory)			4 Launière families		BRIÈRE
Annapolis Royal: François Jermain (3rd signatory)			3 families Bernard Joseph Lesourd, Laporte		DENIS
Passamaquoddy: Thomas Outine (Obin ? Aubin ?)			3 families St-Aubin Étienne (St-Aubin)		JENNISS
					LAUNIERE
Coast/Côte: Jacques Denis (3rd signatory); Louis Lavoint, Jean Pinet			Other families St. Laurent (St-Aubin)		NICOLAS, NICHOLAS
			Reny Noël		OBIN, AUBIN, ST-OBIN, ST-AUBIN
			Paul Joseph (widow Élisabeth Gervais Therrien). Francis Grey Laporte, Picard, etc		TOMAS, THOMAS, TOMAH, TOMMERS

This overview has not considered the many alliances that bind these families together, either by marriage or otherwise, nor that new families are joining with the contemporary Nation, increasing diversity and sometimes conflict. The sole purpose of this examination has been to show that certain families have been, over an extended period of time, deeply involved with the aspirations, expression, and transmission of Maliseet culture.

The status members of the Wolastoqiyik Wahsipekuk Maliseet Nation in present-day Québec: The diaspora continues

At the time of writing (2019), the Maliseet First Nation of Viger has 1,202 registered members, divided into two linguistic groups: 1,057 francophones and 145 anglophones. There are slightly more females (622) than males (580). Beyond these data, the Maliseet First Nation of Viger, now the Walastoqiyik Wahsipekuk, stands out widely scattered over Québec, Canada, and even the United States (see table 15). This dispersal is a direct consequence of the absence of an "occupiable" territory that can accommodate those who wish to return in the community to which they belong.

It should be noted that this dispersal has increased since 1870, when 68.2 percent of members of the Nation resided within Wolastokuk. Today, only 20.4 percent of the members live within its boundaries.

Currently, status members of the Walastoqiyik Wahsipekuk live in all administrative regions of Québec except Northern Québec (Nord-du-Québec). A majority of the status members are found within the boundaries of Wolastokuk (240) or in contiguous regions (see map 53). The regions of North Shore (Côte-Nord; 251); Lower St Lawrence (Bas-Saint-Laurent; 176); National Capital (Capitale-Nationale; 139), Saguenay-Lac-Saint-Jean (88), and Chaudière-Appalaches (53) contain 707 registered members, representing 68.9 percent of the total number of status members living in Québec (1,037). The Montréal (53) and Lanaudière (58) regions also have several members.

It must be admitted that the process of municipalization achieved its goal. Within the boundaries of Wolastokuk are 205 municipalities with a population of 447,060, including 240 Maliseet. Map 54 clearly shows that this territory is highly municipalized. Seven undeveloped territories (territoires non organisés) remain under the jurisdiction of regional municipalities (MRCs).

Even though the Wolastokuk territory is highly municipalized, 7,212 square kilometres of Crown land (exclusive of marine areas) remain of the total area of 32,990 square kilometres. This is traditional Maliseet

7. FROM DISPERSAL TO THE REBIRTH OF THE WOLASTOQIYIK NATION

territory to which title has not been extinguished, according to the 1973 Malouf decision. Part of this Crown land is also undeveloped territory, as mentioned above (see map 55. Finally, some of the Crown land is located within the Rivière du Loup and Madawaska River watersheds and the transitional territory between the two (the Rivière des Trois-Pistoles watershed and part of that of the Saint John River) located within the boundaries of the Wolastokuk territory and in Québec.

TABLE 15 – Distribution of registered members by place of residence, 2019

TERRITORY OF RESIDENCE	NUMBER	PERCENTAGE
United States	**97**	**8.3 %**
Arizona	3	
California	7	
Colorado	2	
Connecticut	7	
Florida	7	
Georgia	3	
Massachusetts	1	
Maine	54	
Missouri	1	
North Carolina	1	
New Hampshire	3	
Nevada	1	
New York	2	
Ohio	1	
Oregon	2	
Texas	2	

TERRITORY OF RESIDENCE	NUMBER	PERCENTAGE
Québec	1,037	88.3 %
Elsewhere in Canada	40	3.4 %
Alberta	4	
British Columbia	2	
New Brunswick	4	
Nova Scotia	3	
Ontario	23	
Northwest Territories	3	
Total	1,174	100 %

Note: Only status members for whom we had complete postal addresses are included. Source, Wolastoqiyik Wahsipekuk First Nation (WWFN)

Within the undeveloped and municipalized territories outlined above, there are certainly places where the Walastoqiyik Wahsipekuk First Nation and the municipalities could partner in the development of regional projects such as housing and the protection and enhancement of hunting, fishing, and trapping activities. The eventual creation of a) future Territorial Regime will require an exhaustive study of plans for the use of Crown land, MRC development plans, and municipal land-use plans in order to better understand future directions for development, land use, and infrastructure. The creation of a regional municipality must also occur in consultation with the members of the Nation.

7. FROM DISPERSAL TO THE REBIRTH OF THE WOLASTOQIYIK NATION 225

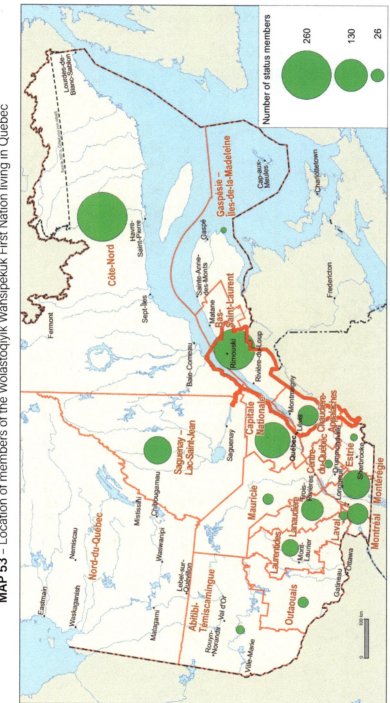

MAP 53 – Location of members of the Wolastoqiyik Wahsipekuk First Nation living in Québec

MAP 54 – Evolution of municipalization, 2019

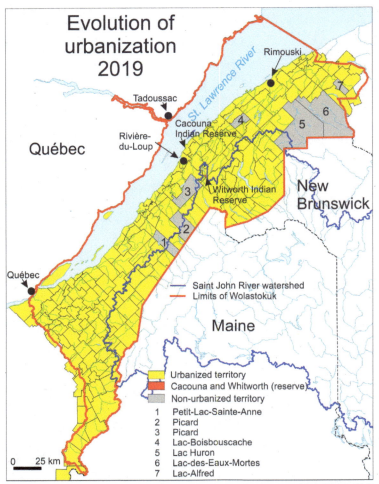

7. FROM DISPERSAL TO THE REBIRTH OF THE WOLASTOQIYIK NATION

MAP 55 – Land ownership, 2019

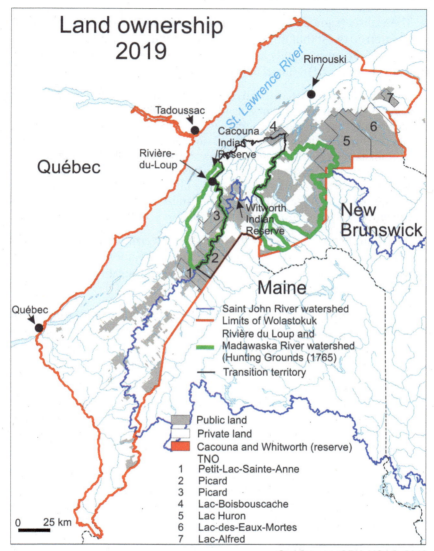

Restoring the nation-to-nation relationship

The Maliseet signed a framework agreement with the federal government on 5 March 2019. At that time, Grand Chief Jacques Tremblay pointed out that talks had begun as early as 2000 and then resumed in 2017 to prepare the final document. He stated in his speech that

> this is the first time we have been recognized in this way by the Government of Canada. The agreement allows us to negotiate with Canada on a nation-to-nation, government-to-government basis. It will allow us to start planning other agreements [...]. Although we have always lived and continue to live on this land, for too long our rights, our traditions, and our way of life have been violated. Fortunately, members of our First Nation have stood up and fought for recognition. About thirty years ago, the Maliseet of Viger First Nation was officially recognized by Canada and Québec (our translation; Signing of framework agreement, Maliseet/Government of Canada, 5 March 2019, see Appendix 2019).

According to the First Nation, the Canadian government was recognizing not only the existence of the Maliseet of Viger First Nation (now the Walastoqiyik Wahsipekuk First Nation) but also the ancestral rights stemming from different treaties.

Like the Grand Chief of the Maliseet of Québec, the federal minister of Crown-Indigenous Relations and Northern Affairs Canada, Carolyn Bennett, stressed the importance for the government to change its approach to Indigenous Peoples and to adapt to the priorities of each Indigenous Nation:

> It is the first step in a process towards self-determination. It is a recognition of rights, a mark of respect, a cooperative approach and a true partnership [...]. It's very important to have a flexible approach and to focus on the priorities of each nation (Signing of framework agreement, Maliseet/Government of Canada, 5 March 2019).

The agreement enabled further development of a commercial fishery that had been underway since the 2000s. New land-acquisition projects, the port of Cacouna and adjacent lands, and microenterprise development could also proceed (Calderhead 2011).

New resources could be allocated to economic, social, and cultural development. The development of a Passamaquoddy-Maliseet-French dictionary would promote the teaching and learning of the spoken and written language. Resources would be available to promote Maliseet arts in Québec in theatre, painting, music, cinema, and new media (web pages, web applications, and smartphone language-learning applications).

On the political level and regarding the assertion of the rights of Indigenous Peoples, representatives of the Maliseet, Innu, Abenaki and, Attikamek signed an international agreement on 6 June 2019 in Québec (city). The Chiefs affirmed in a solemn treaty their right to self-determination and self-government on their ancestral lands (see map 56. The joint declaration states

> that the relationship between our signatory First Nations be based on the recognition and respect of our rights, needs and culture, while promoting mutual assistance, cooperation, exchange and partnerships, as our ancestors would have done; That our signatory First Nations be the guardians of these commitments and ensure their implementation (Lebel 2019; Appendix 7: Solemn Declaration of Mutual Respect and Inter-Nation Alliance, 16 May 2019).

This agreement, based on the right to self-determination and the inherent right to self-government, demonstrates a clear commitment to confirm and solidify the relationship between Nations. It binds the Innu First Nations of Pekuakamiulnuatsh (Mashteuiatsh), Essipit, Pessamit, the W8banaki Nation of Wôlinak and Odanak, the Wolastoqiyiq Wahsipekuk First Nation, and the Attikamek Nations of Manawan and Wemotaci.

230 ALLIANCES AND TREATIES WITH INDIGENOUS PEOPLES OF QUÉBEC

MAP 56 – Ancestral lands covered by the 2019 declaration

Representation of ancestral territories
- Innu First Nations of Pessamit, Essipit and Mashteuiatsh
- Attikamekw Nation (Manawan and Wemotaci)
- W8banaki Nation (Wôlinak and Odanak - Canadian portion of the territory)
- Wolastoqiyik Wahsipekuk First Nation (WWFN)

0   50   100 km

1:5 500 000

General conclusion

THE MALISEET PEOPLE, FROM FIRST CONTACT TO THE NINETEENTH CENTURY: A PEOPLE OF ALLIANCES AND TREATIES

This study has shown that the Maliseet/Wolastoqiyik Wahsipekuk First Nation has occupied its territory for millennia. This is confirmed by the presence of several archaeological sites along the coast and near rivers that they traditionally occupied. Encounters with European fishermen allowed the Maliseet and their neighbours and relations, the Mi'kmaq, Abenaki, and Innu, to initiate exchanges with the Other, strangers who had arrived by sea.

At the time of first contact, especially from 1603 onward, the Innu, the Etchemin/Maliseet, and the Algonquin were France's main allies. The king of France, Henri IV, following prolonged meetings between his representatives and Indigenous leaders near Tadoussac (27 May to 9 June 1603), formalized, in the commission of 8 November 1603, France's policy toward Indigenous Peoples, a policy of alliance with local Peoples.

FRENCH REGIME: A POLICY OF ALLIANCES AND TREATIES

"To trade, to contract to the same effect peace, alliance and Confederation, good friendship [...] with the aforementioned peoples and their Prince [*sic*]" were the terms of the policy toward Indigenous Peoples and Nations under the French regime. Champlain worked hard throughout his career to meet with Chiefs and define the territories of Indigenous Nations by mapping their lands around the rivers and lakes he had inventoried. He initiated contact and then negotiated endlessly to ensure the sustainability of alliances and treaties that confirmed shared sovereignty over territory while ensuring peace, settlement, and the movement of people and goods over an immense territory that was difficult to access. Despite conflicts and setbacks, the principle of alliances, of sharing territory and resources, remained central to French policy because France could not claim it had conquered unless it formed alliances with the Indigenous Nations that occupied the immense northern territory of New France.

Champlain stayed in contact with the Innu who had concluded the first alliance on their territory, but after 1608 activities more often took place at Québec, where Champlain had founded a colony following his failure in Acadia, especially on Sainte-Croix Island, site of his first attempt at settlement. At Québec, a traditional Innu territory, Champlain continued to operate in consultation with Innu representatives who collaborated in the management of their territories.

After that, the Algonquin (Anishinabek) and the Huron (Wendat), who concluded alliances with Champlain as early as 1609 took over the fur trade, a logical outcome of these alliances. As a result, the Maliseet disappeared in the context of the general colonial history.

In the present study, the Maliseet and their allies, the Mi'kmaq and the Abenaki, are key players in the initial implementation of France's policy of alliance with Indigenous Peoples in Acadia. It was in these territories that Champlain, as specified in the commission of 8 November 1603, had received permission to found a colony. The Acadia of that time included the Maliseet Nations of present-day Québec, New Brunswick (created in 1784), and Maine, as well as the Mi'kmaq Nations of Québec and Nova Scotia, including the Abenaki of Québec and the Penobscot of the United States, a Nation related to the Abenaki.

Champlain, with the help of Maliseet Chiefs Bessabez and Cabahis, who acted as mediators with Chiefs of these same Nations, described the main routes along which they lived and travelled. He forged alliances with several Chiefs of the Saint John River (Ouygoudy), an immense waterway that runs from the north to the south of the Maliseet territory (673 kilometres in length with a watershed of 55,000 square kilometres). He met others who controlled the Kennebec River, Passamaquoddy Bay (Maine), and St. Croix Island. The territory of Norembègue and its river is also associated with this "Cadie" found on Champlain's first maps.

Although he used various terms to describe the Peoples he encountered—*Etchemin, Armouchiquois, Pentagouet* (Penobscot, Passamaquoddy)—Champlain asserted that they shared the same way of life, like the *Canadiens* (Mi'kmaq, Innu? Malécite?) or the Souriquois (Mi'kmaq).

The Etchemin/Maliseet whom Champlain met practised hunting, sea fishing, and fresh-water fishing. Champlain stated that they also practised agriculture. They had their own village, where they resided in accordance with their customs and traditions. Both the French and Indigenous Peoples occupied the land according to their customs and their needs.

Champlain reminded us on several occasions that these Peoples were related and that they collaborated on defence and on management of conflict. The Maliseet, Mi'kmaq, and Abenaki, despite the usual conflicts that exist in any relationship, managed conflicts co-operatively, whether internal or against the Iroquois, the French, or the English. The creation of the Wabanaki Confederacy around the 1680s was part of this relationship of collaboration between the Maliseet, Mi'kmaq, and Wabanaki Nations to find common solutions to common problems (Moreau 1866).

In the treaties that followed, the French confirmed with the Iroquois (French-Iroquois treaties of 1665–1666 and later) that land was available to Indigenous Nations that wished to adopt a settled lifestyle and take up agriculture. Territories were opened to Indigenous families in Montréal, Trois-Rivières, and Québec.

The *Grande Paix de Montréal* of 1701 completed the implementation of the alliance policy initiated by Champlain on the shores of Tadoussac on 27 May 1603. The goal of these alliances and treaties was to ensure peace and the free movement of people who were sharing territory and resources while respecting local populations.

In the subsequent treaties between the Maliseet and the British between 1725–1726 until 1760, the lands continued to be shared, consistent with the norms of the French regime.

Traditional Indian lands were protected and reserved for the Nations that developed them. Each Indigenous Nation undertook to respect the traditional lands of other Nations. In border areas, rules were more difficult to enforce. The management of Indian territories outside urban areas with larger populations would never truly be controlled by the French or British Crown. Regulations were applied in a general way, for example, by delineating the King's Domain of the Innu or by strictly regulating trading posts. But inposts located on fur-trading routes, in border areas, or along the St. Lawrence River, as was the case in Tadoussac, it was impossible to control everyone's comings and goings.

A comparison of the management of seigneuries under the French (1603–1760) and British regimes (1760, until the introduction of townships in 1854), shows how French division for sharing land differed from those under the British regime.

Under the French regime, the entire territory of New France was initially seen as Indian territory. To enable the private ownership of land, the seigneurial system was established. However, under the French regime, seigneurial tenure was restricted to the St. Lawrence Lowland, where the soil had agricultural potential. This was the case within Wolastokuk, where a small portion of the seigneurial territory granted was developed for agriculture. In addition, several seigneuries had the right to trade with the *Sauvages* compensated for the lack of agricultural revenues. This meant that, in most of Wolastokuk (traditional territory of the Nation), the Maliseet could move around freely and practise their customary activities.

THE BRITISH REGIME: RECOGNITION AND THE CONSTRUCTION OF A DISCOURSE OF CONTINUING EXCLUSION

Under the British regime, new borders were established for the Province of Québec. Two new principles were added: lands that were reserved for "Indians or Tribes" could be ceded or sold, but only to the Crown, which could use the lands for agriculture or settlement. Traditional Indian lands, to which Indigenous Peoples and Nations held a title of possession, were identified as *Hunting Grounds*, which the limitations that this implied in its interpretation. The British Crown, according to the Royal Proclamation of 1763, could not extinguish this title unless the lands were ceded or sold, which remained an Indigenous prerogative. In 1765, the British authorities recognized the traditional lands of the Maliseet, which were located partly within the borders of the Province of Quebec as established in 1763. By setting these boundaries and officially recognizing the "Indian territory" by name, the British committed themselves to continuing the nation-to-nation relationship that France had maintained. However, they limited it in an important way because they opened the door to the concept of extinguishment of rights to territory by stating that the traditional lands of Indigenous Peoples could be ceded or sold to the Crown.

Despite the stipulation that lands reserved for Indians had to be ceded or sold to the Crown, the recognition of Indian territory decreased following changes in their boundaries (1774, 1791, and 1840). Commissions of inquiry strove to develop an official discourse that supported the Indian policy being introduced in legislation passed in the United Province of Canada in the 1850s. These laws forced Indigenous Nations to leave their traditional lands and settle on reserves, which fit perfectly into the already well-developed process of municipalization of the territory.

After the Royal Proclamation of 1763 and following the clarifications made by the Crown regarding the recognition of the traditional territories of the Maliseet (1765) and the Innu (1767) both inside and outside the province of Québec, the boundaries and status of Indigenous territory in Québec were modified on several occasions. From the Quebec Act onward, there was no further mention of Hunting Grounds. They had disappeared. Whether this omission was intentional or not, the result was that Indigenous People could no longer claim a right to their lands. The British Crown was not respecting its commitments when it removed the underlying title to the lands recognized in the Royal Proclamation of 1763. As a result, successive governments (Lower Canada, United Province of Canada, and the Canadian federation) believed they were justified in pursuing the objective of confining Indigenous Nations to tiny reserves as part of the process of municipalization.

UNITED PROVINCE OF CANADA AND THE CANADIAN FEDERATION: FROM OBLIVION TO MANIPULATED MEMORY, OR WHEN HUNTING GROUNDS BECOME "RESERVES" AND INDIGENOUS NATIONS BECOME "INDIAN BANDS" UNDER TRUSTEESHIP

In the 1850s, the first laws defining Indian territory dealt with reserved lands (890 square kilometres), which became reserves for which Indians with "status" had to register if they wanted to live there. In doing so, governments amended the Royal Proclamation of 1763 and implied, by simple omission, that Hunting Grounds would be the exclusive property of the Crown. The Constitution Act, 1867, and the Indian Act of 1876 confirmed this interpretation by deeming reserves the only territory belonging to Indians and inserting the notion of surrendering reserved lands (extinguishment/*extinction*) as the only way for Indigenous Peoples to occupy territory. This subterfuge continued as the boundaries of Québec were extended in 1898 and 1912. It was not until Justice Malouf called the governments to order in 1973 (Malouf, 1973) that the Crown was reminded that the rights of Indigenous Peoples had never been extinguished in Québec. Justice Malouf stated that any change to the boundaries of the province of Québec had to take into account the Indian territories recognized in the Royal Proclamation of 1763.

The *civilization policy* that arose from the commissions of inquiry in the 1820s was intended to civilize and assimilate Indigenous Peoples by forcing them to settle on agricultural land, leaving other members of Indigenous Nations without any real recognition of their traditional territory. The system of reserves helped to erase the memory of the traditional territories of

Indigenous Peoples, who protested that their lands were not for sale or to be ceded as a way of eliminating their fundamental rights. What was important to Indigenous Nations was the protection of their *traditional lands, whether for traditional activities or for more permanent ownership.* The Crown was still incapable of establishing effective control over this territory.

Under the regime in place in the United Province of Canada from the 1850s onward, the notion of belonging to the culture and identity of an Indigenous Nation disappeared, and the status of the Indian was no longer that of a member of a Nation but that of an individual. Membership in a Nation metamorphosed into individual membership in an "Indian band." This loss of the status of ally and Nation became embedded in a new collective memory that trapped Indigenous Peoples in what John Leslie (1985) described as the development of an *institutional memory* that had led to the creation of the Department of Indian Affairs (quoted in Giokas 1995, 2). This *administrative memory* was based on several historical omissions, including those relating to alliances and treaties. Changes in vocabulary imposed by the commissions of inquiry and new laws that introduced new words and phrases, such as *Indian, band, enfranchisement,* and *reserved land,* contributed to the exclusion of Indigenous Peoples from Confederation in 1867.

Reducing the Indigenous question to an administrative matter and creating a discourse that supported this, the discourse of the Canadian federation, while imposing a legislative framework beginning in the 1850s, was a major shift that sought to replace colonial history by a Canadian history that created its own *endocolonialism* and excluded Indigenous Peoples (on colonial thinking, Matamoros 2007). With the amnesia as a foundation of their administrative framework, the founders of the Canadian federation continued a collective discourse that would create a collective memory, a discourse that would justify the exclusion of Indigenous Peoples from citizenship. It is this legacy of planned amnesia that explains the near disappearance of the Maliseet of Québec as an Indigenous Nation until 1987.

THE MALISEET/WOLASTOQIYIK WAHSIPEKUK NATION OF QUÉBEC: FROM FORGOTTEN MEMORIES (DISPERSAL IN 1869) TO REBIRTH AND RECOGNITION (1987)

After they lost their village in 1869, the Maliseet scattered throughout Québec and elsewhere. The sale of the Viger lands caused the dismantling of the Nation and accelerated the dispersal of its population. In 1870, 68 percent of the members of the Viger Maliseet First Nation had lived within the boundaries of Wolastokuk. In 2019, the municipalization of their territory had reduced this proportion to 20 percent. The Nation's current claims concern reappropriation of their traditional territory and reconstruction of their identity. Repossessing their traditional territory, Wolastokuk (which has never been ceded or sold), and their identity involves the economic, social, and cultural development of the Wolastoqiyik Wahsipekuk Nation of Québec.

The oblivion caused by their dispersal has prevented the Maliseet from asserting themselves and from submitting claims. A People of alliances and treaties since first contact, the Etchemin/Maliseet, Wolastoqiyik of the St. Lawrence, are speaking out, thanks to the actions of leaders from families that are resisting and are seeking to regain their rightful place in Québec and Canadian history, which must come to understand why the Maliseet Nation has been forgotten from historical discourse.

APPENDICES

APPENDIX 1
Commission of the King to the Sieur de Monts, for the habitation of the lands of the Cadie, Canada and other places in New France (November 8, 1603)

Source: Marc Lescarbot, *Histoire de la Nouvelle-France*, vol. II, Toronto, The Champlain Society, 1911, p. 490-494.

Commission du Roy au sieur de Monts, pour l'habitation ès terres de la Cadie, Canada, & autres endroits en la Nouvelle-France.

Title: Commission du Roy au sieur de Monts, pour l'habitation des terres de la Cadie, Canada et autres endroits en la Nouvelle-France (8 novembre 1603)

Commission du Roy au sieur de Monts, pour l'habitation ès terres de la Cadie, Canada, & autres endroits en la Nouvelle-France. Ensemble les defenses à tous autres de traffiquer avec les Sauvages desdites terres.

Henry, par la grace de Dieu Roy de France & de Navarre, A nôtre cher & bien amé le sieur de Monts, Gentilhomme ordinaire de nôtre Chambre, Salut. Comme nôtre plus grand soin & travail soit & ait toujours été, depuis nôtre avenement à cette Couronne, de la maintenir & conserver en son ancienne dignité, grandeur, & splendeur, **d'étendre & amplifier autant que légitimement se peut faire, les bornes & limites d'icelle: Nous étans dés long temps a, informez de la situation & condition des païs & territoire de la Cadie,** Meuz sur toutes choses d'vn zele singulier & d'vne devote & ferme resolution que nous avons prinse, avec l'aide & assistance de Dieu, autheur, distributeur & protecteur de tous Royaumes & Etats; de faire convertir, amener & instruire les peuples qui habitent en cette contrée, de present gens barbares, athées, sans foy ne religion, au Christianisme, & en la creance & profession de nôtre foy & religion: & les retirer de l'ignorance & infidélité où ilz sont. **Ayans aussi dés long temps reconu sur le rapport des Capitaines de navires, pilotes, marchans & autres qui de longue main ont hanté, fréquenté, & traffiqué avec ce qui se trouve de peuples ésdits lieux, combien peut étre fructueuse, commode & vtile à nous, à nos Etats & sujets, la demeure, possession & habitation d'iceux pour le grand & apparent profit qui se retirera par la grande frequentation & habitude que l'on aura avec les peuples qui s'y trouvent, & le traffic & commerce qui se pourra par ce moyen seurement traiter & negocier. Novs, pour ces causes à plein confians de vôtre grande prudence, & en la conoissance & experience que vous avez de la qualité, condition & situation dudit païs** de la Cadie: pour les diverses navigations, voyages, & frequentations que vous avez faits en ces terres, & autres proches & circonvoisines: nous asseurans que cette nôtre resolution & intention, vous étans commise, vous la sçaurés attentivement, diligemment & non moins courageusement, & valeureusement **executer & conduire à la perfection que nous desirons, Vous avons expressement commis & établi, & par ces presentes signées de nôtre main, Vous commettons, ordonnons, faisons, constituons & établissons nôtre Lieutenant general, pour representer nôtre personne aux païs, territoires, côtes & confins de la Cadie:** A commencer dés le quarantième degré, jusques au quarante-sixième. Et en icelle étenduë ou partie d'icelle, tant & si avant que faire se pourra, établir, étendre & faire conoitre nôtre nom, puissance & authorité. Et à icelle **assujettir, submettre & faire obeïr tous les peuples de ladite terre, & les circonvoisins:** Et par le moyen d'icelles & toutes autres voyes licites, les appeler, faire instruire, provoquer & émouvoir à la conoissance de Dieu, & à la lumière de la Foy & religion Chrétienne, la y établir: & en l'exercice & profession d'icelle **maintenir, garder & conserver les dits peuples, & tous autres habituez esdits lieux, & en paix, repos & tranquilité** y commander tant par mer que par terre: Ordonner, decider, & faire executer tout ce que vous jugerez se devoir & pouvoir faire, pour maintenir, garder & conserver lesdits lieux souz nôtre puissance & authorité, par les formes, voyes & moyens prescrits par nos ordonnances. Et pour y avoir égard avec vous, commettre, établir & constituer tous Officiers, tant és affaires de la guerre que de Iustice & police pour la premiere fois, & de là en avant nous les nommer & presenter, pour en estre par nous disposé & donner les lettres, tiltres & provisions tels qu'ilz seront necessaires. Et selon les occurrences des affaires, **vous mémes avec l'avis de gens prudents & capables, prescrire souz nôtre bon plaisir, des loix, statuts & ordonnances autant qu'il se pourra conformes aux nôtres**, notamment és choses & matieres ausquelles n'est pourveu par icelles: traiter & contracter à méme effet paix, alliance & confederation, bonne amitié, correspondance & communication avec lesdits peuples & leurs Princes, ou autres ayans pouvoir & commandement sur eux: Entretenir, garder & soigneusement observer les traittés & alliances dont vous convie(n)drés avec eux: pourveu qu'ils y satisfacent de leur part. Et à ce defaut, leur **faire guerre ouverte pour les contraindre & amener à telle raison que vous jugerez necessaire pour l'honneur, obeissance & service de Dieu, & l'établissement, manutention & conservation de nôtre**

dite authorité parmi eux: du moins pour hanter & frequenter par vous, & tous noz sujets avec eux en toute asseurance, liberté, fréquentation & communication, y negocier & trafiquer amiablement & paisiblement. Leur donner & octroyer graces & privileges, charges & honneurs. Lequel entier pouvoir susdit, voulons aussi & ordonnons que vous ayez sur tous **nosdits sujets & autres qui se transporter ont & voudront s'habituer, trafiquer, negotier & resider esdits lieux; tenir, prendre, reserver, & vous approprier ce que vous voudrez & verrez vous étre plus commode & propre à vôtre charge, qualité & vsage desdites terres, en departir telles parts & portions, leur donner & attribuer tels tiltres, hõneurs, droits, pouvoirs & facultez que vous verrez besoin étre, selon les qualitez, conditions & merites des personnes du païs ou autres. Sur tout peupler, cultiver & faire habituer lesdites terres** le plus promptement, soigneusement & dextrement que le temps, les lieux, & commoditez le pourront permettre: **en faire ou faire faire à cette fin la découverte & reconoissance en l'étenduë des côtes maritimes & autres contrées de la terre ferme**, que vous ordonnerez & prescrirez en l'espace susdite du quarantiéme degré iusques au quarante-sixième, ou autrement tant & si avant qu'il se pourra le long desdites côtes, & en la terre ferme. Faire soigneusement rechercher & reconoitre toutes sortes de mines d'or & d'argent, cuivre & autres metaux & mineraux, les faire fouiller, tirer, purger & affiner, pour étre convertis en vsage, disposer suivant que nous avons prescrit par les Edits & reglemens que nous avons faits en ce Royaume du profit & emolument d'icelles, par vous ou ceux que vous aurés établis à cet effet, NOVS RESERVANS seulement le dixiéme denier de ce qui proviendra de celles d'or, d'argent, & cuivre, vous affectans ce que nous pourrions prendre ausdits autres metaux & mineraux, pour vous aider & soulager aux grandes dépenses que la charge susdite vous pourra apporter. Voulans cependant, que vôtre seureté & commodité, & de tous ceux de noz sujets qui s'en iront, habituëront & trafiqueront esdites terres: comme generalement de tous autres qui s'y accommoderont souz nôtre puissance & authorité, **Vous puissiez faire batir & construire vn ou plusieurs forts, places, villes & toutes autres maisons, demeures & habitations, ports, havres, retraites, logemens que vous conoitrez propres, vtiles & necessaires à l'execution de ladite entreprise. Etablir garnisons & gens de guerre à la garde d'iceux**. Vous ayder & prevaloir aux effets susdits des vagabõs, personnes oyseuses & sans avoeu, tãt ésvilles qu'aux chãps, & des condamnez à banissemens perpetuels, ou à trois ans au moins hors nôtre Royaume, pourveu que ce soit par avis & consentement & de l'authorité de nos Officiers. Outre ce que dessus, & qui vous est d'ailleurs prescrit, mandé & ordonné par les commissions & pouvoirs que vous a donnez nôtre tres-cher cousin le sieur d'Ampville, Admiral de France, pour ce qui concerne le fait & la charge de l'Admirauté, en l'exploit, expedition & execution des choses susdites, faire generalement pour la conquéte, peuplement, habitation & conservation de ladite terre de la Cadie, & des côtes, territoires circonvoisins & de leur appartenances & dependances souz nôtre nom & authorité, ce que nous-mémes ferions & faire pourrions si presens en persone y étions, jaçoit que le cas requit mandement plus special que nous ne le vous prescrivõs par cesdites presentes: Au contenu desquelles, Mandons, ordonnons, & tres-expressement enjoignons à tous nos iusticiers, officiers & sujets, de se conformer: Et à vous obeïr & entendre en toutes & chacunes les choses susdites, leurs cir-constances & dependances. Vous donner aussi en l'execution d'icelles tout ayde & confort, main-forte & assistance dont vous aurez besoin, & seront par vous requis, le tout à peine de rebellion & desobeïssance. Et à fin que persone ne pretende cause d'ignorance de cette nôtre intention, & se vueille immiscer en tout ou partie de la charge, dignité & authorité que nous vous donnons par ces presentes: **Nous avons de noz certaine science, pleine puissance & authorité Royale, revoqué, supprimé & declaré nuls & de nul effet ci-apres & des à present, tous autres pouvoirs & Commissions, Lettres & expeditions donnez & delivrez à quelque persone que ce soit, pour découvrir, conquerir, peupler & habiter en l'étenduë susdite desdites terres situées depuis ledit quarantième degré, iusques au quarantesixiéme quelles qu'elles soient.** Et outre ce, mandons & ordonnons à tous nosdits Officiers de quelque qualité & condition qu'ilz soient, que ces presentes, ou *Vidimus* deuëment collationné d'icelles par l'vn de noz amez & feaux Conseillers, Notaires & Secretaires, ou autre Notaire Royal, ilz fact à votre requéte, poursuite & diligence, ou de noz Procureurs, lire, publier & registrer és registres de leurs jurisdictions, pouvoirs & détroits, cessans en tãt qu'à eux appartiendra, tous troubles & empéchements à ce contraires. Car tel est nôtre plaisir. Donné à Fontainebleau le huitième jour de Novembre; l'an de grace mille six cens trois: Et de nôtre regne le quinziéme. Signé, HENRI, Et plus bas, Par le Roy, POTIER. Et seellé sur simple queuë de cire iaune.

[COMMISSION DE MONSIEUR L'ADMIRAL

CHARLES de Mont-morancy seigneur de Dampville & de Meru, Comte d'Escondigni, Viconte de Meleun, Baron de Chasteau-neuf, Gonnord, Mesles & Savoisi, Chevalier des ordres du Roy, Conseiller és Conseil d'Etat & privé de sa Majesté, Capitaine de cet homme d'armes de ses ordonnances, Admiral de France & de Bretagne: A tous ceux qui ces presentes lettres verront, Salut. Le sieur de Monts nous a fait entendre; que poussé du singulier desir & devotion qu'il a toujours euë au service du Roy, & recherchant toutes occasiõs d'e(n) pouvoir de nouveau re(n)dre quelque fidele preuve à sa Majesté: Il auroit iugé ne lui en pouvoir donner vn plus certain témoignage à present (page 5) qu'il a pleu à Dieu pourvoir son Royaume d'vne bonne & heureuse paix, que de s'appliquer à la navigation, cõme il a des-ja fait cy devant, à découvrir quelques côtes & terres lointaines **dépourveuës de peuples, ou habitées par gens encor Sauvages, Barbares, & dénuez de toute religion, loix & civilité, pour s'y loger & fortifier, & tacher d'en amener les nations à quelque profession de la Foy Chrétienne, civilization de mœurs, reglement de leur vie, pratique & intelligence avec les François pour l'vsage de leur commerce.** Et en fin à leur reconoissance & submission à l'authorité & domination de cette Couronne de France; & specialement pour la découverture & habitation des côtes & contrées de la Cadie, tant pour la temperature des lieux, bonté des terres, commodité de la situation de ladite province, communication & amitié ja encommencée avec aucuns des peuples qui se trouvent en icelle: Que sur l'avis & rapport nagueres fait par les Capitaines qui en sont derniers retournez, de nombre & quantité de bonnes mines qui y sont, lesquelles estant ouvertes pourront apporter beaucoup de profit & commodité. Surquoy considerant combien ce vertueux & loüable dessein dudit sieur de Monts est digne & recommandable, & combien l'heureuse issuë qui en peut proceder souz la conduite d'vn personage de telle valeur & merite, & poussé d'vne si bonne affection, pourra vn jour estre commode & vtile au bien du service de sa Majesté, profit de ses sujets, & honneur de la France. Et outre ce ayant receu divers avis, qu'aucuns étrangers designent d'aller dresser des peupleme(n)s & demeures vers les dites contrées de la Cadie, si comme elles ont esté jusque icy, elles restent encore quelque temps desertes & abandonnées. POVR ces causes & estans bien & deuement informez du vouloir & inte(n)tion de sa Majesté, qui sur la remonstrance par nous à elle de ce faite, a donné vn tres-prompt & favorable consentement à l'effect de cette entreprise: & concedé audit sieur de Monts, la découverte & peuplement de toutes lesdites côtes & contrées maritimes de la Cadie, depuis le quarantiéme degré, jusques au quarante sixiéme, et de tout ce qu'il pourra avant dans les terres; & ce comme nôtre Vic'-Admiral & Lieutenant general tant en mer qu'en terre en tous lesdits païs. Nous en vertu de nôtre pouvoir & authorité d'Admiral, tant suivans les Édits anciens & modernes de la marine, & sur le reglement ce jourd'huy sur ce pris au Conseil d'Etat de sadite Majesté, Avons commis, ordonné & deputé, com-mettons, ordonnons & deputons par ces presentes iceluy sieur de Monts, pour nôtre Vic'-Admiral & Lieutenant general en toutes les mers, côtes, iles, raddes & contrées maritimes qui se trouveront vers ladite province & region de la Cadie, depuis les quarantiéme degrez, jusques au quarantesixiéme, & si avant dans les terres qu'il pourra découvrir & habiter: Avec pouvoir d'assembler par lui, tant cette premiere année que les suivantes, tels Capitaines & Pilotes, mariniers & artisans, & tel nombre de vaisseaux pourveuz, & telle quantité d'armes, agrets, vivres & munitions qu'il iugera necessaire, pour les mener & conduire par toutes lesdites côtes, mers, iles, rades, & contrées, ainsi qu'il trouvera estre plus expedient, pour l'accomplissement de ladite entreprise. Et selon les occasiõs, distribuer, departir ou laisser les vaisseaux és endroits que le besoin pourra requerir: Soit pour la reconoissance des lieux, découverte de mines, garde des places & avenues, ou pour la traite avec les Sauvages, vers la baye sainct Cler, riviere de Canada, ou autres païs: Construire des forts & forteresses, ainsi & en tels endroits qu'il verra estre plus commode: Comme aussi dresser des ports, havres & autres choses necessaires pour la seure retraite (page 6) des vaisseaux François contre tous desseins d'ennemis & incursions de pirates: Etablir és places susdites tels Capitaines & Lieutenans que besoin sera: Ensemble des Capitaines & gardes des côtes, iles, havres & avenuës: & pareillement commettre des officiers pour la distribution de la iustice & entretien de la police, reglemens & ordonnances: Et en somme gerer & negotier, & se comporter par icelui sieur de Monts en la function de ladite charge de nôtre Vic'Admiral & Lieutenant general, pour tout ce qu'il iugera estre de l'avancement desdites reveuës, conquétes & peuplement: & pour le bien du service de sa Majesté & établissement de son authorité vers lesdites mers, provinces & regions: Avec méme pouvoir, puissance & authorité que nous ferions si nous y estions en persone, & comme si le tout estoit ici & par expres & plus particulierement specifié & declaré. De ce faire lui avons donné & donnons par ces presentes toute charge, pouvoir, commission & mandement special. Et pource l'avons substitué & subrogé en nôtre lieu & place, à la charge de faire aussi soigneusement observer par ceux qui seront souz sa charge & authorité en toute l'execution de cette entreprise, les Edits & ordonnances de la marine. Et faire prendre noz congez particuliers par tous les Capitaines des vaisseaux qu'il voudra mener avec luy tant au dessein de la découverture de ladite côte & contrée de la Cadie, que de ceux qu'il voudra envoyer pour la traite de la Pelleterie à lui permise par sa Majesté pour dix ans vers la Baye de sainct Cler & riviere de Canada. Et nous faire bon & fidele rapport à toutes occasions, de tout ce qui aura esté fait & exploité au susdit dessein; pour en rendre par nous prompte raison à sadite Majesté. Et y apporter par nous ce qui pourra estre requis ou d'ordre ou de remede. Si prions & requerons tous Princes & Potentats & seigneurs étrangers, leurs Lieutenans generaux, Admiraux, Gouverneurs de leurs provinces, chefs & conducteurs de leurs gens de guerre tant par mer que par terre, Capitaines de leurs villes & forts maritimes, ports, côtes, havres & détroits. Mandons & ordōnons à nos autres Vic'Admiraux, Lieutenans generaux & particuliers, & autres officiers de nôtre Admirauté, Capitaines des côtes & de la marine & autres estās souz nótre pouvoir & authorité chacun endroit soy, & si comme à lui appartiendra: dōner audit sieur de Monts pour le plein & entier effect, execution & accomplissement de ces presentes, tout support, secours, assistance, retraite, main-forte, faveur & aide si besoin en a, & en ce qu'ils en pourront par lui estre requis. En témoin de ce, Nous avons à cesdites presentes, signées de notre main, fait mettre le seel de nos armes. A Fontaine-bleau le dernier jour d'Octobre, l'an de grace mil six cens trois. Signé, CHARLES DE MONTMORANCY. Et sur le reply, Par Monseigneur l'Admiral, signé, de Gennes, & seellé du seel des armes dudit Seigneur.]

(LESCARBOT #2)

(page 1, title page)

Date: December 18, 1603

Title: LETTRES PATENTES qui accordent au sieur de Monts & ses associés la traite exclusive des pelleteries dans l'Acadie & le golfe Saint-Laurent & des deux côtés du fleuve du Canada.

Source: *Mémoires des Commissaires du Roi et de Sa Majesté Britannique sur les possessions et les droits respectifs des deux Couronnes en Amérique*, vol. 2, 1755, p. 446-447 (page 2) X.

APPENDIX 1 – COMMISSION OF THE KING TO THE SIEUR DE MONTS

LETTRES PATENTES qui accordent au ieur de Monts & à es aocués, la Traite excluive des pelleteries dans l'Acadie & golfe Saint-Laurent, & des deux côtés du fleuve du Canada, du 18 décembre 1603.

Hiftoire de la Nouvelle-France, par l'Efcarbot, *p. 424.*

(page 2, 1st column)

HENRY, par la grace de Dieu, Roi de France & de Navarre: A nos amés & féaux Confeillers les Officiers de notre Admirauté de Normandie, Bretagne, Picardie & Guienne, & à chacun d'eux en droit foi, & en l'étendue de leurs refforts & jurifdictions; SALUT. Nous avons pour beaucoup d'importantes occafions, ordonné, commis & établi le fieur de Monts, Gentilhomme ordinaire de notre Chambre, notre Lieutenant général, pour **peupler & habiter les terres, côtes & pays de l'Acadie, &** *autres circonvoiins*, en l'étendue du quarantième degré jufqu'au quarante-fixième, & là établir notre autorité, & autrement s'y loger & affurer; en forte que nos fujets desormais y puiffent être reçus, y **hanter, réfider & trafiquer avec les Sauvages habitans defdits lieux**, comme plus expreffément nous l'avons déclaré par nos lettres patentes, expédiées.

(page 2, 2nd column)

& délivrées pour cet effet audit fieur de Monts le huitième jour de novembre dernier, fuivant les conditions & articles, moyen- nant lefquelles il s'eft chargé de la conduite & exécution de cette entreprife. Pour faliciter laquelle, & à ceux qui s'y font joints avec lui, & leur donner quelque moyen & commodité d'en fupporter la dépenfe; Nous avons eu agréable de leur promettre & affurer qu'il ne feroit permis à aucuns autres nos fujets, qu'à ceux qui entreroient en affociation avec lui pour faire ladite dépenfe, de trafiquer de pelleterie & autres marchandifes durant dix années, ès terres, pays, ports, rivières & avenues de l'étendue de fa charge; ce que nous voulons avoir lieu. Nous, pour ces caufes & autres confidérations à ce nous mouvans, vous mandons & ordon-nons que vous ayez, chacun de vous en l'étendue de vos pouvoirs, jurifdictions & détroits, à faire de notre

.........comme

(page 3, 1st column)

de notre pleine ....& autorité Royale, nous faifons très- expreffes inhibitions & défenfes à tous marchands, maîtres & Capitaines de navires, matelots & autres nos fujets de quelque état, qualité & condition qu'ils foient, autres néanmoins & fors à ceux qui font entrés en affociation avec ledit fieur de Monts pour ladite entreprife, felon les articles & conventions d'icelles, par nos arrêtés, ainfi que dit eft; d'équiper aucuns vaiffeaux, & en iceux aller ou envoyer **faire trafic & troque de pelleterie, & autres chofes avec les Sauvages, fréquenter, négocier & communiquer durant ledit temps de dix ans, depuis le cap de Raze, jufqu'au quarantième degré, comprenant** *toute la côte de l'Acadie, terre & Cap-Breton, baie de*

Saint-Cler , de Chaleur , ifles percées , Gafpay , Chichedec , Mefamichi , Lefquemin , Tadouffac & la rivière de Canada , tant d'un côté que d'autre , & **TOUTES LES BAIES ET RIVIÈRES QUI ENTRENT AU DEDANS DESDITES COSTES**, à peine de defobéiffance, & confifcation entière de leurs vaiffeaux , vivres , armes & marchandifes, au profit dudit fieur de Monts & de fes affociés , & de trente mille livres d'amende.

(page 3, 2nd column)

Pour l'affurance & acquit de laquelle , & de la cohertion & punition de leur defobéiffance, vous permettrez, comme nous avons auffi permis & permettons , audit fieur de Monts & affociés, de faifir, appréhender & arrêter tous les contrevenans à notre préfente defenfe & ordonnance , & leurs vaiffeaux , marchandifes , armes & victuailles , pour les amener & remettre ès mains de la juftice , & être procédé, tant contre les perfonnes que contre les biens defdits defobéiffans, ainfi qu'il appartiendra: ce que nous voulons, & vous mandons & ordonnons de faire incontinent publier & lire par tous les lieux & endroits publics de vof dits pouvoirs & jurifdictions où vous jugerez befoin être, à ce qu'aucun de nofdits fujets n'en puiffe prétendre caufe d'ignorance , ains que chacun obéiffe & fe conforme fur ce à notrevolonté; de ce faire nous vous avons donné & donnons pouvoir & commiffion & mandement fpécial: Car tel eft notre plaifir. DONNÉ à Paris, le dix-huit décembre, l'an de grace mil fix cens trois, & de notre règne le quinzième, ainfi figné HENRY. *Et plus bas*, Par le Roi, POTIER. Et fcellé du grand fcel de cire jaulne.

APPENDIX 2
Treaties signed by New France with the Iroquois in 1666

TRAITEZ
DE PAIX CONCLUS
ENTRE S.M. LE ROY DE FRANCE

ET LES INDIENS DU CANADA,

PAIX AVEC LES IROQUOIS DE LA Nation Tsonnont8an. *A Quebec le vingt deuxiéme May* 1666.

PAIX AVEC LES IROQUOIS DE LA Nation d'Onnei8t. *A Quebec le douziéme Juillet* 1666.

PAIX AVEC LES IROQUOIS DE LA Nation d'Onnontague. *Le treiziéme Decembre* 1666.

A PARIS,
Par SEBASTIEN MABRE-CRAMOISY
Imprimeur du Roy.

M' DC. LXVII.
De l'exprés commandement de Sa Majesté.

PAIX

ACCORDE'E PAR L'EMPEREUR
de France, aux Iroquois de la Nation
Tſonnont8an.

A Quebec le vingt-deuxiéme May 1666.

LE vingt-deuxiéme du mois de May de l'année 1666. les Iroquois de la Nation de Tſonnont8an, Superieure d'Onnontaé, eſtans deſcendus à Quebec pour y demander la Paix par dix de ſes Ambaſſadeurs, nommez Garonhiaguerha, Sago8ichi8tonk, Oſend8t, Gachioguentiaxa Hotiguerion, Hondeg8araton, So8end8annen, Tehaend8anha8enion, Honagueta8i, Tehonneritaguente, Tſohahin, aprés avoir fait entendre par la bouche de l'Orateur Garanhiaguerha leur Chef, le ſujet de leur Ambaſſade par trente-quatre paroles, exprimées par autant de preſens, ont unanimement demandé, qu'ayant toûjours eſté ſous la protection de Tres Haut, Tres Excellent, & Tres-Puiſſant Prince LOUIS Quatorziéme, par la grace de Dieu Roy Tres-Chreſtien de France & de Navarre, depuis que les François ont découvert leurs Terres, il pluſt à Sa Majeſté de la leur continuer, & de les recevoir au nombre de ſes fidelles Sujets, demandans que le Traité fait, tant pour la Nation d'Onnontaé, que pour la leur, ayt pour eux pleine force & ſon entier effet; le ratifiant de leur part en tous ſes points & articles, dont lecture leur a eſté faite par Joſeph Marie Chaumonot, Preſtre & Religieux de la Compagnie de JESUS, nommé en Langue Huronne, Hechou : Ajoûtans en outre à tous leſdits Articles, qu'ils proteſtent effectuer de bonne foy ce qu'ils ont offert par leurſdits preſens, ſur tout de faire paſſer à Quebec, aux Trois Rivieres, & à Mont-Real, de leurs Familles, pour

A

servir de lien plus eſtroit de leurs perſonnes & de leurs volontez, aux Ordres de ceux qui auront en ce Païs l'autorité dudit Seigneur Roy, qu'ils reconnoiſſent dés-à-preſent comme leur Souverain. Demandans reciproquement entre toutes autres choſes, qu'on tranſmette chez eux des Familles Françoiſes, & quelques Robes Noires, c'eſt à dire, des Jeſuites, pour leur preſcher l'Evangile, & faire connoître le Dieu des François, qu'ils promettent aymer & adorer ; avec aſſeurance que non ſeulement ils leur prepareront des Cabannes pour les loger, mais encore qu'ils travailleront à leur conſtruire des Forts pour les mettre à couvert des incurſions de leurs Ennemis communs les Andaſtoaeronnons, & autres. Et pour que le preſent Traité fait de leur part en ratifiant le precedent, ſoit ſtable & notoire à tous, ils l'ont ſigné de la Marque differentielle & diſtinctive de leurs Familles, aprés que ce qu'ils ont demandé audit Seigneur Roy leur a eſté accordé en ſon nom par Meſſire Alexandre de Prouville, Chevalier, Seigneur de Tracy, Conſeiller du Roy en ſes Conſeils, Lieutenant General des Armées de Sa Majeſté, & dans les Iſles & Terre Ferme de l'Amerique Meridionale & Septentrionale, tant par Mer que par Terre, en vertu du Pouvoir à luy donné, dont eſt fait mention au preſent Traité, en preſence & aſſiſté de Meſſire Daniel de Remy, Seigneur de Courcelle, Conſeiller du Roy en ſes Conſeils, Lieutenant General des Armées de Sa Majeſté, & Gouverneur de l'Acadie, Iſle de Terre Neuve, & de Canada ; & de Meſſire Jean Talon, auſſi Conſeiller de Sa Majeſté, & Intendant de Juſtice, Police & Finances de la nouvelle France, qui ont ſignez avec ledit Seigneur de Tracy. Et comme Témoins François le Mercier, Preſtre, Religieux & Superieur de la Compagnie de JESUS, & Joſeph Marie Chaumonot, auſſi Preſtre & Religieux de la même Compagnie, Interpretes des Langues Iroquoiſe & Huronne. Fait à Quebec le 25. May 1666.

3

AUTRE PAIX

ACCORDE'E PAR L'EMPEREUR DE FRANCE
aux Iroquois de la Nation d'Onnei8t.

A Quebec le douziéme Juillet 1666.

LE septiéme du mois de Juillet de l'année 1666. les Iroquois de la Nation d'Onnei8t, ayant appris par les Agneronnons leurs Voisins & Alliez, & par les Hollandois du Fort d'Orange, qu'au mois de Fevrier de la mesme année, les Troupes de LOUIS Quatorziéme, par la grace de Dieu Roy Tres Chrestien de France & de Navarre, avoient porté sur les neiges & les glaces les Armes de Sa Majesté jusqu'au Fort d'Orange en la nouvelle Hollande, sous la conduite de Messire Daniel de Courcelle, Lieutenant General de ses Armées, par les Ordres qu'elles avoient receus de Messire Alexandre de Prouville, Chevalier, Seigneur de Tracy, Conseiller de Sa Majesté en ses Conseils, & Lieutenant General de ses Armées, & dans les Isles & Terre Ferme de l'Amerique Meridionale & Septentrionale, tant par Mer que par Terre, de combattre & détruire lesd. Agneronnons, ce que probablement elles auroient fait, si la méprise de leurs Guides ne leur avoit fait prendre un chemin pour l'autre, sont descendus à Quebec pour y demander la Paix, tant en leur nom qu'en celuy des Agneronnons, par dix de ses Ambassadeurs, nommez Soenves, Tsoensersanne, Ak8ehen, Gaunonk8enioton, Asarag8an, Achiunhara, Jogonk8aras, Olxaragete.
Et aprés avoir fait entendre par la bouche de l'Orateur Soenres leur Chef, le sujet de leur Ambassade, par dix paroles, exprimées par autant de presens, & nous avoir rendu les Lettres des Officiers de la Nouvelle Hollande, ont unanimement demandé, que connoissant la force des Armes de Sa Majesté, la foiblesse des leurs, & l'estat des

A ij

4

Forts avancez vers eux : & sçachans d'ailleurs que les trois Nations Iroquoises Superieures, se sont toûjours bien trouvées de la Protection qu'elles ont cy-devant reçûë dudit Seigneur Roy, il plust à Sa Majesté de leur faire la même grace qu'à elles, en leur accordant cette même Protection, & les recevant au nombre de ses fidelles Sujets, demandans que les Traitez cy-devant faits tant par lesdites Nations que par la leur, ayent même force & vertu pour celle d'Agnez, qui les a requis de nous en supplier avec grande instance; ce qu'elle auroit fait elle-même par le moyen de ses Ambassadeurs, si pour eux elle n'avoit apprehendé un mauvais traitement de nostre part, ratifiant de la leur tous lesdits Traitez en tous leurs points & articles, dont lecture leur a esté faite en Langue Iroquoise, par Joseph Marie Chaumonot, Prestre & Religieux de la Compagnie de JESUS. Ajoûtans en outre à tous lesdits Articles, qu'ils protestent effectuer de bonne foy ce qu'ils ont offert par leursdits presens; sur tout de rendre tous les François Algonquins & Hurons qu'ils tiennent captifs parmi eux, de quelque condition & qualité qu'ils soient, & si long-temps qu'il y ait qu'ils y soient detenus, mesme de la part des Agneronnons, de faire passer des Familles d'entr'eux, pour servir de mesme que les Familles des autres Nations, de lien plus estroit de leurs personnes & de leurs volontez, aux Ordres de ceux qui auront en ce Païs l'autorité dudit Seigneur Roy, qu'ils reconnoissent dés à present comme leur Souverain. Demandans reciproquement entre toutes autres choses, qu'on leur rende de bonne foy tous ceux de leur Nation qui se trouveront prisonniers à Quebec, à Mont-Real, & aux Trois Rivieres; Qu'on transmette chez eux des Familles Françoises, & quelques Robes Noires, c'est à dire des Jesuites, pour leur prescher l'Evangile, & leur faire connestre le Dieu des François, qu'ils promettent aimer & adorer : Mesme que le Commerce & la Traitte leur soient ouverts avec la Nouvelle France, par le Lac du S. Sacrement, avec asseurance que de leur part ils donneront chez eux une retraite seure, tant ausdites Familles, qu'aux Marchands, Traittans, non seulement en leur pre-

5

parant des Cabanes pour les loger ; mais encore en travaillant à conftruire des Forts pour les mettre à couvert de leurs Ennemis communs les Andaftoaeronnons, & autres. Et pour que le prefent Traité fait de leur part en ratifiant le precedent, foit ftable & notoire à tous, ils l'ont figné de la Marque differentielle & diftinctive de leurs Familles, aprés que ce qu'ils ont demandé audit Seigneur Roy, leur a efté accordé en fon nom par Meffire Alexandre ce Prouville, Chevalier, Seigneur de Tracy, Confeiller du Roy en fes Confeils, Lieutenant General des Armées de Sa Majefté, & dans les Ifles & Terre Ferme de l'Amerique Meridionale & Septentrionale, tant par Mer que par Terre, en vertu du pouvoir à luy donné, dont eft fait mention au precedent Traité, en la prefence & affifté de Meffire Daniel de Remy, Seigneur de Courcelle, Confeiller du Roy en fes Confeils, Lieutenant General des Armées de Sa Majefté, & Gouverneur de l'Acadie, Ifle de Terre Neuve & de Canada ; & de Meffire Jean Talon, auffi Confeiller de Sa Majefté, & Intendant de Juftice, Police & Finances de la Nouvelle France, qui ont fignez avec ledit Seigneur de Tracy. Et comme Témoins François le Mercier, Preftre, Religieux & Superieur de la Compagnie de JESUS, à Quebec, & Jofeph Marie Chaumonot, auffi Preftre & Religieux de la même Compagnie, Interpretes des Langues Iroquoife & Huronne. Fait à Quebec, le douziéme de Juillet 1666.

C113482

6

TROISIESME PAIX
ACCORDE'E PAR L'EMPEREUR de France, aux Iroquois de la Nation d'Onnontague.

Le treiziéme Decembre 1666.

ARTICLES de la Paix demandée par six Ambassadeurs Iroquois, Garakontie, Ahonnonh8araton, Gatiennonties, Hotre8ti, Ha8endaientak, Te Gannontie, de la Nation d'Onnontague, tant au nom de ladite Nation, qu'en celuy des deux Superieures, Goio8en, Tsonnont8an : Ensemble par Achinnhara, de la Nation d'Onnei8t ; les interests de laquelle il a stipulé, aprés s'estre joint ausdits Ambassadeurs : Et accordez au nom & de la part du Roy Tres-Chrestien, par Messire Alexandre de Prouville, Chevalier, Seigneur de Tracy, Conseiller du Roy en ses Conseils, Lieutenant General des Armées de Sa Majesté, & dans les Isles & Terre Ferme de l'Amerique Meridionale & Septentrionale, tant par Mer que par Terre, de ce suffisamment autorisé en vertu du Pouvoir à luy donné par les Lettres Patentes de Sa Majesté, en datte du   en la presence & assisté de Messire Daniel de Courcelle, Conseiller du Roy en ses Conseils, Lieutenant General des Armées de Sa Majesté, & Gouverneur de l'Acadie, Isle de Terre Neuve & de Canada ; & de Messire Jean Talon, aussi Conseiller de Sa Majesté, & Intendant de Justice, Police & Finances de la Nouvelle France.

AU NOM DE DIEU qui a tout fait. Soit notoire à tout l'Univers, que comme cy-devant les Roys Tres-Chrestiens, de glorieuse memoire, auroient souvent avec

C 113 475

7

peril, peine & dépenses, envoyez leurs Sujets à la découverte des Païs inconnus, & occupez par les Nations Sauvages, Barbares & Infidelles ; Cependant avec si peu de succez que jusqu'au Regne de Tres Haut, Tres Excellent, & Tres Puissant Prince LOUIS Quatorziéme, par la grace de Dieu Roy Tres-Chrestien de France & de Navarre, les Armes de leurs Majestez ne se seroient portées que jusques à l'Isle de Mont-Real, dans le grand Fleuve de S. Laurens : Mais que sous le Regne dudit Seigneur Roy LOUIS Quatorziéme, Dieu par sa Misericorde soûtenant les pieux desseins de Sa Majesté, fortifiant ses genereuses entreprises, & benissant ses Armes d'ailleurs victorieuses, auroit ouvert aux François ses Sujets le chemin aux habitations des quatre Nations Iroquoises Superieures, & introduits en ces Contrées voisines du Lac Ontario les mesmes François, tant pour y establir le nom de CHRIST, que pour y assujettir à la domination Françoise les Peuples Sauvages qui les habitent : Les Ambassadeurs cy-devant nommez, ne sont pas venus demander une nouvelle Paix, ne pretendant pas que la premiere union des Iroquois avec les François soit rompuë ou blessée ; mais seulement supplier que l'on confirme la premiere, en leur accordant la continuation de la mê-me protection qu'ils ont cy-devant receuë des Armes de Sa Majesté, & de ses Sujets qui ont habité Onnontague durant plusieurs années ; Sur quoy il a esté convenu & arresté ce qui ensuit.

PREMIEREMENT.

Que puisque les quatre Nations d'Onnontague, Goiogen, Tsonnontsan, & Onneist, supplient tres-humblement ledit Seigneur Roy, d'enterrer avec les François massacrez la memoire de tous les torts, excez, injures, & violences : Iceux Iroquois aussi remettant de leur part tous les eschets & déplaisirs qu'ils ont receus, soit des Hurons, soit des Algonquins Sujets dudit Seigneur Roy, ou vivant sous sa Protection, par infraction de Traitez de Paix autrefois faits avec eux, par le massacre de leurs Ambassadeurs, ou par la détention de leurs presens, sans y répondre par d'autres de pareille nature.

II.

Que lesdits Hurons & Algonquins habituez au Nort du Fleuve de Saint Laurens, depuis les Esquimaux & Berriamites, en remontant jusqu'au grand Lac des Hurons, ou Mer douce, & au Nort du Lac Ontario, ne pourront à l'avenir estre inquietez dans leur Chasse par les quatre Nations Iroquoises, ou troublez dans leur Commerce en descendant par la Traitte à Mont-Real, aux Trois Rivieres, à Quebec, ou par tout ailleurs, soit par Terre dans les Bois, ou par Eauë dans leurs Canots, sous quelque pretexte que ce puisse estre; Ledit Seigneur Roy declarant dés à present qu'il les tient tous, non seulement sous sa Protection, mais comme ses propres Sujets, s'estans une fois donnez à Sa Majesté à titre de sujettion & vasselage, ains au contraire que lesdites Nations Iroquoises seront obligées de les assister en tous leurs besoins, soit en Chasse, soit en Paix ou en Guerre, & que les divisions & inimitiez qui ont esté entre lesdits Algonquins & Hurons, & entre les Iroquois, cessantes par le present Traité, il y aura une amitié & un secours mutuel entre toutes lesdites Nations, qui s'uniront comme freres pour leur commune deffense, sous la protection dudit Seigneur Roy.

III.

Que lesdites Nations Iroquoises ayant rendu des témoignages du respect & de la forte consideration qu'elles avoient pour le nom François, en la personne du nommé le Moyne, Habitant du Mont-Real, Sujet dudit Seigneur Roy, par elles pris en Guerre, qu'elles ont soigneusement conservé & ramené de mesme sein & entier jusques dans son propre Foyer, avec un autre François leur prisonnier, ledit Seigneur Roy leur remettra une femme Iroquoise, Captive des Algonquins demeurans aux Trois Rivieres, comme dés à

C113470

9
à prefent il fait une Femme Huronne d'une Famille refugiée à Tfonnont8an, laquelle fe trouve prefentement Captive dans le Fort des Hurons à Quebec.

IV.

Que conformément à leurs defirs, & à leurs inftantes prieres, il leur fera accordé deux Robes Noires, c'eſt à dire deux Peres Jefuites, l'un defquels fera fucceffeur des charitables foins que le feu Pere le Moyne a pris de leur inftruction ; Qu'auſſi en échange elles auront pour lefdites deux Robes les mefmes fentimens de reconnoiffance qu'elles ont témoignez à la memoire dudit feu Pere, la mort duquel elles ont declaré avoir apprife paſſant aux Trois-Rivieres avec un fenfible déplaifir, ayant mefme fait un prefent pour le reffufciter. Pareillement qu'il leur fera envoyé au Printemps prochain un Armurier, pour remettre leurs Armes rompuës en eſtat de fervice contre leurs Ennemis; & un Chirurgien pour penfer leurs malades & leurs bleffez; ce qu'elles ont ardemment defiré, & ce que ledit Seigneur leur accorde volontiers, pour leur témoigner non feulement le zele qu'il a de procurer chez elles l'avancement du Chriftianifme, l'établiſſement de la Foy, & leur falut, en les faifant inftruire des Principes & Myfteres de noftre Religion ; mais la bonté & charité qui porte Sa Majefté à leur donner les fecours temporels qui leur font fi neceffaires, ou fi utiles contre les maladies, leurs Ennemis domeftiques, & contre l'attaque des Eftrangers.

V.

Que puifque les quatre Nations Iroquoifes reconnoiſſent les avantages qu'elles ont receus de l'union des François, & de la communication qu'ils avoient avec elles, tandis qu'elles les ont eus dans leurs Habitations, & que les efperans pareils, elles demandent que ledit Seigneur Roy faſſe paſſer à Onnontague, Goiog8en & Tfonnont8an, des Familles Françoiſes pour s'habituer dans leur Païs, offrant

B

10

d'aider à leur eftabliffement, & de les appuyer de leurs forces contre les Nations qui voudroient s'y oppofer ou le retarder, Sa Majefté s'engage d'y en envoyer au Printemps prochain, avec les Ambaffadeurs qui doivent apporter la Ratification du prefent Traité de la part des quatre Habitations, à condition que dans chacune d'icelles il fera donné des Champs propres à former des Cabanes, pour y mettre lefdites Familles à couvert, & nourrir du Bled d'Inde, qui fera fourni pour femence en échange d'autres denrées, qui feront à cet effet portées de la part des François qui en fourniront aux Nations Iroquoifes. Que la Chaffe & la Pefche feront communes aux Familles Françoifes, qui d'ailleurs recevront des Iroquoifes tous les fecours & les affiftances favorables, que de veritables Freres doivent s'entrerendre les uns aux autres.

VI.

Que pour rendre l'union defirée des Nations Iroquoifes avec la Françoife, plus forte & plus folide, la Paix plus ferme & perdurable, & la correfpondance plus aifée, il fera envoyé de chacune des quatre Nations Superieures à Mont-Real, aux Trois Rivieres, & à Québec, deux des principales Familles Iroquoifes, aufquelles il fera donné des Champs, & des Bleds d'Inde & François, outre le benefice de la Chaffe & de la Pefche commune, qui leur fera accordé: & ce pour nourrir & fomenter d'autant plus cette Paix fouvent faite & fi fouvent rompuë, & engager mieux ledit Seigneur Roy à continuer fa protection à toute la Nation en general, à laquelle ce moyen eft offert pour feconder les bonnes intentions qu'elle a, de ne tenir pas les François par l'extremité de la robe & par la frange feulement, mais les embraffer fortement par le milieu du corps.

VII.

Que fur l'affeurance donnée au nom des quatre Nations, qu'il ne fera fait aucun acte d'hoftilité fur les François Al-

C 113 473

II

-gonquins & Hurons, la Hache defdits François Algonquins & Hurons, demeurera refpectivement fufpenduë à l'egard defdites Nations Iroquoifes, jufqu'au retour des Ambaffadeurs avec la Ratification du prefent Traité. Bien entendu que comme il y a des Onnei8teronnons & Gaigneigronnons en parti de Chaffe & de Guerre; Si, qu'à Dieu ne plaife, ils attaquoient ou par hazard ou par malice les François Algonquins ou Hurons, il fera permis à ceux-cy de repouffer la force par la force, & d'avoir recours aux Armes pour mettre leurs vies en feureté, fans que pour la mort ou défaite defdits partis, on puiffe imputer leur jufte refiftance à infraction de Traité.

VIII.

Que comme on ne peut excufer les Gagneigronnons de n'avoir pas fceu l'arrivée des François, les Forts par eux conftruits & avancez fur la Riviere de Richelieu, & dans le voifinage de l'habitation defdits Gagneigronnons, leur ayant deu fuffifamment apprendre, on ne peut auffi les excufer de n'avoir pas envoyé des Ambaffadeurs pour demander la Paix, de mefme que les autres Nations Superieures; Qu'ainfi cette Nation feule fera excluë de ce Traité pour le prefent, le Seigneur Roy fe refervant de l'y comprendre, s'il le juge à propos, lors qu'elle envoyera de fa part luy demander la Paix & fa Protection.

IX.

Que pour le prefent Traité demeure feure, ferme & inviolable, & qu'il foit accompli en tous les points & articles y contenus, traitez, accordez & ftipulez, entre Meffire Alexandre de Prouville, en prefence & affifté comme deffus, & les fix Ambaffadeurs cy-deffus nommez, il fera refpectivement figné de part & d'autre, pour demeurer autentique & y avoir recours en cas de befoin; Aprés que lecture en aura efté faite en Langue Iroquoife, & que dans quatre Lunes la Ratification en fera apportée de la part des quatre Nations

12

Superieures, par le retour des mêmes Ambassadeurs, qui ne pouvant signer se sont volontairement obligez de mettre la Marque distinctive de leurs Familles, l'Ours, le Loup & la Tortuë, en presence de François le Mercier, Religieux, Prestre & Superieur de la Compagnie de JESUS, à Quebec, de Joseph Marie Chaumonot, autre Prestre & Religieux de la même Compagnie, & de Charles le Moyne, Habitant de Mont Real, tous Interpretes des Langues Iroquoises & Huronnes, lesquels ont signé comme témoins. Fait à Quebec le treizieme Decembre 1666.

APPENDIX 3
La Grande Paix de Montréal, 1701

Signed on 4 August 1701 in Montréal

Louis-Hector de Callières, signatory (New France) & representatives of several Indigenous nations.[1]

Modern spelling.

Ratification de la Paix faite au mois de septembre dernier entre la colonie de Canada, les Sauvages ses alliés, et les Iroquois dans une assemblée générale des chefs de chacune de ces nations convoquées par monsieur le chevalier de Callières, gouverneur et lieutenant général pour le roi en la Nouvelle-France, à Montréal le quatre août 1701.

Comme il n'y avait ici l'année dernière que des députés des Hurons et des Outaouais lorsque je fis la paix avec les Iroquois pour moi et tous mes alliés, je jugeai qu'il était nécessaire d'envoyer le sieur de Courtemanche et le r[évérend] p[ère] [E]njalran chez toutes les autres nations mes alliés qui étaient absents pour leur apprendre ce qui s'était passé et les inviter à descendre des chefs de chacune avec les prisonniers iroquois qu'ils avaient afin d'écouter tous ensemble ma parole.

C'est une extrême joie de voir ici présentement tous mes enfants assemblés, vous Hurons, Outaouais du Sable [Akonapi], Kiskakons, Outaouais Sinago, nation de la Fourche [Odawas Nassawaketons], Saulteurs [Ojibwés], Potawatomis, Sauks, Puants [Ho-Chunk], Folles-Avoines [Menominees], Renards [Meskwaki], Mascoutens,

---

1. Source: <https://fr.wikisource.org/wiki/Grande_Paix_de_Montréal>. See the essentials Gilles Havard, 1992, La Grande Paix de Montréal de 1701: les voies de la diplomatie franco-amérindienne, Recherches amérindiennes au Québec, p. 189-195. National Archives of France, Fonds de colonie, C11A, vol. 19, folio, 41-44.

Miamis, Illinois, Amikwas, Népissingues, Algonquins, Témiskamingues, Cristinaux [Cris], gens des Terres, Kickapous, gens du Sault [Mohawks de Kahnawake], de la Montagne, Abénais, et vous nations iroquoises, et que m'ayant remis les uns et les autres vos intérêts entre les mains, que je puisse vous faire vivre tous en tranquillité.

Je ratifie donc aujourd'hui la paix que nous avons faite au mois d'août dernier, voulant qu'il ne soit plus parlé de tous les coups faits pendant la guerre, et je me saisis de nouveau de toutes vos haches, et de tous vos autres instruments de guerre, que je mets avec les miens dans une fosse si profonde que personne ne puisse les reprendre, pour troubler la tranquillité que je rétablis parmi mes enfants, en vous recommandant lorsque vous vous rencontrerez de vous traiter comme frères, et de vous accommoder ensemble pour la chasse, de manière qu'il n'arrive aucune brouillerie les uns avec les autres.

Et pour que cette paix ne puisse être troublée, je répète ce que j'ai déjà dit dans le traité que nous avons fait, que s'il arrivait que quelqu'un de mes enfants en frappasse un autre, celui qui aura été frappé ne se vengera point, ni par lui ni par aucun de sa part, mais il viendra me trouver pour que je lui en fasse faire raison, vous déclarant que, si l'offensant refusait d'en faire une satisfaction raisonnable, je me joindrai avec mes autres alliés à l'offensé pour l'y contraindre; ce que je ne crois pas qui puisse arriver, par l'obéissance que me doivent mes enfants qui se ressouviendront de ce que nous arrêtons présentement ensemble.

Et pour qu'ils ne puissent l'oublier, j'attache mes paroles aux colliers que je vais donner à chacune de vos nations afin que les anciens les fassent exécuter par leurs jeunes gens. Je vous invite tous à fumer dans ce calumet de paix où je commence le premier, et à manger de la viande et du bouillon que je vous fais préparer pour que j'aie comme un bon père la satisfaction de voir tous mes enfants réunis. Je garderai ce calumet qui m'a été présenté par les Miamis afin que je puisse vous faire fumer quand vous viendrez me voir.

Après que toutes les nations ci-dessus eurent entendu ce que monsieur le chevalier de Callières leur dit, ils répondirent comme il suit:

Le chef des Kiskakons:

Je n'ai pas voulu manquer, mon père, ayant su que vous me demandiez les prisonniers des Iroquois, à vous les amener. En voilà quatre que je vous présente pour en faire ce qu'il vous plaira. C'est avec cette porcelaine [wampum] que je les ai déliés, et voici un calumet que je présente aux Iroquois pour fumer ensemble quand nous nous rencontrerons. Je me réjouis de ce que vous avez uni la terre qui était bouleversée, et je souscris volontiers à tout ce que vous avez fait.

Les Iroquois:

Nous voilà assemblés, notre père, comme vous l'avez souhaité. Vous plantâtes l'année dernière un arbre de paix et vous y mîtes des racines et des feuilles pour que nous y fussions à l'abri. Nous espérons présentement que tout le monde entende ce que vous dites, qu'on ne touchera point à cet arbre. Pour nous, nous vous assurons par ces quatre colliers, que nous suivrons tout ce que vous avez réglé. Nous vous présentons deux prisonniers que voici, et nous vous rendrons les autres que nous avons. Nous espérons aussi, présentement, que les portes sont ouvertes pour la paix, qu'on nous renverra le reste des nôtres.

Les Hurons :

Nous voilà ici comme vous l'avez demandé. Nous vous présentons douze prisonniers, dont cinq veulent retourner avec nous ; pour les sept autres vous en ferez ce qu'il vous plaira. Nous vous remercions de la paix que vous nous avez procurée, et nous la ratifions avec joie.

Jean le Blanc, Outaouais du Sable :

Je vous ai obéi, mon père, aussitôt que vous m'avez demandé, en vous ramenant deux prisonniers dont vous êtes le maître. Quand vous m'avez commandé d'aller à la guerre je l'ai fait, et à présent que vous me le défendez j'y obéis. Je vous demande, mon père, par ce collier, que les Iroquois délient mon corps qui est chez eux, et qu'ils me le renvoient (c'est-à-dire les gens de sa nation).

Sangouessy, Outaouais Sinago :

Je n'ai pas voulu manquer à vos ordres, mon père, quoique je n'eusse point de prisonniers. Cependant, voilà une femme et un enfant que j'ai rachetés, dont vous ferez ce qu'il vous plaira, et voilà un calumet que je donne aux Iroquois pour fumer comme frères quand nous nous rencontrerons.

Chichicatalo, chef des Miamis :

Je vous ai obéi, mon père, en vous ramenant huit prisonniers iroquois pour en faire ce qu'il vous plaira. Si j'avais eu des canots, je vous en aurais amené davantage. Quoique je ne voie point ici des miens qui sont chez les Iroquois, je vous ramènerai ce qui m'en reste si vous le souhaitez, ou je leur ouvrirai les portes pour qu'ils s'en retournent.

Onanguisset, pour les Sakis :

Je ne fais qu'un même corps avec vous, mon père. Voilà un prisonnier iroquois que j'avais fait à la guerre ; souffrez qu'en vous le présentant je lui donne un calumet pour emporter chez les Iroquois et fumer quand nous nous rencontrerons. Je vous remercie de ce que vous éclairez le soleil qui était obscur depuis la guerre.

Onanguisset, chef des Potawatomis :

Je ne vous ferai point un long discours, mon père ; je n'ai plus que deux prisonniers que je mets à vos deux côtés pour en faire ce qu'il vous plaira. Voilà un calumet que je vous présente, pour que vous le gardiez ou que vous le donniez à ces deux prisonniers afin qu'ils fument dedans chez eux. Je suis toujours prêt à vous obéir jusqu'à la mort.

Misgensa, chef des Ontagamis:

Je n'ai point de prisonniers à vous rendre, mon père, mais je vous remercie du beau jour que vous donnez à toute la terre par la paix. Pour moi, je ne perdrai jamais cette clarté.

Les Maskoutains:

Je ne vous amène point d'esclave iroquois parce que je n'ai pas été en parti contre eux depuis quelque temps, m'étant amusé à faire la guerre à d'autres nations; mais je suis venu pour vous obéir et vous remercier de la paix que vous nous procurez.

Les Folles-Avoines:

Je suis seulement venu, mon père, pour vous obéir et embrasser la paix que vous avez faite entre les Iroquois et nous.

Les Sauteux et les Puants:

Je vous aurais amené, mon père, des esclaves iroquois si j'en avais eu, voulant vous obéir en ce que vous m'ordonnerez. Je vous remercie de la clarté que vous nous donnez et je souhaite qu'elle dure.

Les Népissingues:

Je n'ai pas voulu manquer à me rendre ici comme les autres pour écouter votre voix. J'avais un prisonnier iroquois l'année passée que je vous ai rendu. Voilà un calumet que je vous présente pour le donner aux Iroquois si vous le souhaitez, afin de fumer ensemble quand nous nous rencontrerons.

Les Algonquins:

Je n'ai point de prisonniers à vous rendre, mon père. L'Algonquin est un de vos enfants qui a toujours collé à vous, et qui y sera tant qu'il vivra. Je prie le maître de la vie que ce que vous faites aujourd'hui dure.

L'Amikois:

N'ayant point d'autre volonté que la vôtre, j'obéis à ce que vous venez de faire.

L'Abénaquis:

Quoique je parle des derniers, je ne suis pas moins à vous, mon père. Vous savez que je vous ai toujours été attaché. Je n'ai plus de haches; vous l'avez mise dans une fosse l'année dernière et je ne la reprendrai que quand vous me l'ordonnerez.

Les Gens du Sault :

Vous n'ignorez pas, vous autres Iroquois, que nous ne soyons attachés à notre père, nous qui demeurons avec lui et qui sommes dans son sein. Vous nous envoyâtes un collier il y a trois ans pour nous inviter à vous procurer la paix; nous vous en envoyâmes un en réponse. Nous vous donnons encore celui-ci pour vous dire que nous y avons travaillé; nous ne demandons pas mieux qu'elle soit de durée faite aussi de votre côté ce qu'il faut pour cela.

Les Gens de la Montagne :

Vous avez fait assembler ici, notre père, toutes les nations pour faire un amas de haches et les mettre dans la terre avec la vôtre. Pour moi qui n'en avais pas d'autre, je me réjouis de ce que vous faites aujourd'hui, et j'invite les Iroquois à nous regarder comme leurs frères.

APPENDIX 4
Indigenous Peoples' treaties, Mi'kmaq, Maliseet, etc., 1725-1776[1]

The submission and agreement of the Delegates of the Eastern Indians[2]

(December 15, 1725, Boston, New England, British possession)

Whereas the several Tribes of the Eastern Indians viz the Penobscot, Narridgwolk, St. Johns Cape Sables & other Tribes Inhabiting within His Majesties Territorys of New England and Nova Scotia, who have been Engaged in the present War, from whom we Sauguaaram alias Loron Arexus Francois Xavier & Meganumbe are Delegated & fully Impowered to Enter into Articles of Pacification with His Majties Governments of the Massachusetts Bay New Hampshire & Nova Scotia Have contrary to the several Treatys they have Solemnly Entered into with the said Governments made an open Rupture & have continued some years in Acts of Hostility Against the subjects of His Majesty King George within the said Governments, They being now sensible of the Miseries and Troubles they have involved themselves in, and being Desirous to be restored to His Majesty's Grace & Favour & to live in Peace with all His Majesties Subjects of the said three Governmts & the Province of New York and Colonys of Connecticut & Rhode Island, and that all former Acts of Injury be forgotten Have Concluded to make and we Do by these presents In the Name and behalf of the said Tribes make our Submission unto Hist Most Excellent Majesty George by the Grace of God of Great Britain France and Ireland King Defender of the Faith & C. in as full and ample manner as any of our Predecessors have heretofore done.

---

1. Cap Breton University. "Treaties" (2023): <https://www.cbu.ca/indigenous-initiatives/lnu-resource-centre/treaties/>.
2. Cap Breton University. "Treaty of 1725" (2023): <https://www.cbu.ca/indigenous-initiatives/lnu-resource-centre/treaties/treaty-of-1725/>.

And we do hereby Promise and Engage with the Honorable William Dummer Esqr as he is Lieutenant Governor & Comander in Chief of the said Province for the time being That is to say.

We the said Delegates for and in behalf of the several Tribes aforesaid Do Promise and Engage that at all times forever from and after the date of these presents We and they will lease and forbear all Acts of Hostility Injuries and Discords towards all the Subjects of the Crown of Great Britain, & not offer the lease hurt Violence or Molestation to them or any of them in their Persons or Estates, But will hence forward hold & maintain a firm and Constant Amity and Friendship with all the English and will never Confederate or Combine with any other Nation to their prejudice.

That all the Captives taken in this present War shall at or before the time of the further Ratification of this Treaty be Restored without any Ransom or payment to be made for them or any of them.

That His Majesties Subjects the English shall and may peaceable and Quietly Enter upon Improve & forever Enjoy all & Singular their rights of Land and former Settlements Properties & possessions within the Eastern parts of the said Province of the Massachusetts Bay Together with all Islands Islets, Shoars Beaches and Fishery within the same, without any Molestation or Claims by us, or any other Indians, and in no ways Molested Interupted, or disturbed therein.

Saving unto the Penoscot, Narridgewalk And other Tribes within His Majesties Province aforesaid and their Natural descendants respectively All their Lands liberties & properties not by them Conveyed or sold to, or possess'd by any of the English subjects or aforesaid As also the Privilege of Fishing, Hunting & Fowling as formerly.

That all Trade and Commerce which hereafter may be allowed betwixt the English & Indians shall be under such Management & Regulation, as the Government of the Massachusetts Province shall direct.

If any Controversy of difference at any time hereafter happen to arise between any of the English & Indians for any real or supposed wrong or injury done on either side, no private Revenge shall be taken for the same, but proper Application shall be made to His Majesty's Government upon the place for remedy or Redress there in a due Course of Justice we submit Our selves to be Ruled and Governed by His Majesties Laws and desiring to have the Benefit of the same.

We also the said Delegates in behalf of the Tribes of Indians Inhabiting within the French Territorys who have assisted us in this War, for whom we are fully Impowered to Act in this present Treaty. Do hereby Promise and Engage that they and every of them shall henceforth lease and forbear all Acts of Hostility Force & Violence towards all and every the Subjects of His Majesty the King of Great Britain.

We do further in behalf of the Tribe of the Penobscot Indians Promise & Engage That if any of the other Tribes Intended to be included in this Treaty, shall notwithstanding refuse to Confirm & Ratify this present Treaty Entered into on their behalf & Continue or renew Acts of Hostility against the English in such case the said Penobscot Tribe shall Joyn their Young Men with the English in reducing them to reason.

In the next place we the aforenamed Delegated Do Promise and Engage with the Honorable John Wentworth Esqr as he is Lieutt Governor & Comander in Chief of His Majesties Province of New Hampshire & with the Governors & Comanders in Chief of the said Province for the time being, That we & the Tribes we are Deputed from, willhenceforth lease & Forbear all Acts of Hostility Injuries and Discords towards all the subjects of His Majesty King George within the said Province. And we do understand and take it that the said Government of New Hampshire is also Included and Comprehend in all and every the Articles aforegoing, Excepting that respect the Regulating the Trade with us.

And further we the aforenamed Delegates Doe Promise & Engage with the Honoble Lawrence Armstrong Esqr Lt Governor & Comander in Chief of His Majesties Province of Nova Scotia or Accadie to live in peace with his Majesty's Good Subjects & their Dependants in that Government according to the Articles agreed upon with Majr Paul Mascarene Commissioner for that purpose & further to be Ratified as mentioned in the said Articles.

That this present Treaty shall be Accepted Ratified & Confirmed in a Public and Solemn Manner by the Chiefs of the several Eastern Tribes of Indians Including therein at Falmouth in Casco Bay so time in the Month of May next In whereof we have signed these present Affixed our Seals.

Dated in the Council Chamber in Boston in New England the fifteenth day of December Anno Domini One thousand seven hundred and Twenty five Annoq. RRS Georgii Magna Britanix &c Duodecimo.

Done in the presence of the Great & General Court or Assemble of the Province of the Massachusetts Bay Aforesaid

Being first read distinctly & Interpreted by Capt. John Giles Capt. Saml Jordan & Capt. Joseph Bane sworn Interpreters.

Att J Willard Secry
Sauguaaram Alt Loron
Arexies
Francois Xavier

Ratification of 1725 Treaty[3]

Whereas by the Articles of Peace and agreement Made & concluded upon att Boston in New England the Fifteenth Day of Dec^r: One Thousand Seven Hundred & twenty five by our Delegates & Representatives Sanguarum (allias Laruns) Alexis Francois Xavier & Meganumbe as appears by the Instruments then Sign'd Seal'd & Exchanged in the Presence of the Great & Generall Court or Afsembly of ye Mafsachusetts Bay by our Said Delegates in behalf of us the Said Indians of Penobscot, Norridgewolk, St Johns, Cape Sable, and the other Indian Tribes belonging to & inhabiting within these His Majesty of Great Britains Territories [of] Nova Scotia & New England & by Maj^r: Paul Mascarene Comifsioner from this Said Province in behalf of His Majesty by which Agreem^t itt being requir'd that the Said Articles Shou'd be ratified [?] att His Majesty's Fort of Annapolis Royall Wee the Chiefs & Representatives of the Said Indians with Full Power & Authority by Unanimous Consent 2 desire of the Said Indian Tribes are Come in Complyance with ye Articles Stipulated by our Delegates as aforesaid and do in Obedience thereunto Solemnly Confirm & ratifie ye Same & in Testimony thereof with Hearts full of Sincerity. Wee have Signed & sealed the following Articles being Conform to what was requir'd by the Said Maj^r Paul Mascarene & Promife to be perform'd by our Said Delegates.

Whereas His Majesty King George by the Concefsion of the Most Christian King made att the Treaty of Utrecht is become ye Rightfull Profsefsor of the Province of Nova Scotia or Acadia According to its ancient Boundaries wee the Said Chiefs & Representatives of ye Penobscott, Norridgewolk S^t. Johns, Cape Sables, & of the Other Indian Tribes Belonging to & inhabiting within This His Majesties Province of Nova Scotia or Acadia & New England do for our Selves & the Said Tribes Wee represent acknowledge His Said Majesty King George's Jurisdiction & Dominion Over the Territories of the Said Province of Nova Scotia or Acadia & make our Submifsion to His Said Majesty in as ample a Manner as wee have formerly done to the Most Christian King.

That the Indians shall nott molest any of His Majesty's Subjects or their Dependants in their Settlements already made or Lawfully to be made or in their carrying on Their Trade or Other Affaires within the Said Province.

That If there Happens any robbery or outrage Committed by any of Our Indians the Tribe or Tribes they belong to Shall Cause Satisfaction to be made to ye partys Injur'd.

That the Indians Shall nott help to convey away any Soldiers belonging to His Majesty's Forts butt on the Contrary Shall bring back any Soldier they Shall find Endeavouring to run away.

---

3. New Brunswick Aboriginal Peoples Council (2022), "Ratification of 1725 Treaty", <https://nbapc.org/treaty-of-1726/>.

APPENDIX 4 – INDIGENOUS PEOPLES' TREATIES

That in Case of any Mifsunderstanding Quarrell or Injury between the English & the Indians no Private revenge Shall be taken, butt Application Shall be made for redrefs According to His Majestys Laws.

That if any English Prisoners amongst any of our aforesaid Tribes wee faithfully promifs that the said Prinsoners shall be releas'd & Carefully Conducted & Deliver'd up to this Governmen^{mt}, or that of New England.

That in Testimony of our Sincerity wee have for our Selves & in behalf of Our Said Indian Tribes Confirmes to what was Stipulated by our Delegates att Boston as aforesaid this day Solemnly Confirm'd & ratified each & ratified each & every One of the aforegoing Articles which Shall be Punctually observ'd & duly perform'd by Each & all of us the Said Indians.

IIn Wittnefs Whereof wee have before the [?] [?] John Doucett & Councill for this His Majesty Said Province & the Deputies of the ffrench Inhabitants of Sd Province hereunto Sett our Hands & Seals att Annapolis Royall this 4th Day of June 1726 & in the Twelveth Year of His Majestys Reign.

Chief of
[?] Nipimoit
Nicholas X **S^t. Johns** [notre soulignement]
Chief of
[?] Paul Tecumart X one of ye
Cape Sables
Joseph Ounaginitish X of
Cape Sables
Marquis X of St. Johns [note: marque d'un X de St-Jean]
Obin^a X
Piere X Benoit
Denis X
Puize X Paul
Louis X
Francois X
St Castine X
Jofeph X St Obin
Andre X
Simon X
Joseph X
Joseph [totem]
Joseph [totem]
Francois X
Francois X
Francois X
Michel X
Joseph [totem]

Piere Benoit X
Charles X
Andre X
Chief of
Jean Baptist [totem] Pon
Chichabenady
Jean [totem] Baptist
Etiene fils de Baptist Pon
of
Piere X Martine Chief
Refhiboucto
Jirom X of Attanas Chief
Gidiark
Joseph Martine X
Chief of
Piere X Armquarett
Minis
Chief of
Philip X Eargomot
Chikanicto
Michel [tm] Eargamet
Mark [tm] Antoine
Joseph [totem le Grand
Claud X Grand Glode
Rene X Grand Glode
Francois X Grand Glode
of
Jean Baptist X Chief
Cape Sables
Matthew X Muse
Joseph X Miductuk
from
Jacque X Pemeriot
Pentaquit
Petit Jermain X
Piere Pisnett X
Antoin X Nimquarett
from
Lewis X Pemeroit
Pentaquit
Etien X Chegau
Reny X Nectabau
Piere X Nimcharett
of ye River Indians
Baptist X Tomus Chief

of Annapolis Royal
Jean X Pisnett
Francois X Jermain
from
Francois X Xavier
Pentaquit
Noel X Shomitt
Pafsmaquoddy
Piere X Nimcharett
Piere X Chegau
Francois X Chickarett
Antoine X Tecumart
Philip X Tecumart
Bernard X S^t aboqmadin
Tomas X Outine
Chief of ye Eastern
Antoine X Egigish
Coast
Jean X Quaret
Simon X Nelanoit
Jacque X Denis
Francois X Spugonoit
Jacque X Nughquit
Claud X Begamonit
Jacque Penall
Claud X Migaton
Simon X Spugonoit
Louis X Lavoinst
Jean X Pinet
from ye Cape
Joseph X Chigaguisht
Breton
Jacque X Chegan
[Signed]
Otho Hamilton
Richard Bull
James Ershine
Geo^e Baker
Hugh Campbell

Robert Wroth
Eras: T. Philipps
[Produced by Atlantic Policy Congress of First Nation Chiefs Secretariat, 1999]

Treaty of 1749

In behalf of the Chiefs of the Indian Tribes we Represent have Subscribed and affixed our Seals to the Same and engage that the siad Chiefs shall Ratify this Treaty at St. Johns. Done in Chibucto Harbour the fifteenth of August One Thousand Seven hundred and forty nine.[4]

In Presence of

L. E. HOPSON,
T. MASCARENCE,
ROBT. ELLISON,
JAMES T. MERIER,
CHAS. LAWRENCE
ED. HOW,
JOHN GORHAM,
BENJ. GREEN,
JOHN SALUSBURY,
HUGH DAVIDSON,
Wm STEELE

JOANNES PEDOUSAGHTIGH, (totem) [notre soulignement]
FRANCOIS ARODORVISH, (totem)
SIMON SACTARVINO, (totem)
JEAN BAP.T MADDOUANHOOK, (totem)

The Articles of Peace on the other Side, Concluded at Chebucto, to the fifteenth of August, one thousand Seven hundred and forty-nine, with His Excellency Edward Cornwallis Esqr., Capt. General., Governour and Commander in Chief of His Majes^{ts} Province of Nova scotia or Accadie and Signed by our deputies, having been communicated to us by Edward How, Esqr., one of His Majes^{ts}Council for Said Province, and faithfully Interpreted to Us by Madame De Bellisle Inhabitant of this river nominated by us for that purpose. We the chiefs and Captains of the River St. Johns and places adjacent do for ourselves and our different tribes confirm and ratify the same to all intents and purposes. Given under our hands at the River St. Johns this fourth day of September one thousand Seven hundred and forty-nine in the presence of the under written witnesses.

ED. HOW. of his Majesty's Council
NATH DONNELL
JOHN WEARE
JOSEPH WINNIETT
JOHN WENN
Robert Mc Koun
MATT WINNIETT
JOHN PHILLIPPS

---

4. Cap Breton University. "Treaty of 1749" (2023): <https://www.cbu.ca/indigenous-initiatives/lnu-resource-centre/treaties/treaty-of-1749/>.

MICHELL (TOTEM) NARREYONES *Chief,* [notre soulignement]
NNOLA (TOTEM) NEGUIN *Capt.,*
FRANçOIS (TOTEM) DE XAWIER ARCHIBANO MARQILLIE,
PIERRE (TOTEM) ALEXANDER MARGILLIE,
AUGUSTA (TOTEM) MEYAWET, *Maitre Clef de la Rio.,*
FRANÇOIS (TOTEM) MAYAWYAWET, *Maitre Serure Dt.,*
RENE (TOTEM) NEYUM,
NEPTUNE (TOTEM) PIERRE PAUL, *Chief of Capneyneidy,*
SUAPAU (TOTEM) PAPANLONET
FRANÇOIS (TOTEM) GORMAM, *Capt.,*
PIERRE (TOTEM) BENNOIT, *Capt.,*
FRANÇOIS (TOTEM) DRINO, *Capt.,*
RENE (TOTEM) FILIE DAMBROUS, *Capt.*

[Produced by the Atlantic Policy Congress of First Nation Chiefs Secretariat 1999].

Treaty of 1752

Enclosure in letter of Governor Hopson to the Right Honourable The Earl of Holdernesse 6th of Dec. 1752[5]

Treaty or Articles of Peace and Friendship Renewed

BETWEEN

His Excellency Peregrine Thomas Hopson Esquire Captain General and Governor in Chief in and over His Majesty's Province of Nova Scotia or Acadie Vice Admiral of the same & Colonel of One of His Majesty's Regiments of Foot, and His Majesty's Council on behalf of His Majesty,

AND

Major Jean Baptiste Cope Chief Sacham of the Tribe of Mick Mack Indians, Inhabiting the Eastern Coast of the said Province, and Andrew Hadley Martin, Gabriel Martin and Francis Jeremiah members & Delegates of the said Tribe, for themselves and their said Tribe their heirs and the heirs of their heirs forever. [nous soulignons]

Begun made and Concluded in the manner form & Tenor following, viz.

1. It is agreed that the Articles of Submission & Agreements made at Boston in New England by the Delegates of the Penobscot Norridgwolk & St. John's Indians in the Year 1725 Ratifyed and Confirmed by all the Nova Scotia Tribes at Annapolis Royal in the Month of June 1726 and lately Renewed with Governor Cornwallis at Halifax and Ratifyed at St. John's River, now read over Explained & Interpreted shall be and are hereby from this time forward renewed, reiterated, and forever Confirmed by them and their Tribe, and the said Indians for themselves and their Tribe, and their Heirs aforesaid do make and renew the same Solemn Submissions and promises for the strict Observance of all the Articles therein contained as at any time heretofore hath been done.

2. That all Transactions during the Late War shall on both sides be buried in Oblivion with the Hatchet, And that the said Indians shall have all favour, Friendship & Protection shewn them from this His Majesty's Government.

---

5. Cap Breton University. "Treaty of 1752" (2023): <https://www.cbu.ca/indigenous-initiatives/lnu-resource-centre/treaties/treaty-of-1752/>.

3. That the said Tribe shall use their utmost Endeavours to bring in the other Indians to Renew and Ratify this Peace, and shall discover and make known any attempts or designs of any other Indians or any Enemy whatever against his Majesty's Subjects within this Province so soon as they shall know thereof and shall also hinder and Obstruct the same to the utmost of their power, and on the other hand if any of the Indians refusing to ratify this Peace shall make War upon the Tribe who have now Confirmed the same; they shall upon Application have such aid and Assistance from the Government for their defence as the Case may require.

4. It is agreed that the said Tribe of Indians shall not be hindered from, but have free liberty of Hunting and Fishing as usual and that if they shall think a Truck house needful at the River Chibenaccadie, or any other place of their resort they shall have the same built and proper Merchandize, lodged therein to be exchanged for what the Indians shall have to dispose of and that in the mean time the Indians shall have free liberty to being to Sale to Halifax or any other Settlement within this Province, Skins, feathers, fowl, fish or any other thing they shall have to sell, where they shall have liberty to dispose thereof to the best Advantage.

5. That a Quantity of bread, flour, and such other Provisions, as can be procured, necessary for the Familys and proportionable to the Numbers of the said Indians, shall be given them half Yearly for the time to come; and the same regard shall be had to the other Tribes that shall hereafter Agree to Renew and Ratify the Peace upon the Terms and Conditions now Stipulated.

6. That to Cherish a good harmony and mutual Correspondence between the said Indians and this Government His Excellency Peregrine Thomas Hopson Esq. Capt. General & Governor in Chief in & over His Majesty's Province of Nova Scotia or Acadie Vice Admiral of the same & Colonel of One of His Majesty's Regiments of Foot hereby promises on the part of His Majesty that the said Indians shall upon the First Day of October Yearly, so long as they shall Continue in Friendship, Receive Presents of Blankets, Tobacco, and some Powder & Shot, and the said Indians promise once every year, upon the first of October, to come by themselves or their Delegates and Receive the said Presents and Renew their Friendship and Submissions.

7. That the Indians shall use their best Endeavours to save the Lives & goods of any People Shipwrecked on this Coast where they resort and shall Conduct the People saved to Halifax with their Goods, and a Reward adequate to the Salvage shall be given them.

8. That all Disputes whatsoever that may happen to arise between the Indians now at Peace and others His Majesty's Subjects in this Province shall be tryed in His Majesty's Courts of Civil Judicature, where the Indians shall have the same benefits, Advantages & Priviledges an any others of His Majesty's Subjects.

In Faith & Testimony whereof the Great Seal of the Province is hereunto appended, and the Partys to these Presents have hereunto interchangeably Set their Hands in the Council Chamber at Halifax this 22nd day of Nov. 1752 in the 26th Year of His Majesty's Reign.

P.T. Hopson
Chas. Lawrence
Benj. Green
Jno. Collier
Jno. Salusbury
Willm. Steele
Jean Baptiste
Cope X
Andrew Hadley X
Francios X
Gabriel X

[Produced by the Atlantic Policy Congress of First Nation Chiefs Secretariat, 1999].

Treaties of 1760-1761

Whereas Articles of Submission and Agreement were made and concluded at Boston in New England in the Year of Our Lord 1725 by Sauguaaram alias Loron Arexus Xavier and Meganumbe, Delegates from the Tribes of Penobscott Naridgwalk St. Johns and other tribes inhabiting His Majesty's Territories of Nova Scotia and New England, in manner and form following Vizn.[6]

Articles of Submission and Agreement at Boston in New England by Sauguaaram als Loron Arexus Francois Xavier and Meganumbe Delegates from the Tribes of Penobscot Naridgwalk St. Johns Cape Sable and other Tribes of the Indians inhabiting within His Majesty's Territories of Nova Scotia and New England.

Whereas His Majesty King George by the Concession of the most Christian King made at the Treaty of Utrecht is become the Rightfull possessor of the Province of Nova Scotia or Accadie according to its ancient Boundaries We the said Sauguaram als Loron Arexus Francois Xavier and Megamumbe Delegates from the said Tribes of Penobscot Naridgwalk St. Johns, Cape Sables and other Tribes inhabiting within His Majesty's said Territories of Nova Scotia or Accadie and New England So in the Name and behalf of the said Tribes we represent acknowledge his Said Majesty King Georges Jurisdiction and Dominion over the Territories of said Province of Nova Scotia or Accadie and make our Submission to his Said Majesty in as ample a manner as We have formerly done to the Most Christian King.

And we further promise in behalf of the said Tribes we represent that the Indians shall not molest any of His Majesty's Subjects or their Dependants in their Settlements already or lawfully to be made or in their carrying on their Trade and other affairs within said Province.

That if there happens any Robbery, or outrage Committed by any of the Indians the Tribe or Tribes they belong to shall cause Satisfaction and Restitution to be made to the Parties injured.

That the Indians shall not help to convey away any Soldiers belonging to His Majesty's Forts, but on the contrary shall bring back any soldier they find endeavouring to run away.

That, in case of any misunderstanding Quarrel or Injury between the English and the Indians no private Revenge shall be taken but application shall be made for Redress according to his Majesty's laws.

---

6. Cap Breton University. "Treaties of 1760-1761" (2023): <https://www.cbu.ca/indigenous-initiatives/lnu-resource-centre/treaties/treaties-of-1760-1761/>.

That is the Indians have made any Prisoners belonging to the Government of Nova Scotia or Accadie during the course of the War they shall be released at or before the Ratification of the Treaty.

That this Treaty shall be Ratified at Annapolis Royal.

Dated at the Council Chamber at Boston in New England this fifteenth day of December An Dom, one thousand Seven hundred and twenty five Annog R.R. Georgy Mag Britan and Duodecimo.

Which Articles of Submission and Agreement were renewed and confirmed at Halifax in Nova Scotia in the Year of Our Lord 1749 by Joannes Pedousaghugh Chief of the Tribe of Chignecto Indians and Francois Aroudourvish, Simon Sactarvino and Jean Baptiste Maddouanhook, Deputies from the Chiefs of the St. Johns Indians in manner and form following Vizn.

I Johannes Pedoudaghugh Chief of the Tribe of Chignecto Indians for myself and in behalf of my Tribe my Heirs and their heirs for ever and We Francois Aroudorvish, Simon Sactarvino and Jean Baptiste Maddouanhook Deputies from the Chiefs of the St. Johns Indians and invested by them with full powers for that purpose Do in the most solemn manner renew the above Articles of Agreement and Submission and every Article thereof with His Excellency Edward Cornwallis Esq. Captain General and Governor in Chief in and over His Majestys Province of Nova Scotia or Accadie Vice admiral of the Same Colonel in His Majestys Service and one of his bed Chamber in Witness whereof I the said Johannes Pedousaghugh have Subscribed this Treaty and affixed by Seal and We the said Francois Aroudorvisah Simon Sactarvino and Jean Baptiste Maddouanhook in behalf of the Chiefs of the Indian Tribes we Represent have Subscribed and affixed our Seals t the Same and engage that the said Chiefs shall Ratify this Treaty at St. Johns. Done in Chibucto Harbour the fifteenth of August One Thousand Seven hundred and forty-nine.

In Presence of P. Hopson, Mascarence, Robt ellison, Iam T. mercer, Chas. Lawrence, Edn How, Edm. Gorham, Benj. Green, John Salusbury, Hugh Davidson, William Steele (Members of the Council for Nova Scotia)

Johannes Pedousaghsigh
Francois Arodorvish
Simon Sactarvino
Jean Bap.t Maddouanhook

And the same was according Ratified at St. Johns in manner and form following Vizn.

The Articles of Peace on the other Side Concluded at Chibucto to the fifteenth of August One Thousand Seven hundred and forty nine with His Excellency Edward Cornwallis Esq.r Cap.t Gen. Gov.r & Commander in Chief of His Majesty's Province of Nova scotia or Accadie and Signed by our Deputies having been communicated to Us by Edward How esq.r One of His Majestys Council for Said province, and

APPENDIX 4 - INDIGENOUS PEOPLES' TREATIES

faithfully Interpreted to Us by Madam DeBelliste inhabitant of this River nominated by Us for that purpose We the Chiefs and Captains of the River St. John and places adjacent do for ourselves and our different tribes Confirm and Ratify the same to all Intents and purposes.

Given under our Hands at the River St. Johns the fourth day of September One Thousand Seven hundred and forty nine in presence of the under written Witnesses

Michell/Narragonis chief [nous soulignons]
Nicola/Neguin Capt
Francois/De Xavier Archibano Marqillie
Pierr/Alexander Margillie
Augustin/Meyacvet, Maitre Chief de Riv St. Jean
Francois/Mayanyarvet, Maitre Lerure D.
Rene/Neguin
Neptune/Pierre Paul Chief Pasmequody
Luafin/Papanlouet
Francois/Germain Capt
Pierre/Bennoit Capt
Francois/Drino Capt
Rene/fille D'ambroise Capt
Ed.d Hon. One of His Majesty's Council

nath Dennal
John Beare
Joseph Winniett
John Wonn
Rob McKoun
Matt Winniett
John Phillipps

And Whereas the said Articles of Submission and Agreement, so made and concluded, renewed, confirmed and ratified have notwithstanding been since violated contrary to the good Faith therein engaged for the constant and strict Observation and performance thereof and to the Allegiance due from the said Tribes to His Majesty Our Sovereign Lord King George We Mitchel Neptune Chief of the tribe of Indians of Passamaquody, and Ballomy Gloade Captain in the Tribe of Indians of St. John's River Delegates from the said Tribes and by them fully authorised and empowered to make and conclude with His Excellency Chas Lawrence Esq.[r] His Majesty's Captain General and Governor in Chief of the Province of Nova Scotia or Accadie in behalf of His Majestys Government of the Said Province a Treaty for the renewal and future firm Establishment of Peace and Amity between the said Tribes of Passamaquody and St. Johns River Indians and His Majesty's other subjects and to renew the Acknowledgement of the Allegiance of the said Tribes and their engagements to a perfect and constant Submission and Obedience to His Majesty King George the Second his Heirs and Successors Do accordingly in the name and behalf of the said Tribes of Passamaquody and St. Johns herby renew and Confirm the aforesaid Articles of Submission and Agreement, and every part thereof and do so solemnly promise and engage that the same shall for ever hereafter be strictly observed and performed.

And We the said Mitchel Neptune and Ballomy Glode, for ourselves and in the name and behalf of the said Tribes of Passamaquody and St. Johns Indians Do respectively further promise and engage that no person or persons belonging to the said Tribes shall at any time hereafter aid or Assist any of the Enemies of His most Sacred Majesty King George the Second or of his Heirs and successors nor shall hold any Correspondence or Commerce with any such His Majestys Enemies in any way or manner whatsoever and that, for the more effectually preventing any such Correspondence and Commerce with any of His Majestys Enemies the said Tribes shall at all times hereafter Trafic and barter and exchange Commodities with the Managers of such Truckhouses as shall be established for that purpose by his Majesty's Governors of this Province at Fort Frederick or elsewhere within the Said Province and at no other place without permission from his Majestys Geovernment of the said Province. And We do in like manner further promise and engage that for the more effectually securing and due performance of this Treaty and every part thereof a certain Number, which shall not be less than Three from each of the aforesaid tribes, shall from and after the ratification hereof constantly reside in Fort Frederick at St. Johns or at such other place or places within the Province as shall and at no other place without permission from His Majestys Government of the said Province. And We do in the manner further promise and engage that for the more effectually securing and due performance of this Treaty and every part thereof a certain Number, which shall not be less than Three from each of the aforesaid tribes, shall from and after the Ratification hereof constantly reside in Fort Frederick at St. Johns or at such other place or places within the Province as shall be appointed for that purpose by His Majestys Governors of the said Province as Hostages, which Hostages shall be exchanged for a like Number of others or of the said Tribes when requested.

And We do further promise and engage that this Treaty and every part therof shall be ratified by the Chiefs and Captains and other principal persons of the said Tribes at Fort Frederick aforesaid on or before the 20th May next.

In Faith and Testimony whereof We have Signed these Presents and caused the Seal of the Province to be hereunto affixed, and the said Michel Neptune and Ballomy Glode have hereunto put their Marks and Seals in the Council Chamber at Halifax in Nova Scotia the Twenty third Day of February in the Year of our Lord One Thousand Seven hundred and sixty and in the Thirty third Year of His Majesty's Reign.

A true Copy.

By His Excell.ys Comm
Rich.d Bulkeley, Sec.y

Treaties of 1760-1761

Treaty of Peace and Friendship concluded by [His Excellency Charles Lawrence] Esq. Govr and Com^r. in Chief in and over his Majesty's Province of Nova Scotia or Accadia with Paul Laurent chief of the LaHave tribe of Indians at Halifax in the Province of N.S. or Acadia.

I, Paul Laurent do for myself and the tribe of the LaHave Indians of which I am Chief do acknowledge the jurisdiction and Dominion of His Majesty George the Second over the Territories of Nova Scotia or Accadia and we do make submission to His Majesty in the most perfect, ample and solemn manner.

And I do promise for myself and my tribe that I nor they shall not molest any of His Majesty's subjects or their dependents, in their settlements already made or to be hereafter made or in carrying on their Commerce or in any thing whatever within the Province of His said Majesty in any thing whatever within the Province of His said Majesty or elsewhere and if any insult, robbery or outrage shall happen to be committed by any of my tribe satisfaction and restitution shall be made to the person or persons injured.

That neither I nor any of my tribe shall in any manner entice any of his said Majesty's troops or soldiers to desert, nor in any manner assit in conveying them away but on the contrary will do our utmost endeavours to bring them back to the Company, Regiment, Fort or Garrison to which they shall belong.

That if any Quarrel or Misunderstanding shall happen between myself and the English or between them and any of my tribe, neither I, nor they shall take any private satisfaction or Revenge, but we will apply for redress according to the Laws established in His said Majesty's Dominions.

That all English prisoners made by myself or my tribe shall be sett at Liberty and that we will use our utmost endeavours to prevail on the other tribes to do the same, if any prisoners shall happen to be in their hands.

And I do further promise for myself and my tribe that we will not either directly nor indirectly assist any of the enemies of His most sacred Majesty King George the Second, his heirs or Successors, nor hold any manner of Commerce traffick nor intercourse with them, but on the contrary will as much as may be in our power discover and make known to His Majesty's Governor, any ill designs which may be formed or contrived against His Majesty's subjects. And I do further engage that we will not traffick, barter or Exchange any Commodities in any manner but with such persons or the managers of such Truck houses as shall be appointed or Established by His Majesty's Governor at Lunenbourg or Elsewhere in Nova Scotia or Accadia.

And for the more effectual security of the due performance of this Treaty and every part thereof I do promise and Engage that a certain number of persons of my tribe which shall not be less in number than two prisoners shall on or before September next reside as Hostages at Lunenburg or at such other place or places in this Province of Nova Scotia or Accadia as shall be appointed for that purpose by His Majesty's Governor of said Province which Hostages shall be exchanged for a like number of my tribe when requested.

And all these foregoing articles and every one of them made with His Excellency C.L., His Majesty's Governor I do promise for myself and on of sd part – behalf of my tribe that we will most strictly keep and observe in the most solemn manner.

In witness whereof I have hereunto put my mark and seal at Halifax in Nova Scotia this day of March one thousand & c.

Paul Laurent

I do accept and agree to all the articles of the forgoing treaty in Faith and Testimony whereof I have signed these present I have caused my seal to be hereunto affixed this day of march in the 33 year of His Majesty's Reign and in the year of Our lord – 1760.

Chas Lawrence

The above Treaty was signed 15 days after the Maliseet and Passamaquoddy signed a similar worded Treaty.

Documented adhesions to this treaty were signed by the Mi'kmaq of Richibucto – March 10, 1760, Mouscadaboet – March 10, 1760, Shediac – June 25, 1761, Pokemouche – June 25, 1761, Cape Breton – June 25, 1761, Miramichi – June 25, 1761, La Heve – November 9, 1761.

In the Executive Council minutes there are also references to treaties signed with other communities though no copy of the Treaty has been found. These communities are: Chignecto – July 8, 1761 and Pictou – October 12, 1761.

[Both items produced by the Atlantic Policy Congress of First Nation Chiefs Secretariat, 1999].

APPENDIX 4 – INDIGENOUS PEOPLES' TREATIES

Treaty 1776

A Treaty of Alliance and Friendship entered into and concluded by and between the Governors of the State of Massachusetts Bay, and the Delegates of the St. John's & Mickmac Tribes of Indians.[7]

Whereas the United States of America in General Congress Assembled have in the name, and by the Authority of the Good people of these Colonies Solemnly published and declared, that these United Colonies are, and of Right ought to be free and Independent States; that they are absolved from all Allegiances to the British Crown; and that all political connection between them and the State of Great Britain is and ought to be dissolved; and that as Free and Independent States they have full power to Levy War, conclude Peace, contract Alliances established Commerce, and to do all other Acts and things which Independent States may of Right do;

We the Governors of the State of Massachusetts Bay do by virtue hereof, and by the powers vested in us enter into and conclude the following Treaty of Friendship and Alliance, viz.

1st. We the Governors of the said State of Massachusetts Bay and on behalf of said States, and the other United States of America on the one part, and Ambrose var, Newell Wallis, and Francis, Delegates of the St. John's Tribe, John Denaquara, Charles, Mattahu Ontrane, Nicholas, John Battis, Peter Andre, and Sabbatis Netobcobwit Delegates of the Mickmac Tribes of Indians, inhabiting within the Province of Nova Scotia for themselves, and in behalf of the said Tribes on the other part do solemnly agree that the people of the said State of Massachusetts Bay and of the other United States of America, and of the said Tribes of Indians shall hence forth be at peace with each other and be considered as Friends and Brothers united and allied together for their mutual defence Safety and Happiness.

2nd. That each party to this Treaty shall, and will consider the Enemies of the other as Enemies to themselves, and do hereby solemnly promise and engage to, and with each other that when called upon for that purpose, they shall, and will to the utmost of their abilities, aid and assist each other against their public Enemies, and particularly, that of the People of the said Tribes of Indians shall and will afford, and give to the people of the said State of Massachusetts Bay and the people of the other United States of America during their present War with the King of Britain, all the aid and assistance within their power. And that they the people of said Tribe of Indians shall not, and will not directly or indirectly give any aid, or assistance to the Troops or Subjects of the said King of Great Britain, or others adhering to him or hold any correspondence or carry on any Commerce with them during the present War.

---

7. Cap Breton University. "Treaty of Watertown" (2023): <https://www.cbu.ca/indigenous-initiatives/lnu-resource-centre/treaties/treaty-of-watertown/>.

3rd. That if any Robbery, or Outrage happens to be committed by any of the Subjects of said State of Massachusetts Bay, or of any other of the United States of America upon any of the people of said Tribes, and said State shall upon proper application being made, cause satisfaction and restitution speedily to be made to the Party injured.

4th. That if any Robbery, or Outrage happens to be committed by any of the said Tribes of Indians upon any of the Subjects of the said State or of any other of the United States of America the Tribe to which the Offender or Offenders shall belong, shall upon proper application being made, cause satisfaction and Restitution speedily to be made to the Party injured.

5th. That in case any Misunderstanding, Quarrel, or injury shall happen between the said State of Massachusetts Bay, or any other of the United States of America and the said Tribes of Indians, or either of them, no private revenge shall be taken but a peaceable application shall be made for Redress.

6th. That the said Tribes of Indians shall and will furnish and supply 600 Strong Men out of the said Tribes, or as many as may be, who shall without delay proceed from their several homes up to the Town of Boston within this State, and from thence shall march to join the Army of the United States of America now at New York under the immediate command of his Excellency General Washington, there to take his Orders.

7th. That each of the Indians who shall by their respective Tribes be appointed to join the Army of the United States of America shall bring with them a good Gun, and shall be allowed on Dollar of the use of it; and in case the Gun shall be lost in the service, shall be paid the Value of it. And the pay of each Man shall begin from the time they sail from Machias for Boston, and they shall be supplied with provisions and a Vessel or Vessels for their passage up to Boston. Each private Man shall receive the like pay as is given to our own private Men. The Indians shall be formed into Companies when they arrive in Boston, and shall engage, or enlist for long a time as General Washington shall want them; not exceeding the term of three years, unless General Washington and they shall agree for a longer time. And as Joseph Denaquara, Peter Andre, and Sabbatis Netobcobwit have manfully and Generously offered to enter immediately into the War they shall be sent as soon as may be to Gen. Washington to join the Army, and shall be considered as entering into our pay at the time of arrival at New York.

8th. The Delegates above named, who may return to their Homes, do promise and engage, to use their utmost influence with the Passamaquoddy, and other Neighbouring Tribes of Indians to persuade them to furnish and supply for the said service as many strong of their respective Tribes as possible, and that they come along with those of the Tribes of St. John's (and) Mickmac. And the said Governor of the said State of Massachusetts Bay to hereby engage to give to such of the Passamaquoddy or other Neighbouring Indians, who shall enter into Service of the United States of America, the same pay and encouragement, in every particular, as is above agreed to be given to the St. John's, or Mickmac Indians, and to consider them as our friends, and Brothers.

9th. That the said State of Massachusetts Bay shall, and will furnish their Tuckmaster at Machias as soon as may be with proper articles for the purpose of supplying the Indians of said Tribes with the necessities and conveniences of life.

10th. And the said Delegates do hereby annul and make void all former Treaties by them or by others in behalf of their respective Tribes made with any other power, State of person so far forth as the same shall be repugnant to any of the Articles contained in this Treaty.

In Faith & Testimony whereof we the said Governors of the said state of Massachusetts Bay have signed these presents, and caused the Seal of said State to be hereunto affixed and the said Ambrose Var, Newell Wallis, and Francis, Delegates of the St. John's Tribe, Joseph Denaquara, Charles, Mattahu Ontrane, Nicholas, John Battis, Peter Andre, and Sabbatis Netobcobwit, Delegates of the Mickmac Tribes of Indians have hereunto put their Marks, and Seals in the Council Chamber at Watertown in the State aforesaid the Nineteenth day July in the year of our Lord One thousand and seven Hundred, and seventy-six.

[Produced by the Atlantic Policy Congress of First Nation Chiefs Secretariat, 1999].

APPENDIX 5
Maliseet claim, 1765, and the Governor's reply. Letter of January 19, 1765 and the Governor's reply published as an official document in The Quebec Gazette

THE QUEBEC GAZETTE. / LA GAZETTE DE QUEBEC.

Nº. 32.

THURSDAY, JANUARY 24, 1765.   JEUDY, le 24 de JANVIER, 1765.

GENOA, *September 8.*

ON the third Instant, at Night, this Republic received an Express from Calvi, advising, that two Genoese armed Barks, and two Feluccas, fell in with, on the 26th past, two Corsican armed Barks, one Tartan, and three Feluccas, in the Gulph of St. Fiorenzo. The Corsicans immediately attacked the Genoese; but after an Engagement of Two Hours, the largest of the Corsican Barks (said to have mounted 18 Guns, and 150 Men) sat a-shore. During this Engagement they likewise took the Tartan, which had one Gun of 18 Pound Shot, and two others of a smaller caliber, and several Wall Pieces: When this Vessel was taken, there were only eight Corsicans found alive on board, and two dead. One of the Corsican Feluccas, either designedly or casually, blew up whilst it was engaged with one of the Genoese Feluccas, and the greatest Part of the Crews of both perished, or were wounded. After this Defeat of the Corsicans, the Barks proceeded up the Gulph, and landed the Succours they had on board for the Besieged in St. Fiorenzo, and retired to Calvi to refit, &c.

Vienna, August 29. According to Advices from Hungary, a Body of 10,000 Spahis [Turkish Horse] is actually in March from the Environs of Belgrade towards Moldavia and Wallachia; so that there are at present not 60,000 Turks on the Confines of Transylvania and Poland.

Madrid, August 29. Letters from Lisbon advise, that an Express extraordinary is arrived there from England, whose Dispatches have occasioned the holding of several Councils; from whence we conclude they have brought very important Advices. Besides which we know, that in Portugal they are fortifying all the Frontier Places, and providing them with all Necessaries; that the Troops are recruiting with Vigour, and that such Preparations are making as if we were upon the Eve of a War. All this, joined with what is further said, namely, that the Court of Lisbon has agreed with that of London, for the Purchase of several Ships, and Materials for building more, gives some Umbrage to our Court (Madrid) and causes Enquiry to be made for what End these Preparations are carrying on.

Paris, September 8. Although the Edicts and Arrets of the French Monarch are as strict as the Acts of Commerce and Navigation of other States, as to prohibiting Foreigners from trading in their Islands and Colonies in America, nevertheless they do not think their Laws ought to remain unalterable, according to the Maxim of the Medes and Persians; for it having been represented that the Dutch, from their late prudent Encouragement of Foreigners in the West-Indies, have engrossed a certain very lucrative Trade with the Spaniards, and even English, discretionary Powers have lately been transmitted to several Officers in that Part of the World, to dispense with all such Laws as shall appear for the Benefit of the Colonies, and without Prejudice to the Trade and Navigation of France.

Hague, September 30. It is rumoured here, that no less than three different Memorials of Complaints have lately been presented to the States-General. One from Genoa, that the Malcontents of Corsica are underhand supplied with Ammunition and Warlike Stores by Dutchmen. France complains that the same injurious Traffick is carried on by the Subjects of the Republick with the pyratical States, with whom they are at War; while England pretends to take Exceptions at some late Contracts with the Merchants of Amsterdam, &c. whereby some Thousand Tons of Ordnance, Ship-Timber, Cordage, and other Naval Stores, are to be furnished for the Use of the French Marine.

LONDON, *September 20.*

Printed Bills are stuck up in several Parts of the Town, and in different Prisons, offering 30l. per Month Wages, and Expences borne to Portsmouth, to any Sailor who will immediately enter to serve on Board the Fleet at present fitting out there.

September 25. A Person of a scheming Turn, has a Plan to lay before the Government, whereby he proposes a Saving of 50,000l. Sterling annually, without any new Taxes.

A Courier is arrived from the Court of France, who brings Advice that they are about to declare War against the Government of Algiers, and requiring us to concur with them in that Measure, or at least to engage not to furnish the Algerines with Warlike Stores, or afford them any other Assistance whatever.

The following Naval Expeditions are now said to be resolved on: A Commodore, with three Ships of the Line, and two Frigates, for the Coast of Guiney: An Admiral, with five Sail of the Line, and three Frigates, for Newfoundland: An Admiral, with six Line of Battle Ships, for the East-Indies, to touch at the Spanish Philippines: A Commodore in the Mediterranean, and another to reinforce the Fleet already on the West-India Station.

Extract of a Letter from Plymouth, September 8.

"Yesterday Evening arrived here the Spy Sloop of War, Captain Philips, in 13 Days from Newfoundland, came Express for London. By this Ship we hear, that the French have [what they never had before on that Station] a Fleet of Men of War, consisting of a Ship of 60 Guns, one Frigate of 36, two Store Ships of 40 Guns, a Sloop of 14 Guns, and upwards of 80 Sail of large Ships employed in fishing, carrying from 10 to 20 Guns each, and above 5000 People curing Fish on Shore; and it was thought they intended to fortify St. Peter's, which, at present, we are not able to prevent, being much inferior to them in Force.

QUEBEC, January 24.

By the Post from Montreal we learn, That on Wednesday the 16th Cur. about 5 o'Clock in the Evening, a Party of Men, 25 or 30 in Number, with fixed Bayonets, came to the Gaol in said Town, and carried off 3 Men who were confined therein; they were immediately followed by another Party, who took the Prisoners from them, and returned them again to Prison: Notwithstanding this, they returned about Midnight, broke open the Gaol on the Back-side, and carried off the three Prisoners, who had not been heard of when the Post came away.

ADVERTISEMENTS.

SECRETARY's-OFFICE, Quebec, 19th January, 1765.

WHEREAS by an Ordinance of His Excellency the Governor and Council, for the better suppressing unlicenced Houses, *It is Ordained and Declared*, That if any Person or Persons presume to sell Rum, Brandy, Ale, or other Liquors, without a Licence, they should incur the Penalty of TWELVE POUNDS. And whereas many Persons keeping Publick Houses, and others, have neglected to take out such Licence, This is therefore to give Notice, that the same are ready to be delivered at this Office; and unless they are called for within one Month from the Date hereof, the Persons so neglecting as aforesaid, will be prosecuted as in the said Ordinance is directed.

N. B. LEWIS METRAL, Esq; at Trois-Rivieres, and Mr. William Wier, at Montreal, will give Licences to all such Persons as may find it inconvenient to come to Quebec. J. GOLDFRAP, D. Sec.

Du Secrétariat de Québec, le 19 de Janvier 1765.

COMME il est ordonné et déclaré par une Ordonnance de Son Excellence le Gouverneur et du Conseil, pour la suppression des maisons où se vend des boissons sans permis, Que toutes personnes ou personne qui présumeront de vendre du rum, de l'eau de vie, de l'ale ou autres liqueurs sans licence, encourront une amende de DOUZE LIVRES; et vû que plusieurs personnes qui tiennent des auberges, ainsi que plusieures autres personnes on negligé de prendre des permis de cette espéce. Ceci est donc pour avertir que les dites licenses sont prêtes à livrer dans ce bureau, et que si on ne les demande pas dans un mois, à compter de la date d'icelui, les personnes coupables de negligence comme il est dit ci-dessus, seront poursuivies comme la dite Ordonnance porte.

N. B. Louis Metral, Écuyer, aux Trois Rivières, et le Sieur *Guillaume Wier*, à Montréal, donneront des licenses à toutes personnes qui trouveront qu'il leur seroit incommode de venir à Québec.

J. GOLDFRAP, D. Sec.

SECRETARY's-OFFICE, 19th January, 1765.

QUEBEC, ss. WHEREAS the Nation of Maricitte Indians, by the following Paragraph, of a Petition to His EXCELLENCY the Governor of this Province, have represented that they are incroached upon by the Canadian Inhabitants, hunting Beaver on the Lands therein mentioned, which have ever belonged to, and are the Property of the said Nation: This therefore is to give Notice, That the Privilege prayed for, by the said Indians, will be allowed and confirmed to them, unless any Person or Persons can shew just Cause to the Contrary, by Memorial to His Excellency the Governor and Council, directed to the Secretary of this Province, on or before the first Day of May next.

By Command of His EXCELLENCY,

J. GOLDFRAP, D. Sec.

" Your Petitioner also has the Honor to represent to Your Excellency, that his Brethren Indians find themselves reduced to the lowest Ebb of Misery by the unwarrantable Incroachments of the Canadian Inhabitants, hunting Beaver on the Lands belonging to the Nation by which your Petitioner has been deputed; which Tract begins at the Great Fall of St. John's, and runs as far as Temisquata, including the Wolf-River (or Riviere du Loup) and the River Madawaska, which Rivers discharge themselves into the River St. John's; making a Space of about Twenty Leagues, on which the Nation, whose Grievances your Petitioner has the Honor to lay before Your EXCELLENCY, always had an exclusive Privilege of hunting Beaver in the Time of the French Government, therefore your Petitioner humbly requests in the Name of his Nation, that Your Excellency will be pleased to continue their Privilege by forbiding the Inhabitants of this Province to hunt Beaver on said Grounds."

QUEBEC, à Savoir. *Du Secrétariat le 19 de Janvier, 1765.*

COMME la nation de *Sauvages Maricittes*, a représenté par le paragraphe qui suit, d'une requête présentée à son Excellence le Gouverneur de cette Province, que les habitans Canadiens empiétent sur eux, en faisant la chasse du Castor sur les terres spécifiées dans la dite requête, qui ont toujours appartenu à la dite nation, et des quels ils ont de tous tems été censés les propriétaires. Ceci est donc pour avertir, que le privilege qu'ils démandent par leur requête leur sera alloué et confirmé, à moins que quelques personnes ou personne n'alleguent de bonnes raisons à ce contraires, en forme de memoire au Gouverneur et au Conseil, adressé au Secretaire de cette Province, au premier jour de Mai prochain ou avant.

Par Son EXCELLENCE,

J. GOLDFRAP, D. Sec.

" Le Suppliant a aussi l'honneur de représenter à Votre Excellence que les Sauvages de sa nation se trouvrent réduits à la dernière misère, par la chasse illicite du castor, que font les habitans Canadiens sur les terres appartenantes à sa dite nation, à prendre depuis le grand sault de la rivière de St. Jean jusques à Temisquata, ce qui fait un espace d'environ vingt lieues, y comprennant la rivière du Loup et celle de Madawaska, qui se déchargent dans la rivière de St. Jean, où il étoit de tous tems défendu aux François de faire la chasse du castor, comme cette chasse a toujours été réservée aux Sauvages de la nation dont il a l'honneur de représenter les griefs à Votre Excellence. Il supplie donc Votre Excellence au nom de ses frères, qu'il vous plaise de continuer leur privilege en ordonnant qu'il soit défendu aux habitans Canadiens de faire la chasse du castor sur ces terres."

transport de 20 canons chaque, d'un bateau de 14, et d'au dessus de 80 voiles de gros navires employés à la pesche, armés de 10 à 20 piéces de canon chaque, et au dessus 5000 personnes employés à appréter du poisson à terre, et on croioit qu'ils avoient intention de fortifier l'Isle de St. Pierre, à quoi nous ne pouvons pas nous opposer à présent comme notre force est bien inférieure à la leur.

QUEBEC, *le 23 de Janvier.*

Nous apprenons par le courier de Montréal, qu'une bande de personnes, au nombre de 25 à 30, ont été à la prison de la dite ville avec la bayonette au bout du fusil, le 16 du courant vers les cinq heures du soir, d'où ils enleverent 3 hommes qui y étoient enfermés; un autre parti les poursuivit immédiatement, qui leur tira les prisonniers d'entre les mains, et qui les remit en prison: Nonobstant quoi, ils revinrent vers minuit, et ils enfoncerent la prison du côté de derrière, d'où ils enleverent encore les trois prisonniers, et on ne sçavoit point ce qu'ils étoient devenus quand le courier partit.

AVERTISSEMENTS.

THIS IS TO GIVE NOTICE,

THAT a Court of Common-Pleas, agreeable to the Ordinance of the 17th September, 1764, for the District of Quebec, was this Day (being the 21st January, 1765) held at the Council Chamber, and stands adjourned till the 28th Instant, at 10 o'Clock in the Morning, and that Messrs. Kluck & Panet, Clerks of the said Court for that District, upon Application made to them, at their respective Offices in the Upper-Town (where Attendance will be given every Day, from 10 o'Clock in the Morning till One o'Clock in the Afternoon) will give the proper Summons, &c.

W. KLUCK, } Clerks.
PANET,

21st January, 1765.

CECI est pour avertir, Que la Cour des Plaidoyers Communes, pour le District de Québec, s'est tenue à la chambre du Conseil ce jour, le 21 de Janvier, 1765, conformément à l'Ordonnance du 17 de Septembre, 1764; que la dite cour est ajournée jusques au 28 du courant à dix heures du matin: Et que les Sieurs *Kluck* et *Panet*, Greffiers de la dite cour pour ce District, accorderont les assignations, &c. qui conviendront, en s'adressant à eux à leurs bureaux respectifs, à la Haute Ville, où on donnera les soins nécessaires tous les jours depuis dix heures du matin jusques à une heure après midi.

Le 21 de Janvier, 1765. W. KLUCK, } Greffiers.
PANET,

THOMAS WILLMOT,

BEGS leave to acquaint his Friends and the Publick, That he has opened a Manufactory of Candles, next Door to Captain ALLGEO's, in Sault au Matelot Street, Lower-Town, Quebec, where all Gentlemen, Merchants, Families, &c. may be supplied with the best Sort of Wax and Tallow Candles, either dipt or moulded, Wholesale or Retail. Those Gentlemen, Merchants, &c. that will honour him with the Favour of their Commands, may depend on being faithfully served, and their Favours thankfully acknowledged.

He likewise gives the most Money for Wax, raw or rendered Tallow.

N. B. A Person who understands making of Hard-soap, may hear of Employment, with good Encouragement, by applying as above.

THOMAS WILMOT,

PREND la liberté d'informer ses amis et le public, qu'il a ouvert une manufacture de chandelles à la porte attenante à celle du Capitaine *Algeo*, dans la rue du Sault au Matelot, à la Basse Ville de Québec, où tous les messieurs, négocians, &c. et les familles particuliéres pourront être fournis de bougies de la meilleure espéce, ainsi que des chandelles de suif moulées ou faites à la baguette, en gros ou en detail. Les messieurs, négocians, &c. qui l'honoreront de leurs commandemens peuvent être assurés d'être servis fidélement, et qu'il aura de la reconnoissance de leurs faveurs.

Il donne pareillement un bon prix pour de la cire et du suif crud ou fondu.

N. B. Une personne qui sçait faire du savon dur, pourra s'informer d'une place où elle sera employée et encouragée en s'adressant au dit *Wilmot*.

SECRETARY's-OFFICE, 23d January, 1765.

QUEBEC, ss. WHEREAS His Excellency the Governor and Council, have appointed the following Persons to serve the Office of Bailiffs and Sub-Bailiffs, in the different Parishes throughout this Province; they are in Obedience thereto required forthwith to qualify themselves for the said Office, by taking the proper Oaths before any one or more of His Majesty's Justices of the Peace, that live nearest to their respective Habitations; whereof they are not to fail, as they will answer the Contrary at their Peril.

By His EXCELLENCY's Command,

J. GOLDFRAP, D. Sec.

QUEBEC, à Savoir. *Du Secrétariat le 23 de Janvier, 1765.*

COMME Son Excellence le Gouverneur et le Conseil de sa Majesté ont constitué les personnes qui suivent, pour servir dans les emplois de Baillis et de Sous-baillis dans les différentes paroisses de cette Province, elles sont donc requises par obéissance à icelle, de se mettre incessamment en état d'exercer les dites charges, en prêtant les sermens convenables, par devant un ou plusieurs des Juges de Paix de sa Majesté les plus voisins de leurs habitations respectives, à faute de quoi ils repondront à leurs risques et perils.

Par Son EXCELLENCE,

J. GOLDFRAP, D. Sec.

St. Joseph et St. François de la Bauce,	Jean Boldue, Bailli. Pierre Bureau, sub do. Pierre Poulin, sub do.
St. Marie de la Beauce,	Claude Paris, Bailli. Etienne Paumerteau, sub do. Jacques Parent, sub do.
St. Henry,	Michel Aubois, Bailli. Remy Biton, sub do. Pierre Noël Nabaud, sub do.
Soulange,	Albert Palonde, Bailli. Martin de le Vue, sub do. René le Pue, sub do.

APPENDIX 6
Manuscript document, Maliseet and the loss of the Viger territory, August 4, 1869

Annexe: Document sur la perte de Viger, 4 août 1869

FULL TRANSCRIPTION of the handwritten document on the Viger cession by the Amalecite (Maliseet) People, transcribed from records provided by the Ottawa Archives, Land Register (Xo17354), accepted for "Distribution," 15 Aug. 5 58, '73, see Appendix 1869.14.50_I.1.6.38 Land Grant 1869 - copy.

Header page in document provided by the Ottawa Archives, in which the terms "Reserve" and "Surrender" are used to identify the land and the deed of Cession.

Sachez tous par ces présentes que Nous [underlined words in the text are included in our transcription]

François Etienne St-Aubain, premier chef,
Jean Athanas, second chef,
Joseph Laurent,
Jean Athanas, senior,
James Grey,
Antoine Athanas
Joseph Nicolas,
Jean Bernard,
Thomas Athanas,
Jean Denis,
Noël Denis,
Laurent Athanas
Félix Etienne St-Aubain
Baptiste Denis,
François Grey,
Paul Joseph,
Elizabeth Terrien, vve Paul Joseph

Chefs [na souligné dans le texte] *et Principaux de la Tribu des Sauvages Amalécites résidant à l'Isle Verte, à la Rivière du Loup, à Cacouna, et dans les places environnantes* représentant notre Peuple et agissant pour lui et en son nom, assemblés en conseil ce quatrième jour de Aâut dans l'année de Notre Seigneur, mil huit cent soixante et neuf à Cacouna dans le comté de Témiscouata dans la Province de Québec, dans la Puissance du Canada, pour et en considération (deuxième page version Ottawa) avantage [sic]et profits qui devront résulter pour Notre Peuple de la vente des terres qui ont été réservées pour nous, dans le Township de Viger, dans la dite Province de Québec, dans la dite Puissance du Canada, <u>transportons et cédons</u> par les présentes, à <u>Notre Souveraine Dame la Reine</u> Victoria ses héritiers et successeurs, en <u>fidéicommis</u>, pour être vend(ues) au profit de Notre dit Peuple, et à la condition que les deniers provenant de cette vente soient (dédu(ction) faite d'une proportion raisonnable pour les frais d'arpentage et d'administration), convertis en bons sur l'Etat (Dominion Stock) portant intérêt à raison de six pour cent, par année, lequel intérêt sera divisé à époque fixée en parts égales entre les Sauvages qui résident actuellement dans aucune des localités plus haut en premier lieu mentionnées (et dont les noms se <u>trouvent insérés dans la liste annexée à ces présentes)</u> [nt encadré dans le texte] *et leurs descendants à toujours; Cette <u>réserve</u> dans le dit Township Viger, telle que marquée sur le plan daté -Département des terres de la Couronne, le vingt Février, mil-huit cent cinquante huit et représentée sur le dit plan comme étant de la contenance d'environ trois mille six cent cinquante acres ou arpents, ainsi qu'il appert de la copie du dit plan annexé (troisième page) à ces présentes pour mieux montrer et expliquer la position de l'étendue des terres transportées et cédées par ces présentes dans le but qu'elles soient vendues.*

A la condition en outre que chacun de nous soit rémunéré sur évaluation faite par une personne duement autorisée à cet effet, par le Surintendant général des affaires des Sauvages pour les améliorations qu'il pourra avoir faites sur aucuns des lots situés dans cette partie de la Réserve maintenant transportée, lorsque ces dits lots ou aucun d'eux seront vendus c'est-à-dire que la valeur intrinsèque de chaque lot formera partie du fond commun, et que les améliorations qui peuvent être faites sur aucun des dits lots, appartiendront aux ci-devant possesseurs Indiens comme il est ci-dessus exprimé.

<u>Pour avoir et posséder Sa dite Majesté la Reine</u>, *ses héritiers et successeurs en* <u>fidéicommis</u>, *les terres ci-dessus spécifiées et à elle transportées par ces présentes et en faire l'usage plus haut mentionné.*

<u>En foi de quoi Nous chefs et principaux</u> *de la Tribu des Sauvages Amalécites comme sus-dit agissant pour et au nom de Notre Peuple, lequel a sanctionné et approuvé en Conseil Général le* [illisible dans le manuscrit microfilmé] *(quatrième page) dit Transport et y avons apposé nos noms et sceaux aux lieu et jour plus haut mentionnés.*

(Signatures)

François Etienne X (sa marque) St-Aubain, premier chef
Jean X (sa marque) Athanas, second chef

APPENDIX 6 – MANUSCRIPT DOCUMENT

Joseph X (sa marque) Laurent,
Jean X (sa marque) Athanas, sr,
James X (sa marque) Grey,
Nom biffé
Antoine X (sa marque) Athanas
Jean Bernard, X (sa marque) Bernard
Thomas X (sa marque) Athanas,
Jean X (sa marque) Denis,
Noël X (sa marque) Denis,
Laurent X (sa marque) Athanas
Félix Etienne X (sa marque) St-Aubain
Baptiste X (sa marque) Denis,
François X (sa marque) Grey,
Paul X (sa marque) Joseph,
Elizabeth X (sa marque) Terrien, veuve Paul Joseph
Joseph Nicholas

Je soussigné, accepte, pour et au nom de l'Honorable Secrétaire d'Etat du Canada, surintendant général des affaires des Sauvages ayant duement été par lui autorisé à le représenter et à agir comme tel à cette fin, le Transport ou Instrument comportant la cession qui précède.

Exécuté en présence des témoins soussignés Chas Bertrand M. P. N. Cyrias Pelletier,

J. Laz Marceau ??

Curé de l'Isle Verte Missionnaire ???

(cinquième page)

Nous soussignés certifions que les procédés ci-dessus & des autres parts ont été faits en notre présence et que le tout est correct & que ladite cession a été signé [sic] par François Etienne St- Aubain premier Chef & Jean Athanas fils second Chef & autres Sauvages.

J. Laz. Marceau, Ptre, Curé Curé de l'Isle-Verte &

Missionnaire S.A.T.V.

Assermenté devant moi Juge de la Cour Supérieure à l'Isle-Verte, District de Kamouraska le vingt deux octobre mil huit cent soixante et neuf, (signé) F.O. Gauthier J.C.S.

Jean x (sa marque) Athanas 2e Chef

J. Laz. Marceau, P.C. Curé de l'Isle-Verte Missionnaire des Sauvages

Amalécites de Viger

Dans la version fédérale, une copie en anglais suit la version française ainsi qu'un plan de terrain, ou réserve, concerné. [See as well: Appendix1987.3.1_1987-1995_ FondsRecherche_RevendicationsTerritoriales_12161344, p. 103 ss with reference to the documents: *Archives de l'Archidiocèse de Rimouski, Fonds Ar, cote A -20, Thèmes: Aff. Ind.; Réserve Viger.*]

APPENDIX 7
Solemn Declaration of Mutual Respect and Inter-nation Alliance among Indigenous Peoples in Québec, May 16, 2019, in Québec City[1]

DÉCLARATION SOLENNELLE DE RESPECT MUTUEL ET D'ALLIANCE INTERNATIONS

SOLEMN DECLARATION OF MUTUAL RESPECT AND INTER-NATION ALLIANCE

ATTENDU QUE nous, les Premières Nations signataires, occupons et utilisons le territoire depuis des temps immémoriaux et constituons des sociétés organisées possédant une culture distinctive;

ATTENDU QUE nous, les Premières Nations signataires, possédons un droit inhérent à l'autonomie gouvernementale et à l'autodétermination;

ATTENDU QUE nous, les Premières Nations signataires, détenons le droit d'occuper et d'utiliser le territoire et ses ressources ainsi que d'y établir nos priorités et stratégies de mise en valeur, et ce, dans l'exercice de notre droit inhérent à l'autonomie gouvernementale et à

WHEREAS our signatory First Nations occupy and use the territory since immemorial time in organized societies with a distinctive culture;

WHEREAS our signatory First Nations have inherent rights of self-government and self-determination;

WHEREAS our signatory First Nations have the right to the land and use his resources, and to establish our development priorities and strategies, in the exercise of our right to self-government and self-determination;

---

1. <https://www.mashteuiatsh.ca/messages-aux-pekuakamiulnuatsh/actualites/3150-signature-de-la-declaration-solennelle-de-respect-mutuel-et-d-alliance-internations.html>;<https://www.newswire.ca/fr/news-releases/signature-de-la-declaration-solennelle-de-respect-mutuel-et-d-alliance-internations-899399579.html>.

l'autodétermination;	
ATTENDU QUE nous, les Premières Nations signataires, détenons le droit d'entretenir et de développer des relations et des liens entre Nations, notamment quant à l'occupation, l'utilisation et la mise en valeur du territoire, sans que ces relations ou liens ne soient interprétés de manière à diminuer ou à nier nos droits respectifs;	WHEREAS our signatory First Nations have the right to maintain and develop relationships and links between them, particularly with regard to the occupation, use and development of the territory, without these relationships or links being interpreted in such a way as to diminish or deny our rights;
ATTENDU QUE depuis des temps immémoriaux, nous, les Premières Nations signataires, coexistons pacifiquement en tant que Nations souveraines, coexistence au cours de laquelle nous avons forgé des liens durables, notamment à travers le commerce, les mariages et les valeurs politiques, culturelles et traditionnelles communes;	WHEREAS since immemorial time, our signatory First Nations coexist peacefully as sovereign nations, coexistence during which we have forged lasting ties through trade, marriage and common political, cultural and traditional values;
ATTENDU QUE nous, les Premières Nations signataires, souhaitons continuer notre coexistence pacifique au moyen d'une approche unie visant à équilibrer le développement du territoire avec nos besoins, valeurs et culture respectifs ainsi que par la perpétuation d'une relation axée vers le futur basée sur le respect mutuel, la bonne foi, le partenariat, la participation active, ainsi que des échanges économiques et sociaux mutuellement bénéfiques;	WHEREAS our signatory First Nations wish to continue our peaceful coexistence through a united approach aims at balancing the development of the territory with our needs, values and culture as well as through the perpetuation of a future-oriented relationship based on mutual respect, good faith, partnership, active participation and mutually beneficial economic and social exchanges;
ATTENDU QUE nous, les Premières Nations signataires, avons eu dans le passé, avons actuellement et aurons encore dans le futur à partager une histoire et des activités communes comme Premières Nations;	WHEREAS our signatory First Nations have had in the past, have now and will still have in the future to share a common history and activities as First Nations;
ATTENDU QUE nous, les Premières Nations signataires, jugeons important d'affirmer et de solidifier nos relations afin de s'entraider mutuellement dans un contexte contemporain, comme l'ont fait nos ancêtres, dans l'intérêt des générations actuelles et futures;	WHEREAS our signatory First Nations consider it important to affirm and strengthen our relationships in order to help each other in a contemporary context, as our ancestors did, for the benefit of current and future generations;
ATTENDU QUE nous, les Premières Nations signataires, jugeons nécessaire d'affirmer par écrit notre engagement dans une relation internations empreinte de respect mutuel et de collaboration par la	WHEREAS our signatory First Nations deem it necessary to affirm in writing our commitment to an Inter-Nation relationship of mutual respect and cooperation through this Declaration;

présente Déclaration;	
IL EST CONVENU :	IT HAS BEEN AGREED:
Que notre alliance soit scellée par la signature de la présente Déclaration, sur la base de notre droit à l'autodétermination et notre droit inhérent à l'autonomie gouvernementale que nous détenons et affirmons;	That our signatory First Nations seal our alliance by signing this Declaration on the basis of our right to self-determination and our inherent right to self-government that we hold and affirm;
Que cette Déclaration témoigne de notre engagement, comme Premières Nations signataires, à prendre les moyens pour affirmer et solidifier nos relations, notamment en concluant des accords ou arrangements favorisant notre coexistence harmonieuse sur le territoire;	That this Declaration testifies to the commitment of our signatory First Nations to take the necessary steps to affirm and strengthen our relations, especially by concluding agreements or arrangements that promote our harmonious coexistence on the territory;
Que les relations entre nous, les Premières Nations signataires, soient fondées sur la reconnaissance et le respect de nos droits, besoins et culture respectifs, tout en favorisant l'entraide, la collaboration, l'échange et le partenariat, comme l'auraient fait nos ancêtres;	That the relationships between our signatory First Nations be based on the recognition and respect of our rights, needs and culture while promoting mutual assistance, cooperation, exchange and partnerships, as our ancestors would have done;
Que nous, les Premières Nations signataires, soyons les gardiennes de ces engagements et en assurions la mise en œuvre.	That our signatory First Nations be the guardians of these commitments and ensure their implementation.

EN CONSÉQUENCE, EN CE 16 MAI 2019, ONT SIGNÉ, AU NOM DES PREMIÈRES NATIONS SUIVANTES :

THEREFORE, IN THIS MAY, 16 2019 HAVE SIGNED IN THE FIRST NATIONS' NAME:

Clifford Moar
Chef des Pekuakamiulnuatsh

Martin Dufour
Chef des Innus d'Essipit

René Simon
Chef des Innus de Pessamit

Michel R. Bernard
Chef des Abénakis de Wôlinak

APPENDIX 8
Timeline

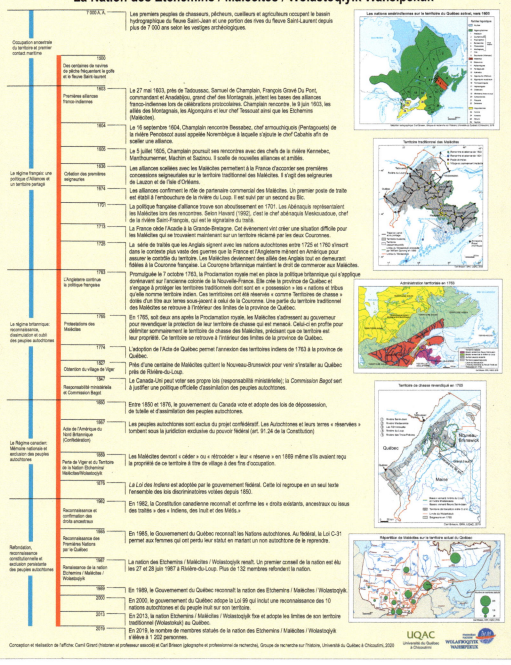

Bibliography

APPENDICES

Documents sur l'histoire des peuples autochtones au Québec (Canada), le Groupe de recherche sur l'histoire (GRH-UQAC). Deposited with the Wolastoqiyik Wahsipekuk First Nation.

Appendix, 1603: Commission du Roy 1603.
   Commission du Roy au sieur de Monts, pour l'habitation des terres de la Cadie, Canada et autres endroits en la Nouvelle-France (8 novembre 1603). In Marc Lescarbot, Histoire de la Nouvelle-France, vol. II, Toronto, The Champlain Society, 1911, p. 490-494 (in PDF).

Appendix, 1603: Champlain Des Sauvages.
   Samuel de Champlain, 1603, *Des Sauvages, ou voyage de Samuel de Champlain, de Brouage, fait en la France nouvelle*, Paris, at Claude de Montreuil with the privilege of the king (Henri IV), <https://archive.org/details/cihm_90062/page/n5>.

Appendix, 1666: Traités Nouvelle-France Iroquois.
   Sa Majesté le Roi de France, 1666, Traitez de Paix conclu entre le Roy de France et les Indiens du Canada, paix avec les Iroquois de la Nation Tsonnont8an à Québec, 22 mai, 1666; paix avec la Nation d'Onnei8t, Québec 12 juillet, 1666; paix avec les Iroquois de la Nation Onnontague, 13 décembre 1666, Imprimé à Paris, Sébastien Marre-Cramoisy, Imprimeur du Roi, 1667, of His Majesty's express command.

Appendix, 1684: Extrait d'une lettre du roi à de Meulles, 1684.
   Library and Archives Canada.
   <https://recherche-collection-search.bac-lac.gc.ca/fra/Accueil/Recherche?q=de%20meulles%201684&>

Appendix, 1701: Grande Paix Montréal de 1701.
   Collectif, Recherches amérindiennes au Québec, 2001, *Le temps des alliances. La Grande Paix de Montréal de 1701*, vol. XXXI, no. 2.

Appendix, 1725 to 1776: Treaties...
Full text of treaties signed by Indigenous Nations, including the Maliseet, with the English between 1725 and 1776. <https://www.cbu.ca/indigenous-initiatives/lnu-resource-centre/treaties/treaty-of-1725/>

Appendix, 1759, 1791: Documents constitutionnels Doughty et Shortt.
Adam Shortt and Arthur G. Doughty, 1921, *Documents relatifs à l'histoire constitutionnelle du Canada, 1759-1791*, Ottawa, National Archives of Canada., <https://archive.org/details/documentsrelati1v2arch>.

Appendix, 1763: Proclamation royale 1763.
Royal Proclamation, 1763: *Revised Statutes of Canada, 1985, Appendices*, Prepared under the authority of the statute Revision Act, Appendice II, no. 1, The Royal Proclamation, 7 October 1763, Ottawa, the Queen's Printer.

Appendix, 1763: Traité de Paris 1763.
Adam Shortt and Arthur G. Doughty, 1921, Archives publiques. Documents relatifs à l'histoire constitutionnelle du Canada, 1759-1791, Proclamation royale, p. 83-99, <https://archive.org/details/documentsrelati1v2arch>.

Appendix, 1765: Décret Gazette de Québec.
Gazette de Québec, January 24, 1765, Positive response to a request from the Maliseet to respect their traditional hunting territories. <https://numerique.banq.qc.ca/patrimoine/details/52327/4265872>.

Appendix, 1767: Murray Domaine du Roi Territoire indien (in French and English).
Letter from Governor Murray to the Board of Trade, 26 May 1767, regarding the King's Domain known as the Tadoussac Trade, in J. Murray, *State of the Posts of the King's Domain in Canada with an Abstract of the Proceedings relating thereto since the Reduction of that Country*, 26 mai 1767, Archives du Canada, C.O. 42, vol. 6, p. 117; see In the Privy Council, *In the matter of the boundary between the dominion of Canada and the colony of Newfoundland in the Labrador peninsula*, vol. VI, p. 2766. Quoted in Brian Slattery, *The Land Rights of Indigenous Canadian Peoples*, Ph. D. Oxford University, 1979, p. 224.

Appendix, 1767: Schulze 1997.
David Alexandre Schulze, 1997, « L'application de la Proclamation royale de 1763 dans les frontières originales de la Province de Québec: la décision du Conseil privé dans l'affaire Allsopp. » *Revue judiciaire Thémis*, Montréal, Université de Montréal.

Appendix, 1774: Acte de Québec – 1774.
Adam Shortt and Arthur G. Doughty, 1921, Public Archives. Documents relatifs à l'histoire constitutionnelle du Canada, 1759-1791, Proclamation royale, p. 552-558, <https://archive.org/details/documentsrelati1v2arch>.

Appendix, 1791: Acte constitutionnel de 1791.
   Adam Shortt and Arthur G. Doughty, 1921, Public Archives. Documents relatifs à l'histoire constitutionnelle du Canada, 1759-1791, Proclamation royale, p. 1013-1032, <https://archive.org/details/documentsrelati1v2arch>.
Appendix, 1826: 14.51_I.1.6.40: DemandeTerrainsCréationViger1826.
   Demande des Malécites pour un village, 1826, manuscript document.
Appendix, 1840: Acte d'union du Haut et du Bas-Canada, 1840.
Appendix, 1839: Rapport Durham, 1839.
   <https://archive.org/details/cihm_32373>.
Appendix, 1844.2001: Commission Bagot (1844) et autres commissions d'enquête.
   Camil Girard et Jessica Thibeault, 2001, *Rapports sur les questions autochtones. Canada 1828-1870*, 3 vol., Chicoutimi, Alliance Recherche-Université (ARUC), Monts Valin Monts Otish (CRSH), Groupe recherche sur l'histoire (GRH)-Université du Québec à Chicoutimi. Paginated reports of commissions of inquiry, including appendices, copy of the commissions and documents in English and French.
Appendix, 1850: Loi Réserves Terres Bas-Canada 1850.
   L'Acte pour mieux protéger les terres et les propriétés des sauvages dans le Bas-Canada (10 août1850), lois du Canada, 13 et 14e Victoria, cap. 41-42, p. 1267-1269.
Appendix, 1851: Acte Abrogation Terres Bas-Canada 1851.
   Acte pour mettre à part certaines étendues de terre pour l'usage de certaines tribus de sauvages dans le Bas-Canada (30 août 1851), laws of Canada, 13 et 14e Victoria, cap. 58-59, p. 1851-1852.
Appendix, 1851: Article Fortin et Frenette Création des réserves RAQ 1989.
   Gérald L. Fortin et Jacques Frenette, 1989, « L'acte de 1851 et la création de nouvelles réserves indiennes au Bas-Canada en 1853 », *Recherches amérindiennes au Québec*, vol. XIX, no. 1, p. 31-37.
Appendix, 1851: Protestation et revendication des Innus 2003.
   Camil Girard, 1851 (2003), « Un document inédit sur les droits territoriaux. Le protêt des Innus du comté de Saguenay en 1851 », *Saguenayensia*, vol. 45, no. 1, January-March, p. 35-43.
Appendix, 1851: Protêt officiel des Innus. Texte intégral 1851.
   Camil Girard, 2016, Le protêt logé par les Innus du Saguenay en 1851 : revendication sur le titre aux terres du domaine indien, Groupe de recherche sur l'histoire, UQAC, 2016.
Appendix, 1851: Réserves des Terres Bas-Canada 1851.
   Canada-Uni, Acte pour mettre à part certaines étendues de terre pour l'usage de certaines tribus de sauvages dans le Bas-Canada (30 août 1851), laws of Canada, 14 et 15e Victoria, cap. 105-106, p. 2036-2037.

Appendix, 1857: Acte de «civilisation et d'émancipation» des «Sauvages» au Canada 1857.

Canada-Uni, Acte pour encourager la Civilisation graduelle des Tribus Sauvages en cette Province, et pour amender les Lois relatives aux Sauvages. 10 juin 1857, laws of Canada, 14 et 15ᵉ Victoria, cap. XXVI, p. 87-91. https://caid.ca/GraCivAct1857.pdf

Appendix, 1867: Constitution du Canada 1867.
<http://laws-lois.justice.gc.ca/fra/Const/Const_index.html>.

Appendix, 1869: Acte sur l'émancipation des *Sauvages* au Canada 1869.

Acte pourvoyant à l'émancipation graduelle des Sauvages, à la meilleure administration des affaires des Sauvages et à l'extension des dispositions de l'acte trente-et-un Victoria, chapitre quarante-deux. Cap. 6, Canada, Sanctioned on 22 June 1869.

Appendix, 1869: 14.50_I.1.6.38 Concession de terres 1869, Viger.

Registre des terres indiennes, *Viger, 1869*, Ottawa, Land register, nu X017354, Québec, Viger, no. 4; copy made available on 15 August 1973. Manuscript document.

Appendix, 1871: Loi constitutionnelle de 1871/ Constitutionnal Act 1871.

Loi constitutionnelle de 1871 (Acte de l'Amérique du Nord britannique, 1871), 34-35 Victoria, ch. 28 (R.-U.). Actes concernant l'établissement des Provinces dans la Puissance du Canada [29 June 1871].

Appendix, 1876: Loi des Sauvages 1876: exemplaire en français et en anglais.

Acte pour amender et refondre les lois concernant les Sauvages. Chap. 18, Gouvernement du Canada/Indian Act, 1876 [sanctioned on 12 April 1876].

Appendix, 1876: Indian Act 1876, Article Holmes, Joan, 2002.

Joan Holmes, 2002, *The original intentions of the Indian Act* (Canada 1876), Ottawa, Joan Holmes et Associés, Conference held 17-18 April 2002 by the Pacific Business and Law Institutes. <http://www.joanholmes.ca/Indian%20Act%20Paper%20Final.pdf>.

Appendix, 1898: Extension des frontières du Québec 1898.

Frontières de la province, *Loi concernant la délimitation des frontières nord-ouest nord et nord-est de la province de Québec*, Government of Canada, 27 CHAP. VI [sanctioned on 15 January 1898], p. 27-28.

Appendix, 1912: Extension des frontières du Québec et de l'Ontario 1912/français, anglais.

Loi de l'extension des frontières de la province de Québec, The Quebec Boundaries Extension Act, 1912, 2 George V, Chapter 45 An Act to extend the Boundaries of the Province of Quebec [fn – See the B.N.A. Act, 1871, also c. 3 of the Statutes of 1898, and also c. 6 of the Statutes of Quebec, 1898. See also 1946, c. 29, infra.] CANADA, 2 GEORGE V, CHAPTER 40, An Act to extend the Boundaries of the Province of Ontario, [Sanctioned on 1st April, 1912]. p. 97-98, <http://www3.sympatico.ca/rd.fournier/inter.canada/doc/qb-1912.htm>.

Appendix, 1915: Speck Wabenaki Confederation Speck1915.
Speck, F. G., 1915, The Eastern Algonkian Wabanaki Confederacy, *American Anthropologist, New Series,* vol. 17, no. 3 (July-Sept. 1915), p. 492-508. Published by: Wiley on behalf of the American Anthropological Association. <https://www.jstor.org/stable/660500>.

Appendix, 1925: Ricard Politique Alliance Mexique 16ᵉ siècle.
Ricard, Robert, 1925, « Sur la politique des alliances. La conquête du Mexique par Cortès », *Journal de la Société des américanistes.*

Appendix, 1927: La frontière du Labrador (carte) 1927.
Carte sur les Concessions au Labrador et à Terre-Neuve par les Français.

Appendix, 1969: Politique indienne au Canada ou *Livre blanc*, 1969.
Chrétien, Jean, 1969, *La politique indienne du gouvernement du Canada*, Ottawa (connue sous le titre du *Livre blanc*...), <https://www.aadnc-aandc.gc.ca/fra/1100100010189/1100100010191>.

Appendix, 1973: Œuvres de Champlain (Fides).
Champlain, Samuel de, 1973, *Œuvres de Samuel de Champlain*, Montréal, Éditions du Jour, 3 vol.

Appendix, 1973: Jugement Malouf.
Malouf, Albert, 1973, Jugement dans Gros-Louis et al. v. la Société de développement de la Baie-James et al. [1974] Québec. P.R. 38, Québec, Superior Court, Malouf J., 15 November 1973.

Appendix, 1975: Traité moderne: *La Convention de la Baie-James et du Nord québécois*, Convention CBJNQ-français, 1975, <http://www.aenq.org/fileadmin/user_upload/syndicats/z77/Stock/Francais/Documents/Conv_Baie_James/ConventionBaieJamesComplet.pdf>.

Appendix, 1982: Revendication des Autochtones sans statut/AAQ, Brief presented to the Ministère de la Chasse, Québec, 1982.

Appendix, 1982: Fernand Chalifoux Entrevue RAQ 1982.
Chalifoux, Fernand, 1982, « Entrevue par Gaétan Gendron, Alliance laurentienne des Métis et Indiens sans statut », *Recherches amérindiennes au Québec*, vol. XII, no. 2.

Appendix, 1982: Profil leaders de l'Alliance autochtone du Québec, RAQ 1982.
Couture, Gilles *1982*, « Visages et profils... », *Recherches amérindiennes au Québec*, vol. XII, no. 2.

Appendix, 1983: René Lévesque, Ottawa, Extraits des propos du PM René Lévesque.
Lévesque, René 1983, Conférence des premiers ministres sur les questions constitutionnelles intéressant les Autochtones, *Accord constitutionnel de 1983 sur les droits des Autochtones*, doc. 80c-17/41 révisé, Federal Government, Ottawa, 15-16 March 1983.

Appendix, 1983: 15 principes qui reconnaissent les nations autochtones du Québec. 1983.

Chevrette, Guy 2003, Pour la négociation d'un traité juste et équitable. Rapport du mandataire spécial du gouvernement du Québec, M. Guy Chevrette. Concernant la proposition d'entente de principe d'ordre général avec les Innus de Mamuitun et de Nutashkuan, Gouvernement du Québec, p. 45.

Appendix, 1983: Revendication des autochtones sans statut/AAQ Assemblée nationale, Mémoire, affaires intergouvernementales, 1983.

Alliance autochtone du Québec (AAQ), 1983, Mémoire présenté à la Commission parlementaire à la présidence du conseil, de la constitution et des affaires intergouvernementales, Sans lieu. Copy from the Université de Sherbrooke.

Appendix, 1983: Correspondance PM René Lévesque à M. Fernand Chalifoux, AAQ, 12 septembre 1983. *Fonds privé, Fernand Chalifoux, 2016.*

Appendix, 1985: Consolidation, Loi sur les Indiens, 1985/Codification Indian Act, 1985.

<https://laws-lois.justice.gc.ca/PDF/I-5.pdf>.

Appendix, 1985: Motion de l'Assemblée nationale du 20 mars 1985 qui reconnaît les nations autochtones du Québec 1985.

Chevrette, Guy 2003, Pour la négociation d'un traité juste et équitable. Rapport du mandataire spécial du gouvernement du Québec, M. Guy Chevrette. Concernant la proposition d'entente de principe d'ordre général avec les Innus de Mamuitun et de Nutashkuan, Gouvernement du Québec, p. 47.

Appendix, 1986: 5.1_19860930_Demande Financement_12161344.

Nation Malécite du Québec, Viger, 1986, *Première assemblée de la Nation malécite du Québec depuis 1869,* internal document Maliseet of Viger First Nation.

Appendix, 1987: 3.1_1987-1995_Fonds Recherche_Revendications Territoriales_12161344.

PNMV, 1987-1995, Série documentaire sur les revendications de la Première Nation Malécite de Viger, internal documents.

Appendix, 1987: 27–28 June Assemblée Fondation MAV-000901.

Première Nation Malécite de Viger, 1987, *La Renaissance des Malécites.* Cacouna, 1987. Internal document.

Appendix, 1989: Québec Reconnaissance Nation Malécite 890530.

Assemblée nationale du Québec, 1989, *Reconnaissance de la nation malécite,* vol. 30, no. 118, 6079, 6080.

Appendix, 1991: Les Autochtones/Historique des lois discriminatoires à leur endroit.

Moss, Wendy, and Elaine Gardner O'Toole, 1987, revised, 1991, *Les Autochtones: historique des lois discriminatoires à leur endroit,* Ottawa, Division du droit et du gouvernement, <https://www.worldcat.org/title/autochtones-historique-des-lois-discriminatoires-a-leur-endroit/oclc/813343512>.

Annexe1993PartnersRoyalCommissionrcap-441.pdf
  Royal Commission on Aboriginal Peoples, 1993, *Partners in Confederation. Aboriginal Peoples, Self-Government, and the Constitution*, Ottawa, Ministry of Supply and Services Canada.
Appendix 1993 Appendix, 1993: CRPA Partenaires Confederation1993 rcap-466.
  Commission royale sur les peuples autochtones du Canada CRPA), 1993, *Partenaires au sein de la Confédération. Les Peuples autochtones, l'autonomie gouvernementale et la Constitution*, Ottawa, Groupe communication Canada.
Appendix, 1993: Lechasseur Histoire BSL Les Malécites 19ᵉ siècle.
  Lechasseur, Antonio, « Les Malécites au XIXᵉ siècle : établissement en réserve et disparition, » in Jean-Charles Fortin, Antonio Lechasseur, 1993, *Histoire du Bas-Saint-Laurent*, Les Éditions de l'IQRC, Québec, Presses de l'Université Laval, 225-250.
Appendix, 1994: 14.22_19940000_RéserveViger_Laurence Johnson_12161344.
  Johnson, Laurence, 1994, « La réserve malécite de Viger : Qui va à la chasse perd sa place…, » *Actes du 25ᵉ Congrès des algonquinistes*, Ottawa, Université Carleton.
Appendix, 1994: Commission royale Peuples autochtones Canada. Comment conclure des traités Canada. Commission royale sur les Peuples autochtones du Canada (CRPA), 1994, *Conclure des traités dans un esprit de coexistence. Une solution de rechange à l'extinction du titre ancestral*, Ottawa, Groupe communication Canada.
Appendix, 1996, RCPAEnglish
  Royal Commission on Aboriginal Peoples. 1993, *Partners in Confederation: Aboriginal Peoples, Self-Government and the Constitution*. Ottawa: Canada Communication Group.
  Royal Commission on Aboriginal Peoples. 1994. *Treaty Making in the Spirit of Co-Existence: An Alternative to Extinguishment*. Ottawa: Canada Communication Group.
  Royal Commission on Aboriginal Peoples. 1996. *Looking Forward, Looking Back*. Vol. 1 of *Royal Commission of Aboriginal Peoples*. Ottawa: Canada Communication Canada.
Appendix, 1996: CRPA Chap. 9 Un passé un avenir-2, 1996.
  Commission royale sur les Peuples autochtones, Canada, 1996, *Un passé, un avenir, chapitre 9 : La Loi sur les Indiens*, Ottawa, p. 274-359.
Appendix, 1996: 14.24_19960000_Origine Réserve Requête_Laurence Johnson_12161344.
  Johnson, Laurence, 1996, « À l'origine de la réserve de Viger, une requête malécite de 1826 », *Recherches amérindiennes au Québec*, vol. XXVI, no. 2.

Appendix, 1996: William C. Wicken John Read Treaty.

Wicken, William, C., John G. Reid, 1996, An Overview of the eighteenth-century treaties signed between the Mi'kmaq and Wuastukwiuk Peoples and the English Crown, 1693-1928, Report presented at the Land and Economy Royal Commission on Indigenous Peoples.

Appendix, 2000: Québec, *Loi 99, droits fondamentaux et État du Québec*, 21 November 2000.

Projet de loi n° 99 (réimpression), *Loi sur l'exercice des droits fondamentaux et des prérogatives du peuple québécois et de l'État du Québec*, M. Joseph Facal, Ministre délégué aux Affaires intergouvernementales canadiennes, Éditeur officiel du Québec, 21 November 2000.

Appendix, 2001: 2.2_20010607_Mémoire_Malécites_Vente Réserve_LJohnson_12161344.

Johnson, Laurence, 2001, *La vente de la réserve Viger. Pressions, tractations douteuses et conséquences*, Brief presented to the Maliseet of Viger First Nation.

Les Classiques des sciences sociales, UQAC, <http://classiques.uqac.ca/contemporains/Johnson_Laurence/La_vente_de_la_reserve_Viger/La_vente_de_la_reserve_Viger.html>.

Appendix, 2002: *Alliance 1603, Régime français*, Dossier documents (2 documents).

Girard, Camil, et Édith Gagné, 2001, Première alliance interculturelle entre Montagnais (Ilnus) et Français, Pointe Saint-Mathieu (près de Tadoussac) (27 mai-9 juin 1603), Mashteuiatsh, Musée amérindien de Mashteuiatsh and Groupe de recherche sur l'histoire, Université du Québec à Chicoutimi.

Girard, Camil, Édith Gagné, 2001, *Le Régime français. Traités, chartes de compagnies, lettres patentes*, Mashteuiatsh, Musée amérindien de Mashteuiatsh and Groupe de recherche sur l'histoire, Université du Québec à Chicoutimi.

Appendix, 2003: Identité et territoire Trappe aux Castors.

Girard, Camil, Marc-André Bourassa et Gervais Tremblay, 2003, *Identité et territoire. Les Innus de Mashteuiatsh et la trappe au castor sur la rivière Péribonka*, Groupe de recherche et d'intervention régionale (GRIR), Université du Québec à Chicoutimi.

Appendix, 2003: 9.13_20030404_Mémoire_Souverainetés_Laurence Johnson_12161344.

Johnson, Laurence, 2003, Souverainetés concurrentes. Politique et diplomatie au XVIIIe siècle canadien, Brief presented to the Maliseet of Viger First Nation.

Appendix, 2004: Le potentiel récréotouristique Monts-Valin.

Désy, Jean, Camil Girard, Gilles Lemieux et Alain Nepton, *Le potentiel récréotouristique du Moyen-Nord québécois. L'axe des Monts Valin-Monts Otish, Saguenay-Lac-Saint-Jean.* Groupe de recherche et d'intervention régionale (GRIR), Université du Québec à Chicoutimi.

Appendix, 2004: 31 mars, EPOG, Approche commune Innus.

Gouvernements, 2004, *Entente de principe et d'ordre général connue aussi sous le nom d'Approche commune*, entre les Premières Nations de Mamuitun et de Nutashkuan et le gouvernement du Québec et le gouvernement du Canada.

Appendix, 2005: Viger Manquement obligation Fiduciaire.2.35_Revendication Perte de Viger.

Première Nation Malécite de Viger, 2005, Revendication particulière à la couronne du chef du Canada, cession de la réserve de Viger et conséquences. Première partie: le manquement à l'obligation fiduciaire. Document PNMV.

Appendix, 2009: Clatworthy loi C-31-1985, impact et peuples autochtones Québec. 2009.

Clatworthy, Stewart, 2009, «Modifications apportées en 1985 à la *Loi sur les Indiens*: répercussions sur les Premières Nations du Québec», *Cahiers québécois de démographie*, vol. 38, no. 2, p. 253-286. <https://www.erudit.org/revue/cqd/2009/v38/n2/044816ar.html>.

Appendix, 2012: ONU Repenser DÉCOUVERTE – Mai 2012.

United Nations, 2012 and Shawn A-in-chut Atleo, chef national, La Doctrine de la découverte: son impact durable sur les peuples autochtones et le droit à réparation pour les conquêtes passées (articles 28 et 37 de la Déclaration des Nations unies sur les droits des peuples autochtones), lecture delivered at the United Nations Permanent Forum on Indigenous Issues, New York, 7-18 May 2012. Joint statement by the Assembly of First Nations, Chiefs of Ontario, Grand Council of the Crees (Eeyou Istchee), Amnesty International, Canadian Quaker Relief Services and KAIROS.

Appendix, 2013: J.-Y. Morin: René Lévesque et droits fondamentaux des peuples autochtones.

Morin, Jacques-Yvan, 2013, *René Lévesque et les droits fondamentaux des autochtones du Québec*, Site Fondation René-Lévesque, accessed on 16 September 2013: <http://fondationrene-levesque.org/rene-levesque/ecrits-sur-rene-levesque/jacques-yvan-morin-rene-levesque-et-les-droits-fondamentaux-des-autochtones-du-quebec/*>.

Appendix, 2013: Résolution Première Nation Malécite de Viger.

Première Nation Malécite de Viger, 25 April 2013, Territoire ancestral de la Première Nation Malécite de Viger. Revendication territoriale globale de la Première Nation Malécite de Viger. Recognition of Wolastokuk.

Appendix, 2015: Commission vérité réconciliation

Commission de vérité et réconciliation, 2015, *Honorer la vérité, réconcilier pour l'avenir*, Sommaire du rapport final de la Commission de vérité et réconciliation du Canada, bibliothèque Archives Canada. Available online.

Appendix, 2015: Entrevue Fernand Chalifoux, ancien chef de l'Alliance autochtone du Québec 2015.

Girard, Camil, et Martin Simard, 2015, *Récit de vie de M. Fernand Chalifoux, ancien Grand Chef de l'Alliance autochtone du Québec: ses rencontres avec*

René Lévesque, interview conducted by Martin Simard, 25 February 2015, under the direction of Camil Girard, GRH-UQAC. Published with permission.

Appendix, 2015: Archéologie Paysage Tourisme Pointe aux Alouettes.
Sans nom, Pointe-aux-Alouettes, Baie-Sainte-Catherine, Characterization study of seven territories of interest in the Charlevoix-Est MRC. https://www.notrepanorama.com/uploads/Pointe-aux-Alouettes.pdf

Appendix, 2016: Commémoration Traité 1725 Nation malécites.
Premières Nations malécites, Commémoration du Traité de 1725-1726, plaque commémorative signée par 8 chefs des Nations malécites, 4 June 2016, memorial date.

Appendix, 2016: Saganash Projet Loi C-262.
Saganash, Roméo, 2016, Projet de loi C-262, Loi visant à assurer l'harmonie des lois fédérales avec la Déclaration des Nations unies sur les droits des peuples autochtones, Ottawa, Parliament of Canada.

Appendix, 2017: Beverley McLachlin Génocide Culturel Autochtones Canada.
McLachlin, Beverley, «La Constitution canadienne. Allocution prononcée par la très honorable Beverley McLachlin, C.P., juge en chef du Canada», *L'Encyclopédie du Canada*. <https://www.thecanadianencyclopedia.ca/fr/article/beverley-mclachlin>.

Appendix, 2019: Entente Cadre Malécite Gouvernement fédéral.
Tremblay, Jacques, 5 March 2019, grand chef de la Première Nation Malécite de Viger, Allocution lors de la signature d'une entente-cadre renouvelant la relation entre le Canada et la Première Nation Malécite de Viger, en présence de la ministre Carolyn Bennett, ministre des Relations Couronne-Autochtones, Government of Canada, Cacouna, Québec, Canada.

Appendix, 2018: 1129 Potentiel Archeologique V.4.
Treyvaud, Geneviève, chargée de projet, David Bernard, Jean-Nicolas Plourde et Hadrien Bois, 2018, *Étude du potentiel archéologique du Wolastokuk pour la Nation Malécite de Viger*, Grand Conseil de la Nation Wabanaki, Research Paper.

Appendix, 2019: Génocide Enquête nationale sur les femmes et les filles autochtones disparues et assassinées.
Enquête nationale sur les femmes et les filles autochtones disparues et assassinées, *Rapport supplémentaire, Génocide*, Legal analysis of genocide, without location. <https://www.mmiwg-ffada.ca/fr/final-report/?fbclid=IwAR3g9BuhzVoeVMdE8G8NnGq82Qg74OLEFKZp8TW7OKo-XRC0hsc-mZnWZeLk>.

OTHER REFERENCES

Act to Encourage the Gradual Civilization of the Indian Tribes in the Province, passed on 10 June 1857. https://caid.ca/GraCivAct1857.pdf

Act of Union, 1840. https://www.uottawa.ca/clmc/union-act-1840

Actes de colloque. D'Amérique et d'Atlantique. 2000. Tadoussac, QC: Cégep de Baie-Comeau; Les Presses du Nord.

Agreement, 2004, *Agreement-in-Principle of General Nature between the First Nations of Mamuitun and Nutashkuan and the Government of Quebec and the Government of Canada*, Ottawa, Québec. https://www.rcaanc-cirnac.gc.ca/eng/1100100031951/1539797054964

Alliance laurentienne des Métis et Indiens sans statut du Québec. 1982. "Mémoire présenté à la Commission parlementaire du Loisir, de la Chasse et de la Pêche, 16–18 novembre 1982". Gatineau, QC: Alliance laurentienne des Métis et Indiens sans statut du Québec. https://www.bibliotheque.assnat.qc.ca/DepotNumerique_v2/AffichageFichier.aspx?idf=135931.

Approche commune (EPOG), 2004, *Entente de Principe d'ordre général entre les Premières nations de Mamuitun et de Nutashkuan et le Gouvernement du Québec et le Gouvernement du Canada*, Ottawa, Québec. https://www.rcaanc-cirnac.gc.ca/fra/1100100031951/1539797054964

Archéologie Paysage Tourisme Pointe aux Alouettes, 2015. *Pointe-aux-Alouettes, Baie-Sainte-Catherine*, Characterization study of seven territories of interest in the Charlevoix-Est MRC. https://www.notrepanorama.com/uploads/Pointe-aux-Alouettes.pdf

Assemblée legislative [Legislative assembly, United Province of Canada]. 1852. *Pièces et documents relatifs à la tenure seigneuriale, demandée par une adresse de l'Assemblée législative.* Québec: Imprimerie d'E.R. Fréchette.

Assemblée legislative [Legislative assembly, Province of Canada]. 1854. *Édits, ordonnances royaux, déclarations et arrêts du Conseil d'État du Roi concernant le Canada.* Québec: Imprimerie d'E.R. Fréchette.

Assemblée Nationale du Québec, 2003, « Consultation générale sur le document intitulé Entente de principe et d'ordre général entre les premières nations de Mamuitun et Nutashkuan et le gouvernement du Québec et le gouvernement du Canada, » *Journal des débats de la Commission permanente des institutions*, 21 January, vol. 37, no. 194. https://www.assnat.qc.ca/Media/Process.aspx?MediaId=ANQ.Vigie.Bll.DocumentGenerique_167135&process=Original&token=ZyMoxNwUn8ikQ+TRKYwPCjWrKwg+vIv9rjij7p3xLGTZDmLVSmJLoqe/vG7/YWzz

Assemblée nationale du Québec. 1985. *Journal des débats* 28, no. 38: 32nd legislature, 5th session, 19 March 1985. Québec: Gouvernement du Québec.

Bagot, Charles, 1844-1845, *Rapport sur les Affaires des Sauvages en Canada, section ère et 2ème. Mis devant l'Assemblée législative, le 20 mars 1845, Appendice E.E.E,* publié par ordre de Charles Bagot, Gouverneur-Général de l'Amérique Britannique du Nord, 8 Victoriae. See Girard and Thibeault, 2003, with pagination, II, 88-132. http://classiques.uqac.ca/classiques/Bagot_Charles/Rapport_Bagot_Francais/Rapport_Bagot_Francais.html

Bagot, Charles, 1844-1845, *Report on the Affairs of the Indians in Canada, laid before the Legislative Assembly, 20th March, 1845,* Appendix EEE, publish by order of Charles Bagot, Governor General of British North America, 8 Victoria. See Girard and Thibeault, 2003, with pagination, II, 42-87. http://classiques.uqac.ca/classiques/Bagot_Charles/Report_Bagot_English/Report_Bagot_English.html

Barkham, Selma. 1984. "The Basque Whaling Establishments in Labrador 1536–1632" *Arctic* 37 (4): 515–19.

Barriault, Yvette. 1971. *Mythes et rites chez les Indiens montagnais.* Québec: Société historique de la Côte-Nord.

Battiste, Marie. 2016. *Living Treaties. Narrating Mi'kmaw Treaty Relations.* Sydney, NS: Cape Breton University Press.

Baudot, Georges, and Tzvetan Todorov. 2009. *La Conquête: Récits aztèques.* Paris: Seuil.

Bayrou, François. 1994. *Henri IV, le roi libre.* Paris: Flammarion.

Beaulieu, Alain. 2003. "La paix de 1624: Les enjeux géopolitiques du premier traité franco-iroquois." In *Guerre et paix en Nouvelle-France,* edited by Alain Beaulieu, 53–101. Québec: Les Éditions GID.

Bélanger, Édith. 2019. *Être Wolastoqey: Entre tradition et modernité: Histoire, culture et légendes.* Cacouna, QC: Malecite of Viger First Nation.

Bélanger, René. 1971. *Les Basques dans l'estuaire du Saint-Laurent.* Sainte-Foy, QC: Presses de l'Université du Québec.

Beltrán, Gonzalo Aguirre. 1992. *Obra antropologica VI: El proceso de Aculturacion y el Cambio cultural en México.* Mexico: Universidad Veracruzana; Instituto nacional indigenista; Gobierno del Estado de Veracruzana; Fondo de cultura economica.

Beltrán, Gonzalo Aguirre. 2009. *Régiones de refugio. El desarrollo de la comunidad y el proceso dominical en Mestizoamérica.* Veracruz, Mexico: Universidad Veracruzana.

Bernard, Louis, 2003, see Bibliography: Assemblée Nationale du Québec, 21 January.

Bideaux, Michel, ed. 1986, *Relations, by Jacques Cartier.* Bibliothèque du Nouveau Monde. Montréal: Presses de l'Université de Montréal.

Biggar, H.P. 1965. *The Early Trading Companies of New France.* New York: Argonaut Press.

Bissonnette, Alain, ed. 1993. "Des alliances fondatrices aux traités modernes." *Recherches amérindiennes au Québec* 23 (1).

Boily, Maxime. 2006. "Les terres amérindiennes dans le régime seigneurial: Les modèles fonciers dans les missions sédentaires de la Nouvelle-France." Master's thesis, Université Laval.

Borrows, John. 2010. *Canada's Indigenous Constitution*. Toronto: University of Toronto Press.

Boucher, Nathalie. 2005. "La transmission intergénérationnelle des savoirs dans la communauté innue de Mashteuiatsh: Savoir-faire et savoir-être au cœur des relations entre les Pekuakamiulnuatsh." Master's thesis, Université Laval.

Bréard, Charles, and Paul Bréard. 1889. *Documents relatifs à la Marine normande et à ses armements aux xvie et xviie siècles* [...]. Rouen, France: Société de l'histoire de Normandie.

Brown, George W. ed. 1996. *Dictionary of Canadian Biography*. Vol. 1, *1000 to 1700*. Québec: Presses de l'Université Laval; Toronto: University of Toronto.

Burke, Adrian L. 2000. "Lithic Procurement and the Ceramic Period Occupation of the Interior of the Maritime Peninsula." PhD. diss., University at Albany, State University of New York.

Burke, Adrian L. 2001. "Temiscouata: Traditional Maliseet Territory and Connections between the St. Lawrence Valley and the St. John River Valley." In *Actes du trente-deuxième congrès des algonquinistes*, edited by J.D. Nichols, 61–73. Winnipeg: University of Manitoba.

Burke, Adrian L. 2009. "L'archéologie des Malécites: Passé, présent et future." *Recherches amérindiennes au Québec* 39 (3): 7–24.

Calderhead, Manon. 2011. "La reconstruction identitaire et territoriale d'une communauté dispersée: L'ère de restitution pour les Malécites de Viger." Master's thesis, Université de Montréal. https://archipel.uqam.ca/4319/1/M12085.pdf.

Campbell, Patrick. (1793) 1937. *Travels in the Interior Inhabited Parts of North America in the Years 1791 and 1792*, edited by H.H. Langton. Toronto: Champlain Society.

Campeau, Lucien, ed. 1967. *Monumenta Novae Franciae I: La première mission d'Acadie (1602–1616)*. Québec: Presses de l'Université Laval.

Canada. 1891. *Indian treaties and surrenders, from 1680 to 1890*. Ottawa: Brown Chamberlin.

Caron, Abbé Adrien. 1980. *De Canada en Acadie: Le Grand Portage*. Cahiers d'histoire 15. La Pocatière, QC: Société historique de la Côte-du-Sud.

Cape Breton University, *Treaties 1725-1761, Treaty of Watertown*. https://www.cbu.ca/indigenous-initiatives/lnu-resource-centre/treaties/

Castonguay, Rachelle. 1980. "Toponymie amérindienne sur les anciennes cartes du Québec conservées aux archives publiques du Gouvernement canadien à Ottawa: 1536–1780." Unpublished manuscript. Québec: Commission de toponymie.

Chalifoux, Éric, and Adrian L. Burke. 1995. "L'occupation préhistorique du Témiscouata (est du Québec), un lieu de portage entre deux grandes voies de circulation." In *Archéologies québécoises*, edited by A.-M. Balac, C. Chapdelaine, N. Clermont, and F. Duguay, 237–70. Paléo-Québec 23. Montreal: Recherches amérindiennes au Québec.

Chalifoux, Éric, Adrian L. Burke, and Claude Chapdelaine. 1998. *La préhistoire du Témiscouata: Occupations amérindiennes dans la haute vallée de Wolastokuk.* Paléo-Québec 26. Montreal: Recherches amérindiennes au Québec.

Champlain, Samuel de. (1603) 1978. *Des Sauvages: A facsimile of the Paris, 1603, edition made from the copy at the John Carter Brown Library.* Introduction by Marcel Trudel. Montréal, Québec: [G. Javitch].

Champlain, Samuel de. (1603) 1993. *Des sauvages*, edited by Alain Beaulieu and Réal Ouellet. Montréal: Typo.

Champlain, Samuel de. 1632. *Les Voyages de la Nouvelle France Occidentale, Dicte Canada* [...]. Paris: Louis Sevestre. https://numerique.banq.qc.ca/patrimoine/details/52327/2022100?docref=Av2OFiCAE3i_CRPDeq_O4w

Charest, Paul, Daniel Clément, and Jacques Frenette. 2004. *Les droits aboriginaux des Mamit Innuat concernant l'exploitation et le commerce des ressources marines.* Sept-Îles, QC: Département des pêches marines du Conseil Mamit Innuat.

Chevrette, Guy, 2003, see Bibliography: Assemblée Nationale du Québec, 21 January.

Chevrette, Guy, 2003, *Pour la négociation d'un traité juste et équitable*, Rapport du mandaraire spécial du Gouvernement du Québec concernant l'Entente de Principe et d'ordre général avec les Innus de Mamuitun et de Nutashkuan, Publication du Gouvernement du Québec. https://numerique.banq.qc.ca/patrimoine/details/52327/44238?docref=7ndBLgjSVUQvqnqNnQ8Rbw

Chopin, Dominique. n.d.-a. "Deuxième generation: Nicolas (2) et Ursule: Nicolas, le deuxième de la ligné." *Généalogie de la famille Jenniss-Malécites.* Accessed 18–19 September 2019. https://genealogiejenniss.weebly.com/?fbclid=IwAR2CyB9nOTysHyftJn3LOr9I2oiVmU5zARqP55MC8a76aiCrkDkM0OY7Jzs.

Chopin, Dominique. n.d.-b. "Première génération: Nicolas Denys." *Généalogie de la famille Jenniss-Malécites.* Accessed 18–19 September 2019. https://genealogiejenniss.weebly.com/?fbclid=IwAR2CyB9nOTysHyftJn3LOr9I2oiVmU5zARqP55MC8a76aiCrkDkM0OY7Jzs.

Clarke, Ernest. 1995. *Siege of Fort Cumberland, 1776: An Episode in the American Revolution.* Montreal and Kingston: McGill-Queen's University Press.

Classiques (Les) des sciences sociales, Université du Québec à Chicoutimi, more than 9000 documents online in free access.

Common Approach, 2004, Entente de Principe d'ordre général entre les Premières nations de Mamuitun et de Nutashkuan et le Gouvernement du Québec et le Gouvernement du Canada, Ottawa, Québec. https://www.rcaanc-cirnac.gc.ca/fra/1100100031951/1539797054964

Constitutional Act, 1982. https://laws-lois.justice.gc.ca/eng/const/

Constitutional Act, 1791. https://www.ola.org/en/visit-learn/about-parliament/history-heritage/timeline/constitutional-act-1791

Correa, Silvio, and Camil Girard. 2006. "La circulation des personnes dans le cadre des alliances franco-amérindiennes: Le don, l'adoption et l'enlèvement au Brésil et au Canada: XVe–XVIe siècles." *Littoral* 1: 27–40.

Correa, Silvio, and Camil Girard. 2007. "Hybridisme culturel et alliances franco-amérindiennes au Brésil et au Québec-Canada (XVIe et XVIIe siècles)." Conference presentation, University of Santa Cruz do Sul, Brasil, 13 November 2007.

Cortés, Hernán. (c. 1520) 1996. *La conquête du Mexique*, edited by Bernard Grunberg. Translated from Spanish by Désiré Charnay. Paris: La Découverte Poche.

Courville, Serge. 1995. *Introduction à la géographie historique*. Québec: Presses de l'Université Laval.

Courville, Serge. 2000. *Le Québec: Genèses et mutations du territoire: Synthèse de géographie historique*. Québec: Presses de l'Université Laval.

Courville, Serge, Serge Labrecque and Jacques Fortin. 1988. *Seigneuries et fiefs du Québec: Nomenclature et cartographie*. Québec: Centre de recherche Cultures – Arts – Sociétés.

Cuena Boy, Francisco. 1998. "Utilización pragmática del derecho romano en dos memoriales indianos del siglo XVII sobre el Protector de Indios." *Revista de estudios historico-juridicos* 20: 107–42.

Cumming, Peter, and Neil H. Mickenberg, eds. 1980. *Native Rights in Canada*. 2nd. ed. Indian-Eskimo Association of Canada; Toronto: General Publishing.

Davenport, F. Gardiner. 1917. *European Treaties bearing on the History of the United States and Its Dependencies to 1648*. Washington DC: Carnegie Institution of Washington.

D'Avignon, Mathieu. 2001. "Samuel de Champlain et les alliances franco-amérindiennes: Une diplomatie interculturelle." Master's thesis, Université Laval.

D'Avignon, Mathieu. 2006. "Champlain et les historiens francophones du Quebec: Les figures du père et le mythe de la foundation." PhD diss., Université Laval.

D'Avignon, Mathieu. 2008. *Champlain et les historiens: Les figures du père et le mythe de la fondation*. Québec: Presses de l'Université Laval.

D'Avignon, Mathieu. 2018. *Samuel de Champlain: Récits de voyages en Nouvelle-France de 1603–1632*. Reprint in modern French. Québec: Presses de l'Université Laval.

D'Avignon, Mathieu, and Camil Girard. 2009. *A-t-on oublié que jadis nous étions "frères"? Alliances fondatrices et reconnaissance des peuples autochtones dans l'histoire du Québec*. Québec: Presses de l'Université Laval.

Débats de l'Assemblée nationale du Québec, 19 March 1985.

Delâge, Denys.1991. *Le pays renversé: Amérindiens et Européens en Amérique du Nord-Est: 1600–1664*. Québec, Boréal.

Delâge, Denys. 2007. "L'alliance franco-amérindienne des XVIIe et XVIIIe siècles: Spécificités, changements de régime, documents." Unpublished manuscript. Québec: Université Laval.

Desjardins, Marc, Yves Frenette, and Jules Bélanger. 1999. *Histoire de la Gaspésie*. 2nd ed. Éditions de l'IQRC; Québec, Presses de l'Université Laval.

Dickason, Olive Patricia. 1984. "The Brazilian Connection: A Look at the Origin of FrenchTechniques for Trading with Amerindians." *Revue française d'histoire d'outre-mer*, 71 (264-5): 129-46.

Dickason, Olive Patricia. 1993a, *Canada's First Nations: A History of Founding Peoples from Earliest Times*. Toronto: McClelland & Stewart.

Dickason, Olive Patricia. 1993b. *Le Mythe du sauvage*. Québec: Septentrion.

Dickason, Olive Patricia. 1996. *Les Premières Nations du Canada*. Québec: Septentrion.

Dionne, Paul, 1891. *La Nouvelle-France. De Cartier à Champlain*, Québec, Darveau.

Dionne, Paul. 1984. "Le titre aborigène des Indiens Attikameks et Montagnais du Québec." Master's thesis, University of Ottawa.

de Encinas, Diego. (1596) 1946. *Cedulario Indiano*, edited by Alfonso Garcia Gallo. Facsimile of the edition of 1596. Madrid: Ediciones Cultura Hispanica.

Durham Report, 1839. <https://archive.org/details/cihm_32373>.

Erickson, Vincent O. 1978. "Maliseet-Passamaquoddy." In *Handbook of North American Indians*. Edited by William C. Sturtevant. Vol. 15, *Northeast*, edited by Bruce G. Trigger, 123-36. Washington, DC: Smithsonian Institution.

First People of America and Canada - Turtle Island. (n.d.). "The Empounded Water: A Malecite Legend." Accessed 29 August 2023. https://www.first-people.us/FP-Html-Legends/TheEmpoundedWater-Malecite.html

Florescano, Enrique. 2004. *Historia de las historias de la nación Mexicana*. Mexico City: Taurus.

Fortin, Jean-Charles, Antonio Lechasseur, and Yves Tremblay. 1993. *Histoire du Bas-Saint-Laurent*. Éditions de l'IQRC; Québec: Presses de l'Université Laval.

Foucault, Michel. 1999. *Les Anormaux: Cours au Collège de France*. Paris: Seuil.

Frenette, Pierre, ed. 1996. *Histoire de la Côte-Nord*. Québec: Presses de l'Université Laval; Éditions de l'IQRC.

Gagnon and Petel 1986. *Hommes effables et bestes sauvages. Images du Nouveau-Monde d'après les voyages de Jacques Cartier*, Montréal, Boréal.

Ganong, William F. 1895. "A Plan for a General History of the Province of New Brunswick." In *Transactions of the Royal Society of Canada*. 2nd ser. 1895-96, vol. 1, sec. 2: 91-102. Ottawa: John Durie and Sons.

Ganong, William F. 1906. "Additions and Corrections to Monographs on the Place-Nomenclature, Cartogra phy, Historic Sites, Boundaries and Settlement-origins of the Province of New Brunswick." In *Proceedings and*

Transactions of the Royal Society of Canada. 2nd ser., 1906-07, vol. 12, sec. 2: 3-88. Ottawa: James Hope & Sons.

Garcini, Ricardo Rendón. 1996. *Breve historia de Tlaxcala.* Mexico City: El Colegio de México; Fideicomiso Historia de las Américas; Fondo de Cultura Económica

Garneau, François-Xavier. (1845) 1996. *Histoire du Canada,* vol. 1. Montréal: Bibliothèque Québécoise; HMH; Leméac.

Gentilcore, R. Louis, and Geoffrey J. Matthews, eds. 1993. *Atlas historique du Canada,* vol. 2. Montréal: Presses de l'Université de Montréal.

Giguère, George-Émile, ed. 1973. *Œuvres de Champlain.* Montréal: Éditions du Jour.

Giokas, John. 1995. *The Indian Act. Evolution, Overview and Options for Amendment and Transition.* Ottawa: [Royal Commission on Aboriginal Peoples].

Girard, Camil. 1997. "Culture et dynamique interculturelle: Trois femmes et trois hommes témoignent de leur vie." Interculture. Report prepared for the Royal Commission on Aboriginal Peoples concerning intercultural relations in contemporary Innu communities. Chicoutimi, QC: Les Éditions JCL. Available online at the site *Les Classiques des sciences sociales.*

Girard, Camil. 2002, *Première alliance interculturelle entre Montagnais (Ilnus) et Français.* Ottawa: Parks Canada; Canadian Heritage.

Girard, Camil. 2003a. "L'Approche commune: Un projet qui s'inscrit dans l'histoire des alliances entre les Innus (Montagnais) et les Couronnes (1603 à nos jours)." Brief presented to the Assemblée nationale du Québec, Parliamentary Commission on the Approche commune.

Girard, Camil. 2003b. "Le début des alliances franco-amérindiennes de 1603 ... Premières Nations et révision des mythes fondateurs de l'histoire." In *Le GRIR, 20 ans de recherche et d'intervention pour le développement local et régional,* edited by Jean Désy, Jules Dufour, Myriam Duplain, Denis Plamondon, and Suzanne Tremblay, 219-60. Revised edition of a report prepared for Parks Canada, 2002 (published with permission). Chicoutimi, QC: Groupe de recherche et d'intervention régionale, Université du Québec à Chicoutimi.

Girard, Camil. 2003c. "Un document inédit sur les droits territoriaux: Le protêt des Innus du comté de Saguenay en 1851." *Saguenayensia* 45 (1) 35-43. Available online at the site Les Classiques des sciences sociales.

Girard, Camil. 2004. "Reconnaissance historique des peuples autochtones au Canada: Territoire et autonomie gouvernementale chez les Innus (Montagnais) au Québec: 1603 à nos jours." Paper presented at the Simposio International sobre Resolucion noviolenta de conflictos en Sociedades Indigenas en America Latina, Yautopec, Morelos, Mexico, March 2004. http://www.uqac.ca/grh/.

Girard, Camil. 2006. "El enfoque común (Approche Commune): Reconocimiento de los derechos ancestrales y del título ancestral de los Innúes Quebec, Canada: La marcha hacia un tratado moderno que se inscribe en la historia de Quebec y de Canadá (1603–1975)." In *El triple desafío: Derechos, instituciones y politicas para la ciudad pluricultural,* edited by Pablo Yanes, Virginia Molina, and Óscar González, 371–418. Mexico City: Secretaria de Desarrollo Social.

Girard, Camil. 2017. "Qualifier pour disqualifier …: Michel Foucault et la gouverne des "marginaux" ou comment les peuples autochtones ont été exclus de la fondation du Canada (1867)." In *Vivre ensemble dans les régions du Québec: Défis et enjeux contemporains,* edited by Marie Fall, Danielle Maltais, and Suzanne Tremblay, 11–27. Chicoutimi, QC: Groupe de recherche et d'intervention régionale (GRIR), Université du Québec à Chicoutimi. Available online at the site Les Classiques des sciences sociales.

Girard, Camil, and Carl Brisson. 2014. *Nistassinan – Notre terre: Alliance et souveraineté partagée du peuple innu au Québec: Des origines à nos jours.* Mondes autochtones. Québec: Presses de l'Université Laval.

Girard, Camil, and Carl Brisson. 2018. *Reconnaissance et exclusion des peuples autochtones au Québec: Du traité d'alliance de 1603 à nos jours.* Québec: Presses de l'Université Laval.

Girard, Camil, and Mathieu d'Avignon. 2000. "Champlain et les Montagnais (Ilnus): Alliances, diplomatie et justice: Ingérence et déférence 1600–1635." In *Actes de colloque: D'Amérique et d'Atlantique,* 29–56. Tadoussac, QC: Cégep de Baie-Comeau; Les Presses du Nord.

Girard, Camil, and Mathieu d'Avignon. 2005. "Samuel de Champlain et les premières alliances franco-amérindiennes (1603–1635): À propos de transferts culturels." *Revue Saguenayensia* 47 (1).

Girard, Camil, and Édith Gagné. 1995. "Première alliance interculturelle: Rencontre entre Montagnais et Français à Tadoussac en 1603." *Recherches amérindiennes au Québec* 25 (3): 3–14.

Girard, Camil, and Jacques Kurtness. 2012. "Premier traité de l'histoire de la Nouvelle-France en Amérique: L'Alliance de 1603 (Tadoussac) et la souveraineté partagée des peuples autochtones du Québec." Groupe internationale de travail pour les peuples autochtones. http://www.gitpa.org/Peuple%20 GITPA%20500/gitpa500-1TEXTREFCGirardJKurt.pdf.

Girard, Camil, and Normand Perron. 1995. *Histoire du Saguenay–Lac-Saint-Jean.* Québec: Presses de l'Université Laval; Éditions de l'IQRC.

Girard, Camil, Jessica Thibeault, 2001. *Rapports sur les questions autochtones: Canada 1828–1870,* 3 vol. Chicoutimi, QC: Alliance de recherche universités-communautés (ARUC); monts Valin-monts Otish (CRSH); Groupe recherche sur l'histoire – Université du Québec à Chicoutimi. Include French and English versions with our pagination to facilitate referencing since most original documents had no pagination). *Charles Bagot Report* included in English, 42–87, in French, 88–132. See online, *Les Classiques des Sciences sociales,* Université du Québec à Chicoutimi. http://classiques.uqac.ca/

Girard, Camil. 2017. "Qualifier pour disqualifier …: Michel Foucault et la gouverne des "marginaux" ou comment les peuples autochtones ont été exclus de la fondation du Canada (1867)." In *Vivre ensemble dans les régions du Québec: Défis et enjeux contemporains,* edited by Marie Fall, Danielle Maltais, and Suzanne Tremblay, 11–27. Chicoutimi, QC: Groupe de recherche et d'intervention régionale (GRIR), Université du Québec à Chicoutimi. Available online at the site Les Classiques des sciences sociales.

Gouvernement du Québec. 1891. *Liste des terrains concédés par la Couronne dans la province de Québec, de 1763 à 31 décembre 1890.* Québec: Charles-François Langlois, Imprimeur de Sa Très Grande Majesté la Reine.

"Governor Murray to Board of Trade," copy. 1767. Great Britain. Colonial Office: Canada, formerly British North America: Original correspondence. CO 42, C-13605, 6: 126–7. 26 May 1767. https://heritage.canadiana.ca/view/oocihm.lac_reel_c13605/142.

Grammond, Sébastien. 1995. *Les traités entre l'État et les peuples autochtones.* Cowansville: QC: Les Éditions Yvon Blais.

Grenier, Benoit. 2015. "Le régime seigneurial au Québec." *Bulletin d'histoire politique* 23 (2): 141–56.

Groulx, Lionel. 1960. *Histoire du Canada français,* vol. 1. Montréal: Fides.

Groulx, Patrice. 1998. *Pièges de la mémoire, Dollard des Ormeaux, les Amérindiens et nous.* Hull, QC: Les Éditions Vents.

Grundset, Eric G, ed., with Briana L. Diaz, Hollis L. Gentry, and Jean D. Strahan. 2008. *Forgotten Patriots: African American and American Indian Patriots in the Revolutionary War. A Guide to Service, Sources and Studies.* 2nd ed. Washington, DC: National Society Daughters of the American Revolution.

Gruzinski, Serge. 1999. *La pensée métisse.* Paris: Fayard.

Gruzinski, Serge. 2004. *Les quatre parties du monde. Histoire d'une mondialisation.* Paris: Éditions de la Martinière.

Hamelin, Jean, ed. 1981. *Histoire du Québec.* Montréal: Éditions France-Amérique.

Harrisse, Henry. [1900] 1968. *Découverte et évolution cartographique de Terre-Neuve et des pays circonvoisins: 1497, 1501, 1760.* Ridgewood, NJ: Gregg Press.

Havard, Gilles. 1992. *La Grande paix de Montréal de 1701: Les voies de la diplomatie franco-amérindienne.* Signes des Amériques. Montréal: Recherches amérindiennes au Québec.

Havard, Gilles. 2003. *Empire et métissage: Indiens et Français dans le Pays d'en Haut: 1660–1715.* Québec: Septentrion; Paris: Presses de l'Université Paris-Sorbonne.

Heidenreich, Conrad, E. and K. Janet Ritch, eds., 2010. *Samuel de Champlain before 1604: Des Sauvages and other, Documents Related to the Period.* Montreal & Kingston: McGill-Queen's University Press for the Champlain Society, Toronto.

Hernández, Natalio. 2009. *De la exclusión al diálogo intercultural con los Pueblos Indígenas.* México City: Ed. Plaza y Valdés. www.plazayvaldes.com.

Humeres, Roxana Paniagua. 1995. "Le Statut de l'Indien au temps de la Conquête: Le débat de Valladolid (1550) et les thèses de Vitoria." *Recherches amérindiennes au Québec* 25 (3): 15–28.

International Court of Justice. Pleadings. 1991. Land, Island and Maritime Frontier Dispute (El Salvador v. Hunduras: Nicaragua intervening). "Public sitting of the Chamber held on Tuesday, 23 April 1991, at 10 a.m., at the Peace Palace, Judge Sette-Camara, President of the Chamber, presiding." Verbatim record C 4/CR 91/7. https://www.icj-cij.org/sites/default/files/case-related/75/075-19910423-ORA-01-00-BI.pdf

Isambert, F.A., A.H. Taillandier, and DeCrusy. 1829. *Recueil général des anciennes lois françaises* [...]. Vol. 15: *Août 1589 – May 1610*. Paris: Belin-LePrieur; Paris: Verdière.

Jaenen, Cornelius J. *The French relationship with the native peoples of New France and Acadia*. Ottawa: Research Branch, Indian and Northern Affairs Canada, 1984 Jaenen, Cornelius J. 1986. "The Meeting of the French and Amerindians in the Seventeenth Century." In *Interpreting Canada's Past*. Vol. 1, *Before Confederation*, edited by J. M. Bumsted. Toronto: Oxford University Press.

James Bay (The) and Northern Quebec Agreement 1975. https://caid.ca/AgrJamBayNorQueA1975.pdf

Johnson, Laurence. 1994. "La réserve malécite de Viger: Qui va à la chasse perd sa place..." *Actes du 25e congrès des algonquinistes*, edited by William Cowen, 236–64. Ottawa: Carleton University.

Johnson, Laurence. 1995. "La réserve malécite de Viger: Un projet-pilote du "programme de civilisation" du gouvernement canadien." Master's thesis, Université de Montréal.

Johnson, Laurence. 1996. "À l'origine de la réserve de Viger: Une requête malécite de 1826." *Recherches amérindiennes au Québec* 26 (2): 77–81.

Johnson, Laurence. 2001. "La vente de la réserve de Viger: Pressions, tractations douteuses et conséquences." Brief presented to the Maliseet of Viger First Nation. Available online at the site Classiques des sciences sociales.

Johnson, Laurence. 2003. "Souverainetés concurrentes: Politique et diplomatie au XVIIIe siècle canadien." Brief presented to the Maliseet of Viger First Nation, second version.

Johnson, Micheline D. (1974). "Aubery, Joseph." In *Dictionary of Canadian Biography*, vol. 3. Québec: Université Laval; Toronto: University of Toronto. http://www.biographi.ca/en/bio/aubery_joseph_3E.html.

Krasowski, Sheldon. 2019. *No Surrender. The Land Remains Indigenous*. Regina: SK: University of Regina Press.

Kurtness, Rémy (Kal'wa). 2000. "De l'alliance entre Innus et Français à un traité de nouvelle génération avec le Kanata et le Kepek." In *Actes de colloque: D'Amérique et d'Atlantique*. Tadoussac, QC: Cégep de Baie-Comeau; Les Presses du Nord.

Kurtness, Remy Kak'wa, 2003, see Bibliography: Assemblée Nationale du Québec, 21 January.

Lacasse, Jean-Paul. 1996. "Le territoire dans l'univers innu d'aujourd'hui." *Les Cahiers de géographie du Québec* 40 (110): 185–204.

Lajoie, Andrée, Jean-Maurice Brisson, Sylvie Normand, and Alain Bissonnette. 1996. "Le statut juridique des peuples autochtones au Québec et le pluralisme." Cowansville, QC: Les Éditions Yvon Blais.

Langevin, Érik. 2000. "Il était une fois l'Anse à la Croix." *Saguenayensia* 42 (3): 3–13.

Leacock, Eleanor. 1981. "Seventeenth-Century Montagnais Social Relations and Values." In *Handbook of North American Indians*. Edited by William Sturtevant. Vol. 6, *Subarctic*, edited by June Hann, 190–5. Washington, DC: Smithsonian Institution.

Lebel, Andréanne. 2019 (5 March). "Signature d'une entente-cadre entre la Première Nation Malécite de Viger et le Canada." *Info Dimanche*. https://www.infodimanche.com.

Lechasseur, Antonio, « Les Malécites aux XIXe siècle : établissement en réserve et disparition, » in Jean-Charles Fortin, Antonio Lechasseur, 1993, *Histoire du Bas-Saint-Laurent*, Les Éditions de l'IQRC, Québec, Presses de l'Université Laval, 225-250. Also en Appendix, 1993)

Léry (de), Jean. (1578) 1994. *Histoire d'un voyage faict en la terre du Brésil (1578)*. Edited by Frank Lestringant. Bibliothèque classique. Paris: Livre de poche.

Lescarbot, Marc. (1609) 1911. *Histoire de la Nouvelle-France*, 3rd ed., edited and translated by W.L. Grant, vol. 2. Toronto: Champlain Society.

Lescarbot, Marc. (1609) 2007. *Voyages en Acadie (1604–1607) suivis de la description des mœurs souriquois comparées à celles d'autres peuples*. Edited by Marie-Christine Pioffet. Québec: Presses de l'Université Laval.

Leslie, John. 1985. "Commissions of Inquiry into Indian Affairs in the Canadas, 1828–1858: Evolving a Corporate Memory for the Indian Department." Ottawa: Department Indian Affairs and Northern Development Canada.

Lestringant, Frank. 1999. *Le Huguenot et le sauvage*. Paris: Klincksieck.

Lestringant, Frank. 2007. "Écrire la Nouvelle-France en 1609: Note sur Marc Lescarbot." Paper presented at the Colloque en hommage à Denys Delâge et Réal Ouellet: Représentation, métissage et pouvoir, Québec, QC, January 2007.

Levaggi, Abelardo. 1993. "Los tratados entre la Corona y Los indios, y el plan de conquista pacifica." *Revista Complutense de Historia de América* 19: 81–91.

Malaurie, Philippe. 2000. *Anthologie de la pensée juridique*. 2nd ed. Paris: Cujas.

Malecite of Viger First Nation. (2010). "Mémoire de la Première Nation Malécite de Viger concernant la participation du Québec au processus de négociation exploratoire, soumis au ministre responsable des Affaires autochtones, ministère du Conseil exécutif." 8 March 2010. Cacouna, QC: Malecite of Viger First Nation.

Malouf, Albert. 1973. *La Baie James indienne: Texte intégral du jugement du juge Malouf.* Edited by André Gagnon. Montréal: Editions du Jour.

Maltais, André, 2003, see Bibliography: Assemblée Nationale du Québec, 21 January.

Mamit Innuat. 2003. "Mémoire des Premières Nations de Mamit Innuat." Commission des institutions chargée de tenir des auditions publiques à l'égard de l'Entente de principe d'ordre générale entre les Premières Nations de Mamuitun et de Nutashkuan et le gouvernement du Québec et le gouvernement du Canada. Québec: Assemblée nationale du Québec. Brief from Mamit Innuat First Nations (749004), January 2003. https://www.bibliotheque.assnat.qc.ca/DepotNumerique_v2/AffichageFichier.aspx?idf=62890

Marie-Victorin, Fr. C. K. 1918. "Le portage du Témiscouata: Notes critiques et documents pour servir à l'histoire d'une vieille route coloniale." *Mémoires et comptes rendus de la Societé royale du Canada, 3rd ser.*, vol. 12: 55–93.

Martinez Baracs, Andrea. 2008. *Un gobierno de indios: Tlaxcala, 1519–1750.* Mexico City: Fundo de Cultura Economica; Colegio de Historia de Tlaxcala; Centro de Investigaciones y Estudios Superiores en Antropologia social.

Matamoros Ponce, Fernando. 2007. *La pensée coloniale: Découverte, conquête et guerre des dieux au Mexique.* Paris: Éditions Syllepse; Puebla, Mexico: Benemérita Universidad Autónoma de Puebla.

Mathieu, Jacques, Serge Courville, and Rénald Lessard. 1987. *Peuplement colonisateur aux XVIIe et XVIIIe siècles.* Sainte-Foy, QC: CELAT, 292.

Mathieu, Jacques, Alain Laberge, and Lina Gouger. 1991. *L'occupation des terres dans la vallée du Saint-Laurent: Les aveux et dénombrement: 1723–1745.* Sillery, QC: Septentrion.

Mauss, Marcel. 1923. "Essai sur le don: Forme et raison de l'échange dans les sociétés archaïquès." *Année sociologique*, 2nd ser., vol. 1: 30–186. See also online in Les Classiques des sciences sociales, Université du Québec à Chicoutimi, <http://classiques.uqac.ca/>.

McLachlin, Beverley, 2015 *Annual pluralism lecture of the Global Centre for pluralism*, Toronto, Canada, 28 May. https://the.akdn/en/resources-media/resources/speeches/2015-annual-pluralism-lecture-global-centre-pluralism-rt-hon-beverley-mclachlin

McLeod, Elsie Jury. 1966. "Anadabijou." In *Dictionary of Canadian Biography*, edited by George W. Brown. Vol. 1, *1000 to 1700*, 61. Québec: Presses de l'Université Laval; Toronto: University of Toronto.

McNeil, Kent. 2007. *La compétence du droit inhérent des gouvernements autochtones.* Centre national pour la gouvernance des Premières Nations, 34.

Michaud, Ghislain. 2003. *Les gardiens des portages: L'histoire des Malécites du Québec.* Québec: Les Éditions GID.

Michaux, Emmanuel. 2007. c. Pêches autochtones. Québec: Université Laval; Centre interuniversitaire d'études et de recherches autochtones.

Milagros Del Vas Mingo, Maria. 1985. "Las Ordenanzas de 1573: Sus antecedentes y consequencias." *Quinto Centenario* 8: 83–101.

Ministère de l'Énergie et des Ressources naturelles, 2015, *Plan d'affectation des terres publiques de Chaudière-Appalaches*, Québec, 292 p.

Moar, Clifford. 2002. « Clifford Moar cache mal son inquiétude », *Progrès-Dimanche*, 27 oct. 2002, A6.

Moar, Clifford, 2003, see Bibliography: Assemblée Nationale du Québec, 21 January.

Moreau, J.A. 1866. *Histoire des Abenakis: Depuis 1605 jusqu'à nos jours*. Sorel, QC: Atelier typographique de la "Gazette de Sorel." See https://numerique.banq.qc.ca/patrimoine/details/52327/2022960

Morin, Michel. 1997. *L'usurpation de la souveraineté autochtone*. Montréal: Boréal.

Morin, Michel. 2004. "La dimension juridique des relations entre Samuel de Champlain et les Autochtones de la Nouvelle-France." *Revue juridique Thémis* 38 (2): 393–426.

Morley, William F.E. 1966. "Pierre de Chauvin de Tonnetuit." In *Dictionary of Canadian Biography*, edited by George W. Brown, 209–10. Vol. 1, *1000 to 1700*. Québec: Presses de l'Université Laval; Toronto: University of Toronto.

Morrison, A.H., and Thomas H. Goetz. 1974. "Membertou's Raid on the Chouacoet 'Almouchiquois': The Micmac Sack of Saco in 1607." In *Papers of the Sixth Algonquian Conference*, edited by William Cowan, 141–79. Ottawa: University of Ottawa Press. See https://www.jstor.org/stable/j.ctv16x92

Moss, Wendy, Elaine Gardner-O'toole, 1987, *The Indigenous People. A History of Laws Discriminating Against Them*, paper prepared for the Canadian Federal Government and Law Division., revised, November 1991. https://publications.gc.ca/Collection-R/LoPBdP/BP/bp175-e.htm

National Inquiry into Missing and Murdered Indigenous Women and Children. 2019. https://www.mmiwg-ffada.ca/final-report/

New Brunswick Aboriginal Peoples Council (NBAPC), *Treaties*, online. https://nbapc.org/treaty-of-1725/

Northeastern (The) Quebec Agreement 1978 [Naskapi]). https://caid.ca/AgrNorEasQueA1974.pdf

Oswald Spring, Ursula, ed. 2004. *Resolución noviolenta de conflictos en sociedades indígenas y minorías*. Mexico: CLAIP, Universidad de Morelos; Colegio de Tlaxcala.

Parent, Raynald. 1981. "L'effritement de la civilisation amérindienne." In *Histoire du Québec*, edited by Jean Hamelin. Montréal: Éditions France-Amérique.

Parent, Raynald. 1985. "Histoire des Amérindiens du Saint-Maurice jusqu'au Labrador: De la préhistoire à 1760." Master's thesis, Université Laval, Québec, QC.

Parliament, Legislative Assembly, 1845, *An Act to repeal certain Ordinances aforesaid and to make better provision for the establishment of local and municipal authorities in Lower Canada*, 8 Victoria, chap. 40. https://bnald.lib.unb.ca/sites/default/files/UnC.1845.ch%2040.pdf.

Pekuakamiulnuatsh Takuhikan. 2019. "Signature de la Déclaration solennelle de respect mutuel et d'alliance internations." *Cision*, news release, 6 June 2019. https://www.mashteuiatsh.ca/messages-aux-pekuakamiulnuatsh/actualites/3150-signature-de-la-declaration-solennelle-de-respect-mutuel-et-d-alliance-internations.html; https://www.newswire.ca/fr/news-releases/signature-de-la-declaration-solennelle-de-respect-mutuel-et-d-alliance-internations-899399579.html.

Picard, Louis-Philippe, Michel Dumais, Alain Prévost, and Josée Vileneuve. 2005. "Étude de potentiel archéologique: Route 132 et infrastructures municipales de la municipalité de Rivière-Ouelle." Projet MTQ 20-3374-8909. Québec: Ministère des Transports.

Première Nation Malécite de Viger. 2013. "Territoire ancestral de la Première Nation Malécite de Viger." Resolution of Conseil de la Nation on the traditional territory of the Maliseet Nation of Québec, le Wolastokuk (Reference map 40)." 25 April 2013. Cacouna, QC: Maliseet of Viger First Nation.

Quebec Act, 1774. https://www.assnat.qc.ca/fr/patrimoine/lexique/acte-de-quebec-(1774).html; https://www.uottawa.ca/clmc/quebec-act-1774

Quebec (The) Gazette, 24 January 1765, 2. https://numerique.banq.qc.ca/patrimoine/details/52327/4265872

Québec. Ministère de l'Énergie et des Ressources naturelles. 2015. *Plan d'affectation des terres publiques du Bas-Saint-Laurent*. Québec: Ministère de l'Énergie et des Ressources naturelles. https://mrnf.gouv.qc.ca/nos-publications/patp-bas-saint-laurent/

Raymond, W.O. (1895) n.d. *The Revolutionary War: Part Played by the St. John River Indians*. Fredericton, NB: Provincial Archives of New Brunswick. https://archives.gnb.ca/Exhibits/FortHavoc/html/Raymond28.aspx?culture=en-CA.

Ricard, Robert. 1925. "Sur la politique des alliances dans la conquête du Mexique par Cortès." *Journal de la Société des américanistes*, n.s., 17: 245–60.

Ricœur, Paul. 2000. *La mémoire, l'histoire, l'oubli*. Paris: Seuil.

de Roquebrune, R. Robert. 1966. "Joseph-Antoin Le Febvre de la Barre." *Dictionary of Canadian Biography*, vol. 1. http://www.biographi.ca/en/bio/le_febvre_de_la_barre_joseph_antoine_1E.html

Ross, Sylvain, 2003, see Bibliography: Assemblée Nationale du Québec, 21 January.

Royal Commission on Aboriginal Peoples, 1993, *Partners in Confederation. Aboriginal Peoples, Self-Government, and the Constitution*, Ottawa, Ministry of Supply and Services Canada.

Royal Commission on Aboriginal Peoples. 1994. *Treaty Making in the Spirit of Co-Existence: An Alternative to Extinguishment.* Ottawa: Canada Communication Group.

Royal Commission on Aboriginal Peoples. 1996. *Looking Forward, Looking Back.* Vol. 1 of *Royal Commission of Aboriginal Peoples.* Ottawa: Canada Communication Canada.

Royal Proclamation, 1763: *Revised Statutes of Canada, 1985, Appendices,* Prepared under the authority of the statute Revision Act, Appendice II, no. 1, The Royal Proclamation, 7 October 1763, Ottawa, the Queen's Printer.

Saint-Pierre, Diane. 1994. "L'évolution municipale du Québec des régions: Un bilan historique." Sainte-Foy, QC: Union des municipalités régionales de comté et des municipalités locales du Québec.

Sanger, David. 2008. "Discerning Regional Variation: The Terminal Archaic Period in the Quoddy Region of the Maritime Peninsula." *Canadian Journal of Archaeology* 32 (1).

Savard, Rémi. 1996. *L'Algonquin Tessouat et la fondation de Montréal.* Montréal: L'Hexagone.

Schulze, David Alexandre. 1997. "L'application de la Proclamation royale de 1763 dans les frontières originales de la Province de Québec: La décision du Conseil privé dans l'affaire Allscopp." *Revue juridique Thémis* 31 (2): 511–74.

Simard, Jean-Paul. 1983. "Les Amérindiens du Saguenay avant la colonisation blanche." In *Les Saguenayens,* edited by Christian Pouyez, Yolande Lavoie, and Gérard Bouchard, 67–94. Québec: Presses du l'Université du Québec.

Slattery, Brian. 1979. "The Land Rights of Indigenous Canadian Peoples." PhD. diss., Oxford University.

Specific Claims Tribunal of Canada, 1973. https://www.sct-trp.ca/en/claims/list-claims

Speck, Frank, G., 1917, "Malecites Tales," *Journal of American Folk-Lore,* XXX, no. 118, 480-481. https://www.jstor.org/stable/534497

Speck, Frank G. 1915. "The Eastern Algonkian Wabanaki Confederacy." *American Anthropologist,* n.s., 17 (3): 492–508. https://www.jstor.org/stable/660500.

Speck, F. G. 1922. Beothuk and Micmac. (Indian Notes and Monographs, Miscellaneous Series, 22.) New York: Museum of the American Indian, Heye Foundation.

Speck, Frank G., and Wendell S. Hadlock. 1946. "A report on tribal boundaries and hunting areas of the Malecite Indian of New Brunswick," *American Anthropologist* 48 (3): 321–74. https://anthrosource.onlinelibrary.wiley.com/doi/epdf/10.1525/aa.1946.48.3.02a00020.

Stavenhagen, Rodolfo, and Mathieu d'Avignon. 2010. *La reconstruction de l'histoire des Amériques.* Entretiens. Québec: Presses de l'Université Laval.

Sterckx, Sébastien. 1966. *Le monde des symboles,* Bayeux, France: Weber.

Sturtevant, William, ed. 1978. *Handbook of North American Indians.* Vol. 15, *Northeast,* edited by Bruce Trigger. Washington, DC: Smithsonian Institution.

Sulte, Beajamin, (1882–1884) 1977. *Histoire des canadiens-français: 1608–1880.* Montréal: Presse Élite.

Supreme Court of Canada, 1973, *Calder et al. v. Attorney-General of British Columbia,* S.C.R. 313.

Supreme Court of Canada. 1999. *R. v. Marshall,* 3 R.C.S. 456.

Thierry, Éric. 2001. *Marc Lescarbot (vers 1570–1641): Un homme de plume au service de la Nouvelle-France.* Paris: Honoré Champion.

Thierry, Éric. 2010. "Les Politiques amérindiennes de Henri IV." In *Les passions d'un historien: Mélanges en l'honneur de Jean-Pierre Poussou,* edited by Reynald Abad, Jean-Pierre Bardet, Jean-François Dunyach, and François-Joseph Ruggiu, 245–54. Paris: Presses de l'Université Paris-Sorbonne.

Todorov, Tzvetan. 1982. *La conquête de l'Amérique: La question de l'autre.* Paris: Seuil.

Tremblay, Victor. 1959. "Anadabijou," *Saguenayensia* 1 (5): 98–101. https://shistoriquesaguenay.com/wp-content/uploads/2023/03/Saguenayensia_vol_01_no_05_1959_complet.pdf

Tremblay, Victor. 1963. "Le traité de 1603," *Saguenayensia* 6 (2): 27–30. https://shistoriquesaguenay.com/wp-content/uploads/2023/03/Saguenayensia_vol_06_no_02_1964_complet.pdf

Trigger, Bruce. 1971. "Champlain Judged by His Indian Policy: A Different View of Early Canadian History." *Anthropologica,* n.s., 13 (1/2): 85–114.

Trigger, Bruce G. 1990. *Les Indiens, la fourrure et les Blancs.* Translated by Georges Khal. Montréal: Boréal. https://www.erudit.org/fr/revues/haf/1991-v45-n1-haf2348/304956ar.pdf

Trudel, Marcel. 1963. *Histoire de la Nouvelle-France.* Vol. 1, *Les vaines tentatives: 1524–1603.* Montréal: Fides.

Trudel, Marcel. 1965. "La Nouvelle-France: 1604–1627." *Revue d'histoire de l'Amérique française* 19 (2): 203–28.

Trudel, Marcel. 1966a. "François Gravé du Pont." In *Dictionary of Canadian Biography,* edited by George W. Brown. Vol. 1, *1000 to 1700,* 345–7. Québec, Presses de l'Université Laval; Toronto: University of Toronto, 1966.

Trudel, Marcel. 1966b. *Histoire de la Nouvelle-France.* Vol. 2, *Le comptoir (1604–1627).* Montréal: Fides.

Trudel, Marcel. 1973a. *La population du Canada en 1663.* Montréal: Fides.

Trudel, Marcel. 1973b. *Le terrier du Saint-Laurent en 1663.* Ottawa: Éditions de l'Université d'Ottawa.

Trudel, Marcel. 1998. *Le terrier du Saint-Laurent en 1674,* 2 vol. Montréal: Éditions du Méridien.

Truth and Reconciliation Commission of Canada. 2015. https://www.rcaanc-cirnac.gc.ca/eng/1450124405592/1529106060525

Turgeon, Laurier. 1982. "Pêcheurs basques et Indiens des côtes du Saint-Laurent au XVIe siècle: Perspectives de recherche." *Études canadiennes/Canadian Studies* 13: 9–14.

Turgeon, Laurier. 2004. "Les Français en Nouvelle-Angleterre avant Champlain." In *Champlain: La naissance de l'Amérique française*, edited by Raymonde Litalien and Denis Vaugeois, 98–112. Québec: Septentrion; Paris: Éditions du Nouveau Monde.

United Nations, 2012 and Shawn A-in-chut Atleo, National Chiefl, *The Doctrine of Discovery: its enduring impact on indigenous peoples and the right to redress for past conquests (article 28 and 37 of the United Nations Declaration on the Rights of Indigenous Peoples,* delivered at the United Nations Permanent Forum on Indigenous Issues, New York, 7-18 May 2012. Joint statement by the Assembly of First Nations, Chiefs of Ontario, Grand Council of the Crees (Eeyou Istchee), Amnesty International, Canadian Quaker Relief Services and KAIROS.

United Province of Canada. 1845. "Report of the Affairs of the Indians of Canada: Laid before the Legislative Assembly, 20th March, 1845" (see Bagot, Charles and Girard, Thibeault, 2001. Les Classiques des Sciences sociales and https://archive.org/details/bp_2289229.

Velasco, Salvador. 2003. "El 'Coloquio de Tlaxcala' de Diego Muñoz Camargo." In *Estudio de Cultura Nahuátl,* 34: 307–29.

Vincent, Sylvie. 1982. La tradition orale montagnaise: Comment l'interroger." *Cahiers de Clio* 70: 5–26.

Vincent, Sylvie. 1991. "La présence des gens du large dans la version montagnaise de l'histoire." *Anthropologie et sociétés* 15 (1): 125–43.

Vincent, Sylvie. 1992. "L'arrivée des chercheurs de terres: Récits et dires des Montagnais de la Moyenne et de la Basse-Côte-Nord." *Recherches amérindiennes au Québec* 22 (2–3): 19–29.

Vincent, Sylvie, and Bernard Arcand. 1979. *L'Image de l'Amérindien dans les manuels scolaires du Québec ou Comment les Québécois ne sont pas des sauvages.* Montréal: Hurtubise HMH, 1979. Available online at the site *Les Classiques des Sciences sociales.*

Vincent, Sylvie, and Joséphine Bacon. 1992. *Première rencontre entre Innus et Français: La tradition de Betsiamites.* Report prepared for Parks Canada. Montréal: Centre de recherche et d'analyse en sciences humaines.

Vincent, Sylvie, and Joséphine Bacon. 1997. *Uepishtikuiau: Récits et dires des Innus sur les premiers contacts avec les Français.* Montréal: Centre de recherche et d'analyse en sciences humaines, 1997. Used with permission of the Institut culturel et éducatif montagnais.

Vincent and Bacon, 2002. *Première rencontre entre Innus et Français: la tradition de Betsiamites,* Montréal, Centre de recherche et d'analyse en sciences humaines.

White, Richard. 2009. *Le Middle Ground: Indiens, empires et républiques dans la région des Grands Lacs, 1650-1815*. Translated by Frédéric Cotton. Toulouse, France: Anacharsis.

Wicken, William C., and John G. Reid. 1996. *An Overview of the Eighteenth Century Treaties Signed between the Mi'kmaq and Wuastukwiuk Peoples and the English Crown: 1693-1928*. [Ottawa]: Royal Commission on Indigenous People.

Zavala, Silvio. 1984-96. *El Servicio personal de los indios en la Nueva Espana*. 8 vol. Mexico City: El Colegio de México; El Colegio Nacional.

de Zurita, Alonzo. (c. 1553) 1840. *Rapport sur les différentes classes de chefs de la Nouvelle-Espagne*. In *Voyages, relations et mémoires originaux pour servir à l'histoire de la découverte de l'Amérique* [...], edited by H. Ternaux-Compans. Unpublished manuscript. Paris: Arthus Bertrand.

Map sources

Map 1. Archaeological sites in Maliseet territory
Source: Grand Council of the Waban-Aki Nation

Map 2. French settlements in America, sixteenth to early seventeenth century (Carl Brisson)
Source: *Atlas of the North American Indian* by Carl Waldman

Map 3. Location of Tadoussac in present-day Québec (Carl Brisson)

Map 4. New France, 1609
Source: Marc Lescarbot, Histoire de la Nouvelle-France contenant les navigations, découvertes & habitations faites pare les François és Indes Occidentales & Nouvelle-France, Paris, Jean Milot, 1609 (map Carter Brown Library). https://upload.wikimedia.org/wikipedia/commons/1/17/Figvre_de_la_terre_nevve%2C_grande_riviere_de_Canada%2C_et_côtes_de_l%27 ocean_en_la_Novvelle_France_1609.jpg.

Map 5. Meeting places, 1604
Source: Samuel de Champlain. 1613. *Les voyages dv sievr de Champlain Xaintongeois, capitaine ordinaire pour le Roy, en la marine, divisez en devx livres: IOVRNAL TRES-FIDELE DES OBSERVAtions faites es deſcouuertures de la Nouuelle France: tant en la deſcriptiõ des terres, costes, riuieres, ports, haures, leurs hauteurs, & pluſieurs declinaiſons de la guide-aymant; qu'en la creãce des peuples, leur ſuperſtition, façon de viure & de guerroyer; enrichi de quantité de figures. 1613.* Paris: Iean Berjon. https://fr.wikipedia.org/wiki/Samuel_de_Champlain#/media/File:Description_of_the_Coasts,_Points,_Harbours_and_Islands_of_New_France_WDL280.png.

Map 6. Indigenous Nations occupying the territory of present-day Québec, about 1600 (adapted by Carl Brisson)
Source: Raynald Parent. "L'effritement de la civilisation amérindienne," in Jean Hamelin (dir.), *Histoire du Québec*, Montréal, Éditions France-Amérique, 1981, p. 35. La limite du Nord-Est est identifiée à la fois à la présence des Esquimaux et des Indiens/Sauvages pour tenir compte des recherches de Barkham (1984) et de Bélanger (1971). See Parent, 1985.

Map 7. The King's Domain, about 1650
Source: Jean-Paul Simard, Les Amérindiens du Saguenay avant la colonisation blanche, dans Christian Pouyez, Yolande Lavoie et collab., *Les*

Saguenayens, Québec, Presses de l'Université du Québec, 1983, p. 67-94; *Relations des Jésuites*, tome 3, 1643.

Map 8. Indigenous Nations and confederacies of northeastern Turtle Island, 1585
Source: See: <https://www.pinterest.ca/pin/370702613068868334>.

Map 9. Travel routes in New Brunswick, 1895
Source: William F. Ganong, Map No. 12 on Pre-Contact Routes of Travel in the Province of New Brunswick and Northern Maine, *From the Transactions of the Royal Society of Canada*, Second Series 1895-96, vol. I, Sect II. John Durie & Sons, Ottawa: Copp-Clark Co., Toronto: Bernard Quaritch. London Englans. 1895. <http://www.maliseettrail.com/GanongRoTMap12.htm>.

Map 10. Boundaries of Maliseet traditional territory in New Brunswick, 1946
Source: Frank G. Speck et Wendell S. Hadlock, 1946, A report on tribal bounderies and hunting areas of the Malecite Indian of New Brunswick, *American antropologist*, vol. 48, July-Sept. no. 3, p. 321-374. <https://anthrosource.onlinelibrary.wiley.com/doi/ epdf/10.1525/aa.1946.48.3.02a00020>.

Map 11. Traditional territory of the Maliseet, 1978
Source: Vincent O. Erickson (1978). « Maliseet-Passamaquoddy », in Bruce G. Trigger (dir.), *Handbook of North American Indians*. vol. 15, *Northeast*: 123-136. Washington, D.C.: Smithsonian Institution.

Map 12. Portages and rivers between the Saint John and St. Lawrence Rivers, 2001
Source: Adrian L. Burke, Temiscouata: Traditional Maliseet Territory and Connections between the St. Lawrence Valley and the St. John River Valley, in *Actes du trente-deuxième Congrès des algonquinistes*, Winnipeg, Université du Manitoba, 2001, p. 61-73.

Map 13. Extract from a map by Lescarbot, 1609
Source: Marc Lescarbot, Histoire de la Nouvelle France contenant les navigations, découvertes & habitations faites pare les François és Indes Occidentales & Nouvelle-France, Paris, Jean Milot, 1609 (Map Carter Brown Library). <https://upload.wikimedia.org/wikipedia/commons/1/17/Figvre_de_la_terre_nevve%2C_grande_riviere_de_Canada%2C_et_côtes_de_l%27ocean_en_la_Novvelle_France_1609.jpg>.

Map 14. Extract from a map by Champlain, 1632
Source: Samuel de Champlain, Paris, 1632 <http://numerique.banq.qc.ca/patrimoine/details/52327/2246880>.

Map 15. Denonville's map, 1685
Source: Jacques-René de Brisay de Denonville, *Chemin de Québec à la Baye Françoise*, 1685, gallica.bnf.fr/Bibliothèque nationale de France.

Map 16. Extract from a map by De Rozier, 1699
Source: Quoted in « L'archéologie des Malécites: passé, présent et futur », Adrian L. Burke *Recherches amérindiennes au Québec*, vol. 39, n° 3, 2009, p. 7-24.

Map 17. Extract from a map of Acadia, 1702
Source: Unknown author, *Carte de l'Acadie*, 1702, gallica.bnf.fr/Bibliothèque nationale de France.

Map 18. Extract from a map by Aubry, 1715
Source: R. P. Aubry, Carte pour les hauteurs des terres et pour servir de Limitte, suivant la Paix, entre la france et l'angleterre, suivant les mémoires du R. P. Aubry, Jésuite, 1715, gallica.bnf.fr/Bibliothèque nationale de France.

Map 19. Extract from a map by Bellin, 1744
Source: Jacques-Nicolas Bellin, *Carte de la partie orientale de la Nouvelle-France ou du Canada*, Paris, 1744, <http://numerique.banq.qc.ca>.

Map 20. Extract from a map by Morris, 1749
Source: Charles Morris, To his excellency William Shirley Esqr., Captain General and Commander in Chief, in and over his Majestys province of the Massachusetts Bay in New England, and Vice Admiral of the same: this draught of the northern English Colonies, together with the French neighbouring settlements; taken partly from actual surveys, and partly from the most approved draughts and other accounts, done at your excellencys request; is most humbly dedicated, Boston, aug 16 1749. <https://collections.leventhalmap.org/search/commonwealth:7h149w97z>.

Map 21. Extract from a map by Mitchell, 1756
Source: John Mitchell, Amérique Septentrionale avec les Routes, Distances en miles, limites et Establissements François et Anglois par le Docteur Mitchell, translated from English in Paris by Le Rouge, ing, geographer to the king, rue des Grands Augustins, 1756. <http://www.davidrumsey.com/maps2898.html>.

Map 22. Extract from a map by Mitchell, 1757
Source: John Mitchell, *A map of the British and French Dominions in North America with the Roads, Distances, limits and Extent of the Settlements*, 1757. <http://www.davidrumsey.com/maps5037.html>.

Map 23. Extract from a map by Delarochette, 1763
Source: Louis Stanislas d'Arcy Delarochette, A new map of North America wherein the British Dominions in the continent of North America: and on the islands of the West Indies, are carefully laid down from all the surveys, hitherto made; and the boundaries of the new governments, as well as the other provinces are shewn. Also extracts from the definitive Treaty of Peace in 1763, relative to the cessions made to his Britannick Majesty on the continent of North America, and to the partition agreed on for the islands, London, John Bowles, 1763.

Map 24. Extract from a map by Jefferys, 1775
Source: Thomas Jefferys, A new map of Nova Scotia and Cape Breton Island with the adjacent parts of New England and Canada from great number of actual surveys and other materials regulated by many new astronomical observations of the longitude as wll as latitude, London, R. Sayer and J. Bennet, 1775.

Map 25. Extract from a map by Franquelin, 1686
Source: Jean-Baptiste Franquelin, Carte gé[né]ralle du voyage que Monsieur De Meulles intendant de la justice, police et finances de la Nouvelle France a fait par ordre du Roy..., 1686. gallica.bnf.fr/Bibliothèque nationale de France.

Map 26. Extract from a map by De Rozier, 1699
Source: William F. Ganong, Additions and Corrections to monographs on the Place-nomenclature, Cartography, Historic sites, Boundaries and Settlement-origins of the province of New Brunswick, Contributions to the History of New Brunswick no. 7, in *Proceedings and Transactions of the Royal Society of Canada*, second series, volume XII, Meeting of May 1906, Ottawa, James Hope and son, p. 60. <https://www.biodiversitylibrary.org/item/41918#page/6/mode/1up>.

Map 27. Extract from a map by Delisle, 1703
Source: Guillaume Delisle, Carte du Canada ou de la Nouvelle France et des Decouvertes qui y ont été faites / Dressée sur plusieurs observations et sur un grand nombre de Relations imprimées ou manuscrites, Paris, 1703. gallica.bnf.fr/Bibliothèque nationale de France.

Map 28. Extract from a map by Aubry, 1713
Source: Nicolas Aubry, Partie du Canada ou nouvelle France et de la Nouvelle Angleterre, de l'Acadie dressée par le P. Aubry jésuite depuis le traité de la paix d'Utrecht (du 22 avril 1713) dessinée par le Sr de Morville sous ingénieur en novembre 1713. gallica.bnf.fr/Bibliothèque nationale de France.

Map 29. Extract from a map of New France, early eighteenth century
Source: Unknown author, *Canada ou Nouvelle France, Nouvelle Angleterre, Terres des Abnaquis*, gallica.bnf.fr/Bibliothèque nationale de France.

Map 30. Extract from a map by Aubry, 1715
Source: R. P. Aubry, *Carte pour les hauteurs des terres et pour servir de Limitte, suivant la Paix, entre la france et l'angleterre*, according to the memoirs of R. P. Aubry, Jésuite, 1715, gallica.bnf.fr/Bibliothèque nationale de France.

Map 31. Extract from a map by Moll, 1720
Source: Herman Moll, A new map of the north parts of America claimed by France under ye ames of Louisiana, Mississipi [i.e. Mississippi], Canada, and New France with ye adjoining territories of England and Spain: to Thomas Bromsall, esq., this map of Louisiana, Mississipi [i.e. Mississippi] & c. is most humbly dedicated, H. Moll, geographer, London, 1720.

Map 32. Extract from a map by the Royal Academy of Sciences, 1729
Source: Unknown author, Canada ou Nouvelle France suivant les Nouvelles Observations de Mess. de l'Académie Royale des Sciences, Paris, A Leide, 1729. gallica.bnf.fr/Bibliothèque nationale de France.

Map 33. Extract from a map by Bellin, 1744
Source: Jacques-Nicolas Bellin, *Carte de la partie orientale de la Nouvelle-France ou du Canada*, Paris, 1744, <http://numerique.banq.qc.ca>.qa

Map 34. Extract from a map by Morris, 1749
Source: Charles Morris, To his excellency William Shirley Esqr., Captain General and Commander in Chief, in and over his Majestys province of the Massachusetts Bay in New England, and Vice Admiral of the same: this draught of the northern English Colonies, together with the French neighbouring settlements; taken partly from actual surveys, and partly from the most approved draughts and other accounts, done at your excellencys request; is most humbly dedicated, Boston, aug 16 1749. <https://collections.leventhalmap.org/search/commonwealth:7h149w97z>.

Map 35. Extract from a map by d'Anville, 1755
Source: Jean-Baptiste Bourguignon d'Anville, Canada, *Louisiane et terres angloises*, Paris, 1755. gallica.bnf.fr/Bibliothèque nationale de France.

Map 36. Extract from a map by Le Rouge, 1755
Source: Georges-Louis Le Rouge, *Canada et Louisiane* / Par le Sr. le Rouge, Ingenieur Geographe du Roy, Paris, 1755. gallica.bnf.fr/Bibliothèque nationale de France.

Map 37. Extract from a map by Jefferys, 1755
Source: Thomas Jefferys, *Nouvelle-Écosse ou partie orientale du Canada*, 1755. <http://collections.musee-mccord.qc.ca/fr/collection/artefacts/W6752>.

Map 38. Extract from a map by Bellin, 1757
Source: Nicolas Bellin, *Carte de l'Accadie et des pais voisins*, 1757. <https://fr.wikipedia.org/wiki/Fichier:Carte_de_l%27_Accadie_et_Pais_Voisins_1757.jpg>.

Map 39. Extract from a map by Bellin, 1764
Source: Jacques-Nicolas Bellin, *La Nouvelle France ou Canada*, 1764. gallica.bnf.fr/Bibliothèque nationale de France.

Map 40. Traditional territory of the Maliseet
Sources: William F. Ganong, Additions and Corrections to monographs on the Place-nomenclature, Cartography, Historic sites, Boundaries ans Settlement-origins of the province of New Brunswick, Contributions to the History of New Brunswick no. 7, in *Proceedings and Transactions of the Royal Society of Canada*, second series, volume XII, Meeting of May 1906, Ottawa, James Hope and son, p. 60.

Adrian L. Burke, Temiscouata: Traditional Maliseet Territory and Connections between the St. Lawrence Valley and the St. John River Valley, dans *Actes du trente-deuxième congrès des algonquinistes*, Winnipeg, Université du Manitoba, 2001, p. 61-73.

Samuel de Champlain, *« Les voyages dv sievr de Champlain Xaintongeois, capitaine ordinaire pour le Roy, en la marine, divisez en devx livres. »:* « *IOVRNAL TRES-FIDELE DES OBSERVAtions faites es deſcouuertures de la Nouuelle France: tant en la deſcriptiõ des terres, costes, riuieres, ports, haures, leurs hauteurs,& pluſieurs declinaiſons de la guide-aymant; qu'en la creãce des peuples, leur ſuperſtition, façon de viure & de guerroyer; enrichi de quantité de figures»*, Paris, France, Iean Berjon, 1613, 434 p.

Vincent O. Erikson (1978). « Maliseet-Passamaquoddy », dans *Handbook of North American Indians*. Vol. 15, *Northeast,* edited by Bruce G. Trigger, 123-136. Washington, D.C.: Smithsonian Institution.

Ghislain Michaud, 2003, Les gardiens des portages, l'histoire des Malécites du Québec, Québec, Édition GID.

Première Nation Malécite de Viger, *Territoire ancestral de la Première nation Malécite de Viger*, Nation's Council Resolution, 25 April 2013.

Map 41. Territory of the Wabanaki Confederacy
Source: Stacy Morin, Wabanaki country, The Wabanaki and their native American neighbors from ancient times to the early 18th century, RDS inc., Orrington, ME.

Map 42. Seigneuries granted by 1663 (Carl Brisson)
Sources: Serge Courville, Serge Labrecque et Jacques Fortin, *Seigneuries et fiefs du Québec, nomenclature et cartographie*, Québec, CELAT, 1988, 202 p.
R. Louis Gentilcore et Geoffrey J. Matthews, *Atlas historique du Canada*, vol. 2, Montréal, Les Presses de l'Université de Montréal, 1993, 185 p.
Gouvernement du Québec, ministère de l'Énergie et des Ressources naturelles, Carte des contraintes l'exploration minière au Québec: limites des cantons et des seigneuries.
Marcel Trudel, *Le terrier du Saint-Laurent en 1663*, Québec, Éditions de l'Université d'Ottawa, 1960, 432 p.
Première Nation Malécite de Viger, *Territoire ancestral de la Première nation Malécite de Viger*, Nation's Council Resolution, 25 April 2013.

Map 43. Seigneuries granted by 1674
Sources: Serge Courville, Serge Labrecque and Jacques Fortin, *Seigneuries et fiefs du Québec, nomenclature et cartographie*, Québec, CELAT, 1988, 202 p.
R. Louis Gentilcore et Geoffrey J. Matthews, *Atlas historique du Canada*, vol. 2, Montréal, Les Presses de l'Université de Montréal, 1993, 185 p.
Gouvernement du Québec, ministère de l'Énergie et des Ressources naturelles, Carte des contraintes l'exploration minière au Québec: limites des cantons et des seigneuries.
Marcel Trudel, *Le terrier du Saint-Laurent en 1674,* tome 2: du lac Saint-Louis à la Gaspésie, Montréal, Éditions du Méridien, 1998.
Première Nation Malécite de Viger, *Territoire ancestral de la Première nation Malécite de Viger*, Nation's Council Resolution, 25 April 2013.

Map 44. Seigneuries granted by 1745 (Carl Brisson)
Sources: Serge Courville, Serge Labrecque and Jacques Fortin, *Seigneuries et fiefs du Québec, nomenclature et cartographie*, Québec, CELAT, 1988, 202 p.
R. Louis Gentilcore et Geoffrey J. Matthews, *Atlas historique du Canada*, vol. 2, Montréal, Les Presses de l'Université de Montréal, 1993, 185 p.

MAP SOURCES

Gouvernement du Québec, ministère de l'Énergie et des Ressources naturelles, Carte des contraintes l'exploration minière au Québec: limites des cantons et des seigneuries.

Jacques Mathieu, Alain Laberge et Lina Gouger, L'occupation des terres dans la vallée du Saint-Laurent: les aveux et dénombrement 1723-1745, Sillery, Septentrion, 1991, 415 p.

Première Nation Malécite de Viger, *Territoire ancestral de la Première nation Malécite de Viger*, Nation's Council Resolution, 25 April 2013.

Map 45. Grants of rights for commercial exploitation (Carl Brisson)
Sources: Gouvernement du Québec, ministère de l'Énergie et des Ressources naturelles, Carte des contraintes l'exploration minière au Québec: limites des cantons et des seigneuries.

Première Nation Malécite de Viger, *Territoire ancestral de la Première nation Malécite de Viger*, Nation's Council Resolution, 25 April 2013.

Assemblée législative, 1852, *Pièces et documents relatifs à la tenure seigneuriale*, demandée par une adresse de l'Assemblée législative, Québec, Imprimerie d'E.R. Fréchette.

Jacques Mathieu, Serge Courville and Rénald Lessard, *Peuplement colonisateur aux XVIIe et XVIIIe siècles*, Sainte-Foy, CELAT, 1987, 292 p.

Map 46. The province of Québec, as specified in the Royal Proclamation of 1763 (Carl Brisson)
Sources: Serge Courville, Serge Labrecque and Jacques Fortin, *Seigneuries et fiefs du Québec, nomenclature et cartographie*, Québec, CELAT, 1988, 202 p.

R. Louis Gentilcore and Geoffrey J. Matthews, *Atlas historique du Canada*, vol. 2, Montréal, Les Presses de l'Université de Montréal, 1993, 185 p.

Maurice Ratelle, Contexte historique de la localisation des Attikameks et des Montagnais de 1760 à nos jours, Appendix 2 Cartographie, Québec.

Gouvernement du Québec, ministère de l'Énergie et des Ressources naturelles, Carte des contraintes à l'exploration minière au Québec: limites des cantons et des seigneuries.

Map 47. Territory claimed in 1765 (Carl Brisson)
Source: Gouvernement du Québec, ministère de l'Énergie et des Ressources naturelles, Carte des contraintes à l'exploration minière au Québec: limites des cantons et des seigneuries.

Première Nation Malécite de Viger, *Territoire ancestral de la Première nation Malécite de Viger*, Nation's Council Resolution, 25 April 2013.

Gazette de Québec, 24 January 1765, Réponse positive à une demande des Malécites pour le respect de leurs territoires traditionnels de chasse.

Map 48. Map by Champlain, 1632
Source: Samuel de Champlain, Paris, 1632. <http://numerique.banq.qc.ca/patrimoine/details/52327/2246880>.

Map 49. Map of the village of Viger, 1847
Source: Jean-Charles Fortin and Antoio Lechasseur, *Histoire du Bas-Saint-Laurent*, 1993, Québec, Institut de recherche sur la culture, 860 p.

Map 50. Evolution of municipalization, 1831 (Carl Brisson)
Sources: Gouvernement du Québec, ministère de l'Énergie et des Ressources naturelles, Carte des contraintes à l'exploration minière au Québec: limites des cantons et des seigneuries.
Gouvernement du Québec, *Liste des terrains concédés par la Couronne dans la Province de Québec, de 1763 à 1890*, Québec, C.-F. Langlois, Imprimeur de Sa Très Grande Majesté la Reine, 1891, 1921 p.
Première Nation Malécite de Viger, *Territoire ancestral de la Première nation Malécite de Viger*, Nation's Council Resolution, 25 April 2013.

Map 51. Evolution of municipalization, 1851 (Carl Brisson)
Sources: Gouvernement du Québec, ministère de l'Énergie et des Ressources naturelles, Carte des contraintes à l'exploration minière au Québec: limites des cantons et des seigneuries.
Gouvernement du Québec, *Liste des terrains concédés par la Couronne dans la Province de Québec, de 1763 à 1890*, Québec, C.-F. Langlois, Imprimeur de Sa Très Grande Majesté la Reine, 1891, 1921 p.
Première Nation Malécite de Viger, *Territoire ancestral de la Première nation Malécite de Viger*, Nation's Council Resolution, 25 April 2013.

Map 52. Evolution of municipalization, 1871 (Carl Brisson)
Sources: Gouvernement du Québec, ministère de l'Énergie et des Ressources naturelles, Carte des contraintes à l'exploration minière au Québec: limites des cantons et des seigneuries.
Gouvernement du Québec, *Liste des terrains concédés par la Couronne dans la Province de Québec, de 1763 à 1890*, Québec, C.-F. Langlois, Imprimeur de Sa Très Grande Majesté la Reine, 1891, 1921 p.
Première Nation Malécite de Viger, *Territoire ancestral de la Première nation Malécite de Viger*, Nation's Council Resolution, 25 April 2013.

Map 53. Location of members of the Wolastoqiyik Wahsipekuk First Nation living in Québec
Sources: Première Nation Malécite de Viger, *Territoire ancestral de la Première nation Malécite de Viger*, Nation's Council Resolution, 25 April 2013.
Première Nation malécite de Viger, Fichier des données sur les membres malécites 06-08-2019.
Ministère des Ressources naturelles, de la Faune et des Parcs, *Base de données géographiques et administratives à l'échelle de 1 / 1 000 000*, Québec, 2003.

Map 54. Evolution of municipalization, 2019
Sources: Ministère des Ressources naturelles, de la Faune et des Parcs, *Base de données géographiques et administratives à l'échelle de 1 / 1 000 000*, Québec, 2003.
Première Nation Malécite de Viger, *Territoire ancestral de la Première nation Malécite de Viger*, Nation's Council Resolution, 25 April 2013.

MAP SOURCES

Map 55. Land ownership, 2019
Sources: Ministère des Ressources naturelles, de la Faune et des Parcs, *Base de données géographiques et administratives à l'échelle de 1 / 1 000 000*, Québec, 2003.
Ministère de l'Énergie et des Ressources naturelles, *Plan d'affectation du Bas-Saint-Laurent*, Québec, 2015, 545 p. <https://mern.gouv.qc.ca/publications/territoire/planification/Cartes_BSL/PATP/bas-saint-laurent-patp.pdf>.
Ministère de l'Énergie et des Ressources naturelles, *Plan d'affectation de Chaudière-Appalaches*, Québec, 2015, 292 p. <https://mern.gouv.qc.ca/publications/territoire/planification/cartes_chaudiere-appalaches/PATP_chaudiere-appalaches_final.pdf>.
Première Nation Malécite de Viger, *Territoire ancestral de la Première nation Malécite de Viger*, Nation's Council Resolution, 25 April 2013.

Map 56. Ancestral lands covered by the 2019 declaration
Source: <https://www.newswire.ca/fr/news-releases/signature-de-la-declaration-solennelle-de-respect-mutuel-et-d-alliance-internations-899399579.html>.